C000176316

THE RUGBY UNION
WHO'S WHO
1991/92

THE RUGBY UNION
WHO'S WHO
1991/92

Compiled and edited by

ALEX SPINK

CollinsWillow
An Imprint of HarperCollins*Publishers*

First published in 1991 by
Collins Willow
an imprint of HarperCollins Publishers
London

A CIP catalogue record for this book is available
from the British Library

ISBN 0 00 218391 9

Cover photographs of John Jeffrey, Simon Geoghegan,
Phil Davies and Rory Underwood by Russell Cheyne/AllSport
Portraits by Russell Cheyne/AllSport, and Colorsport, Inpho, Jim Gidding,
Western Mail and Echo Ltd and ASP

Typeset in Plantin Light by Michael Mepham, Frome

Printed and bound in Great Britain by
Butler & Tanner Ltd, Frome and London

Contents

Preface

Great days indeed for rugby union. But those players responsible for lifting the profile of the sport to its current dizzy heights believe there is still room for improvement and are campaigning for change not only off the park, but now on it as well.

Away from the playing fields, yes, they want the amateurism wrangle straightened out, with some form of reward for their professional levels of commitment to the sport. Yet the best of British and Irish also see the need for a shift in emphasis **on** the field.

For all the sport's success, the players are not enjoying performing as much as they might. That is the general consensus in this the second edition of *The Rugby Union Who's Who*. A year after expunging the theory that players are not interested in financial gain from activities peripheral to the sport, the opinions expressed in this 1991/92 *RUWW* relay another message to rugby's governing bodies: 'Help make the game more exciting for players and spectators alike.'

A remarkable proportion of the four Home Unions' best players have stated that they wish to see the importance of the penalty goal diminished, and the resurrection of try-scoring as the name of the game. England achieved a well-deserved Grand Slam in the Five Nations' Championship, scoring five tries in the process, but Ireland, who failed to win a match, ran in ten. This is not a criticism of England but certainly an indictment, in the players' minds, of today's Game.

Suggested remedies include additional points for a try, all conversions to be taken under the posts, a reduction in the number of offences permitting a kick at goal, a differential between technical (1 point) and physical offences (3 points), and a reduction in the value of the penalty goal; although many players voice the fear that lessening the worth of the penalty across the board would encourage an upsurge in infringements, especially foul play. Other proposals along a similar tack seek to ban all kicking between the two 22-metre lines, and to disallow kicking from hand straight into touch anywhere on the field.

Many hope the 1991 World Cup will prove a watershed for rugby, in that safety-first tactical policies will play second fiddle to flair. However, a large proportion of the players also believe that, as in

1987, the battle for the Webb Ellis Trophy will be marred by the dichotomy in refereeing interpretations in the Northern and Southern hemispheres.

The clarion call is for a worldwide unification of refereeing interpretations – a plea by players, similar to that in the amateurism debate, for grey areas to be repainted black and white, so that they know where they stand rather than going into each game with a trial and error policy. Rucks, mauls, line-outs and scrums all need better, more sympathetic, policing, the players also comment.

This second edition of *The Rugby Union Who's Who* includes a comprehensive results section (pages 321–49), which charts a season of international clashes. There are also reviews of the international season by the captains of the four Home Union nations – Will Carling (England), Rob Saunders (Ireland), David Sole (Scotland) and Paul Thorburn (Wales), although it must be stressed that these were composed before the summer tours.

There are once again over 300 profiles of International players – from U-21 level through to senior status – who represented England, Ireland, Scotland and Wales last season, complete with statistical charts. And to mark the second World Cup, there is a factual reference guide between pages 304–21.

The list of credits of those who, without reward, have contributed to the book include all the players (especially the four International captains) and many club officials, the four Home Unions, Paul Morgan (for his Welsh statistics), Russell Cheyne and the AllSport photographic team, and John Griffiths (whose first-year statistics provided the basis for the updated lists). Finally to Karen, Tom and Jenny, thanks for all your support.

Alex Spink
July 1991

Foreword

P. T. BATEMAN

Chief Executive, Save & Prosper Group

All of us at Save and Prosper were delighted with the success of the first edition of *The Rugby Union Who's Who*.

So it is with great pleasure that I introduce the second edition of this fascinating compendium of rugby and personal information about the current leading players from the four home Unions.

In this exciting World Cup Year we all look forward to some stimulating rugby and, who knows, perhaps some surprises as well.

The 1990/91 International Player's Player of the Year

SERGE BLANCO, the world's most-capped player, is the first winner of the Save and Prosper International Rugby Player's Player of the Year Award, in recognition of a season which, in captaining France, the Biarritz full-back was, quite simply, brilliant.

Every player featured in this book was asked to make his selection and, after a close contest with Gary Armstrong, Simon Geoghegan, Dean Richards and Rob Andrew, it was Blanco who emerged as the most popular vote in the international fraternity of the four Home Union nations.

In what Blanco stated was his last full season of international rugby, the French gloriously escaped the shackles of the forward-orientated game which had taken them into the 1990s with Blanco to the fore in all their most attractive work – as he has been throughout a career which began on the international stage more than 80 caps ago in 1980 with his debut in the French side beaten 15–37 by South Africa in Pretoria.

His spectacular try against Wales in his final Five Nations' appearance at the Parc des Princes, after just two minutes, left an indelible memory not only in the minds of the Welsh players, but in the minds of many others involved in international rugby in the Four Home Unions. World rugby will be a poorer place when Serge Blanco hangs up his boots after the World Cup.

Gary Armstrong, the Scotland scrum-half who played second fiddle to Welshman Robert Jones on the 1989 British Lions' tour to Australia, ran a close second to Blanco after a powerful campaign which confirmed his place among the world's best scrum-halves.

Third place was taken by Simon Geoghegan, surely the find of the season with three tries in his first four Five Nations' matches. The London Irishman, like Blanco, draws gasps of anticipation whenever he touches the ball, or is even in the same vicinity, and that, with the ever-increasing clamour for more expansive rugby, is welcome indeed.

Dean Richards and Rob Andrew, architects in England's first

Grand Slam for eleven years, occupied fourth and fifth places, with young Welsh centre Scott Gibbs, who drew the admiration and heart-felt thanks of a passionate rugby nation by politely rejecting a massive financial overture from Rugby League, in sixth position.

THE TOP 25

1. Serge Blanco (France)
2. Gary Armstrong (Scotland)
3. Simon Geoghegan (Ireland)
4. Dean Richards (England)
5. Rob Andrew (England)
6. Scott Gibbs (Wales)
7. Mike Teague (England)
8. Simon Hodgkinson (England)
9. Rory Underwood (England)
10. Paul Ackford (England)
11. Richard Hill (England)
    Peter Winterbottom (England)
13. Jason Leonard (England)
14. Didier Camberabero (France)
    Grant Fox (New Zealand)
    Craig Innes (New Zealand)
    Olivier Roumat (France)
    David Sole (Scotland)
19. Xavier Blond (France)
    Phil Davies (Wales)
    Jeremy Guscott (England)
    John Jeffrey (Scotland)
    Glyn Llewellyn (Wales)
    Philip Matthews (Ireland)
    Rob Saunders (Ireland)

The Captains review the 1990/91 Season

(Composed prior to summer tours)

ENGLAND

Will Carling

SITTING in the changing rooms under Twickenham after we had beaten France to win the Grand Slam and been chaired off the field, the overwhelming feeling was one of relief. Relief that we had finally fulfilled a nation's expectations.

It was a marvellous moment to look around at the tired faces of a lot of close friends, players and management, knowing that we had achieved a goal we had come so close to but been denied in the previous two seasons. The painful memories of Cardiff 1989 and Murrayfield 1990 could finally be replaced with the triumph of Twickenham 1991.

All season long we were required to prove ourselves; to prove we had what it took to win a Grand Slam, to prove that the summer tour to Argentina, though disappointing results-wise, was not a reflection on the strength of English national rugby. We also came in for criticism for not maintaining the expansive approach we had adopted the previous year.

The centenary Barbarians were our first opponents and although it was a non-cap match, we felt we had to win. A lot of the team, even those who had not toured, were hurt by the criticisms levelled over the Argentine tour, and wanted to put the record straight. The general media impression in Argentina was that it had been a poor tour but they seemed to forget that Argentina are a different proposition when playing with home advantage. We were disappointed with the way we played but the tour was still positive as it brought to light the claims of some of the younger players.

The Barbarians match (won 18–16) was a tough one to play so early in the season, especially as so many of their team were southern hemisphere players who were 'in season'. But there was some great rugby played and we were well satisfied with our contribution.

Argentina (won 51–0) were the next visitors to Twickenham and for us it was a match of double-edged importance. We wanted to state the fact that this was a full England side playing at Twickenham and a different proposition from that which we took to South America, and we also needed to play well because it was our last International before the Five Nations' Championship. It went extremely well. To score 50 points against anyone in international rugby is a great feat and the manner in which we controlled the game – they hardly touched the ball for the first 20 minutes – was particularly pleasing.

Our Five Nations' campaign began in Cardiff (won 25–6) against Wales who, as everyone knew only too well, we had not beaten for twenty-eight years. The team was also well aware of all the hype and we took the conscious decision not to hide away from it all in the build-up. Instead of staying out at St Pierre, we booked into the Crest Hotel in the middle of Cardiff and walked to the ground on match day. It had the desired effect. Apart from the first two or three minutes, we had so much control, and Simon (Hodgkinson) kicked everything. Yet, afterwards, the feeling in the changing rooms was one of disappointment with our performance. We felt that, with 20 minutes to go, when we knew we had won and laid to rest the Cardiff bogey, we could have afforded to use the full force of the side, but did not.

We came in for a lot of bad publicity after the Welsh game, over the decision not to speak to the Press. And after that we took the

England

(H)	v. Barbarians,	won	18–16	(non-cap)
(H)	v. Argentina,	won	51–0	
(A)	v. Wales,	won	25–6	
(H)	v. Scotland,	won	21–12	
(A)	v. Ireland,	won	16–7	
(H)	v. France,	won	21–19	

England B

(H)	v. Namibia,	won	31–16
(H)	v. Emerging Australians,	drew	12–12
(H)	v. Spain,	won	50–6
(H)	v. Italy,	won	12–9
(A)	v. Ireland,	lost	10–24
(H)	v. France,	lost	6–10

England U–21

(H)	v. Ireland U–21,	lost	16–22
(A	v. Netherlands,	won	20–18
(A)	v. French Armed Forces,	lost	7–9

Colts

(H)	v. Italy,	lost	21–22
(H)	v. Argentina,	won	15–12
(H)	v. Wales,	lost	3–32
(A)	v. France,	lost	6–14
(A)	v. Scotland,	lost	7–24

18-Group

(H)	v. Australia,	lost	3–8
(A)	v. Ireland,	won	15–0
(H)	v. France,	won	28–13
(H)	v. Scotland,	won	21–3
(A)	v. Wales,	lost	10–13

16-Group

(A)	v. Italy B,	won	27–16
(A)	v. Italy,	lost	6–7
(H)	v. Spain,	won	10–6

decision to put to one side peripheral matters and concentrate 100 per cent on playing and winning.

It was a problem all season satisfying the critics. Against Scotland in 1990 we had played some lovely rugby and been accused of being tactically naive when we lost. Yet last season when we were tactically superb and exerted tremendous control, we were criticised for doing what those same people said we should have done the previous year.

Because of events at Murrayfield the previous season we were very keen and built-up for the return with Scotland (won 21–12). Indeed, a lot of the team regarded that win as the highlight of the Grand Slam series. It was a very hard game and there was no way we could afford to throw the ball about because they possess such a dangerous team. The only disappointing aspect for us was that, after opening up a 9-point lead (15–6), we let them back into the game. As in the French match, we did not clinically finish off the opposition.

I always knew our visit to Ireland (won 16–7) would be the hardest game of the series because there was no hook on which to hang the build-up. We were expected to win the game – a formality, no problems, a warm-up for the decider with France. As I had suspected, it turned out to be rather different, a nail-biting affair, with us only going ahead in the final 10 minutes. There was the odd vision of doom in my head before Rory (Underwood) scored 7 minutes from time, but we continued to play positively and we were rewarded with victory and England's first Triple Crown for eleven years.

One of the strengths of the England squad throughout the season was control, both on and off the field. Hence there were no excessive nerves before the French game (won 21–19) nor excessive celebrations after it. We were certainly more confident than at Murrayfield the previous year because we were at Twickenham, which these days gives us a massive lift, and because we had beaten France well the year before. Despite having already won the Triple Crown the atmosphere still smacked very much of all-or-nothing. Very little attention, in relative terms, was paid to the Triple Crown, England had to win the Slam. And win it we did. The scenes on the pitch at the final whistle will long remain with me.

However, we cannot dwell on that success, because the World Cup and the opening challenge of New Zealand is upon us. We must improve, get even fitter, before the competition starts, and maintain our gameplan at a certain level. Opening up against the world champions means that we will have to be at our peak for the first game.

I believe the future of the English game is rosy. All the talk of players retiring after the World Cup may be premature. No-one is definitely retiring, but in any event there are a lot of talented players waiting in the wings for their chance to get involved.

IRELAND

Rob Saunders

CIARAN FITZGERALD's appointment as national coach, combined with the new bold attitude of the selectors were the two factors behind Ireland's transformation last season. While it was the players themselves who inspired the turnaround in fortunes, we were inspired by the backing we received off the field.

Prior to the season a lot of the players were cheesed off with the way things had been going and had really got themselves into a stalemate position. So when the chance arose to change the face of the national game, they jumped at it.

Ciaran is a very charismatic leader. He is very much part of the side – not above anybody else – and he puts a lot of work in. His enthusiasm, allied to the selectors' ambitious approach, combined to make the players think: 'Well they have given us their confidence, now let us show them what we can do.'

Okay, ultimately we lost and we shared the wooden spoon, but everyone had expected that to start with so we could afford to experiment without too much fear of criticism. Given the responsibility, we played 15-man rugby and we played it well and now people are all talking about the Irish team again: Simon Geoghegan, Jim Staples, a rejuvenated Brendan Mullin, Philip Matthews back to his best, and so on.

The future looks bright for Ireland but we would be wise not to get too carried away. After all, Ireland have shown fleeting good form in the past – take 1985 when we won the Triple Crown and then got whitewashed the next year – and we have not won anything yet. It is vital now that we do start winning and get into that habit, rather than one of narrowly losing, because, after all, that is what we are there for... to win Triple Crowns, Grand Slams, World Cups. You can play all the attractive rugby you want but at the end of the day winning is what really matters at international level.

I do not think we have seen the best out of Ireland yet, not by a long stretch. I believe there is now a depth of talent there. We have picked a squad of 44 players for the World Cup and any one of those players could take the 1–15 spot. We have virtually got three good sides available which is a very strong position in which to be.

Not that the start to the season hinted at such optimism. Our 20–18 win over Argentina, which was put very much into context by the results achieved against the Pumas by England (51–0) and Scotland (49–3), showed that there was need for changes. From what people tell me, spirits were very low at that point, and many of the players as well as the supporters felt that Ireland did not deserve to win.

Morale, however, did not seem to be a problem when I joined the squad because I was introduced with a new, young and confident batch of players, all of whom had helped Ireland B beat Scotland (16–0).

I would say that that B game in Belfast must have been the turning point of the season because of the amount of players who made reputations playing in it. One of the things that was stressed throughout the season was the need for players to take responsibility and it happened in that game. It would have been very easy to lie down and concede defeat after we were reduced to 14 men after just 14 minutes. Instead of which, as the game progressed everybody took more and more on themselves.

The Algarve training trip was another key period. A lot of good work was done there, conditions were excellent, and everybody got to know one another. We worked so closely together that by the end we had begun to get a feel for each other's abilities and strengths.

We then opened our Five Nations' account against France at Lansdowne Road (lost 13–21) and I do not think the result reflected how close the game was. We were encouraged by our performance because the 'experts' had expected it to be a 20- or 30-point whitewash. Steve Smith's early score got the crowd right behind us and, up until France's late try, I felt the result could have gone either way.

I was very confident that we would beat Wales (drew 21–21) especially as our selectors had made changes in certain positions and given us a back line that was a very good blend. But fair dues to Wales, they did raise their game and it turned out to be a super contest. Obviously, having scored four tries, we were very disappointed not to win but we did not lose and that was important.

The result did not make any difference to the way we approached the visit of England (lost 7–16) to Dublin. England were obviously a great side to win the Grand Slam but I maintain that they did not maximise their potential. I believe the Irish team played all aspects of the game, using every single player on the park. We scored ten tries, we were able to take the ball on in the forwards, we managed to win a lot of ball in the line-outs and we held our own in the scrums. We played 'rugby' while England opted for a distinct gameplan rather than the magical mix they had produced in 1990.

I believe that the previous year England made tactical errors against Scotland (i.e. running penalties and taking scrums instead of kicking goals) that cost them the Grand Slam. Had they taken their goalkicks, they would have beaten Scotland and if they had done that they would not have changed their gameplan this season. They had played very attractive rugby and come very close, and I think they should have stuck with it – the win this time would then have been with more attractive rugby. They've got fabulous players of whom we really did not see enough.

Our final game against Scotland (lost 25–28) was magnificent to play in and I am sure also to watch. But again it was bitterly disappointing and very, very frustrating not to win after such a performance.

I feel that our achievement in scoring ten Championship tries and yet failing to muster a win was down to lacking a prolific placekicker rather than poor defence. Within each game we were maybe one try away from winning the Grand Slam.

For that reason I believe the World Cup has come at just the right time for us. Once the tournament starts, we will study styles of play and adapt our gameplan to the particular style we are up against. But no matter who we are playing, be it Japan, Zimbabwe, Scotland or even New Zealand, we will approach every game in the same mental frame and treat the opposition with an equal amount of respect. If we do not we are asking for trouble.

It is going to be a very long season. But we have training programmes which will allow us to rest between the high points. Last season was also very long but I am not complaining. We are living in exciting times.

Ireland's International season 1990/91

Ireland

(H)	v. Argentina,	won	20–18
(H)	v. France,	lost	13–21
(A)	v. Wales,	drew	21–21
(H)	v. England,	lost	7–16
(A)	v. Scotland,	lost	25–28

Ireland B

(H)	v. Argentina,	won	27–12
(H)	v. Scotland B,	won	16–0
(A)	v. England B,	won	24–10

Ireland U–21

(A)	v. Netherlands,	lost	7–21
(A)	v. England U–21,	won	22–16

18-Group

(H)	v. Australia Schools,	lost	9–13
(A)	v. England 18-Group,	lost	0–15
(A)	v. Wales 18-Group,	lost	11–14
(H)	v. Scotland 18-Group,	won	27–9

SCOTLAND

David Sole

AS CAPTAIN, I found last season a lot tougher than than the previous one. It was not easy to lift the players after winning the Grand Slam and then coming so close to sharing the Test series in New Zealand. With hindsight, there was a little too much looking back as opposed to looking forward: expecting much of the past good work to come out without thinking about and reproducing the commitment that had made it possible in the first place.

It was a superb tour to New Zealand in every sense of the word. We had a great time off the field, which was very important for the gelling of the squad, and we performed well on it. In fact we were only the fourth side to go through New Zealand unbeaten in provincial games and that was a record of which we were particularly proud.

However, after coming so close to beating the All Blacks in the second Test (lost 18–21), where we outscored New Zealand two tries to one, it was very difficult to pick up the pieces and go again in the Five Nations' Championship where, of course, we were defending the Grand Slam.

It would have been very easy to have become complacent and in that respect we did well against Argentina (won 49–3), especially as we once again had to follow on from England. They got first crack at all our opponents during the Grand Slam and again, by beating Argentina 51–0, they set a benchmark for us to follow. But although we performed reasonably against the Pumas I was not so happy with our transition to the Five Nations' Championship.

Against France (lost 9–15), who Scotland had not beaten in Paris for twenty-two years, we were as well prepared as we could have been, yet as we got into the game situation we discovered we were not quite up to the pace of Five Nations' rugby – especially against opponents who had tuned themselves in with two Tests against the All Blacks. I had personally set a silent target, an ambition for the season, of winning in Paris. Even if that was our only win I would have been satisfied because it would have represented an immense achievement. But, on the day, the French were more prepared to adapt to the pace of international rugby and that proved very significant.

Next came the visit of Wales to Murrayfield. Our determination to put things right was total and at times we played as well as we had for a number of years. To be fair we had expected a lot more from their forwards – especially considering their opening performance against England – and they were disappointing. Yet that should not detract from our performance, a lot of which was very pleasing, but again we did not maintain it throughout the game.

So on to Twickenham where England had a very big point to prove and an old score to settle. We had to play a certain style of game to keep things alive but at the end of the day our gameplan fell short. We wanted them to kick to touch, believing we would then win the line-out but, while they did as we wanted, we did not capitalise (lost 12–21).

I must say I don't enjoy playing the kind of rugby which England did in 1991. Everyone plays to win and I sympathise with the English, having come so close the previous year playing outstanding rugby, but last season's was not as enjoyable to watch.

Our final match against Ireland (won 28–25) was a different story altogether. We were extremely lucky to beat them and I don't think we deserved to win because we were pretty poor. We did not tackle well, we did not kick well, our forwards were very loose and we did not even have as much of the game as them. All in all the game taught us a very salutary lesson about what to expect on 12 October when we meet again in the World Cup.

Looking back over the years and seeing how many games we have won in relation to previous Scottish sides, our record stands up very favourably. After our achievements of the previous season there was a great feeling of expectancy in Scotland and that put a lot of pressure on us. Our coaches – Ian McGeechan and Jim Telfer – would never allow complacency to creep in, but over the season we did not perform as well as we could have done, mainly due to injuries and lack of match fitness. I am also worried about the strength in depth of Scottish rugby. Although our A team, a new conception, enjoyed a good win in Spain (39–7), the B side lost their two matches heavily, to Ireland (0–16) and France (10–31).

We always seem to produce good back row players and we have two outstanding hookers in John Allan and Kenny Milne. But in certain other positions we are rather weak. The cover for myself and Paul Burnell is pretty sketchy and we appear thin on the ground in the second row department. It is amazing, though, how these things can turn themselves around.

Hopefully our summer tour to North America will have brought on the younger players. It will have been a tough trip though, not only because twelve of our front line Test players will not have been there, but also because we will have been playing against two emerging nations – the United States and Canada. But it will have provided a great opportunity for some of the younger players to state their cases for inclusion in the World cup squad.

I feel that the World Cup has come at the right time for us. The team is young enough and enthusiastic enough to rekindle for this great occasion.

One of the things we learnt from the first World Cup four years ago was the importance of using the squad in the pool matches. In 1987 we played our first choice team in all three pool games, because we were in a very strong group, and I believe we suffered for that. This time round (with Japan, Zimbabwe and Ireland) we may well use more players in the squad.

Having the World Cup at home will be slightly strange – an internal tour; we will still be apart from our families but perhaps only 20 miles away as opposed to nearer 20,000 previously – and it is imperative that we generate a tour atmosphere. In terms of application, we will become almost professional rugby players during that period, focusing our minds absolutely for the month-long duration of the biggest sporting event in Britain since the 1966 soccer World Cup.

Scotland's International season 1990/91

Scotland

(H)	v. Argentina,	won	49–3
(A)	v. France,	lost	9–15
(H)	v. Wales,	won	32–12
(A)	v. England,	lost	12–21
(H)	v. Ireland,	won	28–25

Scotland A

(A)	v. Spain,	won	39–7

Scotland B

(A)	v. Ireland B,	lost	0–16
(H)	v. France B,	lost	10–31

Scotland U–21

(A)	v. Wales,	lost	15–23

19-Group

(H)	v. Australia U–18s,	lost	12–17
(A)	v. Wales,	lost	20–23
(H)	v. England,	won	24–7

18-Group

(H)	v. Netherlands,	won	21–7
(A)	v. Spain,	lost	19–24

Scottish Schools

(A)	v. France,	lost	8–29
(H)	v. Wales,	lost	4–10
(A)	v. England,	lost	3–21
(H)	v. Ireland,	lost	9–27

15-Group

(A)	v. Wales,	lost	0–42

WALES

Paul Thorburn

I KNEW the 1990/91 season was going to be difficult from the start and unfortunately my fears were borne out as the season unfolded. It was very frustrating because each match gave us a little more hope and yet we were never able to carry on from where we left off in any one game.

We had a strange start to the season in that the Welsh Rugby Union decided to award caps for our match against the centenary Barbarians. I know there was a lot of fuss made in the media but, to be honest, it made no difference to the players. Nobody in the starting line-up was winning his first cap, although Adrian Davies did make his debut as replacement.

It was an unusual game in that they were running the ball from everywhere, which made it hard for us to try and establish some sort of pattern for the forthcoming Five Nations' Championship. It was obviously a good game for me personally as my 21 points was a new Welsh record, but there were signs in the game – notably at the line-out – that we were going to find life every bit as difficult as the previous year.

We started out against an England side (lost 6–25) with two points to prove. They had not won in Cardiff since 1963 and they had lost the previous two Championships at the final hurdle. I considered that it was only a matter of time before they got their act together. I was obviously hoping we would play well against them – as we had two years before when they probably should have won but blew it on the day – and indeed we did in places, especially up front, but unfortunately I missed a load of kicks which perhaps could have cost us the game. However, I think England had plenty in reserve and even had I been more successful, I'm sure they would have stepped up a gear or two.

England might not have won in Cardiff for more than a quarter of a century but, because of our very disappointing last couple of seasons, it was really just another game for us. Had we won every other match and then lost that game in Cardiff it would have been a different matter because everyone would have remembered it as our only defeat. The players around Wales certainly don't talk about it as much as I expected. But maybe in years to come I will be known as the captain who lost them the record after twenty-eight years.

Because the forwards had played well against England – held their own in scrummaging and even pushed England back on one occasion when they themselves were going for the shove – I felt this was an area we could maybe capitalise upon against Scotland (lost 12–32). Yet it was a totally different game up there and they took us apart. Maybe it was an attitude from the forwards' point of view: feeling that because they had done well against England, who were stronger than Scotland on paper, all they had to do was get down together and they would at least hold the Scots. Anyway, it didn't happen like that at all. But the backs did play well, creating plenty of opportunities and at one point, at 12–21, we certainly had Scotland on the rack for a while.

So, after a good forward performance against England and an encouraging display from the backs at Murrayfield, could we put it all together against Ireland? The answer, I'm afraid, was 'no', although, having said that, the Irish game (drew 21–21) was one of the most enjoyable I've played in, because it had a bit of everything.

I told all the players before they went out onto Parc des Princes for our final game against France (lost 3–36) that it would be probably the hardest game they would ever play in, purely because of the atmosphere and the way the French are. They get going, into their stride early on, and they are very difficult to stop, especially with the crowd behind them. And so it proved, although it didn't help that we conceded the first points after all of 35 seconds. Had that up-and-under not bounced the way it did it could have been a

Wales' International season 1990/91

Wales

(H)	v. Barbarians,	lost	24–31
(H)	v. England,	lost	6–25
(A)	v. Scotland,	lost	12–32
(H)	v. Ireland,	drew	21–21
(A)	v. France,	lost	3–36

Wales B

(A)	v. Netherlands,	won	34–12

Wales U–21

(H)	v. Scotland,	won	23–15

Welsh President's (U–21) XV

(H)	v. New Zealand Rugby News XV, won		34–13

Wales Youth

(A)	v. Italy,	won	11–6
(H)	v. France,	won	18–9
(H)	v. Japan,	won	21–9
(A)	v. England,	won	34–3

18-Group

(H)	v. Australia,	lost	0–44
(A)	v. Scotland,	won	10–4
(H)	v. Ireland,	won	14–11
(A)	v. France,	lost	9–24
(H)	v. England,	won	13–10

Tour to Australasia: (1) v. NSW, lost 8–10; (2) v. North Auckland, won
16–6; (3) v. Auckland, won 12–7; (4) v. Manawatu, won 25–10;
(5) v. Wairarapa-Bush, won 12–4; (6) v. Canterbury, won 33–14;
(7) v. New Zealand, won 17–11.

15-Group

(A)	v. Italy,	won	28–10
(A)	v. Italy B,	won	46–0
(H)	v. Scotland,	won	42–0

different matter, but when you are a side without confidence, you
don't get the breaks and I knew it was only a matter of holding on
and keeping the score down. There were again positive aspects,
although we were hammered, but what was disappointing was that
the backs didn't play well. We had a couple of opportunities but
perhaps through over-eagerness, or panicking, we fluffed them.

As regards the World Cup, we all appreciate the levels we have to attain, particularly when you look at what the England players have done. I remember playing against Wade Dooley in the 1987 World Cup and he wasn't anything like the player he is now. But over the last couple of years he has worked hard and become fitter and leaner, and now looks hungry for work. The young players that we have in the squad must realise the standards of fitness and performance that they have to achieve. And, to be honest, I think we still have a fair way to go.

The World Cup will be different from 1987 because we are at home this time; we'll have the luxury of being close to our families and will be able to see them now and again during the tournament, unlike before. And for all the players except one or two of us, it will be a unique experience.

The youngsters in the squad are still bubbly and full of confidence which is the only way to be. There is no point giving in if things are not going well because otherwise you would never get anywhere.

Of our World Cup Pool opponents, Western Samoa will be tough, as they have a number of useful players who play in New Zealand. We beat them 24–6 at the Arms Park in 1988 but I'm sure they will have come on a lot since then, and our side has certainly changed a great deal. Argentina, likewise, will be difficult, as of course will Australia. The bottom line is that nothing whatsoever can be taken for granted when your team has not been winning. That's the way we are at the moment.

I'm confident that if we get our act together we can win Pool Three. But that is a big 'if'. We've got to realise the level of work that we have to put in, and that we have three hard games but that we can win them. We beat Australia (22–21) in the last World Cup (third-place play-off) and we can do it again. We have a vastly changed side but I honestly believe that the potential of the players now is as good as it was then. It only needs something to happen to gel together – one or two players in certain positions getting everyone around them clicking and things could turn out well. It can happen for us as it can happen for anybody.

THE PLAYERS A-Z

KEY TO INDIVIDUAL STATISTICS

Take Joe Soap (below) as an example. Joe made his England B debut in 1981 and last season won two B caps, scoring 4 points. He was first capped at senior England level in 1982, won 4 caps last season (was replacement in one), and has 32 caps in all, with 58 points to his credit. He also played in the non-cap International against the centenary Barbarians last season, landing a conversion. In 1991, Joe toured Australia with England and was included in the preliminary World Cup squad. He is included in England's Development squad for the 1995 World Cup. He won selection to the 1983 British Lions tour to New Zealand but did not play in a Test. However, he played in the 1986 IRB Centenary match in Cardiff (Lions 7, The Rest 15) which has been included as a Lions cap. In 1989 he played one Test in the series against Australia. He switched club allegiances across Severn Bridge last season and played 15 Heineken Welsh League matches, contributing 38 points.

If an uncapped player is selected as bench replacement and does not play, the fact is recorded as 'England (1990/91) 1 rep'.

* The qualification for entry in *The Rugby Union Who's Who* is involvement in one of the four Home Union squads (U-21 up to senior XV) during the 1990/91 season (September 1990–Mae 1991) or selection for either a preliminary World Cup squad or, in England's case, their 1995 Development squad. Players' statistics include summer tours.

	apps	pts
England B (**1981**)		
Last Season	2 caps	4
England (**1982**)		
Last Season	4 caps	0
	1 rep	
v. Barbarians	1 app	2
1991	Tour to Australia	
	World Cup squad	
	1995 Development squad	
Career	32 caps	58
Lions 1983		
1986		
1989	1 Test	0
Heineken 1990/91	15 apps	38

Ackford, P. J.   England

Full Name: Paul John Ackford
1990/91 International category:
England Full
Club: Harlequins
Position: Lock
Height: 6'6" **Weight:** 17st 4lbs
Occupation: Police officer
Born: Hanover, West Germany,
26.2.58
Family: Suzie (wife)
Family links with rugby: Father
played for Army
Former clubs: Plymouth Albion,
Rosslyn Park, Met Police
International debut: England 28,
Australia 19, 1988
Five Nations' debut: England 12,
Scotland 12, 1989
Best moments in rugby: Final
whistle in decisive third Test,
Australia v. 1989 Lions. Winning
1991 Grand Slam
Worst moment in rugby: Losing
1990 Grand Slam decider to
Scotland
Most embarrassing moment:
Losing ball to Rob Andrew in
mauling practice
Most respected opponent:
England lock Wade Dooley –
because he's bigger than me
Serious injuries: Assorted shoulder
and rib injuries

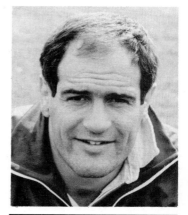

	apps	pts
England B (**1979**)		
Last Season	0 caps	0
England (**1988**)		
Last Season	6 caps	0
v. Barbarians	1 app	0
1991	Tour to Australia	
	World Cup squad	
Career	17 caps	4
Lions (1989)	3 Tests	0

Other sporting achievements: Worst Celebrity-Am golfer on the circuit
Best memory last season: England's Grand Slam
Suggestions to improve rugby: Introduce a compulsory retiring age of 55
for all alickadoos
Other notable landmarks in rugby career: Spotting former *Daily Mail*
Rugby Correspondent Terry O'Connor buying a drink. Being complimented
by a back – it must happen one day
Touchlines: Cooking, eating

Adam, D. R. W.   Scotland

Full Name: Douglas Russell
Wallace Adam
1990/91 International category:
Scotland U-21/B (bench)
Club: Edinburgh Academicals
Position: Centre
Height: 6' **Weight:** 13st 5lbs
Occupation: Student
Born: Nassau, Bahamas, 20.7.70
Family: Single
Family links with rugby: Mother's
family related to Osler brothers
(South African Internationals in
1920s)
International debut (U-21):
Scotland 10, Wales 24, 1990
Best moments in rugby: Playing
for Scotland U-21 and being selected
for 1991 Scotland squad
Worst moment in rugby: Not
making Scotland team during a year
in squad
Most respected opponent:
Scotland centre Sean Lineen
Other sporting achievement: Play
cricket for Stirling County
Best memories last season:
Helping Scotland beat Ireland in

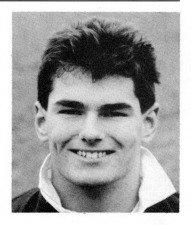

	apps	pts
Scotland U-21 (**1990**)		
Last Season	1 cap	4
Career	2 caps	4
Scotland B (1990/91)	1 rep	

Students international. Playing opposite Ireland caps Brendan Mullin and
Brian Smith for Edinburgh against Leinster. Working with national coach Ian
McGeechan
Suggestions to improve rugby: *On-field* – Encourage tries by devaluing
worth of penalty goal; introduce moving mark to protect full-backs. *Off-field*
– Clarify laws of amateurism and adopt universal regulations
Other notable landmarks in rugby career: Toured New Zealand in 1988
with Scottish Schools. Played for Scotland U-19s (wing) and involved with
U-21s for last three seasons (first on bench). Scored try for Scotland U-21s
in 23–15 loss to Wales U-21s last season. Also played for Edinburgh U-21s.
Represented North and Midlands before having played for Edinburgh
Academicals first team. Ever-present in Scotland Students' 1990/91 team.
Selected as replacement for Scotland B in 10–31 loss to France B at
Hughenden last season

Adams, G. E. England

Full Name: Gareth Edward Adams
1990/1991 International category:
England U-21
Club: Bath
Position: Flanker
Height: 5'11" **Weight:** 14st 4lbs
Occupation: Chemistry student
Born: Wakefield, 12.9.70
Family: Single
Family links with rugby: Brother
(Jonathan) and father (Jack) played
for Sandal
Former club: Sandal
International debut (U-21):
England 16, Ireland 22, 1990
Best moment in rugby: Winning
1991 National Sevens with Bath
Worst moment in rugby: Tearing
knee cartilage in first match of
England 18-Group's 1988 tour to
Australia
Most respected opponent: The
French
Serious injuries: Torn knee
cartilage
Best memory last season: Winning
National Sevens at Bath

	apps	pts
England U-21 (1990)		
Last Season	3 caps	0
Career	3 caps	0

Other notable landmarks in rugby career: Ever-present for England U-21s
last season (three games), captaining side to 20–18 win over Netherlands and
in 7–9 loss to French Armed Forces. Played two seasons for both England
16-Group and 18-Group
Player to watch: Martin Haag (Bath)

Adebayo, A. A.   England

Full Name: Adedayo Adeyemi
Adebayo
1990/91 International category:
England B
Club: Bath
Positions: Wing, centre
Height: 5'11" **Weight:** 14st
Occupation: Student
Born: Ibadan, Nigeria, 30.11.70
Family: Single
Family links with rugby: Brother
(Lecke) played for Devon and South
West
International debut: England B 50,
Spain 6, 1991
Best moment in rugby: Helping
England 18-Group beat Australia
(Canberra, 1988)
Worst moment in rugby: Injuries
Most respected opponent: All of
them
Serious injuries: Torn hamstring,
ankle and knee ligaments
Best memory last season:
Selection to full England squad for
training trip to Lanzarote
Suggestions to improve rugby:

	apps	pts
England B (1991)		
Last Season	3 caps	8
Career	3 caps	8

On-field – Award more points for a try to discourage kicking. *Off-field* – More
drinking
Other notable landmarks in rugby career: Marked England B debut with
two of England's nine tries against Spain at Kingsholm on 20 January, 1991.
Had been selected for England B against Namibia on 2 November, 1990 but
was forced to withdraw with hamstring injury. Played v. Italy and France later
in season. Represented England at 16-Group (two seasons) and 18-Group
(two seasons)
Players to watch: Gareth Adams/Steve Ojomoh (both Bath)

Aherne, L. F. P.   Ireland

Full Name: Leslie Fergus Patrick
Aherne
1990/91 International category:
Ireland (World Cup squad)
Club: Lansdowne
Position: Scrum-half
Height: 5'9" **Weight:** 12st 3lbs
Occupation: Civil engineer
Born: Cork, 16.3.63
Family: Elaine (wife)
Family links with rugby: Father
(Gerald) played for Munster
Former clubs: University College
Cork, Dolphin
International debut: Ireland 10,
England 21, 1988
Five Nations' debut: Ireland 21,
France 26, 1989
Best moment in rugby: Playing for
Ireland v. 1989 All Blacks
Most respected opponent:
Swansea scrum-half Robert Jones
Best memory last season: Winning
Leinster Cup final with Lansdowne
Suggestions to improve rugby:
On-field – Differentiate more
between penalty and try. *Off-field* –
Remuneration for loss of earnings
due to rugby – but guard against
game going professional

	apps	pts
Ireland (**1988**)		
Last Season	0 caps	0
1991	Tour to Namibia	
	World Cup squad	
Career	12 caps	4

Other notable landmarks in rugby career: Played for UCC for four
seasons, captaining them to 1984/85 Munster Senior League title. Made
Provincial bow with Leinster, after breaking into Ireland team and returning
with them from tour of France. Toured with Ireland to North America (1989)
and captained Leinster in 1989/90 Irish Inter-Provincial Championship.
Bench reserve for Ireland B in 27–12 win over Argentina last season
Touchlines: Golf
Player to watch: Conor O'Shea (Lansdowne)

Ainscough, G. C.   England

Full Name: Gerry Christopher Ainscough

1990/91 International category: England B

Club: Orrell

Positions: Centre, fly-half

Height: 5'11" **Weight:** 11st 7lbs

Occupation: Mechanical engineer

Born: Wigan, 7.8.64

Family: Karen (wife)

Family links with rugby: Father and uncle played schoolboy rugby league for Wigan

International debut: Spain 9, England B 31, 1989

Best moment in rugby: Orrell beating Wasps in quarter-finals of 1990/91 Pilkington Cup

Worst moment in rugby: Orrell's defeat by Northampton in semi-finals of 1990/91 Pilkington Cup

Most embarrassing moment: Falling into compost heap whilst retrieving practice ball prior to debut for Wigan Schools Rugby League U-11s (1974)

	apps	pts
England B (**1989**)		
Last Season	1 rep	
Career	1 cap	0

Most respected opponent: Gloucester as a team – locally born players with great pride and immense will to win

Serious injuries: Prolapsed spinal disc, torn medial ligaments

Other sporting achievements: Wigan Schools Rugby League, football and athletics

Best memory last season: The way Orrell played for three-quarters of the season

Suggestions to improve rugby: *On-field* – Simplify rules to reduce number of stoppages and allow a more flowing game. Increase points awarded for tries and conversions – decrease points for penalty and dropped goal. Reduce number of players by eliminating flankers. *Off-field* – Like the off-field status of northern-based rugby players to rival that of those down south. It would have done had Orrell maintained their form to the end of last season in League and Cup

Other notable landmarks in rugby career: Playing at Wembley (1975) for

Wigan Schools Rugby League U-11s. Senior debut for Orrell (1983). Lancashire debut (1985). Dropped goal for Orrell from 45 metres, with 2 minutes remaining in 1988 Lancs Cup semi-final v. Waterloo, to win 9–7. Helped Lancashire win County final at Twickenham and Orrell win first Lancs Cup (1988). North of England debut and England B tour (1989). Scored over 1,200 first-class points in career. Scored 12 points in England B's 32–15 defeat of Spanish Select (1989). Selected as replacement for England B in last season's 31–16 defeat of Namibia at Leicester
Touchlines: Cricket

Allan, J. Scotland

Full Name: John Allan
1990/91 International category:
Scotland Full
Club: Edinburgh Academicals
Position: Hooker
Height: 6′ **Weight:** 14st 8lbs
Occupation: Sales executive for
Save & Prosper
Born: Glasgow, 25.11.63
Family: Single
Family links with rugby: Brothers
both play: William in Italy and
Richard for Empangeni in Durban,
South Africa
Former clubs: Glenwood Old Boys,
Northern Transvaal Defence (SA)
International debut: New Zealand
31, Scotland 16, 1990
Five Nations' debut: Scotland 32,
Wales 12, 1991
Best moment in rugby: Running
out at Murrayfield for Five Nations'
debut against Wales
Worst moment in rugby: Leaving
the pitch injured after 47 minutes of
above match
Most respected opponent:
Springbok hooker Uli Schmidt –
totally dedicated to the game
Serious injuries: Snapped knee
ligaments

	apps	pts
Scotland A (**1990**)		
Last Season	1 cap	0
Career	1 cap	0
Scotland (**1990**)		
Last Season	2 caps	0
	2 reps	
1991	World Cup squad	
Career	3 caps	0

Other sporting achievements: Playing softball for Scotland Schools
Best memory last season: Nearly scoring try for Scotland v. Wales
Suggestions to improve rugby: *On-field* – Stop negative rugby by preventing players from spoiling the opposition's ball. Penalise offenders heavily, perhaps by automatic penalty in front of the posts. *Off-field* – Allow South Africa back into the international rugby fold. SA rugby has been integrated for a long time, they have done everything asked of them and more
Other notable landmarks in rugby career: Warmed Scotland's replacements' bench throughout 1990/91 season, and was replacement for Scotland B against Ireland and France, before making full-debut in first Test at Dunedin on summer tour of New Zealand. Made Five Nations' debut against Wales and again played at Murrayfield against Ireland after missing game in between against England through injury
Touchlines: Reading
Player to watch: Jeremy Thompson – South African centre with great future who played part of last season with Edinburgh Academicals before returning home

Allingham, M. J. de G.   Scotland

Full Name: Michael James De Grey Allingham
1990/91 International category: Scotland B (bench)
Club: Heriot's FP
Position: Scrum-half
Height: 6'0.5" **Weight:** 14st
Occupation: Sports coach
Born: Inverness, 6.1.65
Family: Single
Former clubs: Eastern Suburbs (Aus), Highland, Keynshan
International debut: Scotland Schools v. France Schools (1983)
Best moment in rugby: Playing in North/Midlands team which gave 1988 Wallabies such a good game
Worst moment in rugby: Missing Scotland B debut v. Ireland due to flu
Most embarrassing moment: Losing both contact lenses in course of one match

	apps
Scotland B (1990/91)	1 rep

Most respected opponent: Jed-Forest scrum half Gary Armstrong – great challenge

Other sporting achievements: Cricket – Scottish national squad

Best memory last season: Selection for Scotland B

Suggestions to improve rugby: *On-field* – Current laws offer too much of an advantage to sides who are prepared to organise defence. Any advantage should go to teams endeavouring to exhibit running and handling skills. Increase differential between try and penalty goal

Other notable landmarks in rugby career: Represented North/Midlands for four years in Scottish Inter-District Championship before switching allegiances to Edinburgh last season. Spent season playing in Australia for Sydney club Eastern Suburbs. Selected to make Scotland B debut against Ireland in Belfast (December 1990) but forced out by a bout of flu. Thereafter, lost out to Dundee HSFP's Andy Nicol (who was deputy to me at Heriot's in 1989/90) for following International against France B (March 1991) – only selected to the replacements' bench

Touchlines: Cricket

Player to watch: Andy Macdonald (Heriot's FP)

Amos, J. P. Scotland

Full Name: John Peter Amos
1990/91 International category: Scotland (tour squad)
Club: Gala
Position: Flanker
Height: 6′ **Weight:** 14st
Occupation: Joiner
Born: Bergen, Norway, 25.1.68
Family: Single
Family links with rugby: Brother (Brian) plays for Gala YM
Former club: Gala YM
Best moment in rugby: Making Gala first team debut in 1986 aged 17 v. Middlesbrough
Worst moment in rugby: Having kick charged down by Canada, which led to a try, in last season's Gala Sevens

Most embarrassing moment: As above
Most respected opponent: Stewart's-Melville flanker Finlay Calder

Best memory last season: Gaining
selection for Scotland tour to North
America

Suggestions to improve rugby:
On-field – More points for a try
because penalty goals are ruining
games. Team with most tries wins. *Off-field* – Scottish game is in healthy state.
SRU are doing well although I feel more coaching is needed at younger levels
Other notable landmarks in rugby career: Represented Scotland U-18s
(at centre) and South U-21s. Invited by national selectors to attend National
Squad weekend at St Andrews (March 1991), prior to gaining selection for
Scotland's North American tour. Played v. British Columbia (won 29–9),
Rugby East (won 24–12) and Ontario (won 43–3)
Touchlines: Supporting Rangers and Liverpool
Player to watch: Gregor Townsend (Gala)

Andrew, C. R.   England

Full Name: Christopher Robert
Andrew
1990/91 International category:
England Full
Club: Wasps
Position: Fly-half
Height: 5′9″ **Weight:** 12st 7lbs
Occupation: Chartered surveyor
Born: Richmond, Yorkshire, 18.2.63
Family: Sara (wife) and Emily
(daughter)
Family links with rugby: Brothers
Richard and David playing for
Headingley
Former clubs: Middlesbrough,
Cambridge University (Blues:
1982,83,84), Nottingham, Gordon
(Sydney, Aus)
International debut: England 22,
Romania 15, 1985
Five Nations' debut: England 9, France 9, 1985
Best moment in rugby: Beating France 21–19 at Twickenham to win 1991
Five Nations' Grand Slam decider
Worst moment in rugby: Losing 1990 Grand Slam decider 13–7 to Scotland

Most embarrassing moment:
Missing 9 out of 10 kicks at goal for
Nottingham v. London Welsh in
1986 John Player Cup
Most respected opponent:
Australia fly-half Michael Lynagh
Other sporting achievements:
Played first-class cricket for
Yorkshire 2nd XI and Cambridge
Univ, 1984 and 1985 (as captain).
Scored 101 n. o. for Univ against
Notts at Trent Bridge (1984)
Best memory last season: The
final whistle v. France

	apps	pts
England B (1988)		
Last Season	0 caps	0
England (1985)		
Last Season	7 caps	13
v. Barbarians		
1991	Tour to Australia	
	World Cup squad	
Career	38 caps	142
Lions 1989	2 Tests	8

Suggestions to improve rugby: *On-field* – End season with Five Nations –
later in year (March-April). Remove the 10-yard law for offside for players
in front of ball (revert to old law). Reduce number of offences for which kicks
at goal are permitted. *Off-field* – Allow players to take advantage of off-field
commercial activities. The game is a multi-million pound industry and
therefore should be administered accordingly. Question future of International
Board
Other notable landmarks in rugby career: Established England records for
points scored in an International (21) and penalties kicked (6), in England's
21–18 defeat of Wales at Twickenham in 1986 (both surpassed by Simon
Hodgkinson last season v. Wales). Selection for 1989 Lions and Home Unions.
Captained England v. Romania in Bucharest (May 1989) and Home Unions
v. France in Paris (1989). Divisional rugby both for North (1985, 1987) and
London (1989–90). Most dropped goals by England international. Most
capped fly-half. Captained Wasps to 1989/90 Courage Championship.
Captained London to 1990 Divisional Championship. Stepped down as
Wasps captain at end of last season. Scored first try for England in 28-12 win
over Fiji in Suva last summer.
Touchlines: Gardening, pushing a pram, golf (28-handicap, at least)
Player to watch: Ian Hunter (Northampton) – exceptional pace and strength

Armstrong, G.   Scotland

Full Name: Gary Armstrong
1990/91 International category:
Scotland Full
Club: Jed-Forest
Position: Scrum-half
Height: 5'8" **Weight:** 13st 7lbs
Occupation: Lorry driver
Born: Edinburgh, 30.9.66
Family: Shona (wife) and Darren
James (son)
Family links with rugby: Father
played for Jed-Forest. Brother played
for Jed-Forest and Scotland U-21s
Former club: Jed Thistle
International debut: Scotland 13,
Australia 32, 1988
Five Nations' debut: Scotland 23,
Wales 7, 1989
Best moment in rugby: Beating
England to win 1990 Grand Slam
Most respected opponent: French
scrum-half Pierre Berbizier
Serious injuries: Torn knee, ankle
ligaments, damaged elbow
Best memory last season: Scotland
28, Ireland 25
Suggestions to improve rugby:
On-field – Step up points for try (5)
and conversion (3) to encourage
more open game. Scrap 90-degree

	apps	pts
Scotland B (**1987**)		
Last Season	0 caps	0
Career	2 caps	12
Scotland (**1988**)		
Last Season	5 caps	8
1991	World Cup squad	
Career	18 caps	12
Lions 1989		

scrum wheel law. Referees could do with more rugby at top-level and a more
unified interpretation of the laws. *Off-field* – Quite happy just now. SRU
keeping well in touch with players on amateurism issue
Other notable landmarks in rugby career: Represented Scotland at U-18,
Youth, U-21 and twice at B level in 1988, v. Italy (won 37-0) and France
(won 18–12). Scored hat-trick of tries on B debut v. Italy at Seafield. Selected
to tour Australia with 1989 Lions, playing v. Australia B (won 23–18),
Queensland B (won 30–6), New South Wales B (won 39–19), Australian
Capital Territory (won 41–25) and New South Wales Country (won 72–13),
and accumulating five tries. Integral part of Scotland's 1990 Five Nations'
Grand Slam-winning side
Player to watch: 'Doddie' Weir (Melrose)

Arnold, P. Wales

Full Name: Paul Arnold
1990/91 International category:
Wales Full
Club: Swansea
Position: Lock
Height: 6'5" **Weight:** 16st
Occupation: Builder
Born: 28.4.68
Family: Single
International debut: Namibia 9,
Wales 18, 1990
Best moment in rugby: Going to
Namibia after injured Gareth
Llewellyn withdrew
Worst moment in rugby: Not
being originally picked for Welsh
tour to Namibia
Most respected opponent:
Newport's former Welsh lock David
Waters

Best memory last season: Scoring
try for Wales in 21–21 draw with
Ireland
Suggestions to improve rugby:
On-field – Permit non-powered
scrum if team loses prop. *Off-field* –
Consider introducing win bonuses.
Believe that game will go
semi-professional by next World
Cup
**Other notable landmarks in rugby
career:** In fourth season with
Swansea, having progressed through
All Whites' youth set-up. Also gained
experience playing in New Zealand

	apps	pts
Wales U-21 (**1990**)		
Last Season	0 caps	0
Career	1 cap	0
Wales B (**1990**)		
Last Season	1 cap	0
Career	1 cap	0
Wales (**1990**)		
Last Season	6 caps	4
1991	Tour to Australia	
	World Cup squad	
Career	8 caps	4
Heineken 1990/91	13 apps	4

(summer 1989). Played for Wales U-21s in their 24–10 defeat of Scotland
at Ayr (1990) and followed that with selection for Wales' tour of Namibia,
where won selection to full team for both Tests. Ever-present for Wales last
season
Touchlines: Sunday soccer, indoor 5-a-side, indoor cricket, squash,
swimming
Player to watch: Steele Lewis (Pontypridd)

Back, N. A.   England

Full Name: Neil Antony Back
1990/91 International category:
England B
Club: Leicester
Position: Openside flanker
Height: 5'10" **Weight:** 13st 7lbs
Occupation: Assurance clerk
Born: Coventry, 16.1.69
Family: Single
Former club: Nottingham
International debut: England B 12,
Emerging Australians 12, 1990
Best moment in rugby: Scoring
three tries on England U-21 debut v.
Romania U-21s in Bucharest
Most respected opponent:
England flanker Andy Robinson
Serious injuries: Broken arm (aged
16)
Other sporting achievements:
Cricket for Coventry and
Warwickshire Schools
Suggestions to improve rugby:
Establish worldwide, uniform
guidelines concerning amateurism
**Other notable landmarks in rugby
career:** Represented England U-18s
(1985–87), England Colts
(1987/88), England U-21s
(1988–90) and England XV (1990),
scoring try in 33–15 win over Italy.
Came on as replacement in
Barbarians' 16–18 loss to England (September 1990) and was described by
the *Daily Telegraph's* John Mason as 'the pocket-sized Hercules among
England back row forwards' for a 'masterly' performance. Rewarded with
four B caps
Touchlines: Training five days a week for rugby. Weight training, squash,
badminton

	apps	pts
England U-21 (**1989**)		
Last Season	0 caps	0
Career	3 caps	12
England B (**1990**)		
Last Season	4 caps	0
Career	4 caps	0
England XV (1989/90)	1 cap	4
Barbarians XV		
v. England (1990/91)	1 cap	0

Barley, B.   England

Full Name: Bryan Barley
1990/1991 International category:
England B
Club: Wakefield
Position: Centre
Height: 5'10" **Weight:** 13st 7lbs
Occupation: Insurance broker
Born: Wakefield, 4.1.60
Family: Jayne (wife), Hanna,
Rebecca (daughters) and William
(son)
International debut: England 12,
Ireland 9, 1984
Five Nations' debut: As above
Best moment in rugby: Scoring try
for England v. Fiji (Suva 1988)
Worst moment in rugby: Not
being picked for England v. France
in 1988 after scoring try to help
England B beat England in Trial
Most respected opponent: Former
French centre Didier Codorniou
Serious injuries: Two damaged
knees, broken jaw
Suggestions to improve rugby:
On-field – Make sure skills are
coached in practice rather than
concentrate all the time on fitness and
game plans. Improve consistency of

	apps	pts
England B (1988)		
Last Season	1 cap	0
England (1984)		
Last Season	0 caps	0
Career	7 caps	4

refereeing standards. *Off-field* – Inevitable that game will go professional for a small percentage. I'm happy with my lot but the commitment some players are putting in deserves some reimbursement. It is like having two jobs, and is becoming a single man's game
Other notable landmarks in rugby career: Returning to international rugby after two serious knee operations. Helped England B beat touring Namibians 31–16 at Leicester (November 1990)
Touchlines: Relaxing with family
Player to watch: Philip de Glanville (Bath)

Barrett, D.   Scotland

Full Name: David Barrett
1990/91 International category:
Scotland B
Club: West of Scotland
Position: Full-back
Height: 5'10" **Weight:** 12st 6lbs
Occupation: PE teacher
Born: London, 25.7.63
Family: Wendy (wife) and Amy
(daughter)
Former club: Edinburgh University
International debut (B): Scotland
22, Ireland 22, 1989
Best moment in rugby: Glasgow
securing last-minute victory over
Anglo-Scots to win 1990
Inter-District Championship
Worst moment in rugby: Being
relegated from Scottish first division
in 1989/90 with West
Most respected opponent: Former
Ireland midfield back Mike Gibson
(I was 19, he was 41 and, to this day,
still the best player I have come up
against)
Best memory last season: West
winning promotion back to first
division

	apps	pts
Scotland B (**1989**)		
Last Season	1 cap	0
Career	3 caps	12

Suggestions to improve rugby: *On-field* – Establish a Scottish knock-out cup. Leave points-worth for tries and pens alone. If reduce worth of penalties, more fouls would be committed. *Off-field* – I'm a traditionalist who has always played rugby for fun and always will. Do not really agree with what's happening off the field commercially nor the speed with which it's happening
Other notable landmarks in rugby career: Being invited to tour Canada with West in 1983 and subsequently joining club permanently. Switching from fly-half to full-back in 1988. Represented Scotland B v. Ireland and France in 1989/90 and Ireland again last season in 0–16 defeat in Belfast. Topped Scottish points – scoring charts last season and represented Scotland B v. Ireland B in 16-0 Belfast loss
Touchlines: Golf, cricket, DIY, gardening, looking after Amy
Player to watch: Gregor Townsend (Gala)

Barry, N.   Ireland

Full Name: Nick Barry
1990/1991 International category:
Ireland B
Club: Garryowen
Positions: Wing, fly-half
Height: 5'11" **Weight:** 12st 7lbs
Occupation: BSc student
Born: 5.1.69 **Family:** Single
Family links with rugby: All
family, except females, play
International debut: Ireland B 27,
Argentina 12, 1990
Best moments in rugby:
Captaining Irish Schools. Touring
France with Ireland aged 19. Being
selected for Ireland's 1991 tour to
Namibia
Worst moment in rugby: Losing
Munster Senior Cup final

Most embarrassing moment:
Once playing a match with no boots
Most respected opponent:
Australian wing David Campese –
tremendous ability to attack from
anywhere on field
Serious injuries: Broken hand
Other sporting achievements:
All-Ireland sprint (athletics)
Best memory last season: Kicking
8 points v. Argentina on Ireland B
debut

	apps	pts
Ireland U-21 (**1988**)		
Last Season	0 caps	0
Ireland U-25 (**1990**)		
Last Season	1 cap	14
Ireland B (**1990**)		
Last Season	3 caps	8
Career	3 caps	8
Ireland 1991	Tour to Namibia	
	World Cup squad	

Suggestions to improve rugby:
Move season to May and June to allow a faster game of rugby to be played
Other notable landmarks in rugby career: Toured Australia (with Irish
Schools), Canada and France (with Ireland). Graduated to Ireland B team
after two seasons with U-21s and won caps against Argentina (October 1990)
and England (March 1991) last season. Landed one conversion and two
penalty goals in the 27–12 defeat of the touring Pumas at Thomond Park.
Contributed 14 points to Ireland U-25's 36–17 win over Spain last season.
Invited to tour Namibia with Ireland last summer. Included in preliminary
World Cup squad for World Cup
Touchlines: Greyhound racing

Bates, S. M.   England

Full Name: Steven Michael Bates
1990/91 International category:
England B
Club: Wasps
Position: Scrum-half
Height: 5'10" **Weight:** 13st
Occupation: Teacher
Born: Merthyr Tydfil, 4.3.63
Family: Sarah (wife) and Lottie
(daughter)
Former clubs: West London
Institute, Welwyn
International debut: Romania 3,
England 58, 1989
Best moment in rugby: Winning
first cap in Bucharest
Worst moment in rugby:
Twickenham pitch invasion near end
of Wasps' 1987 John Player Cup
final defeat by Bath. Took dignity
out of occasion as referee was forced
to 'abandon' game
Most respected opponent: Former
New Zealand scrum-half Dave
Loveridge

	apps	pts
England B (**1991**)		
Last Season	1 cap	0
England (**1989**)		
Last Season	0 caps	0
Career	1 cap	0
England XV (**1989/90**)	1 app	0

Serious injuries: Broken jaw
(1983/84) and arm (1986 JP Cup
final), medial ligaments (1990)
Other sporting achievements:
Soccer for Hertfordshire. Golf
(14-handicap)
Best memory last season: Beating Orrell with injury-time score in English
League match
Suggestions to improve rugby: Happy with game on and off the field. After
injury problems last season I am just content to be playing game again
Other notable landmarks in rugby career: Joined Wasps (1981) and
immediately represented Herts. English Colleges (1981–83). Toured Japan
with England Students (1982). Played for London Division since 1986.
England U-23 against Spain (1986). Helped Wasps win 1989/90 English
League Championship. England replacement for first time against 1988
Wallabies and won first cap the following year in 58–3 win over Romania in
Bucharest. Flew out to Argentina to join England tour in summer of 1990 as

replacement. Missed bulk of last season through medial ligament injury. Out for six months after operation (15 Sept). Returned in time to help England B defeat Italy B 12–9 at Waterloo. Toured Australia with London last summer
Touchlines: Photography – built own darkroom

Bayfield, M. C. England

Full Name: Martin Christopher Bayfield
1990/91 International category: England Full
Club: Northampton
Position: Lock
Height: 6′10″ **Weight:** 18st
Occupation: Police constable
Born: Bedford, 21.12.66
Family: Single
Former clubs: Metropolitan Police, Bedford
International debut: Fiji 12, England 28, 1991
Best moments in rugby: Twice representing England B during 1990/91 season
Worst moment in rugby: Bedford's relegation from English first division at end of season 1989/90
Most respected opponent: Harlequins' Paul Ackford
Best memory last season: Bedford beating London Scottish to ease relegation worries in English second division
Suggestions to improve rugby: *On-field* – Lifting should be permitted at the line-out. It is a bit of an art and, anyway, everyone does it. *Off-field* – Put an end to confusion over amateurism. Personally, I believe money spells bad news for rugby. But while there should be no financial reward for playing, there is no reason why players should not be reimbursed for loss of earnings and even given a free holiday with their family each year
Other notable landmarks in rugby career: Played three games for England 18-Group. Represented Midlands Division and British Police for three seasons. Toured with British Police to Italy (1989). Broke into England B

	apps	pts
England (**1991**)		
Last Season	2 caps	0
1991	Tour to Australia	
	World Cup squad	
Career	2 caps	0

set-up last season, playing v. Emerging Australians and Italy. Selected both for England's summer tour to Australia, where made full debut v. Fiji, and their preliminary World Cup squad
Touchlines: Weight training
Player to watch: Neil Back (Leicester)

Booth, A. H. Wales

Full Name: Andrew Howell Booth
1990/91 International category: Wales (World Cup squad)
Club: Cardiff
Position: Scrum-half
Height: 5'10" **Weight:** 13st
Occupation: Financial sales consultant
Born: Swansea, 8.12.68
Family: Single
Family links with rugby: Father played for West Wales
Former clubs: UC Swansea, Neath
International debut (B): France 28, Wales 15, 1989
Best moment in rugby: Replacement for Wales v. 1989 All Blacks (lost 9–34)
Worst moment in rugby: Being dropped from any team
Most respected opponent: Swansea scrum-half Robert Jones
Serious injuries: Cracked ankle ligaments, Achilles tendon
Best memory last season: Cardiff beating Llanelli 43-0
Suggestions to improve rugby: *On-field* – Better understanding of coaching and needs. Boost confidence of all players at all times leading up to a match – criticise constructively

	apps	pts
Wales B (1989)		
Last Season	0 caps	0
Career	1 cap	0
Wales 1991	World Cup squad	
Heineken 1990/91	5 apps	8

Other notable landmarks in rugby career: West Wales U-11s, Welsh Schools U-15s, U-18s, U-21s, Students (scored 15 points), Wales B (v. France, 1989). Played for Cardiff v. 1989 All Blacks. 1989 Cambridge Blue.

Welsh replacement (1989/90) and selected to Wales' preliminary World Cup squad. Captained Wales Students last season
Touchlines: Golf (14-handicap), squash
Player to watch: Rob Saunders (London Irish)

Booth, R. D. England

Full Name: Richard Daniel Booth
1990/91 International category: England U-21
Club: Sale
Position: Scrum-half
Height: 5'8.5" **Weight:** 11st 8lbs
Occupation: Student
Born: Reading, Berkshire, 18.1.70
Family: Single
Family links with rugby: Father (Keith) played for Fylde, Lancashire and North West Counties
International debut (U-21): England 16, Ireland 22, 1990
Best moment in rugby: Helping England Schools beat New Zealand in 1988
Worst moment in rugby: Have not had one ... yet
Best memory last season: Sale retaining their English second division status
Suggestions to improve rugby: *On-field* – Reduce worth of penalty goal to 2 points
Other notable landmarks in rugby career: Won six caps for England

	apps	pts
England U-21 (**1991**)		
Last Season	2 caps	3
Career	2 caps	3

Schools in 1988. Also represented Yorkshire and North Division at Schools and U-21 level. Given England U-21 debut in match v. Ireland at Moseley last season, and landed penalty goal on second appearance, in 7–9 loss to French Armed Forces (May 1991)
Touchlines: Cricket
Player to watch: Laurence Dallaglio (Wasps)

Bowling, S. A.   Wales

Full Name: Stephen Anthony
Bowling
1990/91 International category:
Wales B
Club: Llanelli
Position: Wing
Height: 5'8" **Weight:** 13st
Occupation: Gas board
representative
Born: Swansea, 31.10.66
Family: Jayne (wife)
Former club: Pontarddulais
International debut: Netherlands
12, Wales B 34, 1990
Best moment in rugby: Winning
1990/91 Schweppes Welsh Cup with
Llanelli
Worst moment in rugby: Losing
1988/89 Welsh Cup final to Neath
Most respected opponent: Cardiff
wing Steve Ford
Best memory last season: Being
selected to play in Welsh Cup final
Suggestions to improve rugby:
Off-field – Universal interpretation
of amateur regulations. Not fair that
other nations should get away with
what we are not allowed

Wales B (**1990**)	apps	pts
Last Season	1 cap	0
Career	1 cap	0
Heineken 1990/91	13 apps	23

Other notable landmarks in rugby career: Had trial for Wales at Youth
level. Toured with Wales to New Zealand (1988) and Namibia (1990). Made
Wales B debut in 34–12 win over Netherlands (1990/91)
Touchlines: DIY, keep-fit
Player to watch: Emyr Lewis (Llanelli)

Boyle, L. S.   England

Full Name: Laurence Stuart Boyle
1990/91 International category:
England U-21
Club: Leicester
Position: Centre
Height: 5'10" **Weight:** 13st 1lb
Occupation: Student
Born: Warwick, 29.1.70
Family: Single
Family links with rugby: Brother
played for England U-16s
Former clubs: Leamington,
Moseley
International debut: French
Armed Forces 16, England U-21s
23, 1990
Best moment in rugby: Winning
first cap at England U-16 level
Worst moment in rugby: Losing to
Bath in semi-final of 1989/90
Pilkington Cup
Most respected opponent: Former
England fly-half Les Cusworth –
leadership skills

	apps	pts
England U-21 (**1990**)		
Last Season	2 caps	0
Career	3 caps	0

Other sporting achievements:
Athletics all-rounder for Warwickshire. Javelin at All-England Championships
Best memory last season: Captaining England U-21s v. Ireland
Suggestions to improve rugby: At representative level, tell people who have
been dropped where they went wrong and how they can improve
Other notable landmarks in rugby career: England U-16 Schools v. Italy,
England B U-18 Schools v. Japan, Warwickshire Colts v. Sweden, Midland
Colts v. Italy, Midland U-21s v. NZ U-21s. Won second England U-21 cap
in 16–22 loss to Ireland U-21s at The Reddings last October and third cap
in 20–18 win over Netherlands in May

Bradley, M. T.   Ireland

Full Name: Michael Timothy Bradley
1990/91 International category: Ireland B
Club: Constitution
Position: Scrum-half
Height: 5'10" **Weight:** 13st 2lbs
Occupation: Sales manager
Born: Cork, 17.11.62
Family: Gillian (wife)
Family links with rugby: Father played for Constitution
International debut: Ireland 9, Australia 16, 1984
Five Nations' debut: Scotland 15, Ireland 18, 1985
Best moment in rugby: Captaining Cork Con to 1990/91 All-Ireland League victory
Worst moment in rugby: Ireland losing 3–35 to England at Twickenham in 1988, having led 3-0 at half-time
Most respected opponent: Australian Nick Farr-Jones
Serious injuries: Torn ankle ligaments (1990)
Best memory last season: Winning League

	apps	pts
Ireland B (**1983**)		
Last Season	2 caps	4
Ireland (**1984**)		
Last Season	0 caps	0
	1 rep	
Career	23 caps	16

Suggestions to improve rugby: *Off-field* – Players should receive bonus payments for international matches and reimbursement for loss of earnings
Other notable landmarks in rugby career: Played four games for Irish Schools and captained them on 1980 tour of Australia. Captained Irish U-19s and U-21s. Completed journey up representative ladder with appearances for U-25s and B (1983 v. Scotland). Chosen as replacement for Ireland in 1984 before having played Provincial rugby for Munster. Played in Ireland's 1985 Triple Crown-winning side. Returned to Ireland's B team last season and captained XV to victories over Argentina (October 1990) and England (March 1991). Scored try in 27–12 defeat of touring Pumas. Unused replacement in Ireland's 20–18 win over Argentina (1990/91)
Touchlines: Golf, landscaping in Robert Kennedy's garden (summer house)
Player to watch: Paul McCarthy (Constitution)

Breckenridge, G. M.   Scotland

Full Name: George McLean
Breckenridge
1990/91 International category:
Scotland A (bench)
Club: Glasgow High/Kelvinside
Position: Fly-half
Height: 6′ **Weight:** 12st 2lbs
Occupation: Sales representative
for Gola
Born: Glasgow, 5.9.64
Family: Single
Family links with rugby: Brother
played for Glasgow Schools
Former clubs: St Medard de
Guizeres (Fra), Greytown (NZ)
International debut (B): France
31, Scotland 9, 1990
Best moment in rugby: Scotland B
debut in Oyonnax
Worst moment in rugby: Sitting
out for nine months after damaging
knee ligaments in 1987
Most embarrassing moment:
Playing in 1990 Kilmarnock Sevens,
went to touch ball down for try, but it
bounced off knee and back over my
head. Fortunately still got decisive
touch

	apps	pts
Scotland B (**1990**)		
Last Season	0 caps	0
Career	1 cap	0
Scotland A (1990/91)	1 rep	

Most respected opponent: Melrose fly-half Craig Chalmers
Serious injuries: Damaged knee ligaments
Other sporting achievements: Golf (5-handicap): seventh in 1981
Dumbartonshire County Boys Strokeplay Golf Championship. Won Balmore
GC club members and guests day with fellow GHK player Derek Busby
Best memory last season: Learning that we had stayed in the Scottish first
division despite losing our final game to Hawick in the second minute of injury
time
Suggestions to improve rugby: *On-field* – Increase in the points-worth of
tries to encourage more open games. We want tries to win games not goal
kicking – more exciting for spectators and players alike. *Off-field* – Rugby
should stay amateur but the International Rugby Board should allow players
to get a wee bit back for all their input
Other notable landmarks in rugby career: Played for Glasgow in win

against Fiji and helped them win Scottish Inter-District Championship (both 1989–90). Selected as replacement for Scotland A in 39–7 defeat of Spain (1990)
Touchlines: Reading, travel
Player to watch: Russell Adam (Edinburgh Academicals)

Bridges, C. J. Wales

Full Name: Christopher Jeffrey Bridges
1990/91 International category: Wales Full
Club: Neath
Position: Scrum-half
Height: 5'11" **Weight:** 13st
Occupation: Labourer
Born: Pontypridd, 31.8.68
Family: Sarah (wife) and Daniel (son)
Former club: Beddau
International debut: Namibia 9, Wales 18, 1990
Best moment in rugby: Scoring try on full debut
Worst moment in rugby: Losing to Llanelli in 1988 Welsh Cup final
Most respected opponent: Former Wales scrum-half Jonathan Griffiths
Other sporting achievements: Cricket for Glamorgan U-15s. Won players' golf tournament in Namibia
Best memory last season: Winning Welsh premier division with Neath
Suggestions to improve rugby: *Off-field* – Quite enough changes have already been made to Welsh rugby. But look after players better. We get nothing back for the massive commitment we put in (perhaps semi-pro)

	apps	pts
Wales B (1989)		
Last Season	0 caps	0
Career	1 cap	0
Wales (1990)		
Last Season	5 caps	0
	1 rep	
1991	Tour to Australia	
	World Cup squad	
Career	7 caps	4
Heineken 1990/91	15 apps	24

Other notable landmarks in rugby career: Captained Welsh Youth (1986/87), toured New Zealand with U-19s (1987), Canada with Wales B (1989, playing in 'Test'), Namibia (1990) and Australia (1991) with Wales.

26

Also represented U-21s. With exception of England's visit to Cardiff, was ever-present in Welsh team last season
Touchlines: Golf (25/26-handicap)
Player to watch: Scott Quinnell (Llanelli)

Bryson, D.   Scotland

Full Name: David Bryson
1990/91 International category:
Scotland A (bench)
Club: Gala
Position: Scrum-half
Height: 5'8" **Weight:** 12st 7lbs
Occupation: Textile executive
Born: Galashiels, 5.5.58
Family: Elaine (wife), Kelly and Amy (daughters)
International debut (B): France 44, Scotland 4, 1982
Best moment in rugby: Captaining victorious Gala team at 1987 Gala Sevens
Worst moment in rugby: Missing out on 1982 Scottish tour to France because of injury suffered playing soccer
Most embarrassing moment: Speaking to a local radio correspondent without realising the programme was live on air
Most respected opponent: Former Scotland No.8 Donny McLeod – hard and uncompromising, but not dirty

	apps	pts
Scotland B (**1982**)		
Last Season	2 caps	0
Scotland A (**1990**)	1 rep	

Serious injuries: Torn ligaments (shoulder, knee and ankle), broken collarbone, dislocated shoulder
Other sporting achievements: Played cricket for Gala and South of Scotland. Reduced golf handicap from 14 to 6 in five years
Best memory last season: Fiji's visit to Gala Sevens
Suggestions to improve rugby: *On-field* – Play more in spring/autumn and implement winter break (Dec-Feb). *Off-field* – No problems
Other notable landmarks in rugby career: Hold Scottish record for points scored in a National League match – 34 (three tries and all eleven conversions

27

attempted). Captained Gala seasons 1984/85, 1989/90, 1990/91. Highest try-scorer in Gala's history excluding wings. Capped by Scottish Schools three times. Toured with Scotland to North America (1985). Represented Scotland B in defeats v. Ireland and France last season and was selected as bench reserve for Scotland A's 39–7 defeat of Spain in Seville

Touchlines: Passion for Chinese cookery, woodwork, gardening, snooker and horse racing. Spent numerous summer holidays at Newmarket

Player to watch: Gregor Townsend (Gala)

Buchanan-Smith, G.A.E. Scotland

Full Name: George Adam Edward
Buchanan-Smith
1990/91 International category:
Scotland Full
Club: Heriot's FP
Position: Flanker
Height: 6'2" **Weight:** 15st 2lbs
Occupation: National business
manager for Insurance Courier
services
Born: Edinburgh, 26.7.64
Family: Single
Family links with rugby: Father
played for Army and Edinburgh
Univ. Brother Stuart plays for
London Scottish
Former clubs: Melrose, London
Scottish
International debut: Scotland 38,
Fiji 17, 1989

Best moment in rugby: Coming on
as replacement for Scotland debut v.
Fiji
Worst moment in rugby:
Complicated back injury put me out
of Scotland's North American tour
and jeopardised my World Cup hopes
Most respected opponent:
Glasgow HK's Shade Munro
Serious injuries: Back injury (1991)

	apps	pts
Scotland B (1989)		
Last Season	0 caps	0
Career	1 cap	4
Scotland (1989)		
Last Season	1 cap	0
Career	2 caps	0

Best memory last season: Playing first full International in 49–3 defeat of Argentina (1990)

28

Other notable landmarks in rugby career: Played one season for Scottish Schools. Have also represented Anglo-Scots and Edinburgh in McEwan's Inter-District Championship. Won first senior cap against Fijians after coming on as 65th minute replacement for Graham Marshall. Toured with Scotland to New Zealand (1990). Won second full cap in 49–3 win over Argentina last season

Touchlines: Rock climbing
Player to watch: Stuart Reid (Boroughmuir)

Buckett, I. Wales

Full Name: Ian Buckett
1990/91 International category: Wales B
Club: Swansea
Position: Prop
Height: 6'1" **Weight:** 16st
Occupation: Student
Born: Hollywell, 23.12.67
Family: Single
Former clubs: Swansea University, Wrexham
International debut: Netherlands 12, Wales B 34, 1990
Best moment in rugby: Making Welsh debut v. Welwitschia on 1990 tour to Namibia
Worst moment in rugby: Missing Swansea's game against Barbarians after catching foot in a lawnmower
Most respected opponent: Former Wales prop David Young
Serious injuries: Broken toe in three places in above accident
Best memory last season: Selection to play for Barbarians v. Leicester and Newport
Suggestions to improve rugby: *On-field* – Award less points for penalties

	apps	pts
Wales B **(1990)**		
Last Season	1 cap	0
Career	1 cap	0
Wales 1990	Tour to Namibia	
1991	World Cup squad	
Heineken 1990/91	14 apps	0

Other notable landmarks in rugby career: Represented Welsh Schools U-15s and U-18s and Wales U-21s. Played for Swansea v. 1989 All Blacks (lost 22–37). Toured Namibia with Wales (1990), playing v. Welwitschia

(won 73-0), Central Region (won 43–6) and North Region (won 67–9): scored one try
Touchlines: Cinema-going, lawnmowing!
Player to watch: Robin McBryde (Swansea)

Buckton, J. R.   England

Full Name: John Richard Buckton
1990/91 International category: England B
Club: Saracens
Position: Centre
Height: 6'2" **Weight:** 13st
Occupation: Computer manager
Born: Hull, 22.12.61
Family: Carol (wife)
Family links with rugby: Two brothers (Peter and Nick) play for Liverpool St Helens
Former clubs: Hull and East Riding, Marist Old Boys
International debut: England 28, Australia 19, 1988
Best moment in rugby: Coming on as last-minute replacement v. 1988 Wallabies to win first cap
Worst moment in rugby: Getting injured with England in Australia immediately prior to first Test (1988)
Most embarrassing moment: Missing Yorkshire/Lancashire County game while stuck on train from London to Manchester
Most respected opponent: Saracens' centre Lawrence Smith (in training)

	apps	pts
England B (**1988**)		
Last Season	4 caps	0
England (**1988**)		
Last Season	0 caps	0
Career	1 cap	0
England XV (**1990**)	1 app	4

Best memories last season: Election as captain of Saracens. Club maintaining its English first division status following loss of coach Tony Russ, Floyd Steadman and Jason Leonard
Suggestions to improve rugby: *On-field* – More consistency among referees. Reduce worth of penalty goals to 2 points. *Off-field* – Compensate players for time lost to rugby. Commercially, there are still great avenues for rugby to explore

Other notable landmarks in rugby career: Winning 1987 County Championship with Yorkshire. Helping Saracens win English Second Division (1988/89). Played twice for England B (v. USSR and France) in 1990, during which also helped England XV defeat Italy 33–15 in Rovigo before touring Argentina with England. Last season represented England B v. Italy, France, Emerging Australians and Ireland
Touchlines: Stamp collecting, travel

Budd, M. Wales

Full Name: Michael Budd
1990/91 International category:
Wales (World Cup squad)
Club: Bridgend
Position: Flanker
Height: 6′1″ **Weight:** 14st 8lbs
Occupation: Sales manager
Born: Cardiff, 24.5.63
Family: Debra (wife), Kieron and Leighton (sons)
Family links with rugby: Grandfather and uncle played district rugby
Former club: St Josephs
International debut (B): Wales 12, France 18, 1989
Best moment in rugby: Captaining Bridgend to 23–15 win over Wales XV (1989)
Worst moment in rugby: Giving away a penalty that could have presented Aberavon with a place in 1989/90 Schweppes final. But they missed and Bridgend won semi-final
Most respected opponent: Former Wales scrum-half David Bishop – most complete player ever come up against; could have played any number of positions

	apps	pts
Wales B (1988)		
Last Season	0 caps	0
Career	3 caps	0
Wales 1991	World Cup squad	
Heineken 1990/91	5 apps	0

Serious injuries: Twisted pelvis, pulled hamstrings, damaged neck
Best memory last season: Bridgend beating Cardiff 10–9 at Arms Park – being a Cardiff lad
Suggestions to improve rugby: *On-field* – Law modifications to ruck and

maul to speed up game. Possibly a return to double-banking in line-outs (currently a jungle) for swifter and cleaner possession. Allow passing off floor in rucks if it keeps game flowing. *Off-field* – Pump more money into grass roots of game. Unity among all clubs for good of game as a whole. Still not convinced by Leagues. Welsh rugby was competitive enough beforehand

Other notable landmarks in rugby career: Played for Wales Youth 1980/81, and captained 1981/82 team. Made senior Bridgend debut aged 18. Toured USA with Bridgend (1990). Won three caps for Wales B (two v. France, one v. Canada). Played in four Welsh Cup semi-finals and 1990 final. Damaged neck last November playing v. Neath. Out for five months (traction, scans etc – very worrying). Had just been named in Wales' Five Nations' squad. Played only two further games last season but stepped up training over summer in bid to make World Cup squad

Player to watch: Nathan Jones (Bridgend)

Burnell, A. P. Scotland

Full Name: Andrew Paul Burnell
1990/91 International category: Scotland Full
Club: London Scottish
Position: Tight-head prop
Height: 6' **Weight:** 16st 7lbs
Occupation: Leasing executive
Born: Edinburgh, 29.9.65
Family: Sarah (fiancée)
Former clubs: Marlow, Leicester
International debut: England 12, Scotland 12, 1989
Five Nations' debut: As above
Best moment in rugby: Beating England to win 1990 Grand Slam
Worst moments in rugby: Missing 1989 Japan tour for operation; losing to France in 1989; London Scottish getting relegated from English second division (1988/89); getting dropped

Most respected opponent: Edinburgh Academicals' prop David Sole – good scrummager, great ball player, superb captain
Serious injuries: Serious back injury, requiring surgery
Best memory last season: London Scottish winning Middlesex Sevens
Suggestions to improve rugby: *On-field* – Alter law of the penalty. Side awarded penalty is given throw-in at line-out after ball is kicked to touch.

Off-field – More recognition from the Unions to the amount of time required away from work to meet the standards required to play international rugby. Many clubs are outdated in their administration. Until more people who care about the game are recruited to run clubs financially, rather than committee men who treat the club as their own private 'club', then I am afraid junior and senior rugby will suffer

	apps	pts
Scotland B (1988)		
Last Season	0 caps	0
Career	1 cap	4
Scotland (1989)		
Last Season	5 caps	0
1991	World Cup squad	
Career	14 caps	0

Other notable landmarks in rugby career: Scored on first team debut for Leicester and Scotland B debut in 26–3 win over Italy in L'Aquila (1989). Promotion with London Scottish (1989/90) as English third division champions. Toured New Zealand with Scotland (1990), having been ever-present (No.3) in Grand Slam campaign

Players to watch: David Millard/Fraser Harold/Mark Appleson (all London Scottish) – all have pace and are superb Scotland prospects

Buzza, A. J. England

Full Name: Alan Jan Buzza
1990/91 International category: England B
Club: Wasps
Position: Full-back
Height: 6′ **Weight:** 13st
Occupation: Teacher
Born: Beverley, Yorkshire, 3.3.66
Family: Single
Family links with rugby: Father played scrum-half for Truro and Hertfordshire. First brother plays for Cornwall Schools and second plays for Redruth U-14s
Former clubs: Redruth, Bath, Loughborough Univ and Cambridge Univ
International debut (B): France 15, England 15, 1990

Best moment in rugby: Captaining Cambridge to 22–13 defeat of Oxford in 1989 Varsity match (whole day rather than match)

Worst moment in rugby: Losing 1987 UAU semi-final to Bristol Univ while with Loughborough

Most embarrassing moment: Kick from mark in B match v. France went along ground (unintentional grubber)

	apps	pts
England B (**1990**)		
Last Season	1 cap	0
Career	2 caps	0
England	1995 Development squad	

Most respected opponent: Wasps' Sam Robson

Serious injuries: Ankle ligaments (1990)

Other sporting achievements: Cambridge Univ cricket Blue (1989). Minor Counties Cricket for Cornwall and for Minor Counties U-25s

Best memory last season: Wasps' Pilkington Cup win at Leicester

Suggestions to improve rugby: *On-field* – Moving mark (i.e. mark to be allowed strictly on clean catch). Offside rule from kicks to be that players must be put on-side by the kicker or a runner who started behind him. Maximum four-man line-outs to reduce number of offences while retaining (and promoting) jumping skills

Other notable landmarks in rugby career: Played for England Schools 18-Group, Combined England Students, UAU, Cornwall, South West. England replacement for 23-0 defeat of Ireland (1990)

Touchlines: Reading, maths, piano

Calder, F.   Scotland

Full Name: Finlay Calder OBE
1990/91 International category:
Scotland (World Cup squad)
Club: Stewart's-Melville FP
Position: Flanker
Height: 6′1″ **Weight:** 15st 7lbs
Occupation: Grain shipper
Born: Haddington, 20.8.57
Family: Liz (wife), David (son) and
Hazel (daughter)
Former club: Melrose
International debut: Scotland 18,
France 17, 1986
Best moment in rugby: Winding
up John Jeffrey prior to 1990 Grand
Slam decider v. England
Worst moment in rugby: Being
referred to as 'Buftie' by younger
members of club
Most respected opponent: New
Zealand flanker Michael Jones –
quite simply the best
Other sporting achievements:
Birdie 3 at second hole at Lauder
Golf Club
Best memory last season: Helping
Stew-Mel win at Currie to avoid
relegation from McEwan's Scottish
first division

	apps	pts
Scotland B (1983)		
Last Season	0 caps	0
Scotland (1986)		
Last Season	0 caps	0
1991	World Cup squad	
Career	28 caps	8
Lions 1989	3 Tests	0

Suggestions to improve rugby: *On-field* – Referees must be more
sympathetic to keeping games going. Follow example of French and Southern
Hemisphere officials: far more liberal stances and interested in keeping games
alive for benefit of fans rather than refereeing panels. Too many are out to
score points for themselves these days. Uniformity in laws between two
hemispheres. Take rucking: what is permitted in New Zealand is deemed foul
in Scotland. But good rucking, although it looks ferocious, is as safe as
anything. Referees must acquire a genuine understanding of rugby to be able
to distinguish. *Off-field* – Uniformity desperately needed over amateurism
debate. Work towards a more liberal stance and clear up present grey areas
Other notable landmarks in rugby career: 1989 Scotland captain.
Captained 1989 British Lions to 2–1 Test series win in Australia (Lions first
series win for 15 years). Retired from game after Scotland's 1990 summer

tour to New Zealand but made myself available for 1991 World Cup selection after personal plea from Scotland coach Ian McGeechan

Carling, W. D. C.   England

Full Name: William David Charles Carling
1990/91 International category: England Full
Club: Harlequins
Position: Centre
Height: 5'11" **Weight:** 14st 2lbs
Occupation: Runs own business: 'Inspirational Horizons'
Born: Bradford-on-Avon, Wiltshire, 12.12.65
Family: Single
Family links with rugby: Father (Bill) played for Cardiff
Former club: Durham University
International debut: France 10, England 9, 1988
Five Nations' debut: As above
Best moments in rugby: England beating Australia 28–19 in my first game as captain, and winning 1991 Grand Slam
Worst moment in rugby: Losing 1990 Grand Slam decider to Scotland
Most embarrassing moment: Not touching down try for Harlequins v. Rosslyn Park at Middlesex Sevens
Most respected opponent: French centre Denis Charvet

	apps	pts
England B (**1987**)		
Last Season	0 caps	0
England (**1988**)		
Last Season	7 caps	0
v. Barbarians	1 app	0
1991	Tour to Australia World Cup squad	
Career	26 caps	12

Serious injuries: Fracture of leg (1989)
Best memory last season: Feeling of relief in Twickenham changing room after beating France to achieve Grand Slam
Suggestions to improve rugby: *On-field* – General level of coaching in English club rugby must be raised. We are too stuck in our ways at present. We must learn from other countries. *Off-field* – More constructive appreciation of rugby from the media
Other notable landmarks in rugby career: Turning in one of my best

performances, playing for Durham against Lancashire, in front of the then Northern Division selectors Geoff Cooke and Dave Robinson. Helped England B beat France B 22–9 in 1987. Awarded full England captaincy aged 23 in 1988. Captained England to 1991 Grand Slam
Touchlines: Painting – sketching and inks
Player to watch: Scott Gibbs (Neath)

Carter, A. J.   Wales

Full Name: Alun Jonathan Carter
1990/91 International category: Wales Full
Club: Newport
Positions: No.8, flanker
Height: 6′3″ **Weight:** 14st 4lbs
Occupation: Property developer
Born: Newport, 13.12.64
Family: Emma (daughter)
Former clubs: Pontypool, Millau (Fra)
International debut: Wales 6, England 25, 1991
Five Nations' debut: As above
Best moment in rugby: Wales debut v. England
Worst moment in rugby: Not being selected by Pontypool for game v. 1989 All Blacks
Most respected opponent: Peter Winterbottom (Harlequins)
Best memory last season: Winning first Wales cap at Arms Park
Suggestions to improve rugby: *On-field* – Youngsters should be encouraged to spend a season or two abroad to witness different styles of rugby. Clubs in Britain are too eager to get them and stifle them. *Off-field* – Believe game will turn semi-professional soon because with

	apps	pts
Wales B (**1986**)		
Last Season	0 caps	0
Career	1 cap	0
Wales (**1991**)		
Last Season	2 caps	0
	2 reps	
1991	World cup squad	
Career	2 caps	0
Heineken 1990/91	11 apps	4

the likes of the World Cup and ever-increasing sponsorship deals players will demand a cut; especially those doctors, solicitors and farmers who are losing out financially at present by their commitments to top-level rugby

37

Other notable landmarks in rugby career: Spent season in France playing for Millau. Captained 1983 Welsh Schools to Grand Slam. Won twelve Schools caps in all (two at U-15 level and 10 at U-18). Represented Barbarians last season in Mobbs Memorial match. Also played for Wales B (1986, v. Italy) and Combined Services (1988). Helped Newport gain promotion to Welsh premier division last season and represented Wales v. England and Scotland
Touchlines: Speaking French, golf
Player to watch: Scott Quinnell (Llanelli)

Chalmers, C. M. Scotland

Full Name: Craig Minto Chalmers
1990/91 International category: Scotland Full
Club: Melrose
Position: Fly-half
Height: 5'10" **Weight:** 13st 4lbs
Occupation: Marketing representative for South of Scotland Electricity Board
Born: Galashiels, 15.10.68
Family links with rugby: Father coaches at Melrose
International debut: Scotland 23, Wales 7, 1989
Five Nations' debut: As above
Best moments in rugby: Winning 1990 Grand Slam by beating England; winning 1989/90 Scottish Championship with Melrose
Worst moment in rugby: Being dropped by 1989 Lions, after playing in First Test v. Australia (lost 12–30)
Most respected opponents: Fly-halves Grant Fox (New Zealand) and Michael Lynagh (Australia)
Serious injuries: Torn knee cartilage
Best memories last season: Scoring 'Grand Slam' against Wales: 1 try, 1 con, 1 pen, 1 dropped goal. Winning Border League with Melrose

	apps	pts
Scotland B (1988)		
Last Season	0 caps	0
Career	2 caps	14
Scotland (1989)		
Last Season	5 caps	50
1991	Tour to North America World Cup squad	
Career	16 caps	90
Lions (1989)	1 Test	6

Suggestions to improve rugby: *On-field* – Play game without flankers (give me more room to run). Reduce size of Scottish first division to 10 clubs. Make game more fluid, but not by decreasing worth of penalty goals as that would increase the number of infringements committed. *Off-field* – I do not believe players should be paid to play, but why should we not be permitted to receive money for, say, wearing a particular brand of boots? We are not doing anyone any harm. Encourage more youngsters to get involved in rugby. Work on publicising the game more

Other notable landmarks in rugby career: Youngest player ever to represent Scotland B – scored a try and drop goal on full debut. Earned selection to 1989 Lions tour of Australia and kicked 6 points in first Test. Represented Scotland at U-15, U-18, U-19, U-21 and B levels. Scored 46 points in 1991 Five Nations' Championship (9 v. France, 12 v. Wales, 12 v. England, 13 v. Ireland). Helped Melrose win Border league before touring North America with Scotland last summer, playing against British Columbia and in the 'Tests' v. the United States and Canada

Touchlines: Golf (12-handicap)

Player to watch: 'Doddie' Weir (Melrose)

Childs, G. C.   England

Full Name: Graham Christopher Childs

1990/91 International category: England B (bench)

Club: Wasps

Position: Centre

Height: 6' **Weight:** 13st 10lbs

Occupation: Sales representative for publishing company

Born: Fareham, Hants, 3.4.68

Family: Single

Family links with rugby: Father and brother played for Worthing

Former clubs: Worthing, Northern, Poverty Bay (NZ)

International debut (B): France 15, England 15, 1990

Best moment in rugby: Selection for England's 1990 summer tour of Argentina

Worst moment in rugby: Being

sent off aged 15 (it wasn't my fault, honest!)
Most respected opponent:
England B centre Bryan Barley
Best memory last season: Playing for Poverty Bay against Scotland and Auckland

	apps
England B (1990/91)	1 rep
England 1990	Tour to Argentina

Suggestions to improve rugby: *On-field* – Increase number of points for a try. *Off-field* – Relax laws on amateurism – allow players to receive payment for off-field activities
Other notable landmarks in rugby career: Played mini-rugby at Worthing. Represented South of England Schools and, later, Northumberland (1988–91) in English County Championship. Also North in Divisional Championship (1989–90) and against Soviet Union (1989). Spent summer of 1990 playing for Poverty Bay in New Zealand and then touring Argentina with England. Selected as replacement for England B against Namibia last season. Toured Australia with London last summer
Touchlines: Golf, squash

Clarke, B. B.   England

Full Name: Benjamin Bevan Clarke
1990/91 International category:
England B
Club: Saracens
Position: No.8
Height: 6'5" **Weight:** 17st
Occupation: Student
Born: Bishop's Stortford, 15.4.68
Family: Single
Family links with rugby: Father played for Bishop's Stortford and is club president
Former club: Bishop's Stortford
International debut: England B 50, Spain 6, 1990
Best moment in rugby: Saracens beating Bath last season in English first division

Worst moment in rugby:
Damaging shoulder and missing
England XV's game against an Italy XV (May 1990)
Most respected opponent: Wasps' back row Dean Ryan

Serious injuries: Sprung shoulder joint, tearing ligaments
Best memory last season: Making debut for England B
Suggestions to improve rugby: *On-field* – Better policing of line-outs by referees. *Off-field* – Broken time payments
Other notable landmarks in rugby career: Represented Hertfordshire Colts, U-21 and full teams while with Stortford. Since joining Saracens at start of last season, have played for London Division, Public School Wanderers, Penguins, England Students and England B. Toured Australia with London last summer
Touchlines: Golf, squash, hockey
Player to watch: Dan Dooley (Saracens)

	apps	pts
England B (**1990**)		
Last Season	1 cap	0
	2 reps	
Career	1 cap	0
England	1995 Development squad	

Clarke, J. D. — Ireland

Full Name: Jack David Clarke
1990/91 International category: Ireland Full
Club: Dolphin
Positions: Wing, centre
Height: 6′ **Weight:** 13st 7lbs
Occupation: Pensions assistant
Born: Kisumu, Kenya, 2.9.68
Family: Single
Family links with rugby: Brother (Garoid) plays for Athlone
Former club: Dolphin
International debut: Wales 21, Ireland 21, 1991
Five Nations' debut: As above
Best moment in rugby: Running out at Cardiff on full debut
Worst moment in rugby: Breaking ankle (1984)
Most embarrassing moment: Having to leave field after landing on boil on my backside when tackled
Serious injuries: Broken ankle
Other sporting achievements: Javelin for Irish Schools
Best memory last season: Scoring try on debut for Ireland

Other notable landmarks in rugby career: Spent 12 years in Kenya before moving to Ireland and representing Irish Schools, Munster, Ireland U-21s (v. Italy and New Zealand), Ireland U-25s and, last season, Ireland B (v. Argentina, Scotland B and England B)

Touchlines: Squash, swimming

Player to watch: James Harley (QUB)

	apps	pts
Ireland U-21 (**1989**)		
Last Season	0 caps	0
Career	2 caps	0
Ireland U-25 (**1990**)		
Last Season	1 cap	4
Career	2 caps	4
Ireland B (**1990**)		
Last Season	3 caps	8
Career	3 caps	8
Ireland (**1991**)		
Last Season	2 caps	4
1991	Tour to Namibia	
	World Cup squad	
Career	2 caps	4

Clement, A.   Wales

Full Name: Anthony Clement
1990/91 International category: Wales Full
Club: Swansea
Positions: Fly-half, full-back
Height: 5'9" **Weight:** 13st 8lbs
Occupation: Contract hire consultant
Born: Swansea, 8.2.67
Family: Married
Family links with rugby: Father played for Bonymaen. Brother played for Llanelli
Former club: Morriston Youth
International debut: Wales 46, US Eagles 0, 1987
Five Nations' debut: England 3, Wales 11, 1988
Best moments in rugby: Scoring two tries for Wales on debut.
Helping Wales beat Australia 16–10 in quarter-finals of 1990 Hong Kong Sevens

Worst moment in rugby: Being dropped by Wales for second time (before 1988/89 Five Nations' Championship) when playing well

Most respected opponent: Newport's former Welsh fly-half Paul Turner

Serious injuries: Hamstring strain

Ambition: To play for Wales at full-back – more of a future for me there

Best memory last season: Drubbing Pontypool 63–6 in Heineken Welsh Leagues (they then beat us in Welsh Cup semi-finals – sums up first year of leagues)

Suggestions to improve rugby: *On-field* – Too early to judge new Welsh leagues. We'll find out this year when, hopefully, clubs will be more relaxed and more expansive in their outlook. Last season was win at all costs. Reduce worth of penalty goals (2), drop goals (2) and conversions (1). *Off-field* – Don't put too much store in tradition because it is a stumbling block to progress. There can be no hiding fact that during Five Nations' Championship game is semi-professional for those involved in terms of commitment

Other notable landmarks in rugby career: After playing six games for Welsh Youth (1984), joined Swansea (1985) and captained Wales U-20s. Also represented Wales U-21s, B – twice v. France (1987–88) and v. Netherlands (1990), and Barbarians. Toured South Africa with World XV (1989). Won 11th Welsh cap last season when coming on as 69th minute replacement for Paul Thorburn in 12–32 loss at Murrayfield and 12th in 6–63 loss to Australia

Touchlines: Soccer, cricket

Player to watch: Simon Davies (Swansea)

	apps	pts
Wales B (**1987**)		
Last Season	1 cap	4
Career	3 caps	7
Wales (**1987**)		
Last Season	2 cap	0
	4 reps	
1991	Tour to Australia	
	World Cup squad	
Career	12 caps	11
Lions 1989		
Heineken 1990/91	16 apps	12

Clough, F. J.   England

Full Name: Francis John Clough
1990/91 International category:
England (World Cup squad)
Club: Wasps
Position: Centre
Height: 6'1" **Weight:** 14st 10lbs
Occupation: University research
scientist
Born: Wigan, 1.11.62
Family: Single
Former clubs: Orrell, Durham
Univ, Cambridge Univ
International debut: England 25,
Ireland 20, 1986
Five Nations' debut: As above
Best moment in rugby: Cambridge
beating Oxford 15–10 in 1987
Varsity match

Worst moments in rugby: Missing
England's 1990 summer tour to
Argentina after breaking leg playing
Sevens. Mark Bailey's after-dinner
speaking
Most embarrassing moment:
Holder of world knock-on record for
England v. Japan in 1987 World Cup
Most respected opponent: London
Division treasurer Alan Parker – like
getting blood out of a stone
Serious injuries: Broken leg (1990),

	apps	pts
England B (**1985**)		
Last Season	0 caps	0
England (**1986**)		
Last Season	0 caps	0
1991	World Cup squad	
Career	4 caps	0

ruptured Achilles tendon, recurrent dislocated shoulder
Other sporting achievements: England Schools Rugby League U-16s and
U-19s
Best memory last season: John Olver's first scrummage for England in 51-0
defeat of Argentina
Suggestions to improve rugby: *On-field* – Home and away league matches
in Courage English Championship. *Off-field* – Youthanasia
Other notable landmarks in rugby career: Geoff Cooke's selection as
England manager. Won four Cambridge Blues (1984,85,86,87), captaining
team in 1987. Played for England B three times, twice last season. Came on
as replacement in England's 33–15 defeat of Italy (1989/90). Picked for
England's preliminary World Cup squad. Broken leg, sustained at end of

1989/90 season, kept me out of large bulk of last season. Toured Australia with London last summer
Touchlines: None. Rugby football is my life
Player to watch: Paul Rendall (Wasps) – very experienced for his age!

Collins, R. G. Wales

Full Name: Richard (**Richie**) Graham Collins
1990/91 International category: Wales Full
Club: Cardiff
Position: Flanker
Height: 6'1" **Weight:** 14st 4lbs
Occupation: Policeman
Born: Cardiff, 2.3.62
Family: Single
Former clubs: Pontypridd, Newport, South Wales Police
International debut: Wales 19, England 12, 1987
Five Nations' debut: As above
Best moment in rugby: Wales winning 1988 Triple Crown in Ireland
Worst moment in rugby: Wales' defeats (1990) against England and Ireland
Most respected opponent: Scotland flanker Finlay Calder
Other sporting achievements: Welsh basketball international
Other notable landmarks in rugby career: Played initially to sharpen reflexes and bulk-up for basketball. Spent season playing Wellington club rugby in New Zealand before returning to join Pontypridd, and

	apps	pts
Wales B (**1986**)		
Last Season	0 caps	0
Career	3 caps	4
Wales (**1987**)		
Last Season	1 cap	0
1991	Tour to Australia	
Career	15 caps	0
Heineken 1990/91	15 caps	8

Newport, with whom played in 1986 Welsh Cup final. Scored try on Wales B debut in 24–12 win over Italy (1986). Made full Wales debut as replacement at Cardiff in 1987. Won 14th cap in 6–63 rout by Australia last summer

Corcoran, I.   Scotland

Full Name: Ian Corcoran
1990/91 International category:
Scotland B (bench)
Club: Gala
Position: Hooker
Height: 5'11" **Weight:** 13st 5lbs
Occupation: Carpet fitter/
upholsterer
Born: Edinburgh, 11.5.63
Family: Carrie (wife)
Family links with rugby: Two
brothers play for Gala
International debut (B): France
31, Scotland 9, 1990
Best moment in rugby: Scoring
first ever Scotland try during 1989
tour of Japan
Worst moment in rugby: Being
dropped from senior Scotland squad
(replacement v. Fiji and Romania)
after France B game (1989/90)
Most respected opponent: Former
Gala and Scotland International
Kenny Lawrie
Serious injuries: Damaged knee
ligaments required operation (missed
1988 season)

	apps	pts
Scotland B (1990)		
Last Season	2 reps	
Career	1 cap	0

Other sporting achievements: Cricket for Gala
Best memory last season: Gala's exciting performances in Scottish League
Suggestions to improve rugby: *On-field* – Touch judges must help/consult
more with referees. *Off-field* – Players remunerated for working time lost to
game although must guard against too much money coming in as that would
spoil it
Other notable landmarks in rugby career: Promoted to Scotland B
(1989/90), having previously earned one cap for Scotland U-21s. Bench
reserve for both Scotland B matches (Ireland and France) last season
Touchlines: Squash, badminton, DIY
Player to watch: John Amos (Gala)

Couper, J. A. Scotland

Full Name: John Alan Couper
1990/91 International category:
Scotland U-21
Club: Glasgow High/Kelvinside
Position: Loose-head prop
Height: 5'10" **Weight:** 15st 2lbs
Occupation: Bank officer
Born: Glasgow, 21.10.69
Family: Single
International debut (U-21):
Scotland 10, Wales 24, 1990
Best moment in rugby: Scoring two tries for Scotland U-21s v. Combined Services (1989)
Worst moment in rugby: Scotland U-21s' 1990 defeat by Wales at Ayr
Most respected opponent: Scotland loose-head prop David Sole
Serious injuries: Pulled muscles in back
Other sporting achievements: Cricket for Scotland U-15s and U-16s

Scotland U-21 (1990)	apps	pts
Last Season	1 cap	0
Career	2 caps	0

Best memory last season: Helping Glasgow to share of U-21 Scottish inter-District Championship with South in fourth and final season of eligibility
Suggestions to improve rugby: *On-field* – Revise rucking laws so that person killing ball is penalised rather than man rucking him out. *Off-field* – Continue to ensure that players are put first
Other notable landmarks in rugby career: Represented Scotland U-18s and U-19s against Italy. Unused replacement for Scottish Students against Welsh and English counterparts. Represented Scotland U-21s against Wales for second consecutive year back in April (lost 15–23 at Llanelli)
Touchlines: Cricket
Player to watch: Stuart Reid (Boroughmuir)

Cronin, D. F. Scotland

Full Name: Damian Francis Cronin
1990/91 International category:
Scotland Full
Club: Bath
Position: Lock
Height: 6'6" **Weight:** 17st
Occupation: Sales executive
Born: Wegberg, W. Germany,
17.4.63
Family: Single
Family links with rugby: Father is
president of Ilford Wanderers
Former club: Ilford Wanderers
International debut: Ireland 22,
Scotland 18, 1988
Five Nations' debut: As above
Best moment in rugby: Winning
1990 Grand Slam with Scotland
Worst moments in rugby:
Snapping knee ligaments. Bath's 3–4
defeat by Moseley in quarter-finals
of 1987/88 John Player Cup
Most respected opponent: Wales
lock Robert Norster
Serious injuries: Ligament damage
in both knees. Staple put in right knee
Other sporting achievements:
Drove in celebrity race around
Brands Hatch
Suggestions to improve rugby:
Off-field – Look seriously at
commercialisation of rugby in
support of players

	apps	pts
Scotland B (**1987**)		
Last Season	0 caps	0
Scotland A (**1990**)		
Last Season	1 cap	4
Scotland (**1988**)		
Last Season	4 caps	0
1991	World Cup squad	
Career	21 caps	8

Other notable landmarks in rugby career: Returned to rugby after fracturing base of spine aged 22. Built reputation in Scotland with performances for Anglo-Scots, having become eligible thanks to Lothian-based grandparents. Helped 1987 Anglo's beat French at Cupar and was included in Scottish XV which achieved a similar feat. Toured with Scotland to Zimbabwe (1988) and captained team v. Mashonaland District. Ever-present alongside Chris Gray in Scotland second row during 1991 Five Nations' Championship after missing early season win (49–3) over Argentina through injury

Crossan, K. D.   Ireland

Full Name: Keith Derek Crossan
1990/91 International category:
Ireland Full
Club: Instonians
Position: Wing
Height: 5'7" **Weight:** 11st 4lbs
Occupation: Banker
Born: Belfast, 29.12.59
Family: Joanna (wife), David (son)
and Victoria (daughter)
Family links with rugby: Uncle
(Derek Monteith) captained Ireland
(1947)
International debut: Ireland 21,
Scotland 12, 1982
Five Nations' debut: As above
Best moment in rugby: Being
selected to tour South Africa with
Ireland (1981)
Worst moment in rugby:
Withdrawing from Ireland's match
against Australia (1984) because of
illness
Most embarrassing moment:
Being sick on pitch (too much alcohol
previous night) after scoring two tries
for Instonians against Trinity

	apps	pts
Ireland (1982)		
Last Season	4 caps	4
1991	Tour to Namibia	
	World Cup squad	
Career	37 caps	48

Most respected opponent: Former England wing Mike Harrison – always
scores against me, either for Yorkshire or England
Serious injuries: Broke jaw in two places (1985, out for three months), broken
leg (Nov 1990)
Best memory last season: Scoring try for Ireland in 25–28 loss at
Murrayfield
Suggestions to improve rugby: *On-field* – Change playing season so don't
have to play in depths of winter. Standardise refereeing interpretations.
Off-field – None. All-Ireland League has been a great success
Other notable landmarks in rugby career: Ireland's most capped wing with
36 appearances – broke Trevor Ringland's record of 34 (1981–88) in 7–16
loss to England (1991). Played over 70 times for Ulster but never for Irish
Schools, Ireland U-23 or B. First Irish player to score three tries in one
International at Lansdowne Road (v. Romania, 1986). Ever-present for
Ireland in 1987 World Cup. Toured with Ireland to North America (1989).

Total of 12 Irish tries is third on all-time list behind Brendan Mullin (16) and George Stevenson (14). Missed two and a half months of last season after breaking fibula bone in leg in November. Played in second Test v. Namibia last summer
Touchlines: Try to treat rugby as a 'sport' but this is becoming more difficult as more pressure is put on winning at all costs
Player to watch: Simon Geoghegan (London Irish)

Cunningham, V. J. G.   Ireland

Full Name: Vincent John Gerald Cunningham
1990/91 International category: Ireland Full
Club: St Mary's College
Positions: Centre, fly-half
Height: 5'11" **Weight:** 13st
Occupation: Bank official
Born: Dublin, 14.3.67
Family: Single
Family links with rugby: Father played for (and coached and selected) St Mary's
International debut: Ireland 10, England 21, 1988
Best moment in rugby: Winning first cap in Millennium match
Worst moment in rugby: Breaking hand in training last season to miss Ireland's tour to North America (1989)
Most respected opponent: France full-back Serge Blanco
Serious injuries: Broken hand
Other sporting achievements: Irish Schoolboy Cricket International
Best memory last season: Leinster's back-line performance v. South West division
Suggestions to improve rugby: *On-field* – Award extra point for a try. *Off-field* – Broken time payments

	apps	pts
Ireland U-25 (**1990**)		
Last Season	1 cap	2
Career	2 caps	6
Ireland B (**1990**)		
Last Season	1 cap	3
Career	1 cap	3
Ireland (**1988**)		
Last Season	3 cap	4
	4 reps	
1991	Tour to Namibia World Cup squad	
Career	5 caps	6

Other notable landmarks in rugby career: Outside half in first Irish Schools team to beat Wales. Played in Irish touring side which beat France three seasons ago. Replacement eight times for Ireland, in addition to three caps against England, Italy and, last season, Argentina. Scored Ireland U-25s' try in 12–10 defeat of US Eagles in Limerick (1989/90) and landed conversion in last season's defeat of Spain. Kicked penalty goal in Ireland B's 16-0 defeat of Scotland (1990/91). Regular fixture on Ireland's 1991 Five Nations' bench. Toured Namibia with Ireland last summer, playing in both Tests and scoring try in second
Touchlines: Enjoy horse-racing cricket, golf
Player to watch: Aidan White (St Mary's Coll)

Curtis, D. M. Ireland

Full Name: David Michael Curtis
1990/91 International category:
Ireland Full
Club: London Irish
Position: Centre
Height: 5'10" **Weight:** 13st
Occupation: Civil engineer
Born: Harare, Zimbabwe, 10.4.65
Family: Andrea (wife)
Family links with rugby: Father (Bryan) capped by Ireland against France, England and Scotland in 1950. He was also an Oxford Blue and represented Barbarians
Former clubs: University of Cape Town, Western Province U-20s, Oxford University
International debut: Wales 21, Ireland 21, 1991
Five Nations' debut: As above
Best moment in rugby: Being picked to play for Ireland
Worst moment in rugby: Being injured and having to revert from being a player to a spectator
Most respected opponent: South Africa's Michel du Plessis
Other sporting achievements:

	apps	pts
Ireland B (**1990**)		
Last Season	1 cap	0
Career	1 cap	0
Ireland (**1991**)		
Last Season	5 caps	3
1991	Tour to Namibia	
	World Cup squad	
Career	5 caps	3

Accomplished golfer, cricketer and angler

Best memory last season: Playing first game for Ireland at Lansdowne Road v. England

Suggestions to improve rugby: *On-field* – Greater effort to encourage rugby at schoolboy level. *Off-field* – Some Unions are outdated. Players should have freedom to earn money in non-rugby related activities (e.g. speaking, advertisements)

Other notable landmarks in rugby career: Educated at Falcon College, Esogodine, near Bulawayo and attended university at Cape Town and Oxford, where won a Blue in 1989. Grew up in Zimbabwe and represented Springbok age-group sides and Western Province U-20. Played for Connacht in Ireland's Inter-Provincial Championship. Made Ireland B debut in 16-0 defeat of Scotland in Belfast last December before graduating to full side for drawn match with Wales

Touchlines: Golf, cricket, fly fishing

Player to watch: Simon Geoghegan (London Irish)

Danaher, P. P. A.   Ireland

Full Name: Philip Paul Anthony Danaher

1990/91 International category: Ireland (World Cup squad)

Club: Garryowen

Position: Full-back

Height: 5'11" **Weight:** 13st 10lbs

Occupation: Insurance consultant

Born: Limerick, 5.10.65

Family: Single

Former clubs: Abbeyfeale, Lansdowne

International debut: Ireland 22, Scotland 18, 1988

Five Nations' debut: As above

Best moment in rugby: Winning Schools medal

Worst moment in rugby: Being dropped second time round after France 1990

Most embarrassing moment: Touching ball down behind line and conceding 5-yard scrum against Wales in 1988 (ref was wrong!)

Most respected opponent: French full-back Serge Blanco – naturally brilliant

Serious injuries: Broken both ankles, serious hamstring injuries

Other sporting achievements: Badminton at national level while at school. Played Gaelic Football at county level
Suggestions to improve rugby: Improve coaching of schools and age-group levels
Other notable landmarks in rugby career: Joining Lansdowne and being coached properly for first time. Toured with Ireland to France and North America in 1989

	apps	pts
Ireland B (1990/91)	1 rep	
Ireland (1988)		
Last Season	0 caps	0
1991	World Cup squad	
Career	8 caps	6

Davies, A.   Wales

Full Name: Adrian Davies
1990/91 International category: Wales Full
Clubs: Neath/Cambridge Univ
Position: Fly-half
Height: 5'10" **Weight:** 11st 12lbs
Occupation: Land Economy student
Born: Bridgend, 9.2.69
Family: Single
Family links with rugby: Graham (brother) plays for Neath, Lloyd (brother) plays for Cambridge Univ
Former club: Pencoed Youth
International debut: Wales 24, Barbarians 31, 1990
Best moment in rugby: Helping Neath beat the mighty Pontypool side in the 1986/87 Schweppes Welsh Cup semi-finals
Worst moment in rugby: 1990 Varsity match
Most respected opponent: Bridgend scrum-half Aled Williams
Best memory last season: Coming on as 47th minute replacement for Mark Ring to win first Wales cap v. Barbarians in Cardiff (6 October)
Suggestions to improve rugby: *On-field* – Legalise lifting in line-out if it will make the set-piece less of a mess. *Off-field* – For us to compete with Southern Hemisphere nations we must sort ourselves out off the field. Players do not necessarily have to gain but they must certainly not lose out by playing top-level rugby. It is a joke when nations tour short-handed because certain

players cannot afford time off work
Other notable landmarks in rugby career: Represented Wales U-21s for two years. Kicked four penalty goals for Wales B in 15–28 loss to France B at La Teste (1989). Made full debut for Wales when coming on as 47th minute replacement for Mark Ring during 24–31 loss to Barbarians last season
Touchlines: Cricket, piano, trumpet
Player to watch: Simon Holmes (Cambridge Univ)

	apps	pts
Wales B (1989)		
Last Season	0 caps	0
Career	1 cap	12
Wales (1990)		
Last Season	2 caps	0
1991	Tour to Australia	
	World Cup squad	
Career	2 caps	0
Heineken 1990/91	3 apps	6

Davies, J. D. Wales

Full Name: John David Davies
1990/91 International category: Wales Full
Club: Neath
Position: Tight-head prop
Height: 5'11" **Weight:** 16st
Occupation: Farmer
Born: Carmarthen, 1.2.69
Family: Single
Family links with rugby: Cousin plays for Cwmgwrach
Former club: Cwmgwrach
International debut: Wales 21, Ireland 21, 1991
Five Nations' debut: As above
Best moment in rugby: Making Wales debut v. Ireland
Worst moment in rugby: Neath's 1990/91 Welsh Cup semi-final defeat by Llanelli

Most respected opponent: Wales prop Brian Williams (in training)
Best memories last season: First Wales cap and Neath's win over Bridgend in League decider
Suggestions to improve rugby: *On-field* – More points for a try. More consistent refereeing. Scrap 90-degree scrum wheel law as it slows game down. *Off-field* – Keep game amateur but look after players better
Other notable landmarks in rugby career: Played for Wales Youth

(1987–89) before breaking into Wales U-21 team (1988/89). Represented Wales B for first time in 34–12 win over Netherlands (1990/91) and went on to achieve senior status v. Ireland (drew 21–21) and France (lost 3–36)
Touchlines: Hunting, shooting

	apps	pts
Wales B (**1990**)		
Last Season	1 cap	0
Career	1 cap	0
Wales (**1991**)		
Last Season	2 caps	0
1991	World Cup squad	
Career	2 caps	0
Heineken 1990/91	11 apps	4

Davies, P. T. Wales

Full Name: Philip Thomas Davies
1990/91 International category: Wales Full
Club: Llanelli
Positions: Lock, flanker, prop, No.8
Height: 6'3" **Weight:** 18st
Occupation: Director of packaging company
Born: Seven Sisters, 19.10.63
Family: Caroline (wife), Rebecca and Danikka (daughters)
Family links with rugby: Wife Caroline is Jonathan Davies' sister
Former clubs: Seven Sisters, South Wales Police
International debut: Wales 24, England 15, 1985
Five Nations' debut: As above
Best moments in rugby: Captaining Llanelli to 1988 Schweppes Cup final win v. Neath, and leading Scarlets to the Cup again last season over Pontypool
Worst moment in rugby: Wales' 1990 whitewash
Most embarrassing moment: Having ball knocked from grasp by Kenfig Hill centre while touching down in Cup last season
Most respected opponent: French back row Laurent Rodriguez

	apps	pts
Wales B (**1987**)		
Last Season	0 caps	0
Career	1 cap	0
Wales (**1985**)		
Last Season	3 caps	0
1991	Tour to Australia World Cup squad	
Career	28 caps	16
Heineken 1990/91	14 apps	8

Serious injuries: Broken cheekbone
Other sporting achievements: Swam for West Wales Schools
Best memory last season: Recall to Wales team for Ireland game
Suggestions to improve rugby: *On-field* – Improve general organisation from national viewpoint. *Off-field* – Remuneration for time spent away from work
Other notable landmarks in rugby career: First played for Wales at 16-Group. Former policeman. Broke into full Welsh squad in 1984. Had jaw broken by punch in fiery 1987 clash with England. Dropped after playing in World Cup and became Wales B captain. Left out again last season but recalled for games v. Ireland and France, and included in squads for Australia tour and World Cup. Have also represented Crawshays and Barbarians
Touchlines: Golf
Player to watch: Ian Jones (Llanelli)

Davies, S. L. England

Full Name: Stewart Lyn Davies
International category: England B (bench)
Club: Wasps
Position: Hooker
Height: 5'11" **Weight:** 14st 7lbs
Occupation: Sales consultant
Born: Farnborough, Hants, 5.1.69
Family: Single
Family links with rugby: Father played
Former clubs: Farnborough, Camberley, Rosslyn Park
International debut: Netherlands 3, England U-21 24, 1990
Best moment in rugby: Making debut in English first division for Rosslyn Park v. Wasps last season
Worst moment in rugby: Rosslyn Park losing heavily in League match to Gloucester
Most respected opponent: England development squad member Troy Thacker (Leicester hooker) – after playing him it felt like every bone in my body was broken

	apps	pts
England U-21 (**1990**)		
Last Season	0 caps	0
Career	2 caps	0
England B (**1990/91**)	1 rep	

Serious injuries: Dislocated knee cap
Other sporting achievements: Swimming, cricket and football for school
Suggestions to improve rugby: *On-field* – Concentrating on playing more expansive game, whilst improving rucking and ball retention skills
Other notable landmarks in rugby career: Joining Park from Camberley (1987). Represented England U-21s v. Netherlands and French Armed Forces (both 1989/90). Selected as bench reserve for England B in 31–16 defeat of Namibia (1990/91). Moved from Rosslyn Park to Wasps at end of last season

---

Davis, M. E. Wales

Full Name: Mark Edwin Davis
1990/91 International category: Wales Full
Club: Newport
Position: Loose-head prop
Height: 5′9.5″ **Weight:** 16st
Occupation: Student
Born: Newport, 18.9.70
Family: Single
Former club: Pontypool
International debut: Australia 63, Wales 6, 1991
Best moment in rugby: Promotion to Heineken Welsh premier division with Newport
Most respected opponent: SWP prop Huw Williams-Jones
Best memory last season: Helping WRU President's XV beat New Zealand Youth XV 34–13 at Pontypridd
Suggestions to improve rugby: *On-field* – Better and more sensitive refereeing
Other notable landmarks in rugby career: Helped Newport win Heineken Welsh first division last season. Represented Wales at Schools (1989) and, last season, U-21 level, twice (eligible this season again). Toured Australia with senior Wales squad last summer and earned

	apps	pts
Wales U-21 (**1991**)		
Last Season	1 cap	0
v. New Zealand XV	1 app	0
Career	1 cap	0
Wales (**1991**)		
Last Season	1 cap	0
Career	1 cap	0
	Tour to Australia	
	World Cup squad	
Heineken 1990/91	13 apps	4

selection to Wales' preliminary World Cup squad. Have also represented Gwent Schools, Welsh Tertiary Colleges, British Colleges, Pontypool (one game v. Maesteg) and Wales U-21s in 23–15 win over Scotland (1991)
Touchlines: Reading
Player to watch: Ian Jones (Newport)

Dawe, R. G. R. England

Full Name: Richard Graham Reed Dawe
1990/91 International category: England B
Club: Bath
Position: Hooker
Height: 5'11" **Weight:** 13st 10lbs
Occupation: Farmer
Born: Plymouth, 4.9.59
Family: Liz (wife)
Former club: Launceston
International debut: Ireland 17, England 0, 1987
Five Nations' debut: As above
Best moment in rugby: Winning 1986 John Player Cup final with Bath (25–17 over Wasps)
Worst moment in rugby: Being told that I had been banned by England after 1987 Wales match
Most respected opponents: Orrell's Neil Hitchen and Llanelli's Kerry Towley
Best memory last season: Helping Cornwall win County Championship
Suggestions to improve rugby:
On-field – Abolish law that demands use of same ball that went out of play at line-out. Diminish value of conversion or get rid of it (takes up too much time). *Off-field* – Somehow reduce my travelling

	apps	pts
England (**1987**)		
Last Season	0 caps	0
Career	4 caps	0
England B (**1990**)		
Last Season	4 caps	0
	1 rep	
Career	4 caps	0

Other notable landmarks in rugby career: Played four times for England in 1987 (v. Ireland, France, Wales, and USA in World Cup). Last season played in four of England B's six games (v. Emerging Australians, Spain,

58

Ireland and France). Helped Bath win 1990/91 Courage English League Championship
Touchlines: Bell ringing, cycling, sheep shearing
Player to watch: Phil de Glanville (Bath)

Dear, S. J. England

Full Name: Simon James Dear
1990/91 International category: England B
Club: Rosslyn Park
Position: Lock
Height: 6'8" **Weight:** 17st 4lbs
Occupation: Police officer
Born: Peterborough, 30.1.63
Family: Helen (wife) and Thomas (son)
Family links with rugby: Father played for Peterborough
Former clubs: Southwell (Notts), Chingford, Richmond, Met Police
International debut: England B 31, Namibia 16, 1990
Best moment in rugby: Call-up for my first England B International
Worst moment in rugby: 'Hopu Hopu' army camp, Hamilton, in pouring rain on 1988 tour of New Zealand with British Police and Combined Services
Most embarrassing moment: Captaining a side (Met Police) for the first time in career and losing 66-0 to Stroud

	apps	pts
England B (**1990**)		
Last Season	3 caps	0
Career	3 caps	0
England	1995 Development squad	

Most respected opponent: Harlequins lock Paul Ackford
Best memory last season: Making B debut v. Namibia
Suggestions to improve rugby: *On-field* – Less matches per season. *Off-field* – More publicity for the game (e.g. increased TV coverage)
Other notable landmarks in rugby career: Toured Australia, Canada, USA, New Zealand and Europe. Played in Middlesex side which beat Queensland at Ballymore on 1987 Australian tour. Played for England B on three occasions last season (v. Namibia, Spain and Italy B) and attended

England squad week in Lanzarote. Represented Barbarians on 1990 Easter tour and toured Australia with London last summer
Touchlines: Windsurfing
Player to watch: Chris Brierley (Orrell) – lives in the shadow of Bob Kimmins and has enormous potential

---

De Glanville, P. R.   England

Full Name: Philip Ranulph de Glanville
1990/91 International category: England B
Clubs: Bath/Oxford University
Position: Centre
Height: 6′ **Weight:** 13st
Occupation: Pol/econ student
Born: Loughborough, 1.10.68
Family: Single
Family links with rugby: Father played for Loughborough and Rosslyn Park. Now MD of Rhino scrum machines
International debut (B): Italy 0, England 44, 1989
Best moment in rugby: Replacement for England B in 44-0 defeat of Italy (1989)
Worst moment in rugby: English Students losing 16–6 to Welsh in Cardiff (1989)
Most embarrassing moment: Losing match for Durham Univ on Canadian tour when dropped a goalbound penalty effort beneath posts, and Univ of Victoria scored try from resultant scrum
Most respected opponent: England B centre Fran Clough

	apps	pts
England U-21 (**1989**)		
Last Season	0 caps	0
Career	2 caps	8
England B (**1989**)		
Last Season	2 caps	0
	2 reps	
Career	3 caps	0
England	1995 Development squad	

Serious injuries: Broken arm, dislocated collarbone
Best memory last season: Winning Varsity match with Oxford
Suggestions to improve rugby: Retain County Championship as a meaningful entity
Other notable landmarks in rugby career: Scored two tries in 54–13 win

over Romania on U-21 debut. Made England B debut as a replacement for Barry Evans v. Italy in Piacenza (March 1989) and took tally of caps to three with appearances v. Namibia and Spain last season. Helped underdogs Oxford University win 1991 Varsity match
Touchlines: Windsurfing

Dods, M. — Scotland

Full Name: Michael Dods
1990/91 International category:
Scotland (tour squad)
Club: Gala
Positions: Full-back, wing
Height: 5'11" **Weight:** 11st 2lbs
Occupation: Senior storekeeper
Born: Galashiels, 30.12.68
Family: Louise (wife)
Family links with rugby: Brother
Peter plays for Gala, Scotland and
British Lions
Former club: Gala Wanderers
International debut (U-21):
Scotland 21, Combined Services 4,
1990 (non-cap)
Best moment in rugby: Selection
for North American tour
Worst moment in rugby: Breaking
collarbone before final Scotland
U-19s' trial for International against
Italy
Most embarrassing moment:
Missing penalty goal from in front of
posts against Hawick in Border
League

Scotland U-21 (1989/90)	1 rep	
Scotland B (1990/91)	1 rep	
Scotland 1991	Tour to North America	

Most respected opponent: Hawick wing Tony Stanger
Serious injuries: Broken collarbone (1988), broken nose (1990), thigh strain (1991 – out for a month, missing South of Scotland v. Argentina)
Best memory last season: Playing for Saltires in Dubai Sevens
Suggestions to improve rugby: *On-field* – Award more points for tries to produce a more flowing game. *Off-field* – Let players receive money from advertising etc. and better compensation when away from work on tour. Clarify laws relating to amateurism
Other notable landmarks in rugby career: Represented Scottish Schools

61

at 15 and 18 age-groups. Playing for Gala 1st XV when only 17. Kicking conversion in Scotland U-21 match against Combined Services. Played for Saltires in 1990/91 Dubai Sevens. Shared 100 points with brother Peter on last summer's tour to North America, scoring 44 points myself in three games v. Alberta (2 tries and 10 cons in 76–7 win), Rugby East (2 pens and 3 cons in 24–12 win), and Ontario (1 try in 43–3 win)
Touchlines: Restoring an old house, golf (9-handicap), shooting
Player to watch: Gregor Townsend (Gala)

Dods, P. W.   Scotland

Full Name: Peter William Dods
1990/91 International category: Scotland Full
Club: Gala
Positions: Full-back, centre
Height: 5'9" **Weight:** 12st 8lbs
Occupation: Joiner
Born: Galashiels, 6.1.58
Family: Hazel (wife), Lindsay and Lucy (daughters)
Family links with rugby: Brother Michael plays for Gala
Former club: Gala Wanderers
International debut: Scotland 13, Ireland 15, 1983
Five Nations' debut: As above
Best moment in rugby: Scotland's 1984 Grand Slam
Most respected opponent: French full-back Serge Blanco
Serious injuries: Broken bones in back, cheekbone
Best memory last season: Gala finishing in the Scottish first division's top-four in only second season after winning promotion
Suggestions to improve rugby: *On-field* – Open play up by banning kicking between the 22's. *Off-field* – None, now that touring allowance has risen to £40 per day. When I toured

	apps	pts
Scotland B (**1979**)		
Last Season	0 caps	0
Scotland A (**1990**)		
Last Season	1 cap	11
Scotland (**1983**)		
Last Season	1 cap	0
1991	Tour to North America World Cup squad	
Career	20 caps	186
Lions 1989		

New Zealand in 1981 it was only £6

Other notable landmarks in rugby career: Scotland's 1984 Grand Slam
full-back. After five years in international wilderness, returned in 1989 when
Gavin Hastings was injured and scored 36 points in Five Nations to earn place
on Lions tour. Have scored in every game started for Scotland and represented
them in France, New Zealand, Romania, Australia, United States and Spain.
Once scored 43 points in a game (v. Alberta). Kicked 11 points in Scotland
A's defeat of Spain last season, and won 20th cap when replacing Iwan Tukalo
40 minutes into Scotland 28, Ireland 25. Totalled 56 points in four games on
Scotland's tour of North America last summer, including 21 points (5 pens
and 3 cons) in 41–12 win over United States, and 11 points (3 pens and a 1
con) in 19–24 loss to Canada

Player to watch: Gregor Townsend (Gala)

Donovan, A. W.　　　　　Wales

Full Name: Anthony Wayne
Donovan
1990/91 International category:
Wales U-21
Club: Cardiff
Position: Centre
Height: 6'2" **Weight:** 14st
Born: Bridgend, 10.3.70
Family: Single
Family links with rugby: Cousin
(Richard) won Wales cap as
replacement v. France in 1983
Former club: Llanharan
International debut (U-21): Wales
23, Scotland 15, 1991
Best moment in rugby: Winning
Wales U-21 cap last season
Worst moment in rugby: Losing to
Neath in 1990/91 Welsh Cup
Most respected opponent:
Bridgend wing Glenn Webbe
Best memory last season: Beating
Neath at The Gnoll in Welsh premier
division in final league match
Suggestions to improve rugby:
Allow players to return from Rugby

	apps	pts
Wales U-21 (**1991**)		
Last Season	1 cap	4
v. New Zealand XV	1 app	4
Career	1 cap	4
Heineken 1990/91	8 apps	32

League to Union ... bring back Jonathan Davies!

Other notable landmarks in rugby career: Represented Bridgend and District Youth, Glamorgan, Wales Youth (four times in 1989 v. England, France, Italy and Canada), Wales U-21s (also WRU President's XV in 34–13 win over New Zealand Youth XV at Pontypridd last season)

Touchlines: Training

Player to watch: Ian Jones (Llanelli)

Dooley, W. A.   England

Full Name: Wade Anthony Dooley
1990/91 International category: England Full
Club: Preston Grasshoppers
Position: Lock
Height: 6'8" **Weight:** 17st 9lbs
Occupation: Police constable
Born: Warrington, 2.10.57
Family: Sharon (wife) and Sophie Helen (daughter)
Family links with rugby: Father played Rugby League. Brother also plays for Grasshoppers
Former club: Fylde
International debut: England 22, Romania 15, 1985
Five Nations' debut: England 9, France 9, 1985
Best moment in rugby: Helping England win 1991 Five Nations' Grand Slam

Worst moment in rugby: England losing Grand Slam match to Scotland (1989)
Most embarrassing moment: Being banned for one match for part in violent Wales v. England match (1987)
Most respected opponent: Wasps lock Sean O'Leary

	apps	pts
England (1985)		
Last Season	5 caps	0
v. Barbarians	1 app	0
1991	Tour to Australia	
	World Cup squad	
Career	41 caps	8
Lions 1986		
1989	2 tests	0

Serious injuries: Torn medial ligament (right knee)

Other sporting achievements: Blackpool police division volleyball champions

Best memories last season: England ending 28-year jinx in Cardiff. Seeing Paul Ackford buy a round of drinks

Suggestions to improve rugby: *On-field* – Repeal 90-degree scrummaging law at international level. *Off-field* – Trust funds for international players. Relax regulations on players earning money from promoting goods, sponsors for players etc. Clarification of what players can and cannot do. RFU must get act together

Other notable landmarks in rugby career: Helped 1989 British Lions win Test series 2–1 in Australia

Touchlines: All types of music except jazz. Watching old black and white movies. Fell walking. Eating out. Passion for gardening

Player to watch: Nigel Redman (Bath)

Douglas, S. M. England

Full Name: Stephen Mark Douglas
1990/91 International category:
England U-21 (bench)
Club: Newcastle-Gosforth
Position: Scrum-half
Height: 6′ **Weight:** 13st
Occupation: Accountancy student
Born: Newcastle-upon-Tyne,
21.4.71
Family: Single
International debut (U-19): Italy
Youth 19, England Colts 17, 1990
Best moment in rugby: Scoring
two tries for England Colts in 62–13
defeat of Canada (1990)
Worst moment in rugby: Losing
1990/91 U-21 County
Championship semi-final to
Warwickshire (21–19) after they
scored 12 minutes into injury-time
Most respected opponents:
Scrum-halves Richard Hill (Bath)
and Dewi Morris (Orrell)

	apps
England U-21 (1990/91)	1 rep

Best memory last season: Playing
for Newcastle-Gosforth v. RFU President's XV

Suggestions to improve rugby: *On-field* – More points for a try, less for a penalty goal. *Off-field* – None. Game is going in right direction

Other notable landmarks in rugby career: Played for England Colts

(1989/90) and England Students v. France last season (bench v. Wales). Replacement for England U-21s in 16–22 loss to Ireland U-21s (1990)
Player to watch: Martin Bayfield (Northampton)

Dunn, K. A.   England

Full Name: Kevin Anthony Dunn
International category: England B (bench)
Club: Gloucester
Position: Hooker
Height: 5'9" **Weight:** 13st 10lbs
Occupation: Bricklayer
Born: Gloucester, 5.6.65
Family: Caroline (wife) and Natalie (daughter)
Family links with rugby: Father played for Gloucester Spartans
Former clubs: Gloucester Spartans, Lydney, Warathas (Aus)
International debut: England B 9, Australia 37, 1988
Best moment in rugby: Being selected to England set-up for Australian game (1988)
Worst moment in rugby: Gloucester losing 6–48 to Bath in 1990 Pilkington Cup final
Most respected opponent: All of them

	apps	
England B (1988)		
Last Season	3 reps	
England	1995 Development squad	

Best memory last season: Getting through it injury-free
Suggestions to improve rugby: *On-field* – Scrap 90-degree scrum wheel law. Clamp down on crooked feeds by scrum-halves. More consistent refereeing. *Off-field* – Unions are taking game in right direction
Other notable landmarks in rugby career: Played five times for England B and warmed B bench on nine occasions (three last season, v. Spain, Ireland and France). Unused replacement for Full England team against Australia (1988)
Touchlines: Shooting, golf, weights
Player to watch: Damian Hopley (Wasps)

Edmunds, D. A. — Wales

Full Name: David Alan Edmunds
1990/91 International category: Wales Full
Club: Neath
Position: Wing
Height: 5'11" **Weight:** 12st
Occupation: Carpenter
Born: Neath, 8.10.61
Family: Theresa (wife), Richard (son), Rachel, Rebecca and Regan (daughters)
Former club: Neath Athletic, Aberavon
International debut: Ireland 14, Wales 8, 1990
Five Nations' debut: As above
Best moment in rugby: Coming on as replacement for David Evans in 57th minute at Lansdowne Road to win first cap
Worst moment in rugby: Neath losing 1988/89 Welsh Cup final
Most respected opponent: Wales wing Glenn Webbe
Serious injuries: Torn medial knee ligaments
Other sporting achievements: Cricket for Neath Athletic
Best memories last season: Winning Welsh premier division with Neath, and representing Wales v. Barbarians

	apps	pts
Wales B (1989)		
Last Season	0 caps	0
Career	1 cap	0
Wales (1990)		
Last Season	1 cap	0
Career	2 caps	0
Heineken 1990/91	13 apps	12

Suggestions to improve rugby: *On-field* – More consistency in refereeing. *Off-field* – Relax laws regarding reimbursing players for loss of earnings
Other notable landmarks in rugby career: Played two seasons of Welsh Youth (1980–81), having left school aged 15. Played for Glamorgan Schools. Made Wales B debut in 1989/90 15–28 defeat in France. Scored try for Neath in narrow loss to 1989 All Blacks
Touchlines: Fishing (spinning and worm)
Player to watch: Ian Jones (Llanelli)

Edwards, B.   Scotland

Full Name: Brian Edwards
1990/91 International category:
Scotland A (bench)
Club: Alloa
Position: Centre
Height: 6′ **Weight:** 13st 10lbs
Occupation: Contracts manager
Born: Dunfermline, 3.12.59
Family: Lorna (wife), Philip and
Alastair (sons)
Former clubs: Alloa, Boroughmuir
International debut (B): Italy 3,
Scotland 26, 1988
Best moment in rugby: North and
Midlands beating Glasgow in 1984
at Hughenden
Worst moment in rugby: Sitting
on bench watching Japan beat
Scotland 28–24 in Tokyo, 1989
Most embarrassing moment:
Being unable to make try-line,
playing v. Edinburgh in 1989/90
Scottish Inter-District
Championship, following best break
of season
Most respected opponent: Former
Scotland centre Jim Renwick
Serious injuries: Torn medial
ligaments in knee
Other sporting achievements: Golf (9-handicap)

	apps	pts
Scotland A (1990/91)	1 rep	
Scotland B (**1988**)		
Last Season	0 caps	0
Career	4 caps	0

Best memory last season: Winning McEwan's Scottish division five
championship with Alloa
Suggestions to improve rugby: *On-field* – Cut points for a penalty and
ensure referees send off all players who indulge in foul play. Improve standards
of coaching at lower level. Improve standard of feeder system in Scottish
rugby. Play all league games in first half of season
Other notable landmarks in rugby career: District debut for North and
Midlands (1981), followed by Edinburgh district debut v. Fiji (1982). Toured
North America with Scotland (1985) and Zimbabwe with Public School
Wanderers (1986). Played in both Scotland's B games in 1989/90, v. Ireland
and France, and was promoted to Scotland A squad last season for the game
in Spain

Feats: Managing to see wife and children between September and May
Touchlines: Golf (8-handicap)
Player to watch: Graham Drummond (Boroughmuir)

Egerton, D. W.   England

Full Name: David William Egerton
1990/91 International category:
England B
Club: Bath
Positions: No.8, flanker
Height: 6'5" **Weight:** 16st 10lbs
Occupation: Broker consultant
Born: Pinner, Middlesex, 19.10.61
Family: Single
Family links with rugby: House
called 'Scrummage'. Brother Andy
plays for Saracens. Former dog
called 'Superlative Wing-forward'.
Father played for Wasps 3rd XV
Former clubs: Salisbury,
Loughborough Students, Wasps
(3rd XV)
International debut: Ireland 10,
England 21, 1988
Five Nations' debut: England 23,
Ireland 0, 1990

	apps	pts
England B (**1986**)		
Last Season	1 cap	0
England (**1988**)		
Last Season	0 caps	0
Career	7 caps	4

Best moments in rugby: Winning
first cap in Millennium match.
Helping England beat 1988
Australians
Worst moment in rugby: Being
integrated so slowly into England
team
Most embarrassing moment:
'Scored' try on 22-metre line playing for Bishop Wordsworth's School
Most respected opponents: Bath flanker John Hall (in training), and former
England forward Andy Ripley (in prime)
Serious injuries: Fractured lower back, dislocated kneecap
Other sporting achievements: Shot putt for Dorset and Wilts
Suggestions to improve rugby: Game needs clear guidance. At moment it
is being pulled in all sorts of directions. Involve current players in law changes
Other notable landmarks in rugby career: Influence of coaches Steve

Ralph-Bowman (school) and Jack Rowell (Bath). Won 1984 UAU title with Loughborough against Brian Moore's Nottingham. Unused member of England's 1987 World Cup squad who has earned one England B cap. England's first-choice No.8 for opening 1990 Five Nations' game against Ireland (scored try) but dropped when Mike Teague returned from injury. Missed five months of last season after breaking collarbone v. Neath. Represented England B in 12–9 win over Italy B

Touchlines: Country and Western music fan (esp. Johnny Cash), enjoy playing acoustic guitar. Researcher in ergonomics. Reading science articles and fiction

Emyr, A.   Wales

Full Name: Arthur Emyr (Jones)
1990/91 International category: Wales Full
Club: Swansea
Position: Wing
Height: 6'2" **Weight:** 14st 10lbs
Occupation: Welsh language freelance TV and radio broadcaster/sports journalist
Born: Bangor, 27.7.62
Family: Ana (wife)
Family links with rugby: Two brothers played for Penarth (and younger, for Swansea)
International debut: Wales 12, England 9, 1989
Five Nations' debut: As above
Best moment in rugby: Scoring first try for Wales against Scotland (1990)
Worst moment in rugby: Knee injury, suffered against Maesteg (1987), which required two operations
Most respected opponent: New Zealand wing John Kirwan
Serious injuries: Damaged knee, sprung shoulder joint, ankle ligaments

	apps	pts
Wales B (1985)		
Last Season	0 caps	0
Career	4 caps	24
Wales (1989)		
Last Season	1 cap	0
Career	9 caps	12
Heineken 1990/91	6 apps	0

Other sporting achievements: Welsh International 4 x 100m athlete
Best memory last season: When it ended (wrecked by injury)
Suggestions to improve rugby: *On-field* – Curb endless kicking at goal by awarding 5 points for a try. More freedom to play ball on floor. *Off-field* – More consideration for players and their employers. Current amateur regulations are a farce. So far people are just toying with new ideas. More and more administrators are appearing at clubs on large salaries. Players will soon be looking for the same
Other notable landmarks in rugby career: Career disrupted by serious knee injury (1987) which sidelined me for fourteen months. In and out of Welsh squad since 1983 but finally won first cap in Wales' against-all-odds 1989 defeat of England. Also represented Welsh Universities, Welsh Students, Barbarians, Wales B (scoring five tries v. Spain in 1985). At Sevens, have represented Wales, and Barbarians in Hong Kong. Missed two-thirds of last season due to shoulder and ankle injuries but returned to national side for final Five Nations' match in Paris (lost 3–36)
Touchlines: Going out to cinema
Player to watch: Simon Davies (Swansea – if he works on his strength/physique)

Evans, D. W. Wales

Full Name: David Wyn Evans
1990/91 International category: Wales Full
Club: Cardiff
Positions: Fly-half, centre
Height: 5'9" **Weight:** 11st 8lbs
Occupation: Development officer for Sports Council of Wales
Born: Wootton Bassett, Wilts, 1.11.65
Family: Roberta (wife)
Family links with rugby: Father captained Carnegie College
Former clubs: Swansea and Oxford Universities, Aberaman
International debut: France 31, Wales 12, 1989
Five Nations' debut: As above
Best moment in rugby: Wales defying odds to beat England 12–9 at Cardiff (1989)

Worst moment in rugby: Wales losing 6–34 to England at Twickenham (1990)

Most respected opponent: French centre Philippe Sella

Serious injuries: Dislocated and fractured shoulder, concussion

Best memory last season: Cardiff beating Swansea in opening Heineken Welsh League match

Suggestions to improve rugby: *On-field* – Reduce number of games played by top players. More consistent refereeing. Improve coaching structure

	apps	pts
Wales B (**1989**)		
Last Season	0 caps	0
Career	1 cap	0
Wales (**1989**)		
Last Season	2 cap	3
	4 reps	
1991	Tour to Australia	
	World Cup squad	
Career	9 caps	6
Heineken 1990/91	15 apps	102

Other notable landmarks in rugby career: Partnered Robert Jones at half-back three times for 1984 Welsh Schools, scoring 16 points in 20-0 defeat of France. Also represented Welsh Students, Welsh Universities, Swansea University (1988 UAU final) and Oxford University (1988 Blue). Toured Fiji, Australia, New Zealand and USA with Oxbridge, Japan with Oxford, and Canada with Wales B (where made B debut). Dropped goal for Wales in 24–31 early-season loss to Barbarians (1990/91) before fracturing left shoulder for second time

Touchlines: Learning to speak Welsh and to play Spanish guitar

Player to watch: Scott Gibbs (Neath)

Evans, I. C.   Wales

Full Name: Ieuan Cenydd Evans
1990/91 International category:
Wales Full
Club: Llanelli
Position: Wing
Height: 5'10" **Weight:** 13st 2lbs
Occupation: Leasing executive
Born: Pontardulais, 21.3.64
Family: Single
Family links with rugby: Father
(John) played for Aberavon
Former club: Carmarthen Quins
International debut: France 16,
Wales 9, 1987
Five Nations' debut: As above
Best moment in rugby: Scoring try
that clinched Test series for 1989
Lions in Australia
Worst moment in rugby: Wales'
mis-conceived 1988 tour to New
Zealand
Most respected opponent:
Australian wing David Campese –
can never let him out of your sight
Serious injuries: Recurring
dislocated shoulder, broken leg
Best memory last season:
Winning Schweppes Welsh Cup
with Llanelli
Suggestions to improve rugby:
On-field – When ball is kicked to
touch, allow throw-in to be taken
anywhere behind mark. Award more
points for a try. *Off-field* – Broken time payments

	apps	pts
Wales B (**1985**)		
Last Season	0 caps	0
Career	3 caps	28
Wales (**1987**)		
Last Season	5 caps	0
Career	23 caps	28
1991	Tour to Australia	
	World Cup squad	
Lions 1989	3 Tests	4
Heineken 1990/91	12 apps	28

Other notable landmarks in rugby career: Playing career severely
hampered by injury. Returned with triumphant 1989 Lions from Down Under
but was then forced to miss whole of 1989/90 season through injury. Played
in five matches in 1987 World Cup, scoring four tries in 40–9 defeat of
Canada. Scored six tries for Wales B in 1985 defeat of Spain
Touchlines: Tennis, cricket, squash, golf
Player to watch: Emyr Lewis (Llanelli)

Evans, I. L.   Wales

Full Name: Iwan Luc Evans
1990/91 International category:
Wales U-21
Club: Bridgend
Positions: Full-back, centre
Height: 5'8" **Weight:** 12st
Occupation: Dental student
Born: Treherbert, 13.6.71
Family: Single
Family links with rugby: Father
played for Swansea
Former clubs: Treherbert,
Treorchy
International debut (U-21):
Scotland 10, Wales 24, 1990
Best moment in rugby: Helping
Bridgend beat Wales last season
Worst moments in rugby: Welsh
Schools losing 6–9 to Irish after I
missed a late penalty. Watching
England's Dusty Hare kick late
penalty to beat Wales in 1980
Most embarrassing moment:
Having to run across field to catch
kick while changing shorts, playing
for Bridgend against Gloucester
Most respected opponent: Former
Neath centre Allan Bateman
Other sporting achievements:
Welsh Schools 400m hurdler
Best memory last season: Scored

	apps	pts
Wales U-21 (**1990**)		
Last Season	1 cap	0
v. New Zealand XV	1 app	8
Career	2 caps	7
Wales B (1990/91)	1 rep	
Wales 1991	Tour to Australia	
	World Cup squad	
Heineken 1990/91	10 apps	75

two tries for WRU President's XV in 34–13 defeat of New Zealand Rugby
News U-21 XV last season at Pontypridd
Other notable landmarks in rugby career: Represented Wales Schools
(U-18) in 1989 and Wales U-21 team for last two seasons as an 18-and 19-year
old. Scored two tries for WRU President's (U-21) XV in 34–13 win over New
Zealand Youth XV last season at Pontypridd. Included on Wales B bench for
34–12 defeat of Netherlands last season, and toured Australia with senior
Welsh squad over summer. Included in Wales' preliminary World Cup squad

Field, M. J.   Ireland

Full Name: Maurice John Field
1990/91 International category:
Ireland (World Cup squad)
Club: Malone
Position: Centre
Height: 6' **Weight:** 13st 4lbs
Occupation: Fireman
Born: Greenisland, 24.2.64
Family: Gillian (wife) and Rebekah
(daughter)
Family links with rugby: Father
(John) played for Malone and
Carrickfergus
Former club: North of Ireland
(1983–87)
Best moment in rugby: Selection
to Ireland's 1991 World Cup squad
Worst moment in rugby: Ulster's
performance in defeat by Bath last
season

Ireland 1991   World Cup squad

Most respected opponent: Former
Maori wing Bob Gray
Best memory last season: Scoring
try on Ulster debut v. Irish Exiles
Suggestions to improve rugby:
On-field – More points for a try, less for a penalty goal. *Off-field* –
Reimbursement for time lost to rugby. Clarify what can and cannot be done
Other notable landmarks in rugby career: Appearances for Ulster U-20s
and Young Ulster before breaking into Ulster senior team last season. Spent
five seasons playing for North of Ireland before joining Malone in 1987.
Included in Ireland's preliminary World Cup squad
Touchlines: Golf (16-handicap), swimming, cycling, soccer
Player to watch: Derek McAleese (Ballymena)

Fitzgerald, D. C.   Ireland

Full Name: Desmond Christopher Fitzgerald
1990/91 International category: Ireland Full
Club: Lansdowne
Position: Prop
Height: 6'1" **Weight:** 17st 3lbs
Occupation: National account manager for Digital
Born: Dublin, 20.12.57
Family: Luke (son), Rachel and Rebecca (daughters)
Former club: Dublin University
International debut: England 12, Ireland 9, 1984
Five Nations' debut: As above
Best moment in rugby: Playing for 1986 Lions in Cardiff
Worst moment in rugby: Being dropped by Ireland for first time after 1984 season (missed 1985 Triple Crown)
Most respected opponent: Former Wales prop Jeff Whitefoot
Serious injuries: Dislocated both shoulders, broken ribs, torn hamstrings

	apps	pts
Ireland B (**1983**)		
Last Season	0 caps	0
Ireland (**1984**)		
Last Season	7 caps	0
Career	29 caps	0
Lions 1986		

Other sporting achievements: 1980/81 British and Irish Universities heavyweight boxing champion. Ex-competitive wrestler
Best memory last season: Getting selected for Irish team while playing for Lansdowne 2nd XV
Suggestions to improve rugby: *Off-field* – Address pro-am dilemma. With levels of expectation constantly increasing, administrators must decide how to reward players of the future
Other notable landmarks in rugby career: Injuries postponed Ireland B debut for three years, finally coming in 1983. Toured Romania with Leinster (1980) and South Africa with Ireland (1981). Represented Ireland at loose and tight-head
Touchlines: Golf (18-handicap), shooting
Player to watch: Jim Staples (London Irish)

Fitzgerald, J. J.   Ireland

Full Name: John Joseph Fitzgerald
1990/91 International category: Ireland Full
Club: Young Munster
Position: Loose-head prop
Height: 5'11" **Weight:** 16st 4lbs
Occupation: Business development executive (banking)
Born: London, 31.8.61
Family: Caroline (wife) and Nicole (daughter)
Family links with rugby: Younger brother plays for Shannon
Former club: Tokoroa (NZ)
International debut: Ireland 22, Scotland 18, 1988
Five Nations' debut: As above
Best moment in rugby: Scoring try against Scotland in 1990 Five Nations' Championship
Worst moment in rugby: Being trounced 25–6 by France in Paris in 1988
Most respected opponent: French prop Pascal Ondarts – tough and durable

	apps	pts
Ireland B (1990)		
Last Season	1 cap	0
Ireland (1988)		
Last Season	4 caps	0
	1 rep	
Career	9 caps	4

Best memory last season: Winning Munster Senior Cup with Young Munster
Suggestions to improve rugby: *On-field* – Concentrate on general levels of fitness. *Off-field* – Work on attitude and approach to big-day games
Other notable landmarks in rugby career: Playing in Parc des Princes. Spent a season playing in New Zealand with Tokoroa. Enjoyed living out there for four months during summer 1989 – way of life and manner in which they approach rugby was very interesting
Touchlines: Weight lifting, jogging
Player to watch: Simon Geoghegan (London Irish)

Fitzgibbon, M. J.   Ireland

Full Name: Michael Joseph
Fitzgibbon
1990/91 International category:
Ireland B
Club: Shannon
Position: Open-side flanker
Height: 6'1.5" **Weight:** 14st 7lbs
Occupation: Engineer
Born: Askeaton, Co. Limerick,
2.4.66
Family: Single
Family links with rugby: Uncle
(Basil) played for Munster
Former club: Trinity
International debut (B): Ireland
24, England 10, 1991
**Other notable landmarks in
rugby career:** Won six caps in two
seasons of representing Irish
Schools. Also played for Irish
universities before getting Ireland B
call-up last season. Included in
44-man preliminary Ireland squad
for World Cup
Touchlines: Indoor soccer, all sport

	apps	pts
Ireland B (**1991**)		
Last Season	1 cap	0
Career	1 cap	0
Ireland 1991	World Cup squad	

Ford, S. P.   Wales

Full Name: Stephen Paul Ford
1990/1991 International category:
Wales Full
Club: Cardiff
Position: Right wing
Height: 6′ **Weight:** 12st 7lbs
Occupation: Carpet fitter
Born: Cardiff, 15.8.65
Family: Single with son
Family links with rugby: Phil
(brother) plays Rugby League for
Leeds and Great Britain
Former clubs: Glamorgan
Wanderers, Rumney
International debut: Ireland 14,
Wales 8, 1990
Five Nations' debut: As above
Best moment in rugby: Scoring try
in first International
Worst moment in rugby: Being
banned from Rugby Union for two
and a half years after having Rugby
League trial with Leeds
Most respected opponent: New
Zealand wing John Kirwan
Serious injuries: Damaged Achilles
tendon
Suggestions to improve rugby:
Bring money into game
**Other notable landmarks in rugby
career:** Set Welsh try-scoring record

	apps	pts
Wales B (**1989**)		
Last Season	1 cap	8
Career	2 caps	12
Wales (**1990**)		
Last Season	5 caps	4
Career	8 caps	8
Heineken 1990/91	14 apps	32

by scoring seven for Wales B in 47-0 win over Saskatchewan on 1989
Canadian tour. Played both 'tests' in Namibia on 1990 summer tour and held
my place on Wales wing until final match of last season (v. France). Scored
one of only three Wales tries in last season's Five Nations Championship, in
12–32 loss to Scotland at Murrayfield

Fox, D. C.   Wales

Full Name: David Clifford Fox
1990/91 International category:
Wales (World Cup squad)
Club: Llanelli
Position: Hooker
Height: 5'9" **Weight:** 13st 7lbs
Occupation: Fireman
Born: Swansea, 4.12.59
Family: Sian (wife) and Lynsey
(daughter)
Former club: Bonymaen
Best moment in rugby: Winning
Welsh Cup for third time last season
Worst moment in rugby: All
injuries (missed 1989/90 season
through shoulder operation)
Most respected opponent:
Aberavon hooker Billy James
Serious injuries: Broken ankle
(1987), damaged shoulder (1989/90)
Best memory last season: Llanelli
beating Pontypool in Welsh Cup
final
**Other notable landmarks in
rugby career:** Bench reserve for
Wales 16-Group v. England.
Selected for Wales B v. France four years ago but had to withdraw with
cracked bone in ankle
Touchlines: Keep-fit
Player to watch: Andrew Lamerton (Llanelli)

	apps	pts
Wales 1991	World Cup squad	
Heineken 1990/91	7 apps	4

Francis, N. P.   Ireland

Full Name: Neil Patrick Francis
1990/91 International category: Ireland Full
Club: Blackrock College
Position: Lock
Height: 6'6" **Weight:** 17st 3lbs
Occupation: Banker
Born: Dublin, 17.3.64
Family: Single
Former clubs: London Irish, Manly (Aus)
International debut: Ireland 32, Tonga 9, 1987 (World Cup)
Five Nations' debut: Scotland 37, Ireland 21, 1989
Best moment in rugby: Winning 1981 Schools Cup final with Blackrock
Worst moment in rugby: Being dropped by Ireland on 1989 North American tour
Most respected opponent: French forward Laurent Rodriguez
Serious injuries: Broken vertebrae (out two years)
Other sporting achievements: Javelin for Ireland (national junior and senior champion)

	apps	pts
Ireland (1987)		
Last Season	4 caps	0
1991	Tour to Namibia	
	World Cup squad	
Career	12 caps	4

Other notable landmarks in rugby career: Represented Irish Schools five times (1981–82). Rejoined Blackrock from London Irish in 1989. Made full Ireland debut in 1987 World Cup but not called upon until Oct 1988 when played against Western Samoa, scoring a try. Sole Irish representative in Home Unions team which played Rest of Europe at Twickenham in aid of Romania in 1990. Took tally of caps into double figures last season with starts v. England and Scotland in final two Championship games

Galwey, M. J.　　　　　　　　Ireland

Full Name: Michael Joseph Galwey
1990/91 International category:
Ireland Full
Club: Shannon
Position: Lock
Height: 6'4" **Weight:** 17st
Occupation: Sales representative
Born: Co. Kerry, 8.10.66
Family: Single
Former club: Castle Island
International debut (B): Scotland
22, Ireland 22, 1989
Best moment in rugby: Scoring a
try in Munster Cup final
Worst moment in rugby: Losing
1988/89 Munster Cup final to
Constitution
Most respected opponent: Ireland
lock Donal Lenihan
Serious injuries: Damaged Achilles
tendon
Other sporting achievements:
Winner of All-Ireland Gaelic
Football medal with Kerry in 1986
**Other notable landmarks in
rugby career:** Being selected to play
with Munster U-20 XV whilst a
member of Castle Island. Winning
the Munster Senior Cup in three
successive seasons, and being

	apps	pts
Ireland B (**1989**)		
Last Season	3 caps	4
Ireland (**1991**)		
Last Season	3 caps	0
	1 rep	
Career	3 caps	0

awarded a Shannon RFC cap for the achievement. Played for Ireland U-25s
against United States (won 12–10) in March 1990. Broke into senior team
last season, earning selection for the games v. France and Ireland after warming
bench in season-opener v. Argentina. A regular fixture in the B XV, playing
in all three matches (and wins) v. Argentina (scoring try), Scotland and
England
Touchlines: Fishing the Kerry Lakes

Geoghegan, S. P.   Ireland

Full Name: Simon Patrick
Geoghegan
1990/91 International category:
Ireland Full
Club: London Irish
Position: Wing
Height: 6′ **Weight:** 13st
Occupation: Trainee solicitor
Born: Barnet, Herts, 1.9.68
Family: Single
Former club: Wasps Colts
International debut: Ireland 13,
France 21, 1991
Five Nations' debut: As above
Best moment in rugby: Scoring try
on second full international
appearance for Ireland in 21–21
draw with Wales (1991)
Worst moment in rugby: Losing
all three provincial games with
Connacht last season
Most respected opponent: Rugby
wing Eddie Saunders
Best memories last season: Being
selected for Ireland and maintaining
place through Five Nations'
Championship
Suggestions to improve rugby:
On-field – Alter amount of points
awarded for penalty goals as this
tends to devalue the worth of a try
which, after all, is the essence of
rugby union. *Off-field* – Players
should be properly remunerated for
time spent training at international
squad sessions etc.

	apps	pts
Ireland U-25 (**1990**)		
Last Season	1 cap	4
Career	1 cap	4
Ireland B (**1990**)		
Last Season	1 cap	4
Career	1 cap	4
Ireland (**1991**)		
Last Season	5 caps	12
1991	Tour to Namibia	
	World Cup squad	
Career	5 caps	12

Other notable landmarks in rugby career: Represented Ireland at U-25,
Students, B and Full level. Ran 40 yards for try on Ireland B debut last season
in 27–12 defeat of Argentina at Thomond Park and scored another for Ireland
U-25 in 36–17 win over Spain. Given full Ireland debut v. France opposite
Patrice Lagisquet at Lansdowne Road (2 Feb 1991). Scored tries in next three
Internationals (v. Wales, Ireland and Scotland)

Touchlines: Cinema, reading, swimming, tennis, cricket
Player to watch: Richard Wallace (Garryowen – strong, fast, and steadfast wing who hopefully won't take my place!)

George, G. M. Wales

Full Name: Glen Max George
1990/91 International category: Wales Full
Club: Newport
Position: Flanker
Height: 6′1″ **Weight:** 15st
Occupation: Postal executive
Born: Newport, 30.9.64
Family: Single
International debut: Wales 6, England 25, 1991
Five Nations' debut: As above
Best moment in rugby: Turning Newport around into the side we have now become
Worst moment in rugby: Failing to gain selection for Wales' 1991 summer tour to Australia
Most respected opponent: Pontypool captain Chris Huish
Best memory last season: Making Wales debut v. England at Arms Park

	apps	pts
Wales B (**1990**)		
Last Season	1 cap	0
Career	1 cap	0
Wales (**1991**)		
Last Season	2 caps	0
1991	World Cup squad	
Career	2 caps	0
Heineken 1990/91	11 apps	16

Suggestions to improve rugby:
On-field – Be more sensitive about 90-degree scrum wheel law. Give players chance to use it instead of blowing up straight away. If one side wheels, then give ball to opposite side instead of just awarding fresh put-in.
Off-field – Continue to nurture youngsters into game. The WRU are now trying to encourage youth. Introduce Wales U-23 side
Other notable landmarks in rugby career: Represented Wales at School and Youth level (U-15s, 16s and 19s). Captain of Newport – led them to win against Neath which ended All Black's 51-match unbeaten run. Captained Wales B to 34–12 defeat of Netherlands in Leiden last season prior to making

full debut in 25–6 loss to England. Also represented Barbarians, Monmouthshire (captain), Public School Wanderers and Crawshays
Player to watch: David Llewellyn (Newport)

Gibbs, I. S. Wales

Full Name: Ian Scott Gibbs
1990/91 International category:
Wales Full
Club: Neath
Position: Centre
Height: 5'10" **Weight:** 12st 7lbs
Occupation: TV researcher at
Rugby Vision Ltd
Born: Bridgend, 23.1.71
Family: Single
Family links with rugby: None.
Father (Graham) is a former pole
vaulter and international gymnast
Former clubs: Pencoed, Bridgend
International debut: Wales 6,
England 25, 1991
Five Nations' debut: As above
Best moment in rugby: Welsh
Youth beating England Colts at
Wrexham in 1990
Worst moment in rugby: Losing to
England Colts in 1989 at Torquay
Most respected opponent: French
centre Philippe Sella
Best memory last season: Gaining
revenge over Newport in Welsh Cup
for earlier defeat
**Other notable landmarks in rugby
career:** Made full debut against
England aged 19; first pupil of Ysgol

	apps	pts
Wales B (1990)		
Last Season	1 cap	4
Career	1 cap	4
Wales (1991)		
Last Season	5 caps	0
Career	5 caps	0
Heineken 1990/91	10 apps	12

Gyfun Llanharry to be capped by Wales. Last season was first with Neath, having joined All Blacks from Pencoed, with whom won seven Welsh Youth caps (two seasons) and captained side in 1989/90. Quickly progressed up the representative ladder last season, making Wales B debut in Netherlands (scoring one of five tries in a 34–12 win), before being called into the full side for duration of Five Nations' Championship. Youngest player to be voted

Welsh Player of Year (1990/91). Ended season by rejecting £230,000 offer
from Wigan RLFC to move North
Touchlines: Boxing, music, golf
Player to watch: Scott Quinnell (Llanelli)

Glasgow, I. C.   Scotland

Full Name: Iain Cameron Glasgow
1990/91 International category:
Scotland B
Club: Heriot's FP
Positions: Full-back, wing
Height: 5'7.5" **Weight:** 11st 7lbs
Occupation: Trainee chartered
surveyor
Born: Bridge of Allan, 24.2.66
Family: Single
Family links with rugby: Father
played ten times for Scotland.
Brother Anthony plays for London
Scottish, having previously played
for Army, Blackheath and Royal
Engineers
Former clubs: Edinburgh
Wanderers, Howe of Fife, St
Andrew's Univ, Cambridge Univ
Best moment in rugby: Scoring 39
points for Scotland XV in record
91–8 defeat of Kanto on 1989 tour of
Japan (four short of Peter Dods'
Scottish record for a tour match)
Worst moments in rugby:
Scotland XV losing 1989 Test 24–28
to Japan in Tokyo. Disastrous 1990
Scottish Trial

	apps	pts
Scotland B (**1991**)		
Last Season	1 cap	6
	1 rep	
Career	1 cap	6
Scotland (1989/90)	2 rep	

Most respected opponents: Wales
fly-half David Evans, Australian wing Ian Williams and former Scotland
back row men Jim and Finlay Calder
Serious injuries: Broken cheekbone (five weeks before 1988 Varsity match)
Other sporting achievements: Scottish Junior decathlon champion
Best memory last season: Attending first Hong Kong Sevens with Saltires
Suggestions to improve rugby: *On-field* – Simplify laws to encourage more
expansive play. More points for a try. Alter offside law so that when full-back

receives high kick from opposite number, the opposing players cannot advance until they have been played on-side. *Off-field* – Clarify laws on amateurism so that there is not one rule for one hemisphere and one for the other. Treat top players better

Other notable landmarks in rugby career: Played on right wing for Cambridge in 1988 Varsity match. Toured Fiji, Australia and New Zealand with Oxbridge (1989). Represented Scotland at Schools, U-21 and Student level. Played in 1988 Student World Cup. Kicked two penalty goals for Scotland B v. France B in 10–31 loss at Hughenden (1990/91). Replacement against Ireland B

Touchlines: Golf (11-handicap), tennis

Player to watch: Graham Shiel (Melrose)

Goodey, R. Wales

Full Name: Richard Goodey
1990/91 International category:
Wales B (squad)
Club: Pontypool
Positions: Lock, No.8
Height: 6′4″ **Weight:** 16st
Occupation: Postman
Born: Chepstow, 17.7.65
Family: Helen (wife)
Family links with rugby: Brother plays for Chepstow
Former clubs: Caldicot, Chepstow
Best moment in rugby: Scoring winning try for Pontypool at Cardiff (1988/89)
Worst moment in rugby: Tearing ankle ligaments at Cardiff (1988/89)
Most respected opponent: Wales lock Phil Davies
Serious injuries: Torn ankle ligaments (required operation), cartilage (operation)
Other sporting achievements: Soccer for Chepstow RFC
Best memory last season: Pontypool defeating Swansea in Schweppes Welsh Cup semi-final

	apps	pts
Wales 1991	Tour to Australia World Cup squad	
Heineken 1990/91	12 apps	8

Suggestions to improve rugby: *On-field* – Let rucks continue bit longer where possible. *Off-field* – Unions handling amateurism question quite well... walking very thin line, could not really do any more

Other notable landmarks in rugby career: Played for Ron Waldron's XV v. Lord Mayor's XV (1989/90). Also represented Monmouthshire U-23s and senior team. Selected as reserve for Wales B v. France (1989/90). Last season disrupted by cartilage injury which required operation before Christmas. Included in Wales squad for World Cup and invited to tour Australia last summer after helping Pontypool to final of Welsh Cup

Player to watch: Lyndon Mustoe (Pontypool)

Gray, C. A. Scotland

Full Name: Christopher Anthony Gray

1990/91 International category: Scotland Full

Club: Nottingham

Position: Lock

Height: 6'5" **Weight:** 16st 12lbs

Occupation: Dental surgeon

Born: Haddington, 11.7.60

Family: Single

Family links with rugby: Older brother played and introduced me to game

Former club: Edinburgh Academicals

International debut: Scotland 23, Wales 7, 1989

Five Nations' debut: As above

Best moment in rugby: Winning 1990 Five Nations' Grand Slam

Worst moments in rugby: Losing to Japan 28–24 in unofficial Test (1989). Losing to France 3–19 in Paris (1989) and yet again last season (9–15)

Most embarrassing moment: Destroying half-way marker post on run out at Kingsholm

Most respected opponents: Paul Ackford (England) and Gary Whetton (New Zealand)

Other sporting achievements: Golf (6-handicap)

	apps	pts
Scotland B (1986)		
Last Season	0 caps	0
Scotland (1989)		
Last Season	5 caps	4
1991	World Cup squad	
Career	17 caps	12

Best memories last season: Nottingham's Pilkington Cup semi-final v. Harlequins. Scotland's 32–12 defeat of Wales

Suggestions to improve rugby: *On-field* – Referees should keep in touch (verbally) with captains. *Off-field* – Better communications between top administrators and players. Get amateur laws properly sorted out. What can we do?

Other notable landmarks in rugby career: Played for Notts/Lincs/Derby in 1985 English County Championship final. Captained Anglo-Scots in 1987 Scottish Inter-District Championship. Won four caps for Scotland B. Captained Scotland XV against Goshawks (Zimbabwe, 1988). Captained Nottingham (1989/90). Played for Barbarians. Scored first tries for Scotland during 1989/90 season against Fiji and New Zealand (first Test) and added a third last season in 49–3 win over Argentina at Murrayfield. Member of Scotland's 1990 Grand Slam side

Touchlines: Golf, tennis, relaxing hard

Player to watch: Guy Gregory (Nottingham)

Griffiths, M. **Wales**

Full Name: Mike Griffiths
1990/91 International category: Wales Full
Club: Cardiff
Position: Loose-head prop
Height: 6′ **Weight:** 16st 7lbs
Occupation: Builder
Born: Tonypandy, 18.3.62
Family: Married with two sons
Family links with rugby: Brother plays for Ystrad Rhondda
Former clubs: Ystrad Rhondda, Bridgend
International debut: Wales 24, Western Samoa 6, 1988
Five Nations' debut: Scotland 23, Wales 7, 1989
Best moment in rugby: Winning first Welsh cap against touring Samoans

Worst moment in rugby: Wales losing 6–34 to England at Twickenham (1990)

Most respected opponents: England prop Jeff Probyn (for his technique) and Scotland prop Iain Milne (for his size and strength)

Serious injuries: Broken ribs, fractured arm, twisted shoulder muscles, damaged ankle and knee ligaments
Other sporting achievements: Accomplished soccer player (centre-back)
Suggestions to improve rugby: Look after players better
Other notable landmarks in rugby career: Started career in back-row

	apps	pts
Wales B (**1988**)		
Last Season	0 caps	0
Career	1 cap	0
Wales (**1988**)		
Last Season	3 caps	0
	2 reps	
Career	14 caps	0
Lions 1989		
Heineken	10 apps	0

but moved to front of scrum shortly before joining Bridgend. Moved to Cardiff for new challenges and found them: playing for Crawshays, Wales B, Wales and 1989 Lions. Sole Welsh representative in Home Unions' team which played Europe at Twickenham on behalf of Romanian appeal in 1990

Guscott, J. C. $\qquad$ England

Full Name: Jeremy Clayton Guscott
1990/91 International category: England Full
Club: Bath
Position: Centre
Height: 6'1" **Weight:** 13st 5lbs
Occupation: Public relations officer
Born: Bath, 7.7.65
Family: Married
International debut: Romania 3, England 58, 1989
Five Nations' debut: England 23, Ireland 0, 1990
Best moment in rugby: Try scored for 1989 Lions v. Australia in second Test
Worst moment in rugby: Being dropped by Bath for semi-finals of 1989/90 Pilkington Cup
Most embarrassing moment: Any time I miss a tackle
Most respected opponent: All of them

Best memory last season: Rory Underwood running past Jean-Baptiste Lafond to score crucial try in Grand Slam decider with France

Suggestions to improve rugby:
On-field – Scrap 90-degree scrum wheel law. *Off-field* – Allow players to earn money through off-field activities

Other notable landmarks in rugby career: Started career with Bath's mini-section as a wing, aged seven. Meteoric rise in 1989 saw two caps for England B, mark full England debut in Bucharest with three tries and gain an invitation from Lions.

	apps	pts
England B (1988)		
Last Season	0 caps	0
England (1989)		
Last Season	7 caps	8
Career	13 caps	40
1991	Tour to Australia	
	World Cup squad	
Lions 1989	2 Tests	4

Scored crucial try in Brisbane to keep Lions in hunt. Helped England win 1991 Five Nations' Grand Slam before touring with them to Australia last summer and scoring visitors' only try in 15–40 Test loss to Wallabies

Touchlines: Golf

Player to watch: Philip de Glanville (Bath)

Hall, J. P.   England

Full Name: Jonathan Peter Hall
1990/91 International category: England Full
Club: Bath
Positions: Flanker, No.8
Height: 6′3.5″ **Weight:** 16st 7lbs
Occupation: Lloyds underwriter
Born: Bath, 15.3.62
Family: Single
Family links with rugby: Father (Peter) and grandfather (Harry Vowles) played for Bath
International debut: Scotland 18, England 6, 1984
Five Nations' debut: As above
Best moments in rugby: Winning first England cap and winning 1984 John Player Cup final (10–9 v. Bristol)
Worst moment in rugby: Knee cartilage injury sustained during England's training week in Lanzarote that required operation and put paid to international hopes for season

Most embarrassing moment:
Playing in England U-23 trial at
Bisham Abbey on pitch which also
had soccer markings, I ran to try-line
and triumphantly touched ball
down...only to discover I was still five
metres short!

Most respected opponent: Former
Pontypool and Wales prop Jeff
Squire

	apps	pts
England B (1985)		
Last Season	1 cap	0
Career	2 caps	0
England (1984)		
Last Season	1 cap	4
Career	20 caps	

Serious injuries: Knee cartilage (1990/91)

Best memory last season: Earning England recall in 51-0 win over Argentina
and scoring try

Suggestions to improve rugby: *On-field* – Standards of refereeing
worldwide must fall into line. Present situation (interpretations differing so
markedly between northern and southern hemispheres) is both frustrating and
dangerous. *Off-field* – Guidelines regarding amateurism must be clearly
marked out. No grey areas, but black and white

Other notable landmarks in rugby career: Made full England debut as a
21-year-old in 1984, having missed out on England B. Won first B cap the
following year v. Italy. Won 19th full cap v. Scotland in 1987, and did not
play again until returning v. Argentina (and scoring try) at start of last season.
Knee injury in Lanzarote ended International season prematurely, although
did win second B cap in 12–9 win over Italy in March 1991

Touchlines: Hot air ballooning, cycling

Player to watch: Martin Haag (Bath)

Hall, M. R.   Wales

Full Name: Michael Robert Hall
1990/91 International category:
Wales Full
Club: Cardiff
Positions: Centre, wing
Height: 6'1" **Weight:** 14st 2lbs
Occupation: Surveyor
Born: Bridgend, 13.10.65
Family: Single
Former clubs: Bridgend, Maesteg,
Cambridge Univ
International debut: New Zealand
52, Wales 3, 1988
Five Nations' debut: Scotland 23,
Wales 7, 1989
Best moments in rugby: Selection
for 1989 British Lions. 1990 Hong
Kong Sevens with Barbarians
Worst moment in rugby: England
34, Wales 6 (Feb 1990)
Most embarrassing moment:
Wales' record defeat at Twickenham
(1990)
Most respected opponent: French
centre Philippe Sella
Serious injuries: Hamstring tears
Other sporting achievements:
Schoolboy honours at county level in
soccer, basketball and cricket
Best memory last season: Eagling
9th hole at Mountain Ash Golf Club

	apps	pts
Wales B (1987)		
Last Season	0 caps	0
Career	1 cap	0
Wales (1988)		
Last Season	1 cap	0
1991	Tour to Australia	
Career	13 caps	8
Lions 1989	1 Test	0
Heineken 1990/91	10 apps	24

Suggestions to improve rugby: *On-field* – Simplify rules. Sort out line-out
shambles. *Off-field* – Market game properly. Clear up ambiguities in laws on
amateurism. WRU are doing well (appointing marketing manager etc.)
Other notable landmarks in rugby career: Past captain of British
Universities, Welsh Students and Wales U-21s. Two Blues at Cambridge
(1987,88). Wales B against France in 1987 (lost 0–26). 1989 Lions against
Australia in first Test (lost 12–30). Toured with Wales to New Zealand (1988)
and to South Africa (1989) with World XV. Winning try against England
(1989). Tore hamstring in first appearance last season and having recovered,
did it again. Included in Wales' summer tour to Australia and played in 6–63
International defeat

Halliday, S. J.   England

Full Name: Simon John Halliday
1990/91 International category:
England Full (bench)
Club: Harlequins
Positions: Centre, wing
Height: 6' **Weight:** 14st
Occupation: Stockbroker
Born: Haverfordwest, 13.7.60
Family: Suzanne (wife) and Sophie
(daughter)
Family links with rugby: Father
played for Norfolk and Royal Navy
Former clubs: Oxford Univ., Bath
International debut: England 28,
Canada 0, 1983
Five Nations' debut: England 21,
Wales 18, 1986
Best moment in rugby: Final
whistle of England/Australia (1988)
Worst moment in rugby: Losing
6–33 to Scotland (1986)
**Most embarrassing moments
(almost!):** Leg bandage slipped
down to my ankle as I broke through
to score for England against
Australia (1988). Had my journey
been any longer the support would
have tripped me up. Having my
hairstyle criticised by Will Carling in
commentary of Romania/England match (1989)

	apps	pts
England B (1985)		
Last Season	0 caps	0
England (1986)		
Last Season	0 caps	0
	3 reps	
Career	16 caps	4

Most respected opponent: Former Wales centre Ray Gravell – very tough to
knock down
Serious injuries: Fractured dislocation of left foot, playing for Somerset v.
Middlesex in 1983 County Championship (cost me three years of international
rugby), torn hamstrings
Other sporting achievements: Oxford cricket Blue (1980). Proud owner of
first-class century (113 n.o. v. Kent). Played for Dorset and Minor Counties
Best memory last season: Being part of England's Grand Slam squad

Suggestions to improve rugby: *On-field* – Kicks at goal to be restricted to foul play and deliberate offside. Award 5 points for a try. *Off-field* – Recognition of time players spend away from work – pro-rata compensation. Show players that what they are doing is appreciated. Present situation is still embarrassing

Other notable landmarks in rugby career: Played for Dorset & Wilts U-19s. Won three rugby Blues at Oxford (1979,80,81). Captained South West to victories over USA and Australia (both 1988). Represented Bath in five Cup finals and emerged a winner on each occasion

Touchlines: Golf, DIY

Player to watch: Adedayo Adebayo (Bath) – outstanding 'all-court' player. Man after my own heart. A name to conjure with – Bill McLaren would love it!

Halpin, G. F. Ireland

Full Name: Garrett Francis Halpin
1990/91 International category:
Ireland Full (bench)
Club: Wanderers
Position: Tight-head prop
Height: 5′11″ **Weight:** 17st 4lbs
Occupation: Insurance official
Born: Dublin, 14.2.66
Family: Carol (wife)
Former club: Rockwell College
International debut: England 23, Ireland 0, 1990
Five Nations' debut: As above
Best moment in rugby: Winning first full cap, at Twickenham
Worst moment in rugby: Losing place after above match
Most respected opponent: Lansdowne prop Tom Clancy

Other sporting achievements: Irish International hammer thrower – American Indoor Collegiate champion. Represented Ireland in 1987 in World Athletics Championships (Rome)

Best memory last season: Touring Namibia with Ireland
Suggestions to improve rugby: *On-field* – Scrap 90-degree scrummage wheel law as it slows game down and inspires dubious tactics
Other notable landmarks in rugby career: Joining Wanderers on return

95

from a sports scholarship with University of Manhattan in New York. Played four times for Ireland Schools. Toured North America with Ireland (1989), scoring try in defeat of Mid West in Chicago. Won 1989/90 Leinster League and Cup double with Wanderers. Propped in Ireland B's 27–12 win over Argentina last season. Ever present on

	apps	pts
Ireland B (1990)		
Last Season	1 cap	0
Career	1 cap	0
Ireland (1990)		
Last Season	4 reps	
Career	1 cap	0

replacements' bench for Ireland during 1991 Five Nations' Championship
Player to watch: Simon Geoghegan (London Irish)

Hamilton, G. F.   Ireland

Full Name: Gordon Frederic Hamilton
1990/91 International category: Ireland Full
Club: North of Ireland (NIFC)
Position: Flanker
Height: 6′ **Weight:** 14st 7lbs
Occupation: Shipping and travel agent
Born: Belfast, 13.5.64
Family: Single
Family links with rugby: Father (Jimmy) played for NIFC
Former club: Blackheath
International debut: Ireland 13, France 21, 1991
Five Nations' debut: As above
Best moment in rugby: Running out at Lansdowne Road for first cap
Worst moment in rugby: Ireland's 7–16 loss to England (1991)
Most embarrassing moment: Fell over while running out for team photo prior to full debut. Cut thumb badly and needed stitches
Most respected opponent: Kelso flanker John Jeffrey

	apps	pts
Ireland B (1989)		
Last Season	1 cap	0
Ireland (1991)		
Last Season	5 caps	0
Career	5 caps	0

Best memory last season: Charging down Mark Ring's kick in 21–21 draw with Wales which led to Brendan Mullin's Irish record-equalling try

Suggestions to improve rugby: *On-field* – None, game is in good shape. *Off-field* – Compensation for time lost to work due to rugby

Other notable landmarks in rugby career: Prop at school and had final Ulster Schools trial. But was wrong shape for a prop. Played three seasons for Scottish Universities while at Dundee University. Also played for Blackheath (1986/87) and Kent before returning to join NIFC to become their first international for ten years when was capped against France on 2 February. Also represented Ulster (two years) and Ireland B, in 16-0 defeat of Scotland B on 22 December (selected v. Argentina but withdrew with injured knee)

Touchlines: Sailing (half-tonners), golf

Player to watch: Simon Geoghegan (London Irish)

Hancock, M. E.   England

Full Name: Mark Edward Hancock
1990/91 International category:
England B (bench)
Club: Richmond
Position: Scrum-half
Height: 5'8" **Weight:** 12st 4lbs
Occupation: Chartered surveyor
Born: Southport, 4.4.65
Family: Single
Former clubs: Vale of Lune,
Loughborough Students,
Cambridge Univ, Nottingham
Best moment in rugby: Winning
1987 Varsity match
Worst moments in rugby: Losing
1988 Varsity match. Richmond
being relegated from English second
division last season after being held
to draw by promoted London Irish
in final match

Most respected opponent: New
Zealand scrum-half David Kirk

	apps
England B (1990/91)	1 rep
Career	4 reps

Best memory last season:
Renewing acquaintances with old
clubmates at Nottingham when
Richmond visited Beeston in Pilkington Cup

Suggestions to improve rugby: *On-field* – Make offside laws at ruck/maul clearer: penalise more severely. Hard to instigate laws at first phase to speed game up. Needs to be done at second phase. *Off-field* – Players' personal lives ought to be treated with more respect (by general public and clubs themselves). Clubs should take more of an active involvement with players' families. It is my experience that players perform better on the field when they are happy off it

Other notable landmarks in rugby career: Played for London and Barbarians. Toured Australasia with Combined Oxbridge side in 1989, beating New Zealand Universities side which won inaugural Students World Cup in 1988. Represented Cambridge Univ in 1987 Varsity match and captained them in 1988. Made four appearances on England B bench: three in 1987/88 (Spain, France and Italy) and one (Namibia) last season

Player to watch: Adrian Davies (Neath)

Harriman, A. T.   England

Full Name: Andrew Tuoyo Harriman
1990/91 International category: England (1995 development squad)
Club: Harlequins
Position: Right wing
Height: 6'2" **Weight:** 12st 8lbs
Occupation: Chartered surveyor
Born: Lagos, Nigeria, 13.7.64
Family: Single
Former club: Cambridge Univ
International debut: England 28, Australia 19, 1988
Best moment in rugby: Being informed of England selection
Worst moment in rugby: Playing while injured for Barbarians v. West Midlands (1989)
Most embarrassing moment: Being tackled from behind by a Portuguese prop during Estoril Sevens
Most respected opponent: Former Rosslyn Park wing, now Great Britain Rugby League star, Martin Offiah – always aware of opportunities

	apps	pts
England (1988)		
Last Season	0 caps	0
Career	1 cap	0
	1995 Development squad	

Serious injuries: Right knee cartilage and ligaments
Other sporting achievements: Great Britain U-16 tennis doubles champion. Cambridge athletics Blue
Best memory last season: Winning Pilkington Cup with Harlequins
Suggestions to improve rugby: Allow players to reap off-field benefits to compensate for time and hard work given to game
Other notable landmarks in rugby career: Cambridge Blue (1985). Three Middlesex Sevens trophies. 1988 John Player Cup win v. Bristol. Helped both London (21–10) and England beat 1988 Australians. Also represented Barbarians
Touchlines: Tennis, squash, fives, travelling, listening to music

---

Hastings, A. G. Scotland

Full Name: Andrew Gavin Hastings
1990/91 International category: Scotland Full
Club: London Scottish
Position: Full-back
Height: 6'2" **Weight:** 14st 9lbs
Occupation: Agency surveyor at Richard Ellis
Born: Edinburgh, 3.1.62
Family: Single
Family links with rugby: Clifford (father) played No.8 for Edinburgh XV and Watsonians; Scott (brother) plays for Watsonians, Scotland and British Lions; Graeme (brother) plays centre for Melbourne RFC and Victoria State (Aus); Ewan (brother) plays on wing for Watsonians
Former clubs: Watsonians, Cambridge Univ, London Scottish
International debut: Scotland 18, France 17, 1986
Five Nations' debut: As above
Best moments in rugby: Winning 1990 Grand Slam. 1989 British Lions' 2–1 series win in Australia
Worst moments in rugby: Varsity match 1985 (lost 6–7), England 21, Scotland 12 (1987), British Lions first Test (1989)
Most embarrassing moment: Missing plane home from Ireland after B international

99

Most respected opponents: The All Blacks, because of their record
Other sporting achievements: Appearing on TV in Trail Blazers (1988) and Pro-Celebrity Golf (1990)
Best memory last season: Promotion to Scottish first division with Watsonians
Suggestions to improve rugby: *On-field* – Get fit and stay fit. Practise your weaknesses. Ban the

	apps	pts
Scotland B (1983)		
Last Season	0 caps	0
Career	5 caps	
Scotland (1986)		
Last Season	5 caps	32
1991	World Cup squad	
Career	31 caps	301
Lions 1986		
1989	3 Tests	28

scrum-half dummy pass – how can it be right that you can concede same three points for being duped offside as for foul play. Ban players from charging full-back immediately he has caught high ball. At present they can run to within 10-metre circle and as soon as he catches it nobble him. Whoever kicked the ball should have to play them onside first. All Black Mike Brewer caught me (1990) in the second Test and I reckon it cost Scotland the match. *Off-field* – Play down the clamour for money. We all went into the game for fun, not to make money. However, players should be looked after adequately – certainly not allowed to be disadvantaged for loss of earnings. The SRU are good to players in Scotland, however there is a myth about the Timberland episode. England's players were banned from appearing in a match programme advertising the product yet myself, brother Scott and David Sole were allowed to 'fill their boots' in the Scottish programme. However, all we received in return was a pair of the company's boots, as did every member of the team – the England boys received exactly the same, despite their advert being aborted
Other notable landmarks in rugby career: Attended Cambridge University where played in the 1984 and 1985 Varsity matches. Won five caps for Scotland B before establishing Scottish record with six penalty goals on full debut. Hold Scottish points-scoring record with 301 in 31 Internationals, and Scottish record for most points scored in a Five Nations' season (52 in 1986). Toured with Scotland to North America (1985), the 1987 World Cup (where scored 62 points in 4 games), and New Zealand (May 1990). Scored go-ahead try in second Test for 1989 Lions and 15 points in the Third. Played in '1989 Home Unions' 29–27 win over France (scored 22 points) and for '1989 Barbarians' against All Blacks
Touchlines: Playing golf with Sam Torrance against Ronan Rafferty and Peter Alliss – most nervous I've ever been in my life, including winning first cap at Murrayfield
Player to watch: Fraser Harold (London Scottish)

Hastings, S.   Scotland

Full Name: Scott Hastings
1990/91 International category:
Scotland Full
Club: Watsonians
Positions: Centre, wing, full-back
Height: 6'1" **Weight:** 14st 4lbs
Occupation: Advertising account
executive
Born: Edinburgh, 4.12.64
Family: Jenny (wife)
Family links with rugby: Clifford
(father) played No.8 for Edinburgh
XV and Watsonians; Gavin
(brother) plays for London Scottish,
Scotland and British Lions; Graeme
(brother) plays centre for Melbourne
RFC and Victoria State (Aus); Ewan
(brother) plays on wing for
Watsonians
Former club: Newcastle Northern
International debut: Scotland 19,
France 18, 1986
Five Nations' debut: As above
Best moments in rugby: British
Lions Test series win; winning 1990
Grand Slam with Scotland; playing
in Hong Kong Sevens
Worst moment in rugby:
Sustaining hamstring injury on first
appearance in 1987 World Cup
(55–28 win v. Romania)

	apps	pts
Scotland B (1985)		
Last Season	0 caps	0
Career	1 cap	
Scotland (1986)		
Last Season	5 caps	4
1991	World Cup squad	
Career	30 caps	20
Lions 1989	2 Tests	

Most embarrassing moments: My 1987 World Cup injury and discovering
I did not have any Y-fronts to change into after a match
Most respected opponent: Ireland centre Brendan Mullin – have played
opposite him since we captained our respective countries in a Schools
international
Serious injuries: Torn hamstring, cartilage operation (1985), broken
cheekbone (1987, v. Wales)
Best memory last season: Helping Watsonians win Scottish second division
Suggestions to improve rugby: *On-field* – Put posts on dead-ball line so
penalties cannot be kicked from the halfway line and teams will be more
inclined to run the ball. Increase try-worth to 6 points. *Off-field* – Allow players

to undertake any commercial activity. Why should we not wear and promote a certain brand of boots? It would not hurt anyone

Other notable landmarks in rugby career: John O'Groats. All rugby tours. 1989/90 captain of Watsonians. With Gavin became the first Scottish brothers to play together in a Lions' Test. Played for Barbarians against 1989 All Blacks, and Home Unions against Europe in April 1990. Helped Edinburgh to three Inter-District Championship 'grand slams' between 1986–88. Former captain of Scottish Schools. Played three times for Scotland U-21s. Played on winning team in 1988 Dubai Sevens

Touchlines: Bandit golfer (18-handicap), watching films, viticulture

Player to watch: Neil Back (Leicester)

Hay, J. A.   Scotland

Full Name: James Alan Hay
1990/91 International category: Scotland Full (bench)
Club: Hawick
Position: Hooker
Height: 5'10" **Weight:** 14st 4lbs
Occupation: Finishing manager for knitwear company
Born: Hawick, 8.8.64
Family: Susan (wife)
Family links with rugby: Father played for Hawick and South. Father-in-law played for Hawick before switching to Rugby League
Former clubs: Hawick Wanderers, Hawick Linden
International debut (B): Scotland 14, France 12, 1989
Best moment in rugby: Making debut for Hawick v. Tynedale (1982)
Worst moments in rugby: Being dropped from Scottish squad last season. Dressing-room scene after Hawick had lost fifth successive National League game
Most embarrassing moment: Debut for South of Scotland – being awarded South tie after coming on as a replacement for last 10 seconds

	apps	pts
Scotland B (**1989**)		
Last Season	1 cap	0
Career	2 caps	0
Scotland A (1990/91)	1 rep	
Scotland (1990/91)	1 rep	
1991	World Cup squad	

Most respected opponent: Scotland hooker Kenny Milne – genuine, modest man who has had to work for everything he has achieved

Best memory last season: Bench reserve for England 21, Scotland 12, Twickenham (16 Feb)

Suggestions to improve rugby: *On-field* – Become more professional at club level. Make game flow more – amount of time devoted to stoppages is quite ridiculous. *Off-field* – More consideration for the players as regards to earning potential; do not go whole way but create a finer balance between what is and what is not allowed

Other notable landmarks in rugby career: Made Hawick debut aged 17. Member of winning Public School Wanderers' Seven at London Welsh Centenary tournament. First time on Scottish bench (1989). Toured with Scotland to Zimbabwe (1988) and Japan (1989). Scored only Scottish try in 24–28 defeat by Japan in Tokyo. Scored hat-trick of tries for Hawick v. Boroughmuir (1989/90). Included in Scotland's squads at B, A and Full level last season

Touchlines: Golf (22-handicap), DIY

Player to watch: Stuart Reid (Boroughmuir)

Hembrow, I. L. Wales

Full Name: Ian Lee Hembrow
1990/91 International category: Tour squad
Club: Cardiff
Position: No.8
Height: 6'3" **Weight:** 17st 4lbs
Occupation: Gas board service engineer
Born: Maesteg, 21.6.69
Family: Single
Former club: Maesteg Celtic
Best moment in rugby: Cardiff beating Neath at The Gnoll in final League match (1990/91)
Worst moment in rugby: Being sent-off in Cup final for Maesteg Celtic
Most respected opponent: Newbridge's Hemi Taylor
Best memory last season: Scoring try for Cardiff v. Barbarians

Other notable landmarks in rugby career: Selected to tour Australia with

Wales last summer after only eight games for Cardiff in Heineken premier division
Player to watch: Anthony Donovan (Cardiff)

	apps	pts
Wales 1991	Tour to Australia	
Heineken 1990/91	8 apps	0

Hernan, D. C.   Ireland

Full Name: David Christopher Hernan
1990/91 International category: Ireland B
Club: University College Dublin
Positions: Wing, centre
Height: 6′ **Weight:** 12st
Occupation: Student
Born: County Galway, 1.2.71
Family: Single
Family links with rugby: Brother (Raymond) played for Ireland U-25s. Brother (Robert) played for Ireland U-21s. Both also played for Connacht
International debut (B): Ireland 16, Scotland 0, 1990
Best moment in rugby: Scoring try on Ireland B debut at Ravenhill
Worst moment in rugby: Back injury which sidelined me for post-Christmas part of 1990/91 season
Most respected opponent: Bath wing Adedayo Adebayo
Serious injuries: Haematoma in back
Other sporting achievements: Gaelic football for Galway U-18s (won Provincial medal)

	apps	pts
Ireland U-21 (**1990**)		
Last Season	1 cap	0
Career	1 cap	0
Ireland B (**1990**)		
Last Season	1 cap	4
Career	1 cap	4

Best memory last season: Selection for Ireland B just three months after making debut in senior rugby
Suggestions to improve rugby: *On-field* – Increase worth of try and decrease value of penalty goal
Other notable landmarks in rugby career: Broke into Leinster side last

season, playing three games including debut v. Connacht. Played two seasons with Ireland Schools. Given Ireland U-21 debut in 22–16 win over England last season and soon after called into Ireland B team as late replacement for injured Simon Geoghegan. Scored try in victory made famous by fact that Ireland played 66 minutes with only 14 men

Touchlines: Gaelic football, hurling

Player to watch: Gabriel Fulcher (Univ Coll Dublin)

Heslop, N. J.   England

Full Name: Nigel John Heslop

1990/91 International category: England Full

Club: Orrell

Position: Wing

Height: 5′10″ **Weight:** 12st 7lbs

Occupation: Police officer

Born: Hartlepool, 4.12.63

Family: Denise (wife)

Family links with rugby: Brother plays Rugby League for Leeds Poly

Former clubs: Waterloo, Liverpool

International debut: Argentina 12, England 25, 1990

Best moment in rugby: Scoring only try of match in England's 21–12 defeat of Scotland (1991)

Worst moment in rugby: Letting Wasps' Chris Oti in for winning try in League match v. Orrell (1990/91)

Most embarrassing moment: Tackled by stray dog while playing for Liverpool

Most respected opponent: England wing Rory Underwood

Serious injuries: Dislocated elbow (1986)

Other sporting achievements: Sprinted in Police Championships

Best memory last season: Winning Grand Slam with England

Suggestions to improve rugby:

On-field – Anything to make game flow more; too many stoppages. *Off-field*

	apps	pts
England B (**1989**)		
Last Season	0 caps	0
Career	2 caps	0
England (**1990**)		
Last Season	5 caps	4
1991	Tour to Australia	
	World Cup squad	
1995 Development squad		
Career	7 caps	8

– Quite happy personally but players should be able to benefit from off-field activities
Other notable landmarks in rugby career: Played for England Colts (1980) but then waited nine years for B cap, on summer tour to Spain. Helped Lancashire win 1989/90 County Championship. Played in England XV's 33–15 defeat of Italy XV in Rovigo (May 1990). Toured with England to Argentina (1990), where made full debut (scoring try in 13–15 second Test loss), and Australia (1991). Ever-present in England's 1991 Grand Slam-winning side, scoring decisive try in England's 21–12 win over Scotland
Player to watch: Martin Bayfield (Bedford)

Hill, R. J. England

Full Name: Richard John Hill
1990/91 International category: England Full
Club: Bath
Position: Scrum-half
Height: 5'7" **Weight:** 12st 3lbs
Occupation: Financial consultant
Born: Birmingham, 4.5.61
Family: Married with son and daughter
Former clubs: Exeter University, Salisbury
International debut: South Africa 33, England 15, 1984
Five Nations' debut: Ireland 13, England 10, 1985
Best moment in rugby: Scoring first try for England, in 34–6 defeat of Wales (1990)
Worst moment in rugby: Being banned (as captain) following England's clash with Wales (Cardiff 1987)
Most embarrassing moment: Having pass intercepted by Philippe Sella, who ran in to score from 65 yards, during England's 15–19 Twickenham defeat by France (1987)
Most respected opponent: Former Wales scrum-half David Bishop – he could win matches on his own
Serious injuries: Knee operation (summer 1990)
Best memory last season: Winning Grand Slam
Suggestions to improve rugby: Establish an Anglo-Welsh championship to strengthen fixture lists. Home and away system in League

Other notable landmarks in rugby career: Kept out of England Colts by Nigel Melville but represented England Students whilst at Exeter University. Joined Bath and played England final Trial (1983) and won first full cap following season. Share, with Gareth Chilcott, the distinction of having played in all six of Bath's Cup final teams. Captained England four times (1986–87). Represented England in 1987 World Cup (v. USA). England tours include Argentina (1990) and Australia (1991). Ever-present in 1991 Five Nations' Grand Slam-winning side

	apps	pts
England B (**1986**)		
Last Season	0 caps	0
England (**1984**)		
Last Season	7 caps	4
v. Barbarians	1 app	0
1991	Tour to Australia	
	World Cup squad	
Career	23 caps	8
Lions 1986		

Hill, S. D.   Wales

Full Name: Simon David Hill
1990/91 International category: Wales (World Cup squad)
Club: Cardiff
Position: Centre
Height: 5'11" **Weight:** 13st 2lbs
Occupation: Dentistry student
Born: Barry, South Glamorgan, 27.5.68
Family: Single
Former club: Headingley
Best moment in rugby: Winning 1986/87 Youth Cup with Saffron Major
Worst moment in rugby: Breaking nose and having to leave field after 15 mins of 1990/91 game v. Wasps
Best memory last season: Setting up try on League debut for Cardiff v. Pontypridd
Other notable landmarks in rugby career: Represented Glamorgan and Headingley (while studying in Leeds). Included in Wales' preliminary 1991 World Cup

	apps	pts
Wales B (1990/91)	1 rep	
Wales 1991	World Cup squad	
Heineken 1990/91	7 apps	8

squad. Bench reserve for Wales B during 34–12 win over Netherlands in Leiden last season
Touchlines: Lifeguard in summer

Hilton, D. I. W. England

Full Name: David Ivor Walter Hilton
1990/91 International category: England U-21
Club: Bristol
Position: Loose-head prop
Height: 5'11" **Weight:** 16st 8lbs
Occupation: Butcher
Born: Bristol, 3.4.70
Family: Single
International debut (U-21): England 16, Ireland 22, 1990
Best moment in rugby: Helping Somerset beat Warwickshire in 1988 Colts County Championship final
Worst moment in rugby: Somerset's loss to Warwickshire in 1987 Colts County final
Most respected opponent: Gloucester's Rob Phillips
Best memories last season: Winning Ireland U-21 cap and helping Bristol beat Leicester and Gloucester to retain English first division status
Suggestions to improve rugby: *On-field* – Please, no more rule changes

	apps	pts
England U-21 (**1990**)		
Last Season	1 cap	0
Career	1 cap	0

Other notable landmarks in rugby career: Represented President's XV in England 16-Group, Somerset Colts and Bristol Schools, before receiving England U-21 recognition last season
Touchlines: Waterskiing
Player to watch: Joel Pearson (Bristol)

Hitchen, N.   England

Full Name: Neil Hitchen
1990/91 International category:
England B
Club: Orrell
Position: Hooker
Height: 5'9" **Weight:** 14st 10lbs
Occupation: Farmer
Born: Nantwich
Family: Lynda (wife) and Sarah (daughter)
Former club: Crewe & Nantwich
International debut: Spain 9, England B 31, 1989
Best moment in rugby: Orrell beating Wasps in quarter-finals of 1990/91 Pilkington Cup
Worst moment in rugby: Orrell losing to Northampton in semi-finals of 1990/91 Pilkington Cup semi-finals
Most respected opponent: Bath hooker Graham Dawe – strong, fast and skilful
Serious injuries: Broken leg
Suggestions to improve rugby: *On-field* – Improve fitness. *Off-field* – Promote game better. Improve communication between selectors and players. Players must be told what they have to do to be selected

	apps	pts
England B (**1989**)		
Last Season	1 cap	0
Career	3 caps	0

Other notable landmarks in rugby career: Played over 300 games for Orrell. Toured with England B to Spain (1989), scoring 25-yard try in 32–15 defeat of Spanish Select. Helped England B draw 15–15 with France B (1990)
Player to watch: Neil Back (Leicester)

Hodgkinson, S. D.   England

Full Name: Simon David
Hodgkinson
1990/91 International category:
England Full
Club: Nottingham
Position: Full-back
Height: 5'10" **Weight:** 12st
Occupation: Sales manager
Born: Bristol, 15.12.62
Family: Single
Family links with rugby: Father
played for Thornbury (Bristol) and
Scarborough
International debut: Romania 3,
England 58, 1989
Five Nations' debut: England 23,
Ireland 0, 1990
Best moment in rugby: Winning
1991 Grand Slam with England
Worst moment in rugby:
Performance for England XV in
7–13 defeat by England B XV in
1988 – Final Trial
Most embarrassing moment:
Failing to turn up for a Sevens
quarter-final
Most respected opponent: French
centre Philippe Sella
Other sporting achievements:
Midlands U-15 cricket

	apps	pts
England B (1988)		
Last Season	0 caps	0
England (1989)		
Last Season	5 caps	83
v. Barbarians	1 app	14
1991	Tour to Australia	
	World Cup squad	
Career	13 caps	186

Best memory last season: England's Grand Slam
Suggestions to improve rugby: *On-field* – Get rid of 90-degree scrummage
rule. *Off-field* – Resolve payment to players position. Allow sponsorship
payments to players
Other notable landmarks in rugby career: Established new points-scoring
record in 1991 Five Nations' Championship with 60 (18 pens and 3 cons) in
England's Grand Slam. Took tally to 83 for season with 23 in England's 51-0
rout of Argentina. Was also leading scorer in the 1990 Five Nations'
Championship with 42 points (10 pens and 6 cons). Member of select
gathering to have scored more than 40 points in Championship season. Hold
English record for conversions. Toured with England to Argentina (1990)
and Australia/Fiji (1991) where lost No. 15 jersey to Jon Webber. Scored 14

points for England XV v. both Italy (1990, won 33–15) and Barbarians (1990, won 18–16)
Touchlines: Golf
Player to watch: Stuart Potter (Nottingham)

Hogg, C. D. Scotland

Full Name: Carl David Hogg
1990/91 International category:
Scotland B
Club: Melrose
Positions: No.8, lock, flanker
Height: 6′4″ **Weight:** 15st 7lbs
Occupation: Civil engineering student
Born: Galashiels, 5.7.69
Family: Single
Family links with rugby: Uncle Jim Telfer played for Scotland and Lions
International debut (B): Scotland 10, France 31, 1991
Best moment in rugby: Melrose clinching 1989/90 Scottish First Division against Jed-Forest
Worst moment in rugby: Being well beaten by Randwick in 1990 Melrose Sevens
Most respected opponent: Kelso's Scotland flanker John Jeffrey
Serious injuries: Back operation to remove disc
Best memory last season: Selection for Scotland B
Suggestions to improve rugby: *Off-field* – Greater media coverage of club games. More sponsorship at club level

	apps	pts
Scotland U-21 (**1990**)		
Last Season	0 caps	0
Career	1 cap	0
Scotland B (**1990**)		
Last Season	1 cap	0
	1 rep	
Career	1 cap	0

Other notable landmarks in rugby career: Represented Scotland Schools and U-19s before breaking into Scotland U-21 side (1989/90) and captained side in 10–24 loss to Wales at Ayr. Last season graduated to Scotland B and, after warming bench in Belfast, made debut v. France in Glasgow in unaccustomed surroundings of second row
Touchlines: Golf (15-handicap)
Player to watch: Peter Jorgensen (Queensland)

Holmes, G.   England

Full Name: Gary Holmes
1990/91 International category:
England B
Club: Wasps
Position: Loose-head prop
Height: 5'10.5" **Weight:** 16st 5lbs
Occupation: General manager for
packaging company
Born: Belsize Park, London, 7.7.65
Family: Single
Former club: Old Dunstablians
International debut: England B 31,
Namibia 16, 1990
Best moment in rugby: Selection
for Wasps first team less than 24
hours before 1986 John Player Cup
final (after Paul Rendall pulled out)
Most respected opponent: Wasps'
tight-head Jeff Probyn
Best memory last season: Initial
selection for England B and then
retaining my place
**Other notable landmarks in rugby
career:** Played for England Colts
(1983 v. Italy). Represented Wasps
in 17–25 loss to Bath in 1986 JPC
Final. Helped Wasps win Courage
English League Championship
(1989/90). Made England B breakthrough last season, playing v. Namibia
(debut), Ireland, France and Italy
Touchlines: Horse riding, swimming, weights, spending time with girlfriend
Alison
Player to watch: Graham Childs (Wasps)

	apps	pts
England B (**1990**)		
Last Season	4 caps	0
	1 rep	
Career	4 caps	0

Hooks, K. J.   Ireland

Full Name: Kenneth John Hooks
1990/91 International category:
Ireland Full
Club: Bangor
Position: Right wing
Height: 5'11" **Weight:** 13st 11lbs
Occupation: Mathematics teacher
Born: Markethill, 1.1.60
Family: Ann (wife) and Gareth
(son)
Former clubs: Queen's University
Belfast, Bangor, Ards
International debut: Scotland 10,
Ireland 9, 1981
Five Nations' debut: As above
Best moment in rugby: Captain of
Bangor Grammar School when
winning the Ulster School Cup in
front of 20,000 people
Worst moment in rugby: Having
to leave the field with concussion
during the Ireland/New Zealand
game (1989/90) – especially after
having had to wait so long to make
second appearance
Most embarrassing moment:
Being asked for my autograph by a
schoolboy before my first cap. When

	apps	pts
Ireland B (**1979**)		
Last Season	0 caps	0
Ireland (**1981**)		
Last Season	2 caps	4
Career	6 caps	4

he realised I was not Tony Ward he snatched his book away before I had the
chance to sign
Most respected opponent: Ireland wing Keith Crossan – tremendous change
of pace and deceptively strong
Other sporting achievements: Represented Irish Schools at athletics
Best memory last season: Scoring first ever try for Ireland in 20–18 win
over Argentina
Suggestions to improve rugby: *On-field* – Stop forwards touching or kicking
the ball, except at set pieces – and then only for a maximum 10 seconds!
Clarify situation regarding rucks and players on ground. *Off-field* –
Organisation off-field still very amateur, yet players are still expected to give
professional levels of commitment
Other notable landmarks in rugby career: Replacement for Irish Schools
aged 16 (won 4 caps). Played for Ulster and Ireland B aged 19. First capped

113

for Ireland aged 21, second cap aged 29 – Irish record for the longest break between first and second caps. Member of Ireland team involved in 1989 'Haka incident' when we advanced on All Blacks' Maori ritual. Ards' captain before switching allegiances to Bangor at start of last season. Played v. Argentina and France (lost 13–21) last season

Touchlines: Member of Christians in Sport organisation

Player to watch: Simon Geoghegan (London Irish)

Hopley, D. P.   England

Full Name: Damian Paul Hopley
1990/91 International category:
England Full (bench)
Club: Wasps
Position: Centre
Height: 6′2″ **Weight:** 14st 10lbs
Occupation: Student
Born: London, 12.4.70
Family: Single
Family links with rugby: Brother
(Philip) plays for Wasps and
England Students
Former Club: St Andrews Univ
International debut: England B 12,
Emerging Australians 12, 1990
Best moment in rugby: Wasps
debut v. Harlequins (1990/91)
Worst moment in rugby: Injury v.
Orrell in Pilkington Cup quarter-finals which put me out for ten weeks
Most embarrassing moment:
Being mistaken for Nigel Heslop
when on bench at England/Wales
match in Cardiff (1991)
Most respected opponent:
Harlequins' centre Simon Halliday
Best memory last season: Gaining
selection for England's summer tour to Australia

	apps	pts
England B (1990)		
Last Season	1 cap	0
Career	1 cap	0
England (1990/91)	1 rep	
1991	Tour to Australia	

Suggestions to improve rugby: *Off-field* – Increased commitment towards game – will bring about change, whatever that might be. Reimbursement for working time lost to rugby

Other notable landmarks in rugby career: Won six caps for England Schools (toured Australia and New Zealand). Also represented England Colts

and Scottish Universities (two years). Selected for England U-21s last season but withdrawn and put into B team for debut v. Emerging Australians. Bench reserve for England in Wales before injury (February 23) curtailed season
Touchlines: Playing piano, cricket, soccer
Player to watch: Adedayo Adebayo (Bath)

Howley, R. **Wales**

Full Name: Robert Howley
1990/91 International category:
Wales B (bench)
Clubs: Bridgend/Swansea Univ
Position: Scrum-half
Height: 5'10.5" **Weight:** 12st 5lbs
Occupation: Student
Born: Bridgend, 13.10.70
Family: Single
Best moments in rugby: Selection for Wales B bench for 1990 match v. Netherlands in Leiden. Bridgend beating Cardiff in Heineken League match in Cardiff (1990/91)
Worst moment in rugby: Tearing knee cartilage playing for Swansea Univ v. Cardiff Univ in 1991 UAU final – put me out for rest of season
Other sporting achievements: Cricket for Welsh Schools (1989)
Most respected opponent: Swansea scrum-half Robert Jones
Serious injuries: Torn knee cartilage (1991)
Best memory last season: Scoring winning try in League victory at Cardiff

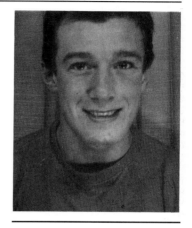

	apps	pts
Wales B (1990/91)	1 rep	
Wales 1991	World Cup squad	
Heineken 1990/91	13 apps	12

Suggestions to improve rugby: *On-field* – Less kicking and more running. Get rid of 'mark' in 22. *Off-field* – None. Bright future for Welsh rugby with some fine young players coming through
Other notable landmarks in rugby career: Welsh Schools U-18 captain (1989), Wales U-21 squad (1989/90). Wales B replacement in Netherlands last season when Wales won 34–12
Touchlines: Cricket
Player to watch: Scott Quinnell (Llanelli)

Hull, P. A.   England

Full Name: Paul Anthony Hull
1990/91 International category:
England B
Club: Bristol
Positions: Fly-half, centre
Height: 5'10" **Weight:** 11st 7lbs
Occupation: RAF PTI
Born: London, 17.5.68
Family: Lesley-Ann (wife)
Former club: Milton Keynes
International debut: England B 12,
Fiji 20, 1990
Best moment in rugby: Being
selected for England tour to
Argentina (1990)
Worst moment in rugby: Missing
Bristol v. Harlequins 1988 Cup final
through injury
Most embarrassing moment:
Being kicked in the privates the first
time my wife watched me play
Serious injuries: Torn ankle
ligaments
Other sporting achievements:
Soccer trials with Southampton
Youth
Best memory last season: Being
appointed vice-captain of Bristol
Suggestions to improve rugby:
On-field – Bring youngsters on with

	apps	pts
England U-21 (**1989**)		
Last Season	0 caps	0
Career	1 cap	0
England B (**1989**)		
Last Season	1 cap	4
Career	2 caps	4
England	1995 Development squad	

aid of fitness advisors and private medical insurance. *Off-field* – Make game
more professional. Clarify laws relating to amateurism
Other notable landmarks in rugby career: Played in inaugural England
U-21 team which swamped Romanian counterparts 54–13 in Bucharest in
1989. Tasted defeat on England B debut v. Fiji in 1989/90 before returning
to winning ways on second appearance, scoring try in 31–16 win over touring
Namibians last season
Touchlines: Soul music, nightlife
Player to watch: Rupert Moon (Llanelli)

Hunter, I.   England

Full Name: Ian Hunter
1990/91 International category:
England B
Club: Northampton
Positions: Full-back, wing, centre
Height: 6'2" **Weight:** 17st 7lbs
Occupation: Student
Born: Harrow, London 15.2.69
Family: Single
Family links with rugby: Father
played in New Zealand
Former clubs: Windermere,
Carlisle, Nottingham
Best moment in rugby: Playing in
Hong Kong Sevens
Worst moments in rugby: Missing
tackle v. France B last season.
Winger went on to score and we
(England B) lost by 4 points. Losing
to Harlequins in extra-time in
1990/91 Pilkington Cup final
Most embarrassing moment:
Falling over for no reason in front of
capacity crowd at Northampton just
before kick-off
Most respected opponent: Wasps'
Steve Pilgrim

	apps	pts
England B (**1990**)		
Last Season	5 caps	8
Career	5 caps	8
England 1991	Tour to Australia	
	World Cup squad	
1995 Development squad		

Best memories last season:
Selection for England's tour to
Australia and Fiji. Reaching Pilkington Cup final with Northampton
Suggestions to improve rugby: *On-field* – Play league games on a home
and away basis. *Off-field* – RFU to sort out their amateur regulations, like
every other nation
Other notable landmarks in rugby career: Included in England's
development squad for 1995 World Cup. Played five games for England B
in 1990/91 (v. Emerging Australians, Spain, Italy, Ireland and France) and
scored two tries v. Spain and Ireland. Helped Northampton win promotion
to first division (1989/90) and into 1990/91 Pilkington Cup final v. Harlequins.
Represented centenary Barbarians (1990/91) and toured Australia with
England last summer
Touchlines: Working for my degree.
Players to watch: Tony Underwood and Neil Back (both Leicester), Rupert
Moon (Llanelli)

Hutton, M. J.   England

Full Name: Michael James Hutton
1990/91 International category:
England U-21
Club: Richmond
Positions: Centre, wing
Height: 6' **Weight:** 15st
Occupation: Medical student
Born: Christchurch, New Zealand,
9.4.70
Family: Single
Family links with rugby: Brother
(Robbie) played for England
Schools last season
International debut (U-21):
England 16, Ireland 22, 1990
Best moment in rugby: Winning
1991 Hospital Sevens with Charing
Cross
Worst moment in rugby: Being
relegated from English second
division last season with Richmond
Most respected opponent: Former
Leicester centre Paul Dodge
Best memory last season: Setting
up both tries for London U-21s in
16–10 defeat of South West U-21s
Suggestions to improve rugby:

	apps	pts
England U-21 (1990)		
Last Season	1 cap	0
Career	1 cap	0

On-field – Possession should go to attacking side at scrummage if defending side intentionally wheels scrum 90-degrees. *Off-field* – Too much politics, not enough rugby
Other notable landmarks in rugby career: Left for New Zealand when aged three. Made senior debut for Richmond six days after turning up at first training session. Played for England B in defeat by Ireland last season at Moseley
Touchlines: Cricket, squash
Player to watch: Damian Hopley (Wasps)

Hynes, M. P. — England

Full Name: Martin Peter Hynes
1990/91 International category:
England B (bench)
Club: Orrell
Position: Prop
Height: 5′9″ **Weight:** 15st 4lbs
Occupation: Electrician
Born: Wigan, Lancs, 23.8.68
Family: Single
Family links with rugby: Father played Rugby League for Wigan Colts
International debut (U-21): Romania 13, England 54, 1989
Best moment in rugby: Making England debut in Bucharest
Worst moment in rugby: Orrell losing to Northampton in semi-finals of 1990/91 Pilkington Cup
Most embarrassing moment: Being sent off for punching v. Bedford
Most respected opponent: England prop Jeff Probyn
Serious injuries: Broken coccyx
Other sporting achievements: Swam butterfly for Wigan Wasps in National Championships

	apps	pts
England U-21 (**1989**)		
Last Season	0 caps	0
Career	1 cap	0
England B (1990/91)	2 reps	

Best memory last season: Orrell beating Gloucester at Gloucester for first time
Suggestions to improve rugby: *On-field* – Scrap 90-degree scrum wheel law. *Off-field* – reimbursement of wages lost through playing rugby
Other notable landmarks in rugby career: Played for Lancashire Colts and was reserve for Northumberland Colts. Played for Lancashire and North of England U-21s and, after Lancashire's 1989/90 County Championship success, toured with county to Zimbabwe last summer. Bench reserve for England B last season v. France B and Italy B
Touchlines: Karate
Player to watch: Neil Ashurst (Orrell)

Isaac, G. R.   Scotland

Full Name: Gary Ronald Isaac
1990/91 International category:
Scotland A
Club: Gala
Position: Prop
Height: 5′10″ **Weight:** 15st 8lbs
Occupation: Surveyor
Born: Dufftown, 15.2.66
Family: Antonya (wife)
Former club: Moray
International debut: Spain 7,
Scotland A 39, 1990
Best moment in rugby: Playing for
Scotland A in Seville
Worst moment in rugby:
Appendix operation which put me
out of Scotland's 1991 tour to North
America
Most respected opponent:
Heriot's prop Iain Milne
Best memory last season: Scotland
A trip
Suggestions to improve rugby:
On-field – Increase value of try to 5
points to encourage more attacking
play. *Off-field* – None. SRU have
got their house in order

	apps	pts
Scotland U-21 (**1986**)		
Career	1 cap	0
Scotland A (**1990**)		
Last Season	1 cap	0
Career	1 cap	0

**Other notable landmarks in rugby
career:** Helped Scotland U-21s
defeat Italy 22–6 in Piacenza (1986). Called into inaugural Scotland A team
last season. Selected to tour North America with Scotland (1991) but forced
to withdraw after appendix operation
Touchlines: Tug-of-war for Elgin (Scottish champions)
Player to watch: John Amos (Gala)

Jardine, I. C.   Scotland

Full Name: Ian Carrick Jardine
1990/91 International category:
Scotland B
Club: Stirling County
Position: Centre
Height: 6'1" **Weight:** 13st 7lbs
Occupation: Civil engineer
Born: Dunfermline, 20.10.64
Family: Anne (wife)
Family links with rugby: Four
brothers play at Stirling
International debut (B): Scotland
22, Ireland 22, 1990
Best moments in rugby: Winning
promotion from Scottish second to
first division (1988/89). Winning
Inter-District Championship with
Glasgow (1989/90). Gaining
selection for Scotland's summer tour
to North America
Worst moment in rugby: Losing
any match
Most respected opponent: Former
Scotland wing Keith Robertson
Best memory last season: Stirling's
early League success (won first six
games), especially wins at Hawick
and Kelso

	apps	pts
Scotland B (**1989**)		
Last Season	1 rep	
Career	1 cap	0
Scotland 1991	Tour to North America	

Suggestions to improve rugby: *On-field* – Award more points for a try.
Off-field – Players compensated for earnings lost due to rugby. Allow us to
advertise rugby-related items – main potential source of earning
Other notable landmarks in rugby career: Replacement for Scotland U-21s
(1986) and Scotland B in Italy (1988/89). Made B debut in 22–22 draw with
Ireland B, and last season was replacement in 0–16 loss to Ireland B. Toured
Canada and the United States with Scotland last summer, appearing v. Alberta
(won 76–7) and Ontario (won 43–3)
Touchlines: Hill walking, cycling
Player to watch: Scott Gibbs (Neath)

Jardine, S.   Scotland

Full Name: Stewart Jardine
1990/91 International category:
Scotland B (squad)
Club: Cardiff Institute
Position: Scrum-half
Height: 5'10" **Weight:** 12st
Occupation: PE student
Born: Edinburgh, 24.12.65
Family: Single
Family links with rugby: Father
played for Edinburgh Academicals
and Scotland B
Former clubs: Edinburgh
Academicals, Glamorgan Wanderers
International debut (B): Ireland
16, Scotland 0, 1990
Best moment in rugby: Touring
Japan with Scotland (1989)
Worst moment in rugby:
Requiring 17 stitches after being
head-butted ten minutes into match
against Kyushu on above tour
Most respected opponent:
Jed-Forest scrum-half Gary
Armstrong
Other sporting achievements:
Cricket for Shropshire 2nd XI. Ran
half-marathon

	apps	pts
Scotland B (**1990**)		
Last Season	1 cap	0
Career	1 cap	0

Best memories last season: Scotland Students beating Ireland Students.
Winning B cap in Ireland
Suggestions to improve rugby: *On-field* – Players should be given individual
training programmes worked around time they have available. *Off-field* –
Work for a better relationship between committee and players. Better
communications between two parties – there are still big gaps between what
players want (e.g. England players' Press-boycott at Arms Park last season)
Other notable landmarks in rugby career: Attended school in South Africa.
Returned aged 19 having played half a season with Crusaders (Port Elizabeth)
and warmed bench for provincial team. Represented Scotland Students for
last five years and played in 1988 Students World Cup (last game v. Fiji).
Made Scotland B debut last season at Ravenhill (Belfast)
Touchlines: Windsurfing, waterskiing, canoeing
Player to watch: Ben Clarke (Saracens)

Jeffrey, J.   Scotland

Full Name: John Jeffrey
1990/91 International category:
Scotland Full
Club: Kelso
Positions: Flanker, No.8
Height: 6'4" **Weight:** 14st 5lbs
Occupation: Farmer
Born: Kelso, 25.3.59
Family: Single
International debut: Scotland 12,
Australia 37, 1984
Five Nations' debut: Scotland 15,
Ireland 18, 1985
Best moment in rugby: Winning
1990 Five Nations' Grand Slam with
Scotland
Worst moment in rugby: Scotland
losing 12–21 to England (April
1988) when playing for Triple
Crown
Most embarrassing moment:
Being 'wound-up' by Fin Calder the
day before the 1990 Grand Slam
decider against England
Most respected opponent:
Scotland scrum-half Gary
Armstrong
Serious injuries: Cartilage
operation whilst at school
Worst memory last season: Kelso's
relegation from Scottish first division

	apps	pts
Scotland B (**1983**)		
Last Season	0 caps	0
Career	3 caps	
Scotland (**1984**)		
Last Season	5 caps	0
1991	World Cup squad	
Career	35 caps	36
Scotland VII (**1991**)	Hong Kong Sevens	
Lions 1986		
1989		

Suggestions to improve rugby:
On-field – Work harder on fitness and enjoy the game more. Do not lose sight
of the fact that we play rugby for enjoyment. *Off-field* – None. Progress in
Scotland is being made. We have a good relationship with the SRU
Other notable landmarks in rugby career: Hold Scottish record for a
forward of nine tries in cap Internationals. Member of both the British Lions
and Five Nations' teams in the 1986 IRB celebration matches. Captained
Kelso to Scottish Division One title in 1988/89. Most capped Kelso
International, with 35. Played five times for 1989 British Lions' midweek team
in Australia and represented 1990 Home Unions XV against Europe. Ever
present for Scotland last season

Jenkins, N. R.   Wales

Full Name: Neil Roger Jenkins
1990/91 International category:
Wales Full
Club: Pontypridd
Position: Fly-half
Height: 5'10" **Weight:** 12st 8lbs
Occupation: Scrapper
Born: Church Village, Pontypridd,
8.7.71
Family: Single
International debut: Wales 6,
England 25, 1991
Five Nations' debut: As above
Best moment in rugby: Full debut
for Wales at Cardiff
Most respected opponent: France
fly-half Didier Camberabero
Best memory last season: Scoring
try in 21–21 draw with Ireland
Suggestions to improve rugby:
On-field – Award less points for
goals

**Other notable landmarks in rugby
career:** Played for East Wales U-11s
v. West Wales, East Glamorgan, and
Wales Youth (1989/90). Last season
broke into Wales U-21s and played
v. Rugby News New Zealand U-21
XV (kicked four conversions and two
penalty goals) and v. Scotland U-21s
(scored try, conversion and three
penalties). Graduated to Wales B
where scored try, four conversions
and two penalties in 34–12 defeat of
the Netherlands in Leiden. Next onto senior status where played 1991 Five
Nations' Championship in No.10 jersey, scoring penalty goal in 6–25 loss to
England and a try and drop goal in draw with Ireland
Player to watch: Scott Quinnell (Llanelli)

	apps	pts
Wales U-21 (**1991**)		
Last Season	1 cap	15
v. New Zealand XV	1 app	14
Career	1 cap	15
Wales B (**1990**)		
Last Season	1 cap	18
Career	1 cap	18
Wales (**1991**)		
Last Season	4 caps	10
1991	Tour to Australia	
	World Cup squad	
Career	4 caps	10
Heineken 1990/91	14 apps	127

Jenkins, R. H. J.   England

Full Name: Rory Harry John Jenkins
1990/91 International category:
England U-21
Clubs: Cambridge Univ/Brixham
Position: Blindside flanker
Height: 6'2" **Weight:** 15st 2lbs
Occupation: Law student
Born: Leicester, 29.6.70
Family: Single
Family links with rugby: Father
(John) played for Cambridge Univ
and Leicester
International debut (U-21):
England 16, Ireland 22, 1990
Best moment in rugby: Helping
England Colts beat Wales Youth
15–11 (1 April 1989)
Worst moment in rugby: England
U-21's defeat by Ireland (1990)
Most respected opponent:
Northampton No.8 Wayne Shelford
Best memory last season:
Selection for England U-21s
Other sporting achievements:
Cricket for Cambridge Univ and
Devon

	apps	pts
England U-21 (**1990**)		
Last Season	1 cap	4
Career	1 cap	4

Other notable landmarks in rugby career: Scored try on debut for England
U-21s in 16–22 defeat by Ireland at Moseley (1990). Ever-present in England
Colts team in 1988/89

John, P.   Wales

Full Name: Paul John
1990/91 International category:
Wales B
Club: Cardiff
Position: Scrum-half
Height: 5'10" **Weight:** 12st 10lbs
Occupation: Student
Born: Pontypridd, 25.1.70
Family: Single
Family links with rugby: Father
played for Pontypool, Penarth,
Pontypridd and Barbarians
Former club: Pontypridd (youth)
International debut: Netherlands
12, Wales B 34, 1990
Best moment in rugby: Helping
Cardiff beat Llanelli in 1989/90
Welsh Cup
Worst moment in rugby:
Dislocating shoulder in Wales U-18
Trial and requiring operation
Most respected opponent:
Swansea scrum-half Robert Jones
Serious injuries: Broken arm,
dislocated shoulder and elbow
**Other notable landmarks in
rugby career:** Represented Wales at
U-15, U-18, U-20 and U-21 levels.
Played for Welsh Students
(1989/90). Captained Wales U-21s
in both matches last season, v. New
Zealand Rugby News XV (won
34–13) and Scotland U-21s (won 23–15), and awarded B debut in
Netherlands
Touchlines: Golf, squash

	apps	pts
Wales U-21 (**1990**)		
Last Season	1 cap	0
v. New Zealand XV	1 app	4
Career	2 caps	0
Wales B (**1990**)		
Last Season	1 cap	0
Career	1 cap	0
Wales 1991	World Cup squad	
Heineken 1990/91	11 apps	20

Johns, P. S.   Ireland

Full Name: Patrick Stephen Johns
1990/91 International category:
Ireland Full
Club: Dublin University
Position: Lock
Height: 6′6″ **Weight:** 16st
Occupation: Dental student
Born: Portadown, 19.2.68
Family: Single
Former clubs: Dungannon,
Newcastle University, Gosforth
International debut: Ireland 20,
Argentina 18, 1990
Best moment in rugby: First match
for Ireland (Schools v. Australia,
1988)
Most embarrassing moment:
Getting my shorts ripped off aged 13
Most respected opponent: New
Zealand lock Alan Whetton – the
best about
Serious injuries: Neck injury,
broken wrist
Best memory last season:
Winning record sixth Irish
Inter-Provincial Championship with
Ulster
Suggestions to improve rugby:
On-field – Less emphasis on
set-play. Encourage more open
rugby

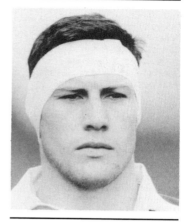

	apps	pts
Ireland B (**1989**)		
Last Season	1 cap	4
Career	2 caps	4
Ireland (**1990**)		
Last Season	1 cap	0
Career	1 cap	0

Other notable landmarks in rugby career: Ulster v. 1989 All Blacks.
. ·ing Canada with Dungannon (1989). Playing for Ireland at U-25, U-21
and schools level. Represented Ireland B v. Scotland B in 1989 (22–22) and
v. England B in 1991 (scoring try in 24–10 win) and in between received a
full cap in defeat of touring Pumas
Touchlines: Cycling

Jones, I. W.   Wales

Full Name: Ian Wynn Jones
1990/91 International category:
Wales (World Cup squad)
Club: Llanelli
Positions: Full-back, wing
Height: 5'10" **Weight:** 12st 3lbs
Occupation: Optics student
Born: Carmarthen, 12.5.71
Family: Single
Best moment in rugby: Scoring try
in Llanelli's Welsh Cup final win
over Pontypool last season
Worst moment in rugby: Missing
Wales U-21 debut v. Scotland
(1990/91) because of tonsillitis
Most respected opponent:
Harlequins' Simon Halliday
Best memory last season:
Winning Welsh Cup final and
earning selection to Wales squad for
tour to Australia
Suggestions to improve rugby:
On-field – Less breaks in play.
Off-field – Ease up on amateur
regulations
**Other notable landmarks in rugby
career:** Represented Welsh Schools
(five caps) in 1987/88. Played for
WRU President's (U-21) XV in
34–13 win over New Zealand Rugby

	apps	pts
Wales U-21 (1990/91)		
Last Season	0 caps	0
v. New Zealand XV	1 app	0
Wales 1991	Tour to Australia	
	World Cup squad	
Heineken 1990/91	11 apps	12

News Youth XV last season at Pontypridd. Tonsillitis put paid to debut v.
Scotland, but ended season on high note with scoring appearance in Welsh
Cup final and selection both to Wales preliminary World Cup squad, and to
summer tour of Australia
Touchlines: Playing violin, piano and golf
Player to watch: Huw Daniels (Cardiff Institute)

Jones, P. M.   Scotland

Full Name: Peter Martin Jones
1990/91 International category:
Scotland B
Club: Gloucester
Position: Prop
Height: 5'11" **Weight:** 15st 8lbs
Occupation: Engineer for Southern
Trent Water
Born: Arbroath, 28.12.64
Family: Sarah (wife)
Former club: Longlevens
International debut (B): Ireland
16, Scotland 0, 1990
Best moment in rugby: Being
picked to play for Scotland B
(1990/91)
Worst moment in rugby: Losing to
Ireland B on debut
Most respected opponent: Former
Gloucester and England prop Phil
Blakeway
Best memory last season:
Becoming first choice in Gloucester
first team

Scotland B (1990)	apps	pts
Last Season	1 cap	0
Career	1 cap	0

Suggestions to improve rugby:
On-field – More consistency in
refereeing. *Off-field* – None. Hope money does not spoil the game. Too much
cash floating about and people will start playing for the wrong reasons
Other notable landmarks in rugby career: Left Scotland aged 8 when
family moved to Gloucester. Selected for England B bench v. Emerging
Australians last season but chose to play for Scotland, who seemed more
genuine, and who gave me B debut in Belfast match v. Ireland
Touchlines: Hillwalking with dog
Player to watch: Dave Sims (Gloucester)

Jones, R. N.   Wales

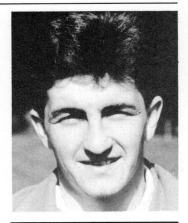

Full Name: Robert Nicholas Jones
1990/91 International category:
Wales Full
Club: Swansea
Position: Scrum-half
Height: 5'7" **Weight:** 11st 3lbs
Occupation: Financial consultant
Born: Trebanos, 10.11.65
Family: Megan (wife)
Family links with rugby:
Father-in-law, Clive Rowlands,
played for Wales and Lions. Brother
has played for Llanelli and Aberavon
International debut: England 21,
Wales 18, 1986
Five Nations' debut: As above
Best moments in rugby:
Captaining Wales. 1989 Lions
winning decisive third Test against
Australia
Worst moments in rugby:
Captaining Wales in 1990 whitewash
– very, very despondent. Defeat by
New Zealand in 1987 World Cup
Most embarrassing moment:
Attempted dropped goal for Wales
against Ireland, hit ground before
ball and sent it 3 yards. Paul Dean
collected and initiated move which
led to Irish try
Most respected opponents:
Scrum-halves Pierre Berbizier and
Gary Armstrong

	apps	pts
Wales B (1985)		
Last Season	0 caps	0
Career	1 cap	0
Wales (1986)		
Last Season	2 caps	0
	3 reps	
1991	Tour to Namibia	
	World Cup squad	
Career	34 caps	4
Lions 1989	3 Tests	0
Heineken 1990/91	14 apps	104

Other sporting achievements:
Represented Wales at cricket at three age-group levels
Best memory last season: Recall to Wales side for England game after losing place v. Barbarians (not one of my best seasons)
Suggestions to improve rugby: *On-field* – Introduce scale within penalty system, depending whether technical or physical infringement. England winning Grand Slam with hardly any tries makes mockery of existing system. *Off-field* – Greater depth of consideration for players. Reconsider amateur issue so that players can benefit away from play. Look after players' employers

with tickets, etc. WRU trying to be more forward-looking than other Unions but they are governed by IRB. Moves still have to be made to improve situation because there are still very few player-benefits considering time put in. Commitments and time involved ever-increasing. Yet athletes are able to benefit from their amateur sport

Other notable landmarks in rugby career: Former Wales captain. First represented All Whites while still at Cwmtawe School, having already played for West Wales U-11s and Wales 12-Group. Enjoyed outstanding World Cup (1987) and toured New Zealand (1988). Partnered Jonathan Davies in twenty-two Internationals. One of key figures in 1989 Lions' series win in Australia. Missed Welsh tour of Namibia last summer through injury

Touchlines: Golf (24-handicap)

Player to watch: Stuart Davies (Swansea)

Kardooni, A. England

Full Name: Aadel Kardooni

1990/91 International category: England B (bench)

Club: Leicester

Position: Scrum-half

Height: 5'8" **Weight:** 11st 8lbs

Occupation: Law & Accounts student

Born: Tehran, Iran, 17.5.68

Family: Single

Former clubs: North Dorset, Wasps

Best moment in rugby: Playing for Leicester (v. Bath) in 1988 Pilkington Cup final

Worst moment in rugby: Losing above match

Most embarrassing moment: Being congratulated on my performance by a Leicester fan when in fact I had not played due to injury

Most respected opponent: Harlequins flanker Peter Winterbottom

	apps
England B (1990/91)	2 reps

Best memories last season: Winning at Bath in Pilkington Cup. Involvement in England B squad

Suggestions to improve rugby: *On-field* – Home and away League system.

131

Reduce number of games players committed to per season. *Off-field* – Players should not be paid for playing. One international rule for all to adhere to
Other notable landmarks in rugby career: Represented England at 16-Group, 18-Group and Students. Selected as replacement by England B for matches v. Ireland and France last season
Touchlines: Cycling, other sports
Players to watch: John Liley, Tony Underwood and Neil Back (all Leicester)

Kembury, A. J.   Wales

Full Name: Andrew John Kembury
1990/91 International category: Wales B
Club: Neath
Positions: Lock, No.8, flanker
Height: 6′8″ **Weight:** 18st 7lbs
Occupation: Trainee site manager with Fairclough Building
Born: Bridgend, 30.7.69
Family: Joanne (fiancee)
Family links with rugby: Grandfather (Norman Pitt) played for Royal Navy
International debut: Netherlands 12, Wales B 34, 1990
Best moments in rugby: Neath beating Bridgend in 1987 Welsh Cup quarter-finals. A good game for me personally – proved to myself that I could make grade. Being involved with Neath squad which beat Llanelli (14–13) to win 1989 Welsh Cup
Worst moment in rugby: Being sent off in 1990 Schweppes Welsh Cup final v. Bridgend. One of those things you have to learn to deal with

	apps	pts
Wales B (**1990**)		
Last Season	1 cap	0
Career	1 cap	0
Wales 1991	World Cup squad	
Heineken 1990/91	8 apps	4

Most embarrassing moment: Coming off injured in every other game
Most respected opponent: Newport's David Waters
Best memory last season: Chatting with Bridgend's Owain Williams about the weather at the back of a line-out at the Brewery Field

Serious injuries: Damaged right shoulder (partly dislocated – played up for next two years)
Other sporting achievements: Hammer for Beddau Athletics Club
Suggestions to improve rugby: *On-field* – Less games per season. *Off-field* – Players should have more of a choice as to what they do away from rugby. It is their own business
Other notable landmarks in rugby career: Six caps for Wales Schools U-18s (1986–87). Toured New Zealand with Wales U-19s. One cap for each of U-20s, U-21s and Wales Students. Made Wales B debut in victory over the Netherlands at Leiden last season
Touchlines: Reading, motocross, music
Player to watch: Scott Quinnell (Llanelli)

Keyes, R. P. Ireland

Full Name: Ralph Patrick Keyes
1990/91 International category: Ireland Full (bench)
Club: Cork Constitution
Position: Fly-half
Height: 5′9″ **Weight:** 12st 7lbs
Occupation: Inspector for life insurance company
Born: Cork, 1.8.61
Family: Married with son and daughter
Family links with rugby: Father played for Cork and Munster
International debut: England 25, Ireland 20, 1986
Five Nations' debut: As above
Best moment in rugby: Being capped v. England at Twickenham
Worst moment in rugby: Sustaining injury in club game seven days after Ireland debut, which forced me out of next game v. Scotland
Most respected opponent: Former Ireland fly-half Paul Dean
Serious injuries: Ripped hamstring
Best memory last season: Winning All-Ireland League with Cork Con

	apps	pts
Ireland B (1984)		
Last Season	1 rep	
Ireland (1986)		
Last Season	1 rep	
1991	World Cup squad	
Career	1 cap	0

Suggestions to improve rugby: *On-field* – Reduce impact of penalty kicks. *Off-field* – Restructure present archaic amateur laws
Other notable landmarks in rugby career: Member of 1983 and 1985 Munster Cup-winning Cork teams. Represented Munster v. 1989 All Blacks. Captaining club in 1989/90 season. Made Ireland B debut in 23–20 defeat of Scotland at Galway in 1984. Bench reserve for Ireland in 1985 and toured Japan that same year. Replaced Paul Dean at half-time of second Test in Tokyo (won 38–15) and again replaced unfortunate Dean when winning first full cap (1986). Regular on Irish replacements' bench since. Last season reserve for Ireland and Ireland B in matches v. Argentina
Touchlines: Golf
Player to watch: Simon Geoghegan (London Irish)

Kiernan, M. J.   Ireland

Full Name: Michael Joseph Kiernan
1990/91 International category: Ireland Full
Club: Dolphin
Positions: Centre, wing
Height: 6′ **Weight:** 14st
Occupation: Company director
Born: Cork, 17.1.61
Family: Anne (wife) and Alison (daughter)
Family links with rugby: Several (father Tom is Ireland's most-capped full-back with 54 appearances between 1960–73)
Former club: Lansdowne
International debut: Ireland 20, Wales 12, 1982
Five Nations' debut: As above
Best moment in rugby: Winning Triple Crown in 1985

Worst moment in rugby: British Lions losing 6–38 to New Zealand in fourth Test (1983)
Most respected opponent: All Black centre Joe Stanley
Serious injuries: Depressed cheekbone (1988)
Other sporting achievements: National 200m sprint champion (1981)
Best memory last season: Helping Dolphin qualify for national leagues
Suggestions to improve rugby: *On-field* – Increase try worth to 5 points. Increase actual playing time (time ball is in play). *Off-field* – Address amateur

dilemma. Danger that if left alone sooner or later it will come to an unpleasant head. IRB must govern – at present there is a lack of cohesion between it and member unions
Other notable landmarks in rugby career: Record points-scorer for Ireland, having taken tally to 308 since winning first cap in 1982 as a replacement against Wales. Set Irish record for overseas tour with 65 on 1985 tour of Japan. Began representative career with Schools cap in 1979 and toured South Africa with Ireland in 1981 and North America (scoring 61 points) in 1989. Scored two tries for World XV in 38–42 loss to Australia in Australian Bicentennial match (May 1988). Landed penalty for Ireland B in 24–10 win over England B last season at Old Belvedere

	apps	pts
Ireland B (**1991**)		
Last Season	1 cap	3
Career	1 cap	3
Ireland (**1982**)		
Last Season	2 caps	25
Career	43 caps	308
Lions 1983	3 Tests	0
1986		

Touchlines: Golf (14-handicap), tennis, athletics
Player to watch: Jack Clarke (Dolphin)

Kimmins, R. England

Full Name: Robert Kimmins
1990/91 International category: England B
Club: Orrell
Position: Lock
Height: 6'8" **Weight:** 18st 5lbs
Occupation: Bricklayer
Born: Wigan, 28.1.62
Family: Julie-Ann (wife) and Stephen (son)
International debut: Spain v. England U-23s, 1984
Best moment in rugby: Being selected by England to tour Argentina (1990)
Worst moment in rugby: Orrell's defeat by Northampton in semi-finals of 1990/91 Pilkington Cup
Most respected opponent: None. I let them respect me

Best memory last season: Orrell's League loss to Wasps; very enjoyable game to play in
Suggestions to improve rugby: *On-field* – Get rid of 90-degree scrummage law. *Off-field* – Not bothered

	apps	pts
England B (1985)		
Last Season	1 cap	0
Career	8 caps	4
England 1990	Tour to Argentina	

Other notable landmarks in rugby career: Made eight appearances for England B (scoring one try), including caps against Spain and Fiji last season. Helped England XV beat Italy XV 33–15 (1989/90)
Player to watch: Martin Hynes (Orrell)
Touchlines: Railway photography

Kingston, T. J.   Ireland

Full Name: Terence John Kingston
1990/91 International category: Ireland Full (bench)
Club: Dolphin
Position: Hooker
Height: 5′10″ **Weight:** 14st 10lbs
Occupation: Computer consultant
Born: Cork, 19.9.63
Family: Single
Former club: Lansdowne
International debut: Ireland 6, Wales 13, 1987 World Cup
Five Nations' debut: Ireland 22, Scotland 18, 1988
Best moments in rugby: Selection for 1987 World Cup and gaining first cap v. Wales during the tournament
Worst moments in rugby: Being dropped from Irish team and Dolphin's failure to qualify for National League in 1989/90 play-off match
Most respected opponent: All of them
Best memory last season: Helping Dolphin qualify for national league
Suggestions to improve rugby: *On-field* – An extra 5 metres should be added to all penalties as an increased deterrent and to encourage team benefiting to take fast, running ball while opposition is retreating
Other notable landmarks in rugby career: Represented Irish Schools

(1982), Ireland U-21s (1984), Ireland U-25s (1987, three caps), Ireland B (v. Argentina last season) and, on nine occasions since debut in 1987 World Cup, Ireland Full. Ever-present on Ireland replacements' bench last season
Touchlines: Golf (18-handicap)
Player to watch: Jack Clarke (Dolphin)

	apps	pts
Ireland B (**1990**)		
Last Season	1 cap	0
Career	1 cap	0
Ireland (**1987**)		
Last Season	5 reps	
1991	Tour to Namibia World Cup squad	
Career	9 caps	8

Kirkpatrick, R. M. Scotland

Full Name: Ronald Mercer Kirkpatrick
1990/91 International category: Scotland (Tour squad)
Club: Jed-Forest
Positions: Flanker, No.8
Height: 6'3" **Weight:** 14st
Occupation: Electronics engineer
Born: Jedburgh 11.5.68
Family: Single
Family links with rugby: Father (Jack) played for Jed-Forest Brother (Jack) plays for Jed-Forest 2nd XV
International debut (U-21): Wales 26, Scotland 18, 1989
Best moment in rugby: Winning Scottish second division championship with Jed-Forest
Worst moment in rugby: Jed's loss to Melrose in 1989/90 Scottish League Championship clincher
Most embarrassing moment: Constantly having surname misquoted
Most respected opponent: Kelso's John Jeffrey
Best memory last season: Representing Scotland in Hong Kong Sevens

	apps	pts
Scotland U-21 (**1989**)		
Last Season	0 caps	0
Career	1 cap	0
Scotland 1991	Tour to North America	
Scotland VII (**1991**)	Hong Kong Sevens	

Suggestions to improve rugby: *On-field* – Contest Scottish League

Championship before Christmas (Jed always seem to lose momentum during winter break). *Off-field* – Lessen demands on top players or compensate them for time lost to work

Other notable landmarks in rugby career: Captained Scotland U-21s v. Wales in 1989 at The Gnoll. Captained South U-18s, and U-21s to Inter-District Championship. Border League winner with Jed-Forest. Selected for Scotland's B International v. France last season but had to withdraw through injury, but toured with Scotland to North America and played in non-cap 'test' defeat by Canada (19–24). Averaged a try a game in three other tour appearances (including brace in 76–6 rout of Alberta). Represented official Scotland side at 1991 Hong Kong Sevens

Player to watch: Rowen Shepherd (Edinburgh Academicals)

Knight, P.   Wales

Full Name: Paul Knight
1990/91 International category:
Wales Full
Club: Pontypridd
Position: Prop
Height: 6' **Weight:** 16st 8lbs
Occupation: Production controller
Born: Tonypandy, 30.4.61
Family: Jennifer (wife) and Nadia
Kylie (daughter)
Family links with rugby: Brother
(Tony) plays for Treorchy
Former clubs: Treorchy, Aberavon
International debut: Namibia 9,
Wales 18, 1990
Five Nations' debut: Wales 25,
England 6, 1990
Best moment in rugby: Winning
first full cap in first Test at Windhoek
Serious injuries: Knee cartilage
Best memory last season: Making
first appearance in Five Nations'
Championship v. England
Suggestions to improve rugby:
On-field – Needs no improving.
Off-field – Become more
professional in administration
Other notable landmarks in rugby

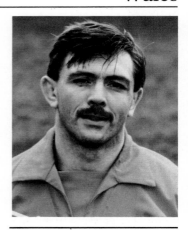

	apps	pts
Wales (1990)		
Last Season	3 caps	0
1991	Tour to Australia	
	World Cup squad	
Career	5 caps	0
Heineken 1990/91	15 apps	0

career: Attended Welsh Youth trials. Represented Mid-District, West Wales, Crawshays and 1990/91 centenary Barbarians v. Argentina at Cardiff. Bench reserve for Wales B in early 1980s. Selected for Wales tour of Namibia (1990) and played in both Tests. Came on as 14th minute minute replacement for Brian Williams in Wales' 24–31 loss to Barbarians last season, and started 1991 Five Nations' matches v. England and Scotland
Touchlines: Gardening, DIY
Player to watch: Neil Jenkins (Pontypridd)

Laing, J. Scotland

Full Name: John Laing
1990/91 International category:
Scotland Full (bench)
Club: Gala
Position: Lock
Height: 6′5.5″ **Weight:** 17st
Occupation: Account manager
Born: Glasgow, 1.4.60
Family: Single
Former clubs: Corstorphine, Aberdeen GSFP
Best moments in rugby: Selection as replacement for Scotland's 49–3 defeat of Argentina last season. Helping South win McEwan's Scottish Inter-District Championship
Most respected opponent: Nottingham lock Chris Gray
Best memory last season: Bench reserve for Scotland
Serious injuries: Torn knee ligaments aged 23 (plaster for eight weeks)

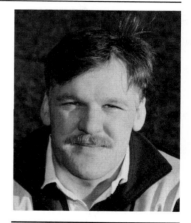

	apps
Scotland Full (1990/91)	1 rep

Suggestions to improve rugby: *On-field* – More consistency in refereeing
Other notable landmarks in rugby career: Played for Corstorphine v. Boroughmuir in final of 1987/88 River Series. Helped South win 1990/91 Inter-District Championship in first season of District rugby. Represented South v. Argentina. Bench replacement for Scotland v. Argentina at Murrayfield last season
Touchlines: Social golf (handicap – my clubs)
Player to watch: Gregor Townsend (Galashiels Academy)

Laity, C.   Wales

Full Name: Colin Laity
1990/91 International category:
Wales (World Cup squad)
Club: Neath
Position: Centre
Height: 5'10" **Weight:** 13st 7lbs
Occupation: Financial consultant
Born: Helston, Cornwall, 19.6.65
Family: Single
Former clubs: Helston, Redruth,
Penarth, Llanelli, South Glamorgan
Institute
Best moment in rugby:
Representing Barbarians v. 1988
Australians
Worst moments in rugby: Neath
losing to Llanelli in 1989 Schweppes
Cup final and suffering concussion
during game
Most respected opponent: Neath
flanker Lyn Jones
Serious injuries: Damaged knee
and ankle ligaments, concussion
Best memory last season: Winning
Heineken League Championship
with Neath

	apps	pts
Wales B (1988)		
Last Season	0 caps	0
Career	1 cap	0
Wales 1991	World Cup squad	
Heineken	14 apps	24

Suggestions to improve rugby:
On-field – Universal interpretation
of rules by referees. *Off-field* –
Adequate reimbursment to players for loss of earnings due to rugby
Other notable landmarks in rugby career: Represented Cornwall, South
and South West Division, Crawshays and Barbarians. Educated at Helston
Comprehensive School, Cornish College of Further and Higher Education
and South Glamorgan Institute where was rugby captain. Played for England
Students in inaugural Students World Cup, scoring two tries in 16–9 defeat
of Scotland. Eligible for England or Wales but chose latter. Included in Wales'
preliminary World Cup squad last season
Touchlines: Cycling, sea-fishing (best is 6lb bass)
Players to watch: Scott Quinnell and Luc Evans (both Llanelli)

Lamerton, A. E.   Wales

Full Name: Andrew Edwin
Lamerton
1990/91 International category:
Wales U-21
Club: Llanelli
Position: Hooker
Height: 6' **Weight:** 14st 2lbs
Occupation: Production operator
Born: Pontypridd, 28.5.70
Family: Single
Former club: Beddau
International debut (U-21):
Scotland 10, Wales 24, 1990
Best moment in rugby: Playing for
Llanelli v. 1989 All Blacks
Worst moment in rugby: Ripping
shorts playing at Cardiff and being
brought out pair two sizes too small.
To everyone's amusement they got
stuck halfway up my legs
Most embarrassing moment:
Attempted to touch loose ball down
behind own try-line at Newport last
season but it bounced over my hands
and Newport wing scored
Most respected opponent:
England B hooker Graham Dawe
Best memory last season: Winning
Schweppes Welsh Cup final with
Llanelli

	apps	pts
Wales U-21 (**1991**)		
Last Season	1 cap	0
v. New Zealand XV	1 app	0
Career	2 caps	0
Heineken 1990/91	13 apps	4

Suggestions to improve rugby: *Off-field* – Take more care of players; better
facilities etc.
Other notable landmarks in rugby career: Played four times for Wales
U-18s (1986/87) and four times for Wales Youth (1987/88). Scored try for
Youth v. Canada. Represented Wales U-21s twice v. Scotland (1990–91)
Touchlines: Golf (26-handicap)
Player to watch: Ian Jones (Llanelli)

Lawlor, P. J.   Ireland

Full Name: Philip John Lawlor
1990/91 International category:
Ireland Full
Club: Bective Rangers
Position: No.8
Height: 6'5" **Weight:** 16st 3lbs
Occupation: Farmer
Born: Kildare, 2.7.65
Family: Single
Former club: Naas
International debut: Ireland 20,
Argentina 18, 1990
Best moment in rugby: Getting
capped v. touring Pumas
Worst moment in rugby: Breaking
ankle playing for Leinster v. South
West Division (Sept 1989)
Most respected opponent:
Northampton No.8 Wayne Shelford
Other sporting achievements:
Gaelic football for Naas
Best memory last season:
Stepping out onto Lansdowne Road
pitch in Ireland jersey
**Other notable landmarks in
rugby career:** Played international
rugby at three levels last season. For
Ireland U-25s v. Spain, for Ireland B
v. Argentina and v. England, and for
Ireland v. Argentina
Touchlines: Gaelic football, horse racing, golf
Player to watch: Mark Coddihy (Naas)

	apps	pts
Ireland B (**1990**)		
Last Season	2 caps	0
Career	2 caps	0
Ireland (**1990**)		
Last Season	1 cap	0
Career	1 cap	0

Leahy, K. T.   Ireland

Full Name: Kelvin Tremaine Leahy
1990/91 International category:
Ireland B
Club: Wanderers
Positions: Flanker, No.8
Height: 6'2.5" **Weight:** 16st
Occupation: Building Society
manager
Born: Cork, 1.9.65
Family: Deirdre (wife)
Family links with rugby: Father
(Mick) played at lock (replacing
Willy-John McBride) for Ireland in
6–15 loss to Wales in 1964
International debut: Ireland B 27,
Argentina 12, 1990
Best moment in rugby: Captaining
Ireland B to 16-0 win over Scotland
B (1990/91)
Most respected opponent:
Wanderers' flanker Philip Matthews
Best memory last season: Beating
Scotland B after being reduced to 14
men inside first 20 minutes
Serious injuries: Shoulder
dislocation (required operation)
Suggestions to improve rugby:
On-field – Award 5 points for a try.
Off-field – Reimburse employers for
lost working hours due to rugby

	apps	pts
Ireland U-25 (**1990**)		
Last Season	1 cap	0
	1 rep	
Ireland B (**1990**)		
Last season	2 caps	0
Career	2 caps	0
Ireland 1991	World Cup squad	

Other notable landmarks in rugby career: Represented 1984 Irish Schools.
Replacement for Ireland U-25s v. US Eagles (1989/90). Captained Leinster
and Ireland U-25s (v. Spain) last season. Captained Ireland B to 16-0 defeat
of Scotland last season, having previously made debut in 27–12 win v. touring
Argentine Pumas. Missed match v. England B with three-month long shoulder
dislocation injury
Touchlines: Swimming, fishing (fly/spinning)
Player to watch: Richard Wallace (Garryowen)

Lenihan, D. G.   Ireland

Full Name: Donal Gerald Lenihan
1990/91 International category:
Ireland Full
Club: Cork Constitution
Position: Lock
Height: 6'4" **Weight:** 17st
Occupation: Building Society
manager
Born: Cork, 12.9.59
Family: Married with son
Former club: University College,
Cork
International debut: Ireland 12,
Australia 16, 1981
Five Nations' debut: Ireland 20,
Wales 12, 1982
Best moments in rugby: Winning
two Triple Crowns with Ireland and
1990/91 All-Ireland League success
with Cork Con
Most respected opponent: Former
England lock Maurice Colclough
Serious injuries: Broken nose,
finger
Best memory last season:
Constitution's All-Ireland League
win
Suggestions to improve rugby:
On-field – Standardise refereeing
interpretations in southern and
northern hemispheres

	apps	pts
Ireland B (**1980**)		
Last Season	0 caps	0
Ireland (**1981**)		
Last Season	2 cap	0
Career	48 caps	4
Lions 1983		
1986		
1989		

Other notable landmarks in rugby career: Made Ireland debut for Schools
(1977) and within four years had graduated through U-23s (1979) and Ireland
B (1980) to full status (1981). Last season captained Ireland to 20–18 defeat
over touring Argentina before sustaining injury which forced absence until
second Test v. Namibia, when won 48th cap in 15–26 defeat

Leonard, J.   England

Full Name: Jason Leonard
1990/91 International category:
England Full
Club: Harlequins
Position: Loose-head prop
Height: 5'10" **Weight:** 16st 7lbs
Occupation: Builder
Born: Barking, London, 14.8.68
Family: Single
Former clubs: Barking, Saracens
International debut: England 12,
Fiji 20, 1989
Best moments in rugby: Playing
against Fiji, and Saracens beating
Bath in English first division
Worst moment in rugby: Two
seasons of Cup defeats with Saracens
Most embarrassing moment: Ball
landing on my head during B match
in France (1989/90)
Most respected opponent:
England prop Jeff Probyn –
technique and physical abilities
Best memory last season: Winning
Grand Slam in first season with
England
Suggestions to improve rugby:
Improve grass roots part of game
**Other notable landmarks in
rugby career:** Helped Barking win
Essex Colts Cup before tasting
success at Twickenham with Eastern
Counties winning U-21 County
Championship. Won English second division title with Saracens (1988/89)
and sat on England U-21 bench in Romania (1989). Broke into England B
ranks 1989/90, winning caps v. Fiji and v. France and warming bench v. USSR

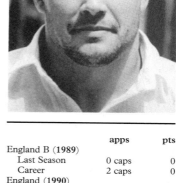

	apps	pts
England B (1989)		
Last Season	0 caps	0
Career	2 caps	0
England (1990)		
Last Season	7 caps	0
v. Barbarians	1 app	0
1991	Tour to Australia	
	World Cup squad	
	1995 Development squad	
Career	9 caps	0

Lewis, E. W. Wales

Full Name: Emyr Wyn Lewis
1990/91 International category:
Wales Full
Club: Llanelli
Positions: Flanker, No.8
Height: 6'4" **Weight:** 16st 9lbs
Occupation: Police officer
Born: Carmarthen, 29.8.68
Family: Single
Former club: Carmarthen Athletic
International debut: Wales 21,
Ireland 21, 1991
Five Nations' debut: As above
Best moment in rugby: Selection
for first cap
Most embarrassing moment:
Running down sidelines in support
of attack v. Northampton (1990/91)
and falling over, twisting ankle in
process
Most respected opponent: Neath
flanker Lyn Jones
Best memories last season: Lifting
Schweppes Welsh Cup with Llanelli,
and running out onto Arms Park for
first time in Wales jersey
Suggestions to improve rugby:
On-field – Award more points for a
try
**Other notable landmarks in rugby
career:** Missed playing for Welsh
Schools because too old by two days.
Could not play for Wales Youth

	apps	pts
Wales B (**1990**)		
Last Season	1 cap	0
Career	1 cap	0
Wales (**1991**)		
Last Season	3 caps	0
	2 reps	
1991	Tour to Australia	
	World Cup squad	
Career	3 caps	0
Heineken 1990/91	12 apps	20

because still at school, but on leaving represented Wales at U-20, U-21, B
(for two minutes as replacement in last season's 34–12 defeat of the
Netherlands) and senior level (last season v. Ireland and France)
Touchlines: Fishing (river spinning), shooting
Player to watch: Ian Jones (Llanelli)

Lewis, S. L.   Wales

Full Name: Steele Lloyd Lewis
1990/91 International category:
Wales B
Club: Pontypridd
Position: Centre
Height: 5'10" **Weight:** 13st 4lbs
Occupation: Roof tiler
Born: Rinteln, Germany, 29.10.64
Family: Alison (wife), Natasha
(daughter)
Former clubs: Gilfach Goch,
Tonyrefail
International debut: France B 28,
Wales B 15, 1989
Best moment in rugby: Selection
by Wales for 1991 tour to Australia
Most respected opponent:
Pontypridd centre Ceri Jones
Best memory last season: Helping
Wales B beat the Netherlands 34–12
in Leiden
**Other notable landmarks in
rugby career:** Made Wales B debut
at La Teste when coming on as 58th
minute replacement for Colin
Stephens during 15–28 loss to
France B. Also represented Mid
District and Glamorgan County.
Invited to join Wales' preliminary
World Cup squad and to tour Australia with the senior team last summer
Touchlines: Swimming
Player to watch: Jason Lewis (Pontypridd)

	apps	pts
Wales B (1989)		
Last Season	1 cap	0
Career	2 caps	0
Wales 1991	Tour to Australia	
	World Cup squad	
Heineken 1990/91	13 apps	4

Liley, J. G. England

Full Name: John Garin Liley
1990/91 International category:
England B
Club: Leicester
Position: Full-back
Height: 5'11" **Weight:** 12st 10lbs
Occupation: Trainee accountant
Born: Wakefield, 21.8.67
Family: Melanie (wife)
Family links with rugby: Father
and grandfather played for
Wakefield. Brother Rob plays in
Cahors (France)
Former clubs: Sandal, Wakefield
International debut: England B 31,
Namibia 16, 1990
Best moment in rugby: Scoring 15
points against Bath in final game of
1989/90 to beat Dusty Hare's
season-scoring record at Leicester
(438) by 1 point
Worst moment in rugby:
Wakefield losing to Headingley in
1987/88 Yorkshire Cup final
Most respected opponent:
Scotland full-back Gavin Hastings
Serious injuries: Pulled hamstrings
Other sporting achievements:
Represented Yorkshire U-14s at

	apps	pts
England B (**1990**)		
Last Season	3 caps	33
Career	3 caps	33
England 1990	Tour to Argentina	
	1995 Development squad	

basketball. Played for 1986/87 England Colleges Rugby League team v. Welsh
Colleges
Best memories last season: Leicester winning at Bath in third round of
Pilkington Cup. Reaching ADT County Championship final with Yorkshire
Suggestions to improve rugby: *On-field* – More consistent refereeing.
Inconsistency makes games frustrating, especially those of importance
Other notable landmarks in rugby career: 1989/90 total of 439 points
topped English scoring charts: 1. Liley 439 (18t, 89c, 63p); 2. A Green
(Exeter) 333; 3. S Burnage (Fylde) 326. Also topped goal-kicking table: 1.
Liley 367; 2. Burnage 310; 3. Green 309. But Green took revenge last season,
heading Unisys Computer lists, with 373 to my 348 (8t, 56c, 67p, 1dg), and
goal-kicking table, 321 to my 316. Played for North of England U-21s v.
Midlands (1987/88). Toured Argentina with England (1990), playing v.

Banco Nacion (lost 21–29), Tucuman Selection (won 19–14), Cuyo Selection (lost 22–21) and Cordoba Selection (won 15–12); contributing 15 points (try, conversion, three penalty goals). Helped Yorkshire reach 1990/91 English County Championship final
Touchlines: Cricket, golf, driving, photography
Player to watch: Damian Hopley (Wasps)

Lineen, S. R. P.   Scotland

Full Name: Sean Raymond Patrick Lineen
1990/91 International category: Scotland Full
Club: Boroughmuir
Position: Centre
Height: 6'1.5" **Weight:** 13st 6lbs
Occupation: Sales and Marketing manager for *Scottish Rugby* magazine
Born: Auckland, New Zealand, 25.12.61
Family: Single
Family links with rugby: Terry (father) played twelve times for New Zealand (1957–60); Troy (brother) represented Auckland at junior level
Former clubs: Pakuranga, Papakura, Counties (all NZ), Bombay, Pontypool
International debut: Scotland 23, Wales 7, 1989
Five Nations' debut: As above
Best moments in rugby: First Scotland cap against Wales, and winning 1990 Grand Slam
Worst moment in rugby: Playing in Scotland XV beaten 28–24 by Japan in 1989

	apps	pts
Scotland (**1989**)		
Last Season	5 caps	0
1991	World Cup squad	
Career	17 caps	4

Most embarrassing moment: Over-indulging on beverages at Gatwick en route to join Boroughmuir after arriving early from New Zealand on 28-hour flight. When collected and taken straight to training with new team mates I brought everything up. So much for Muir's great New Zealand hope!
Most respected opponent: France centre Philippe Sella
Other sporting achievements: Auckland junior badminton

Best memory last season: Boroughmuir's first McEwan's League Championship
Suggestions to improve rugby: *On-field* – Improve refereeing standards; change laws to improve game as a spectacle. *Off-field* – Clear-cut definition of what players can and cannot do regarding rugby-related activities away from the field. At present 90 per cent of earning opportunities for rugby union players have been taken away
Other notable landmarks in rugby career: Helping Counties win first New Zealand National Sevens in 1985. First two performances for Boroughmuir – pleased with my start. Qualified for Scotland through grandfather who came from the Hebrides. Returned to New Zealand on tour with Scotland (1990) and ever-present throughout 1991 Five Nations' Championship
Touchlines: Racket sports, especially squash
Player to watch: Stuart Reid Boroughmuir)

Linnett, M. S. England

Full Name: Mark Stuart Linnett
1990/91 International category: England B (bench)
Club: Moseley
Position: Loose-head prop
Height: 5'11" **Weight:** 17st
Occupation: Policeman
Born: Rugby, 17.2.63
Family: Julie (wife) and Jack (son)
Former club: Rugby
International debut: England 58, Fiji 23, 1989
Best moment in rugby: Scoring try on England debut
Worst moment in rugby: Losing to Bristol and Bath in Cup semi-finals
Most respected opponent: England tight-head prop Jeff Probyn – extremely awkward scrummager

Other sporting achievements: Qualified PTI
Best memory last season: Beating Bristol in 1989/90 Pilkington Cup quarter-finals
Suggestions to improve rugby: *On-field* – English Leagues should operate on home and away basis. Improve standards of refereeing. *Off-field* – None.

If there is any money to be had in terms of compensation for time lost to rugby I will accept it, but I will not go on the scrounge

Other notable landmarks in rugby career: England Colts (1981), England U-23 (1984), England B (1988), England and Barbarians (1989). Scored try against Fiji on full England debut (Nov 1989). Scored tries for England B v. Spain and Italy. Member of England's development squad for 1995 World Cup. Toured Argentina with England (1990), playing v. Banco Nacion, Cuyo Selection and Cordoba Selection

Player to watch: Rupert Moon (Llanelli)

	apps	pts
England B (**1988**)		
Last Season	1 rep	
England (**1989**)		
Last Season	0 caps	0
	1995 Development squad	
Career	1 cap	4

Llewellyn, D. S.   Wales

Full Name: David Stephen Llewellyn
1990/91 International category: Wales U-21 (bench)
Club: Newport
Position: Scrum-half
Height: 5'11" **Weight:** 12st 8lbs
Born: Tredegar, 29.9.70
Family: Single
Family links with rugby: Uncle (David) played for Tredegar Ironsides, Army and Combined Services
Former clubs: Ebbw Vale, Karaka (NZ), Counties (NZ)
Best moments in rugby: Selection to Wales' 1991 World Cup squad. Being told while I was in New Zealand that if I had been a Kiwi I would be an All Black
Worst moment in rugby: Not getting off bench when Wales played Scotland at U-21 level last season
Most respected opponent: Aberavon's Ray Giles

	apps	pts
Wales U-21 (1990/91)	1 rep	
Wales 1991	World Cup squad	
Heineken 1990/91	7 apps	36

151

Best memory last season: Scoring try in Newport's famous win at Neath
Suggestions to improve rugby: *On-field* – End practice of awarding penalty try for scrum wheeling on try-line
Other notable landmarks in rugby career: Played for Wales at U-20 and Students level. Included in Wales Youth, U-21 and senior World Cup squads. Represented New Zealand Barbarians during spell in NZ
Touchlines: Swimming, athletics, weight training
Player to watch: Matthew McCarthy (Aberavon)

Llewellyn, G. O. Wales

Full Name: Gareth Owen Llewellyn
1990/91 International category: Wales Full
Club: Neath
Position: Lock
Height: 6′6″ **Weight:** 17st 7lbs
Occupation: Fitter and turner
Born: Cardiff, 27.2.69
Family: Single
Family links with rugby: Brother (Glyn) plays for Neath and toured Namibia with Wales (1990)
Former club: Llanharan
International debut: Wales 9, New Zealand 34, 1989
Five Nations' debut: England 34, Wales 6, 1990
Best moment in rugby: Winning first Wales cap
Worst moment in rugby: Twice being dropped by Wales
Most embarrassing moment: Almost tripping over when running out at Cardiff for first cap
Most respected opponent: Wales lock Bob Norster
Serious injuries: Dislocated collarbone, damaged pelvis
Best memory last season: Winning Welsh premier division with Neath
Suggestions to improve rugby: *Off-field* – Take better care of players

	apps	pts
Wales B (**1989**)		
Last Season	1 cap	0
Career	1 cap	0
Wales (**1989**)		
Last Season	3 caps	0
1991	Tour to Australia World Cup squad	
Career	7 caps	4
Heineken 1990/91	12 apps	0

Other notable landmarks in rugby career: Capped three times by Wales Youth. Toured New Zealand with Welsh U-19 team. Also played for Crawshays and Barbarians. Represented Wales v. England and v. Scotland last season before losing place to Paul Arnold. Included in Wales squad for summer tour to Australia and for World Cup

Touchlines: Golf, squash, weights

Player to watch: Scott Gibbs (Neath)

Llewellyn, G. D.   Wales

Full Name: Glyn David Llewellyn

1990/91 International category: Wales Full

Club: Neath

Position: Lock

Height: 6′6″ **Weight:** 17st 12lbs

Occupation: Architect

Born: Bradford on Avon, Wilts, 9.8.65

Family: Single

Family links with rugby: Brother (Gareth) plays for Neath and Wales. Father, who was in Army with Will Carling's dad, is qualified WRU coach

Former clubs: Llanharan, Bridgend, London Welsh, Llanelli

International debut: Namibia 9, Wales 18, 1990

Best moment in rugby: Playing with brother in Wales team for first time, v. England at Cardiff (1990/91)

Worst moment in rugby: Welsh Schools defeat by British Columbia during 1983 Canadian tour – until last season, the only time I had ever been on a losing Welsh national team

	apps	pts
Wales (**1990**)		
Last Season	6 caps	0
1991	Tour to Australia World Cup squad	
Career	8 caps	0
Heineken 1990/91	15 apps	0

Most embarrassing moment: Having shorts ripped off when jockstrap-less

Most respected opponent: England B lock John Morrison

Serious injuries: Torn knee ligaments (1987)

Other sporting achievements: Welsh Schools basketball International

Best memory last season: England game (see Best Moment)

Suggestions to improve rugby: *On-field* – More consistency in refereeing. Eliminate line-out barging by preventing anyone from moving until ball has been touched. Once penalty has been awarded move ball on 15 yards from where offence occurred to discourage foul play while also encouraging sides to go for tries. Unification of laws. Present interpretations differ widely between northern and southern hemispheres

Other notable landmarks in rugby career: Spent five years with London Welsh before returning to Wales on obtaining a post in Barry. Won six secondary caps. Ever-present for Wales throughout last season (five games). Included in Wales squad both for summer tour to Australia and for World Cup

Touchlines: Windsurfing, cricket, basketball and weights

Player to watch: Scott Gibbs (Neath)

Lloyd, O. S. Wales

Full Name: Owain Stradling Lloyd
1990/91 International category: Wales U-21
Club: Bridgend
Position: Flanker
Height: 6'3" **Weight:** 16st 3lbs
Occupation: Human movements student
Born: Bridgend, 26.9.70
Family: Single
Former club: East Coast Bays (NZ)
International debut (U-21): Wales 23, Scotland 15, 1991
Best moment in rugby: Playing for Wales U-21s
Best memory last season: Beating Scotland with Wales U-21s
Other notable landmarks in rugby career: Captained Llandovery College to victory over Brecon (1988/89). Represented Caermarthen County U-17s and U-19s and Wales Schools (1988/89) and Welsh Public Schools. Played for WRU President's (U-21) XV in 34–13 defeat of New Zealand Youth

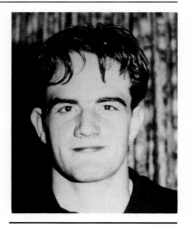

	apps	pts
Wales U-21 (1991)		
Last Season	1 cap	0
v. New Zealand XV	1 app	0
Career	1 cap	0
Heineken 1990/91	1 app	0

XV at Pontypridd last season, prior to winning U-21 cap in match v. Scotland at Stradey Park last April
Touchlines: Golf
Player to watch: Scott Quinnell (Llanelli)

Luxton, C. T.   England

Full Name: Craig Thomas Luxton
1990/91 International category:
England B
Club: Harlequins
Position: Scrum-half
Height: 5'10" **Weight:** 12st
Occupations: International head hunter and part-time tennis coach
Born: Opotiki, New Zealand, 11.3.64
Family: Single
Family links with rugby: Father played for Bay of Plenty (NZ)
Former clubs: Leamington, Cambridge United (NZ)
International debut: England 31, Namibia 16, 1990
Best moment in rugby: Being a Kiwi wearing the red rose of England (B)
Worst moment in rugby: Harlequins losing to Leicester in 1989 Cup semi-final
Most embarrassing moment: Doing a big dive for try-line with no-one in sight and dropping ball
Most respected opponents:

	apps	pts
England B (1990)		
Last Season	1 cap	0
Career	1 cap	0

Waikato's Stephen Putt, England's Richard Hill and Wales' Robert Jones
Serious injuries: Broken knee cartilage, damaged medial ligaments
Other sporting achievements: NZ age-group tennis champion; NZ national development tennis squad; Waikato Schools softball team
Suggestions to improve rugby: *On-field* – Make training as enjoyable and constructive as possible. Don't place heavy demands on players (i.e. not too many games)
Other notable landmarks in rugby career: Spent two seasons with Waikato. Co-coaching local club in NZ to second division Grand Final. Toured Spain

with England B in 1989 but had to wait for the visit of Namibia last season (won 31–16) to win first B cap

Touchlines: Surviving drinking sessions with England flanker Mick 'Munch' Skinner, body surfing, golf

Lyman, N. M.   England

Full Name: Neil Michael Lyman
1990/91 International category: England U-21
Club: Moseley
Position: Tight-head prop
Height: 6'1" **Weight:** 17st
Occupation: Carpenter
Born: Bedford, 6.5.70
Family: Single
Family links with rugby: Father played for Bedford
Former club: Kidderminster Carolians
International debut: Netherlands 3, England U-21 24, 1990
Best moment in rugby: Pulling on England shirt
Worst moment in rugby: Not coming off bench when England U-21s played French Armed Forces (1990)
Most respected opponent: Leicester flanker Neil Back
Serious injuries: Torn bicep (1990)
Other sporting achievements: County soccer for Hereford & Worcestershire

	apps	pts
England U-21 (**1990**)		
Last Season	2 caps	0
Career	3 caps	0

Suggestions to improve rugby: Players should stay on feet more to keep game moving quicker

Other notable landmarks in rugby career: Only started playing rugby five years ago. Joined Moseley from junior club 1989/90. Helped England U-21s beat Netherlands 24–3 away (1989/90) and, last season, represented them in losses to Ireland (16–22) and French Armed Forces (7–9)

McAleese, D. R.   Ireland

Full Name: Derek Raymond McAleese
1990/91 International category: Ireland B
Club: Ballymena
Position: Fly-half
Height: 6'2" **Weight:** 13st 10lbs
Occupation: Estate agent
Born: Limvady, 14.9.64
Family: Married
Former club: Limvady
International debut (B): Ireland 16, Scotland 0, 1990
Best moments in rugby: Completing hat-trick of Ulster Cup wins with Ballymena. Ulster's Inter-Provincial victory over Munster in Cork (1989/90). Winning Ireland B cap
Worst moment in rugby: Not being selected for Ireland's B game v. England (1990/91)
Most respected opponent: Boroughmuir's Graham Drummond
Best memory last season: Making Ireland B debut

	apps	pts
Ireland B (1990)		
Last Season	1 cap	8
Career	1 cap	8

Suggestions to improve rugby:
On-field – More sympathetic and consistent refereeing. We watch Internationals on TV but when we try to emulate what we see, at club level (i.e. rucking), we get penalised. Interpretations must be unified between two hemispheres because rucking is a dead duck in the northern hemisphere.
Off-field – Full compensation for time lost to rugby and travelling expenses for top players
Other notable landmarks in rugby career: Represented Civil Service for three years. Kicked two penalties and a conversion in Ireland B's 16-0 defeat of Scotland at Ravenhill (1990/91). Also represented Ulster U-20s and senior Ulster XV
Touchlines: Golf (9-handicap), summer soccer
Player to watch: Simon Geoghegan (London Irish)

McAndrew, D. C.   Scotland

Full Name: Douglas Cameron McAndrew
1990/91 International category: Scotland U-21
Club: Stirling County
Position: Hooker
Height: 5'9" **Weight:** 12st 8lbs
Occupation: Accountancy student
Born: Stirling, 21.9.69
Family: Single
Family links with rugby: Jack (father) is vice-president of Stirling County
International debut (U-21): Wales 23, Scotland 15, 1991
Best moment in rugby: Debut for Scotland U-21s at Stradey Park
Worst moment in rugby: Stirling County being thrashed by Melrose in 1988 U-18 final at Murrayfield
Most respected opponent: Glasgow H/K hooker Gordon Peterson
Best memory last season: Playing for Stirling County first team in two friendlies

Scotland U-21 (**1991**)	apps	pts
Last Season	1 cap	0
Career	1 cap	0

Suggestions to improve rugby:
On-field – More consistency in refereeing
Other notable landmarks in rugby career: Represented Scotland U-18s v. Scotland Schools (1987). Bench reserve for Scotland U-21s in 15–23 loss to Wales U-21s (Llanelli, 20 April 1991). Played for Stirling County VII in 1991 Melrose Sevens
Player to watch: Andy Ness (Glasgow High/Kelvinside)

McBride, W. D.   Ireland

Full Name: William **Denis** McBride
1990/91 International category:
Ireland Full
Club: Malone
Position: Flanker
Height: 5'11" **Weight:** 14st
Occupation: Mechanical engineer
Born: Belfast, 9.9.64
Family: Catrina (wife)
Family links with rugby: Brother
also plays
Former club: Queen's University
Belfast
International debut: Ireland 9,
Wales 12, 1988
Five Nations' debut: As above
Best moment in rugby: Ireland XV
beating France XV 19–18 at Auch
(1988) in non-cap tour match
Worst moment in rugby: Second
half of Ireland's 3–35 defeat by
England in 1988 when we conceded
35 points without reply
Most embarrassing moment:
Ireland v. England (1988)
Most respected opponents: No.8s
Wayne Shelford (New Zealand) and
Laurent Rodriguez (France)

	apps	pts
Ireland B (**1990**)		
Last Season	1 cap	0
Ireland (**1988**)		
Last Season	1 cap	0
Career	8 caps	8

Other sporting achievements:
Completed the 1982 Belfast City Marathon
Best memory last season: Winning Melrose Sevens with Irish Wolfhounds
Suggestions to improve rugby: *On-field* – More points for a try, less for a
penalty goal. Scrap 90-degree scrummage wheel law. *Off-field* – Better
marketing of the sport. All countries should send teams to Hong Kong Sevens.
Permit players to benefit from off-field activities
Other notable landmarks in rugby career: Ulster v. 1989 All Blacks (lost
21–3). 1989 Hong Kong Sevens with Irish Wolfhounds. Represented Ireland
B in 27–12 win over Argentina B last season before winning eighth cap in
20–18 defeat of touring Pumas at Lansdowne Road
Touchlines: Athletics (400m)
Player to watch: Richard Wallace (Garryowen)

McCarthy, P. D.   Ireland

Full Name: Paul David McCarthy
1990/91 International category:
Ireland B
Club: Cork Constitution
Position: Tight-head prop
Height: 6′ **Weight:** 18st
Occupation: Service engineer
Born: Cork, 27.8.63
Former club: Dolphin
International debut (B): Ireland
16, Scotland 0, 1990
Best moments in rugby: Helping
Ireland B beat England B 24–10
(1991), and Constitution winning
inaugural All-Ireland League
Worst moment in rugby: Injury
Most respected opponent:
Pontypool prop Staff Jones
Best memory last season:
All-Ireland League success
Suggestions to improve rugby:
On-field – Improve refereeing of
scrum
**Other notable landmarks in
rugby career:** Won Schools Junior
and Senior Cup medals.
Represented Munster in Irish
Inter-Provincial Championship and
Ireland B in defeats of Scotland (16-0) and England (24–10) last season
Touchlines: Shooting, fishing
Player to watch: Philip Soden (Constitution)

	apps	pts
Ireland B (**1990**)		
Last Season	2 caps	0
Career	2 caps	0
Ireland 1991	World Cup squad	

McCoy, J. J.   Ireland

Full Name: James Joseph McCoy
1990/91 International category:
Ireland B (bench)
Club: Bangor
Position: Tight-head prop
Height: 6'1" **Weight:** 17st
Occupation: Civil servant
Born: Enniskillen, 28.6.58
Family: Fiona (wife), Nicola
(daughter) and Craig James (son)
Former clubs: Enniskillen,
Dungannon
International debut: Ireland 9,
Wales 18, 1984
Five Nations' debut: As above
Best moment in rugby: Winning
Triple Crown in 1985
Worst moment in rugby: Getting
injured in stupid Irish Trial match
last season
Most respected opponent: All of
them at International level
Serious injuries: Ruptured tendons
in thumb (1989/90)
Best memory last season: Simply
enjoying my rugby
Suggestions to improve rugby:
On-field – Clarify rucking law.
Off-field – Broken time payments

	apps	pts
Ireland B (1979)		
Last Season	1 rep	
Ireland (1984)		
Last Season	0 caps	0
Career	16 caps	0

Other notable landmarks in rugby career: Every game is another landmark
due to Irish selection. Played Irish Schools (1975–76). Won U-23 and B caps
(1979). Became one of only seven players capped at four levels when made
full debut. Toured with Ireland to 1987 World Cup, Japan and France (1988)
and North America (1989). Replacement for Ireland B in 27–12 defeat of
Argentina last season
Touchlines: Walking baby, darts, squash, soccer
Player to watch: Simon Geoghegan (London Irish)

Macdonald, A. E. D.   Scotland

Full Name: Andrew Edward
Douglas Macdonald
1990/91 International category:
Scotland B
Clubs: Heriot's FP
Positions: No.8, lock
Height: 6'8" **Weight:** 17st 10lbs
Occupation: Student
Born: Nairn, 17.1.66
Family: Single
Former clubs: Loughborough
University, London Scottish,
Cambridge University
International debut (B): France
31, Scotland 9, 1989
Best moment in rugby: Winning
1989 Varsity match
Worst moments in rugby: Missing
1988 Varsity match after being
injured five minutes from end of
preceding match. Scotland B's 16-0
defeat by Ireland (1990) after
opposition were reduced to 14 men
only 14 minutes into match
Most embarrassing moment:
Being sent-off and breaking hand
simultaneously in UAU semi-final,
then being headlined as a 'villain' in
Times report

	apps	pts
Scotland B (**1990**)		
Last Season	2 caps	0
Career	4 caps	0
Scotland 1991	Tour to North America	
	World Cup squad	

Most respected opponent: Former Wales lock Robert Norster – constantly
outjumped taller opponents
Serious injuries: Broken hand, ankle ligaments, prolapsed disc (out for three
months)
Other sporting achievements: Bowling Steve James (future cricket star with
Glamorgan) in net practice
Best memory last season: Selection for Scotland B
Suggestions to improve rugby: *On-field* – Eliminate 90-degree scrum wheel
law. Get coaches more involved in selection
Other notable landmarks in rugby career: Capped by Scotland once each
at U-21 and B level. Scotland trial (1990). Represented Scotland B in losses
to Ireland B (0–16) and France B (10–31) last season. Made four appearances
on Scotland's six-match summer tour to North America, including both

non-cap 'tests' v. US Eagles (won 41–12 and scored try) and Canada (lost 19–24)
Touchlines: Keen ukelele player, golf (14-handicap)
Player to watch: Alan Buzza (Wasps)

McDonald, J. P. Ireland

Full Name: John Parker McDonald
1990/91 International category:
Ireland Full
Club: Malone
Position: Hooker
Height: 5'10" **Weight:** 13st 7lbs
Occupation: Civil Servant
Born: Banbridge, Co. Down, 9.4.60
Family: Wendy (wife), Karl and
Lloyd (sons)
Former club: Dungannon
International debut: Ireland 46,
Canada 19, 1987 World Cup
Five Nations' debut: England 23,
Ireland 0, 1990
Best moment in rugby: Making
full Ireland debut in Dunedin
Worst moment in rugby: Having
to pull out of Ireland's 1990 game
with Wales 15 minutes before
kick-off after tearing a calf muscle
warming up. Had even been
included in pre-match team photo!
Most embarrassing moment:
Looking at above photograph
Most respected opponent: Former
Scotland hooker Colin Deans – more
a rugby player than an athlete,
proved size isn't everything

	apps	pts
Ireland B (**1984**)		
Last Season	0 caps	0
Ireland (**1987**)		
Last Season	1 cap	0
Career	4 caps	0

Serious injuries: Torn calf muscle, ankle ligaments (on debut against Canada) and rib cartilage
Best memory last season: Ireland 20, Argentina 18 – result not performance
Suggestions to improve rugby: *On-field* – Diminish value of penalty goal. *Off-field* – Universal uniformity. Why should only some countries' players be afforded luxuries?
Other notable landmarks in rugby career: Influence of former Irish coach

Jimmy Davidson, with whom I played at Dungannon and was coached by with Ulster and Ireland. Made B debut against Scotland (1984/85) and played for Ulster v. Fiji (1985/86). Toured with Ulster to Italy (1986). Called out to 1987 World Cup as second replacement hooker. Toured with Ireland to France (1988) and North America (1989). Involved in perennial battle with Steve Smith for right to play for Ulster and Ireland. Helped Ireland beat Argentina 20–18 in Dublin last season

Touchlines: Weight training, soccer

McGauchie, S.   Scotland

Full Name: Shaun McGauchie
1990/91 International category:
Scotland B
Club: Pontypool
Positions: Fly-half, inside-centre
Height: 5'11" **Weight:** 13st
Occupation: Student
Born: Dumfries, 29.8.64
Family: Single
Former clubs: Annan, Selkirk
International debut (B): Ireland 16, Scotland 0, 1990
Best moment in rugby: Scoring try which put Pontypool into final of 1991 Schweppes Welsh Cup
Worst moment in rugby: Final whistle of Scotland B's 16-0 loss in Belfast
Most respected opponent: Melrose scrum-half Alan Tait
Other sporting achievements: Scottish Schools soccer. Once on books of Queen of the South
Best memory last season: Phone call informing me of my Scotland B selection

	apps	pts
Scotland B (1990)		
Last Season	1 cap	0
Career	1 cap	0

Suggestions to improve rugby:
On-field – Award 5 points for a try to endeavour to make game more expansive. *Off-field* – Authorities must come out and say what can and cannot be done in relation to amateurism question. To many grey areas

Other notable landmarks in rugby career: Did not take up rugby until

aged 17. Captained Scottish Students this season v. Wales and France. Broke into Scotland B team last season
Touchlines: Golf (12-handicap), after-dinner speaking

McIlroy, N. A. Scotland

Full Name: Neil Alexander McIlroy
1990/91 International category: Scotland A (bench)
Club: Jed-Forest
Position: Loose-head prop
Height: 6'2" **Weight:** 15st 11lbs
Occupation: Architectural technician
Born: Gateshead, 19.10.67
Family: Single
Family links with rugby: Brothers Graeme and Alasdair play for Jed
Former club: Jed-Thistle
International debut: Wales U-21 26, Scotland U-21 18, 1989
Best moment in rugby: Selection for Scotland squad
Worst moment in rugby: Being dropped by South last season
Most respected opponent: Heriot's prop Iain Milne
Best memory last season: Selection for Scotland A bench in 39–7 defeat of Spain
Suggestions to improve rugby:
On-field – Greater freedom with rucking: referees are too whistle-happy. *Off-field* – When players are dropped selectors should spend more time explaining reasons why

	apps	pts
Scotland U-21 (**1989**)		
Last Season	0 caps	0
Career	1 cap	0
Scotland A (1990/91)	1 rep	

Other notable landmarks in rugby career: Played for South U-18s and U-21s. Represented Jed-Forest VII last season, and earned selection to Scotland A bench. Previously represented Scotland U-21s in 18–26 loss to Wales U-21s at Neath (1989). Appointed captain of Jed-Forest for this season
Touchlines: Weight training, watching films
Player to watch: Kevin Armstrong (Jed-Forest)

McIntosh, D. L. M.   Scotland

Full Name: Dale Lynsay Manawa
McIntosh
1990/91 International category:
Scotland U-21
Club: Pontypridd
Positions: Flanker, No.8
Height: 6'3" **Weight:** 16st
Occupation: Labourer
Born: Turangi, New Zealand,
23.11.69
Family: Single
Former clubs: King Country (NZ),
Counties (NZ), Hawkes Bay (NZ),
Taupo United (NZ)
International debut (U-21): Wales
23, Scotland 15, 1991
Best moment in rugby: Selection
for Scotland U-21s
Most respected opponent:
Northampton's New Zealand No.8
Wayne Shelford
Best memory last season: Playing
for Pontypridd and touring with
them to America

	apps	pts
Scotland U-21 (1991)		
Last Season	1 cap	0
Career	1 cap	0

Suggestions to improve rugby:
On-field – Standardise refereeing
world-wide. Allow players to get on
with game – too many needless stoppages. *Off-field* – All aspects could be
improved
Other notable landmarks in rugby career: Played two games for New
Zealand U-18s. Qualify for Scotland through grandfather who hails from
Edinburgh
Touchlines: Tennis, weightlifting
Player to watch: Neil Jenkins (Pontypridd)

McIvor, D. J. Scotland

Full Name: David John McIvor
1990/91 International category:
Scotland B
Club: Edinburgh Academicals
Positions: No.8, flanker
Height: 6'1" **Weight:** 16st 8lbs
Occupation: Communications
technician
Born: Kircaldy, 29.6.64
Family: Pauline (wife) and Jamie
(son)
Former clubs: Dunfermline,
Glenrothes
International debut (B): Scotland
10, France 31, 1991
Best moment in rugby: Selection
for B cap at Hughenden
Most respected opponent: Kelso
flanker John Jeffrey
Best memory last season: Helping
North and Midlands beat
Anglo-Scots at Oxford for first win
in McEwan's Scottish Inter-District
Championship since 1984
Suggestions to improve rugby:
On-field – Increase value of try to 5
points and reduce penalty goals to 2
points. Game is so boring at present. *Off-field* – Stay amateur

	apps	pts
Scotland B (1991)		
Last Season	1 cap	0
Career	1 cap	0

Other notable landmarks in rugby career: Played first District game for
North and Midlands in 1986, having represented North and Midlands U-18s
in 1982 and U-21s in 1985. Made Scotland B debut v. France at Hughenden
last season
Touchlines: Golf (14-handicap)
Player to watch: Stuart Reid (Boroughmuir)

McKee, G. T.   Scotland

Full Name: Graham Thomas McKee
1990/91 International category: Scotland U-21
Club: Glasgow High/Kelvinside
Position: Tight-head prop
Height: 5'9" **Weight:** 15st
Occupation: Student
Born: Motherwell, 23.10.69
Family: Single
Former club: Hutchesons
International debut (U-21): Scotland 10, Wales 24, 1990
Best moment in rugby: Being selected for U-21s
Worst moment in rugby: Playing in Scotland Schools side that failed to score with last-minute penalty (run) and, as a result, lost 9–13 to Ireland Schools
Most respected opponent: Scotland loose-head prop David Sole
Best memory last season: Captaining Scotland U-21s and Scotland Students
Suggestions to improve rugby: *On-field* – Revision to rucking laws

	apps	pts
Scotland U-21 (**1990**)		
Last Season	1 cap	0
Career	2 caps	0

so that man obstructing ball on ground should be penalised rather than man trying to get ball (providing no foul is being committed). *Off-field* – Never want to be paid to play but cannot see why players should not be able to benefit, for example, from wearing a certain brand of boots
Other notable landmarks in rugby career: Moved up Scottish representative ladder from Schools (U-18s), Youth, U-19s, Students and Colleges, to U-21s. Captained Scotland U-21s in defeat by Wales at Llanelli
Touchlines: Golf, ten-pin bowling
Player to watch: Leicester wing Tony Underwood

McKee, K. J.   Ireland

Full Name: Kevin John McKee
1990/91 International category:
Ireland U-21
Club: CIYMS, Belfast
Position: Openside flanker
Height: 6'1.5" **Weight:** 13st 7lbs
Occupation: Air conditioning
engineer
Born: Belfast, 13.9.69
Family: Single
Family links with rugby: Father
(Dermot) played for Ulster and was
Ulster senior selector. Grandfather
(Harold) also played for Ulster
International debut: Netherlands
21, Ireland U-21 7, 1990
Best moment in rugby: Helping
Ireland U-21s beat England U-21s
22–16 at Moseley (October 1990)
Best memory last season: Beating
England U-21s

	apps	pts
Ireland U-21 (**1990**)		
Last Season	2 caps	0
Career	2 caps	0

Suggestions to improve rugby:
On-field – Allow more playing ball
on ground. This practice has become
obsolete and has done away with
what being a wing forward is all
about. *Off-field* – Place greater
emphasis on up-and-coming players to nurture them through
Other notable landmarks in rugby career: Captained Ulster U-20s last
season (played v. touring New Zealand team – big thrill). Won two Ireland
U-21 caps, v. Dutch senior team and England U-21s
Touchlines: Golf (15-handicap)
Player to watch: Simon Geoghegan (London Irish)

McKenzie, L.   England

Full Name: Leroy McKenzie
1990/91 International category:
England U-21
Club: Coventry
Position: Wing
Height: 5′9″ **Weight:** 12st 7lbs
Occupation: Estimator (joinery)
Born: Birmingham, 2.9.69
Family: Single
Former clubs: Five Ways, Old
Edwardians
International debut: Netherlands
3, England U-21 24, 1990
Best moment in rugby: Playing
opposite Rory Underwood and
scoring try in only third ever senior
game
Worst moment in rugby: Pulling
both hamstrings playing v. Liverpool
St Helens
Most respected opponents: Jeremy
Guscott (Bath) and Rory
Underwood (Leicester)
Best memory last season: Scoring
winning try for Coventry v. Moseley
for second year running

	apps	pts
England U-21 (1990)		
Last Season	3 caps	4
Career	5 caps	4

Suggestions to improve rugby:
On-field – Less points for a penalty. Instruct TV commentators to get more
excited. *Off-field* – None. In my experience players are treated well. In my
England U-21 matches I have not had to spend a penny. But I think full
internationals should be remunerated for all the extra time they give up to
rugby
Other notable landmarks in career: Played for Greater Birmingham
Schools aged 16 and North Midlands Schools (as flanker). Represented
England U–21s v. French Armed forces (twice), Ireland and Netherlands
(twice – scoring try in 20–18 win in May 1991)
Touchlines: Spending time with girlfriend Julie, listening to soul records
Player to watch: Steve Ojomoh (Bath)

McKinty, S. J.   Ireland

Full Name: Stephen John McKinty
1990/91 International category:
Ireland U-25 (bench)
Club: Bangor
Position: Flanker
Height: 6'4" **Weight:** 15st 3lbs
Occupation: Electrical engineer
Born: Newtownards, 7.7.66
Family: Single
Former club: Edinburgh Univ (four years)
Best moment in rugby: Touring Far East with Edinburgh Univ (1988)
Most respected opponent: Sunday's Well flanker Pat O'Hara
Best memory last season: Bench reserve for Ireland U-25s
Suggestions to improve rugby: *On-field* – More consistent refereeing
Other notable landmarks in rugby career: Won 1985 Ulster Bank Schools Cup at Ravenhill with Bangor GS
Touchlines: Tennis
Player to watch: Simon Geoghegan (London Irish)

	apps
Ireland U-25 (1990/91)	1 rep

Maclean, R. R. W.   Scotland

Full Name: Richard Ruari Willard Maclean
1990/91 International category: Scotland A
Club: Moseley
Positions: Centre, full-back
Height: 5′11″ **Weight:** 13st 7lbs
Occupation: PE teacher
Born: London, 27.9.61
Family: Cindy (wife), Molly (daughter) and Drew (son)
Family links with rugby: Uncle coached Llanelli and is on WRU committee
Former clubs: Old Alleynians, South Glamorgan Institute, Gloucester, Llanelli, Newport
International debut: Spain 7, Scotland A 39, 1990
Best moment in rugby: Helping Anglo-Scots beat France XV 19–16 at Cupar in 1987 (playing opposite Denis Charvet) and being called into Scotland squad for first time afterwards
Worst moment in rugby: Scotland losing 24–28 to Japan (Tokyo 1989)
Most embarrassing moment: Making debut for Moseley against Gloucester – first game since leaving Kingsholm

	apps	pts
Scotland B (**1987**)		
Last Season	1 cap	0
Career	4 caps	0
Scotland A (**1990**)		
Last Season	1 cap	0
Career	1 cap	0

Most respected opponent: Former Wales centre Ray Gravell
Serious injuries: Broken arm, shoulder, leg. Arthritis in back (missed three complete seasons through injuries)
Other sporting achievements: Soccer for Chelsea until aged 15. Qualified tennis coach. Rugby league for Welsh Students
Best memory last season: Captaining Scotland B in 10–31 defeat by France B at Hughenden
Suggestions to improve rugby: *On-field* – Improve sportsmanship in game; it's supposed to be played for enjoyment. Open up game like rugby league has done. Award more points for a try and take any measures necessary to

make the game a better spectacle. Do not be frightened of change. *Off-field* – Clear up pro-am wrangle

Other notable landmarks in rugby career: Injured throughout Schools. Played for Welsh Colleges and captained Welsh Students Rugby League team which beat English counterparts in 1984 for first time. Represented Scotland B four times and, while at Gloucester, Anglo-Scots. Toured with Scotland to Zimbabwe (1988) and Japan (1989). Scotland B v. France B last season marked first occasion when I had ever captained a senior side. Followed up by being appointed captain of Moseley for this season. Helped Scotland A beat Spain 39–7 in Seville (1990). Unavailable for Scotland's 1991 North American tour

Touchlines: Home brew

Player to watch: Neil Martin (Moseley)

Macrae, D. Scotland

Full Name: Duncan Macrae

1990/91 International category: Scotland U-21

Club: Cambridge Univ

Position: Wing

Height: 6′ **Weight:** 13st 10lbs

Occupation: Chemistry student

Born: Bida, Nigeria, 24.12.69

Family: Single

International debut: Wales 26, Scotland 18, 1989

Best moment in rugby: Scoring try for Scotland U-21s in 15–23 loss to Wales U-21s last season

Worst moment in rugby: Being told that I was not going to get a Blue for Cambridge in the 1990 Varsity match – completely gutted

Most embarrassing moment: Listing computing as a favourite hobby in last year's edition of *The Rugby Union Who's Who* – have not heard the end of it!

Most respected opponent: Cambridge Univ/Neath fly-half Adrian Davies

	apps	pts
Scotland U-21 (**1990**)		
Last Season	1 cap	4
Career	2 caps	8

Serious injuries: Concussion (aged 14)
Other sporting achievements: County soccer for Northumberland (until 13)
Best memory last season: Representing Scotland at U-21 level
Suggestions to improve rugby: *On-field* – Award tap-penalty instead of scrummage on certain occasions in bid to keep game flowing. *Off-field* – None. I play rugby for enjoyment ... although if there were any benefits I would be happy to enjoy them too
Other notable landmarks in rugby career: Did not start playing until aged 11. Represented Northumberland U-18s (year young) and Scotland U-18s (two seasons), U-19s and U-21s (two seasons). Scored try for Scotland U-21s in both matches played v. Wales U-21s (1990 and 1991)
Touchlines: Beer
Player to watch: Stuart Reid (Boroughmuir)

Mannion, N. P. S. Ireland

Full Name: Noel Patrick Stephen Mannion
1990/91 International category: Ireland Full
Club: Lansdowne
Positions: No.8, flanker
Height: 6'5" **Weight:** 17st
Occupation: Sales rep
Born: Ballinasloe, 12.1.63
Family: Single
Family links with rugby: Brother plays for Galwegians and Connacht
Former clubs: Ballinasloe, Drumoyne (Aus), Corinthians
International debut: Ireland 49, Western Samoa 22, 1988
Five Nations' debut: Ireland 21, France 26, 1989
Best moment in rugby: Intercepting Welsh kick on own 22 and running ball back for Ireland try in 19–13 win (Cardiff 1989)
Worst moment in rugby: Running a quick penalty for Connacht against Ulster, tripping for no apparent reason, and knocking ball forwards

	apps	pts
Ireland (**1988**)		
Last Season	3 cap	0
	4 reps	
Career	14 caps	4

Most embarrassing moment: As above
Most respected opponent: New Zealand No.8 Wayne Shelford
Serious injuries: Broken collarbone, wrist. Twisted knee
Other sporting achievements: Played one season of Gaelic football for Galway. Came on as replacement in 1987 All-Ireland semi-final replay against Cork
Best memory last season: Winning Senior Cup with Lansdowne
Suggestions to improve rugby: *On-field* – Standardise refereeing in southern and northern hemispheres. Presently too many different interpretations. *Off-field* – Clarify laws regarding amateurism. What, exactly, are we entitled to do? No-one is clear
Other notable landmarks in rugby career: Represented Connacht at Schools and U-20 level before making senior Provincial debut in 1985. Played for Ireland U-25s against Canada following season. Scored famous try in second full appearance. Toured with Ireland to Canada (1989) and was an ever-present. Made Barbarians bow against Newport in 1989/90. Switched clubs from Corinthians to Lansdowne at start of last season. Lost place in Ireland side after 20–18 defeat of Argentina. Ever-present on replacements' bench thereafter but returned to play in both Tests v. Namibia
Touchlines: Music, reading
Player to watch: Simon Geoghegan (London Irish)

Marshall, G. R.   Scotland

Full Name: Graham Robert Marshall
1990/91 International category: Scotland Full
Club: Selkirk
Position: Flanker
Height: 6'3" **Weight:** 15st 7lbs
Occupation: PE teacher
Born: Glasgow, 23.5.60
Family: Anne (wife), Callum (son) and Kirsty (daughter)
Former clubs: Jordanhill, Wakefield
International debut: Scotland 13, Australia 32, 1988
Best moment in rugby: Coming on as replacement for Derek White against Wallabies to win first cap
Worst moment in rugby: Losing 28–24 to Japan (Tokyo 1989)

Most respected opponent:
Whoever playing against next
Serious injuries: Knee (1983)
Best memory last season: Playing for Scotland in 49–3 defeat of Argentina at Murrayfield
Suggestions to improve rugby: *On-field* – Tidy up line-out which is such a mess at present. Perhaps revert to double-banking. *Off-field* – Clarify amateur situation

	apps	pts
Scotland B (**1987**)		
Last Season	0 caps	0
Career	2 caps	0
Scotland (**1988**)		
Last Season	1 cap	0
1991	World Cup squad	
Career	3 caps	0
Scotland VII (**1991**)	Hong Kong Sevens	

Other notable landmarks in rugby career: Toured with Scotland to Japan (1989), New Zealand (1990) and North America (1991). Played in 38–17 win v. Fiji (Oct 1989). Played one season for Scottish Schools. Twice represented Scottish XVs and twice Scotland B (1988). Won third full cap when touring Pumas visited Murrayfield last season. Bench reserve throughout 1991 Five Nations' Championship. Played in first official Scotland VII at 1991 Hong Kong Sevens
Player to watch: Stuart Reid (Boroughmuir)

Matthews, N. J.   England

Full Name: Neil John Matthews
1990/91 International category: England U-21
Club: Gloucester
Position: Fly-half
Height: 5'10" **Weight:** 13st
Occupation: Contracts manager/buyer
Born: Gloucester, 11.4.70
Family: Single
Family links with rugby: Father (Tom) played for Longlevens. Brother (Wayne) plays No.8 for Gordon League
Former club: Longlevens, Cheltenham Colts
International debut (U-21): England 16, Ireland 22, 1990
Best moment in rugby: Earning selection for England Colts
Worst moment in rugby: Breaking

thumb in first half of first International for England Colts (v. Italy) to end my season

Best memory last season: Scoring try for England U-21s v. French Armed Forces

Serious injuries: Broken thumb

Suggestions to improve rugby:
On-field – More points for a try. Less points for a penalty

Other notable landmarks in rugby career: Made debut for England U-21s at fly-half in 16–22 defeat by Ireland U-21s last season, and retained place throughout season, winning further caps v. Netherlands and French Armed Forces (scoring game's only try in 7–9 loss). Started out with Longlevens (until aged 17). Played for Cheltenham, Gloucestershire and England Colts. Invited to tour Portugal with Gloucester (aged 18). Played three seasons at Kingsholm

Touchlines: Pool, golf

Player to watch: Lawrie Beck (Gloucester)

	apps	pts
England U-21 (**1990**)		
Last Season	3 caps	4
Career	3 caps	4

Matthews, P. M.   Ireland

Full Name: Philip Michael Matthews

1990/91 International category: Ireland Full

Club: Wanderers

Position: Flanker

Height: 6′3″ **Weight:** 16st

Occupation: Marketing manager

Born: Gloucester, 24.1.60

Family: Lisa (wife) and Hannah (daughter)

Family links with rugby: Father-in-law is former Ireland International Kevin Flynn (1959–73)

Former clubs: Queen's University Belfast, Ards

International debut: Ireland 9, Australia 16, 1984

Five Nations' debut: Scotland 18, Ireland 15, 1985

Best moment in rugby: Scoring for Barbarians against 1989 All Blacks at Twickenham

Worst moment in rugby: 1987 World Cup – injured in first game
Most respected opponent: None in particular
Serious injuries: Dislocated elbow
Best memory last season: Getting back to playing well after two years suffering from Post-Viral Fatigue Syndrome

	apps	pts
Ireland (1984)		
Last Season	5 caps	0
Career	32 caps	16

Suggestions to improve rugby: *On-field* – More points for a try and reduce value of penalty goal. All conversions to be taken under posts. *Off-field* – Pay players (you have to take extreme line to get any change). Remove shackles of amateurism and take realistic long-term view of what is happening in other sports
Other notable landmarks in rugby career: The Bull & Bear in Hong Kong. Won five Schools caps (1977–78), captaining team three times. Became Ards' first International when capped in 1984. Captained Ireland six times. Irish rugby writers' choice as 'Player of Year' in 1988. Represented Barbarians and Home Unions (against France) in 1989/90. Ever present for Ireland in 1991 Five Nations' Championship campaign. Captained Ireland in Namibia last summer
Touchlines: Golf
Players to watch: Simon Geoghegan/Jim Staples (London Irish)

Milne, D. F.   Scotland

Full Name: David Ferguson Milne
1990/91 International category:
Scotland Full (bench)
Club: Heriot's FP
Position: Prop
Height: 5'11.5" **Weight:** 15st 8lbs
Occupation: Sales manager for
pharmaceutical company
Born: Edinburgh, 7.12.58
Family: Julia (wife) and Rory (son)
Family links with rugby: Brothers
Kenny and Iain play for Heriot's and
Scotland
Former clubs: Bordeaux Students
(France, 1981–82), Worcester,
Stourbridge
International debut (B): France
10, Scotland 12, 1986
Best moment in rugby: Helping
comprise all-Milne front row for
Barbarians v. East Midlands in 1989
Mobbs Memorial match
Worst moment in rugby: Heriot's
throwing away chance of McEwan's
Scottish League Championship with
diabolical team performance in
defeat at hands of champions-to-be
Boroughmuir
Most respected opponent: France
prop Pascal Ondarts

	apps	pts
Scotland B (**1986**)		
Last Season	1 cap	0
	1 rep	
Career	6 caps	0
	2 reps	
Scotland (**1990/91**)	4 reps	
1991	World Cup squad	

Best memory last season: Involvement with Scotland set-up at top level
Serious injuries: Ruptured cruciate ligaments in both knees. Prior to 1990/91
season surgeon advised me to stop playing. Undergone eight knee operations
in all
Suggestions to improve rugby: *On-field* – Differential penalty to judge
between technical and physical violation (worth 1 and 3 points respectively).
Far too easy to score/concede points through technical infringements at
present. Take all conversions in front of posts. *Off-field* – Relax demands on
players at top level to have to play at various representative levels. If selected
for a side one should be trusted more to devise one's own fitness programme
etc. Too many squad sessions – more consideration for players' families
Other notable landmarks in rugby career: Played for Edinburgh Schools

and, later, in Scottish Inter-District Championship, for Anglo-Scots and Edinburgh. First Scotland appearance for U-21s v. British Post Office! Scotland replacement in each of 1991 Five Nations' matches. Also replacement for Scotland B v. Ireland B, but played in 10–31 loss to France B at Hughenden. Toured to North America with Scotland (1991)
Touchlines: Weightlifting, keeping fit
Player to watch: Stuart Reid (Boroughmuir)

Milne, I. G.   Scotland

Full Name: Iain Gordon Milne
1990/91 International category: Scotland Full (bench)
Club: Heriot's FP
Position: Tight-head prop
Height: 6' **Weight:** 17st 9lbs
Occupation: Sales manager in printing industry
Born: Edinburgh, 17.6.58
Family: Marian (wife)
Family links with rugby: Kenny (brother) plays for Heriot's and Scotland. David (brother) plays for Heriot's and Scotland B and is bench reserve for Scotland
Former club: Harlequins
International debut: Scotland 11, Ireland 11, 1979
Five Nations' debut: As above
Best moments in rugby: Winning 1979 Scottish Championship with Heriot's and 1984 Grand Slam with Scotland
Worst moment in rugby: Damaging bones in a foot against Wales in 1989 and missing game against England
Most embarrassing moment: Putting on too much Deep Heat
before first match as Heriot's captain and having to leave for a shower midway through my first pre-match team talk
Most respected opponent: Any French front row forward

	apps	pts
Scotland (**1979**)		
Last Season	1 rep	
1991	World Cup squad	
Career	44 caps	0
Lions 1983		
1986		

180

Best memory last season: Getting back into Scotland team in New Zealand (1990)

Suggestions to improve rugby: *On-field* – Play Internationals later in season. 90-degree wheels: put-in should go to team going forwards. Penalise heavily those players trying to be negative and destructive in pile-up situations. *Off-field* – Too many idiosyncracies between nations over amateurism. Should be unified and carved in tablets of stone

Other notable landmarks in rugby career: First called into national squad as 20-year-old in 1978. Toured New Zealand with 1983 British Lions. With Scotland, toured New Zealand (1981 and 1990), Australia (1982) and North America (1985), and played in 1987 World Cup. Bench reserve for Scotland's 49–3 defeat of Argentina last season. Serious ear infection cut down playing time last season. Intend giving international rugby one more crack in bid to make World Cup

Touchlines: Keen angler (salmon and trout)

Player to watch: Stuart Reid (Boroughmuir)

Milne, K. S. Scotland

Full Name: Kenneth Stuart Milne
1990/91 International category: Scotland Full
Club: Heriot's FP
Position: Hooker
Height: 6′ **Weight:** 15st
Occupation: Sales rep for printing firm
Born: Edinburgh, 1.12.61
Family: Eleanor (wife) and Stuart (son)
Family links with rugby: Iain (brother) plays for Heriot's, Scotland and British Lions. David (brother) plays for Heriot's, Scotland B and is currently in full Scotland squad
International debut: Scotland 23, Wales 7, 1989
Five Nations' debut: As above
Best moment in rugby: 1990 Grand Slam
Worst moment in rugby: Being dropped at any level
Most embarrassing moment: Accidentally flooring the referee when the front rows of Heriot's and Jed-Forest squared up. He let me off!

Most respected opponents:
Scotland's Gary Callender and
England's Brian Moore
Best memory last season: The
reception I received when I ran onto
the pitch at Murrayfield as
replacement for Scotland against
Wales
Suggestions to improve rugby:
On-field – Scottish Inter-District
Championship should be broadened

	apps	pts
Scotland B (1986)		
Last Season	0 caps	0
Career	6 caps	
Scotland (1989)		
Last Season	4 caps	8
	1 rep	
1991	World Cup squad	
Career	15 caps	12

to include likes of Bath and Leicester. A British League of sorts, with stronger
opposition, must be the way forward. *Off-field* – Clarification of amateurism
issue desperately needed
Other notable landmarks in rugby career: Ever-present in 1990
Championship team. Scored first International try against Fiji (Oct 1989).
First Scotland hooker to score two tries in International (in last season's 49–3
defeat of Argentina). Toured North America with Scotland (1991), playing
v. Alberta, Rugby East and Ontario, but losing out to John Allan in non-cap
'test' matches v. US Eagles and Canada
Touchlines: Fly fishing, golf
Player to watch: Andy Nicol (Dundee HSFP)

Moncrieff, M.   Scotland

Full Name: Mark Moncrieff
1990/91 International category:
Scotland A
Club: Gala
Position: Wing
Height: 5'10" **Weight:** 11st 10lbs
Occupation: Sales assistant,
McQueen Ltd
Born: Edinburgh, 19.12.68
Family: Single
Former club: Hutt Old Boys
(Wellington, NZ)
International debut: Spain 7,
Scotland A 39, 1990
Best moment in rugby: Selection
for 1991 Scotland tour to North
America
Worst moment in rugby: Injury

182

preventing participation in Scotland U-19s v. West Germany

Most embarrassing moment: Missing eight weeks rugby after injuring an ankle whilst trying to rescue a neighbour's cat

Most respected opponent: Australia's Ian Williams

Best memory last season: Breaking through into Scotland A team for game in Spain

Suggestions to improve rugby: *On-field* – Award more points for a try and less for a penalty. *Off-field* – Ensure that any future player-benefits are spread equally throughout XV and not hogged by minority

Other notable landmarks in rugby career: Won 4 caps for Scottish Schools (U-18s) and 1 for U-19s (against Italy). Scored only try Australian Schools conceded during tour, for Scotland Schools (U-18s) at Murrayfield. Played for triumphant South in last season's Scottish Inter-District Championship, having previously turned out for South U-21s. Spent summer of 1990 playing in New Zealand. Went to Hong Kong for XVs event prior to Sevens (1991). Made Scotland B debut in 10–31 loss to France B (Hughenden, 1991). Late call-up to Scotland's summer tour of North America and was adjudged one of the successes, winning place in non-cap 'test' side v. US Eagles and Canada. Hat-trick of tries in 76–7 win over Alberta

Touchlines: Hill walking, holidays

Player to watch: Gregor Townsend (Gala)

	apps	pts
Scotland U-21 (1989/90)		
Career	1 rep	
Scotland B (**1991**)		
Last Season	1 cap	0
Career	1 cap	0
Scotland A (**1990**)		
Last Season	1 cap	0
Career	1 cap	0
Scotland 1991	Tour to North America World Cup squad	

Moon, R. H. St J. B.   England

Full Name: Rupert Henry St. John
Barker Moon
1990/91 International category:
England B
Club: Llanelli
Position: Scrum-half
Height: 6′ **Weight:** 13st
Occupation: Student
Born: Birmingham, 1.2.68
Family: Single
Family links with rugby: Brother
(Richard) plays scrum-half for
Rosslyn Park. Sister (Estel) plays
scrum-half/back row for Wasps
Ladies. All three of us have got
winners' medals in national
competitions. Is this a record?
Former clubs: Walsall, Abertillery,
Neath
International debut (U-21):
Romania 13, England 54, 1989
Best moments in rugby: Scoring
first try in above match in Bucharest,
and captaining England Students
Worst moment in rugby: Failed
drop goal in quarter-finals of
1990/91 Welsh Cup
Most embarrassing moment:
Saying my full name on national
television

	apps	pts
England U-21 (**1989**)		
Last season	0 caps	0
Career	1 cap	4
England B (**1990**)		
Last Season	4 caps	8
	1 rep	
Career	4 caps	8
England	1995 Development squad	

Most respected opponents:
Former Wales scrum-half David Bishop and brother Richard
Serious injuries: Popped rib cartilage
Other sporting achievements: Cricket for Walsall. Soccer for Midlands
Schools
Best memory last season: Winning man-of-match award in 1990/91
Schweppes Welsh Cup final
Suggestions to improve rugby: *On-field* – Scrap farcical 90-degree scrum
wheel law. Only allow kicking inside 22. Clarify interpretation of tackle law.
Can you pass ball on ground or not? *Off-field* – Give all Student rugby players
free food vouchers (but never money)
Other notable landmarks in rugby career: Sat on bench for England

Schools, stood on wing for England Students (twice) and Colts. Represented England in 1988 Student World Cup. Included in Neath's squad for Schweppes Cup final defeat of Bridgend. Joined Llanelli at start of last season and proceeded to break into England B team, and scored two tries in 50–6 defeat of Spain. Bench reserve for 12–9 win v. Italy. Helped Llanelli beat Pontypool to win 1990/91 Welsh Cup

Touchlines: Any novelty sports, golf, eating
Player to watch: Jonathan Locke (Cambridge Univ)

Moore, A.   Scotland

Full Name: Alexander Moore
1990/91 International category:
Scotland Full
Club: Edinburgh Academicals
Position: Wing
Height: 5'7" **Weight:** 13st
Occupation: Sales rep
Born: Queensland, Australia,
19.8.63
Family: Gareth and Christopher
(sons)
Former clubs: Livingston, Gala
International debut: New Zealand
21, Scotland 18, 1990
Five Nations' debut: France 15,
Scotland 9, 1991
Best moment in rugby: Winning
first cap in second Test at Auckland
(1990)
Worst moments in rugby: Being
left out of Edinburgh side to play
1988 Australians. Missing Irish
game (1991) with groin/pelvic injury
Most respected opponent:
Scotland wing Iwan Tukalo
Serious injuries: Dislocated collar
bone (1982), groin/pelvic strain
(1991)
Best memory last season: Making
Five Nations' debut in Paris

	apps	pts
Scotland B (**1986**)		
Last Season	0 caps	0
Career	3 caps	4
Scotland (**1990**)		
Last Season	4 caps	4
1991	World Cup squad	
Career	5 caps	8

Suggestions to improve rugby: *On-field* – Differentiate between technical and physical violations. Make 1 point available for 'technical' penalty goals (minor misdemeanour) and 3 for 'physical'. *Off-field* – Carry on with good work. New image rugby and Youth development officers are taking game in right direction

Other notable landmarks in rugby career: Won three Scotland 'B' caps (against Italy, Ireland and France). Toured with Scotland to Zimbabwe in 1988. Winning 1988 Scottish Inter-District Championship with Edinburgh. Selected to tour North America last summer but forced to withdraw with pelvic strain, to be replaced by Gala's Mark Moncrieff. Scored second international try in Scotland's 49–3 defeat of Argentina (1990).

Touchlines: High jump, power weightlifting, golf, budding saxophonist
Player to watch: Stuart Reid (Boroughmuir)

Moore, B. C.   England

Full Name: Brian Christopher Moore
1990/91 International category: England Full
Club: Harlequins
Position: Hooker
Height: 5'9" **Weight:** 14st 2lbs
Occupation: Corporate financier
Born: Birmingham, 11.1.62
Family: Single
Former clubs: Old Crossleyans, Nottingham
International debut: England 21, Scotland 12, 1987
Five Nations' debut: As above
Best moment in rugby: 1989 Lions beating Australia in third Test to clinch series
Worst moment in rugby: Wales 16, England 3, 1987 World Cup quarter-final
Most embarrassing moment: Being forced to watch pre-match team talks on video
Most respected opponent: England lock Wade Dooley's wallet – I have never managed to open it!
Serious injuries: Fractured ego v. Scotland, Murrayfield 1990
Other sporting achievements: Intermediate swimming certificate
Best memory last season: First scrum – England 34, Wales 6
Suggestions to improve rugby: Automatic retirement from RFU Committee

186

at 55. Player representation on all major decision and law-making committees. Major revision of amateurism laws, along with those concerning foul play, line-outs and kickable penalties. Southern hemisphere referees to be prevented from officiating Grand Slam deciders **Other notable landmarks in rugby career:** Beneficiary of Mark Bailey's understating and self-deprecating wit. Missed only 2 of England's last 31 matches. Have captained England B and Nottingham. Voted Whitbread/*Rugby World* 'Player of Year' for 1990/91 season. Ever-present in 1989 Lions' 2–1 series win over Australia. Toured Argentina (1990) and Australia (1991) with England

Touchlines: Not allowed life outside rugby in these amateur days

	apps	pts
England B (1985)		
Last Season	0 caps	0
England (1987)		
Last Season	6 caps	0
1991	Tour to Australia World Cup squad	
Career	31 caps	4
Lions 1989	3 Tests	0

Morris, C. D. England

Full Name: Colin **Dewi** Morris
1990/91 International category: England Full (bench)
Club: Orrell
Position: Scrum-half
Height: 6′ **Weight:** 13st 7lbs
Occupation: Distillery production controller
Born: Crickhowell, Wales, 9.2.64
Family: Single
Former clubs: Brecon, Crewe & Alsager College, Winnington Park, Liverpool St Helens
International debut: England 28, Australia 19, 1988
Five Nations' debut: England 12, Scotland 12, 1989
Best moments in rugby: Scoring try on England debut and winning. Scoring winning try for North in 15–9 defeat of Australia (Oct 1988)
Worst moment in rugby: Losing 9–12 to Wales at Cardiff (March 1989)
Most embarrassing moment: Being dropped by North for match v. US

Eagles after five consecutive International caps and five consecutive Divisional caps

Most respected opponent: Wales scrum-half Robert Jones – possesses perfect pass and kick

Serious injuries: Broken nose (three times), serious ligament damage to left shoulder, both knees and right ankle

	apps	pts
England B (1988)		
Last Season	0 caps	0
England (1988)		
Last Season	0 caps	0
	4 reps	
Career	5 caps	4
1995 Development squad		

Other sporting achievements: Gwent Schools U-19 County cricket finalists

Best memories last season: Selection for England squad again, throughout Grand Slam, and for summer tour to Australia

Suggestions to improve rugby: *On-field* – More consistency among referees. Immediate action for serious offences. Reduce points-worth of penalties to 2 points. Scrap 90-degree scrummaging law

Other notable landmarks in rugby career: Progressing from junior rugby to International level in six months (Winnington Park-LSH-Lancashire-North-England B-England). Toured with England to Argentina (1990) and Australia (1991)

Touchlines: Holidays spent on lazy beaches

Rugby Hates: Reporters who have never played game to any notable standard, let alone on International stage, talking as if they could do better and know all the answers

Player to watch: Martin Hynes (Orrell)

Morris, M. S.   Wales

Full Name: Martyn Stuart Morris
1990/91 International category:
Wales Full
Club: Neath
Position: Flanker
Height: 6′3″ **Weight:** 14st
Occupation: Police officer
Born: Neath, 23.8.62
Family: Rhian (wife) and Emily
(daughter)
Former clubs: Neath Athletic,
South Wales Police
International debut: Scotland 21,
Wales 25, 1985
Five Nations' debut: As above
Best moment in rugby: Being
recalled to Welsh team against
Ireland last season after five years
away
Worst moment in rugby: Being
dropped in first place
Most respected opponents: 1989
All Blacks
Serious injuries: Broken nose
Other sporting achievements:
Cricket for Neath
Best memory last season:
Winning Welsh premier division title
with Neath
Suggestions to improve rugby:
On-field – Better standard of
refereeing in Wales. *Off-field* –
Improved treatment of players

	apps	pts
Wales B (**1983**)		
Last Season	0 caps	0
Career	2 caps	8
Wales (**1985**)		
Last Season	3 caps	0
1991	Tour to Australia	
	World Cup squad	
Career	9 caps	0
Heineken 1990/91	11 apps	8

Other notable landmarks in rugby career: Former vice-captain of Wales
Youth (played No.8) and also represented Wales B before making full debut
in 1985. Rejoined Neath in 1989/90 from SWP. Represented Wales v.
Barbarians, Ireland and France last season
Touchlines: Road running for training, cricket
Player to watch: Kevin Fox (Neath)

Moseley, K.   Wales

Full Name: Kevin Moseley
1990/91 International category:
World Cup squad
Club: Newport
Position: Lock
Height: 6'7" **Weight:** 17st 6lbs
Occupation: Printer
Born: Blackwood, 2.7.63
Former clubs: Blackwood, Bay of
Plenty (NZ), Pontypool
International debut: New Zealand
54, Wales 9, 1988
Five Nations' debut: Scotland 23,
Wales 7, 1989
Best moment in rugby: Winning
first cap for Wales
Worst moment in rugby: Being
sent off playing for Wales against
France at Cardiff last season
Most embarrassing moment: As
above
Serious injuries: Damaged foot
(1988)
Suggestions to improve rugby:
On-field – Award more points for a
try. *Off-field* – Clubs should treat
players' families better
**Other notable landmarks in rugby
career:** A footballer until aged 17.
Began rugby career with home-club
Blackwood, before moving to
Pontypool in 1984. Spent season
playing with Bay of Plenty in New

	apps	pts
Wales B (1984)		
Last Season	0 caps	0
Career	6 caps	0
Wales (1988)		
Last Season	0 caps	0
1991	World Cup squad	
Career	5 caps	0
Heineken 1990/91		
(with Pontypool)	7 apps	0
(with Newport)	5 apps	0

Zealand's Inter-Provincial Championship (14 appearances). Played for Wales
B and toured New Zealand (1988) with Wales. Was unavailable for 1991 tour
to Australia but was included in Wales' preliminary squad for 1991 World
Cup
Touchlines: DIY, walking dog
Player to watch: David Llewellyn (Newport)

Mruk, L. M.   Wales

Full Name: Lee Mark Mruk
1990/91 International category:
Wales U-21
Club: Pontypool
Positions: Lock, back row
Height: 6′4″ **Weight:** 15st 10lbs
Occupation: Production operator
Born: Newport, 17.10.69
Family: Single
Former clubs: Talywain, Pontypool
United
International debut (U-21): Wales
23, Scotland 15, 1991
Best moment in rugby: Scoring
tries on both appearances for Wales
U-21s last season
Worst moment in rugby: Missing
Wales U-21 v. Scotland U-21 in
1990 after breaking thumb
Most respected opponent:
Pontypool's Dean Oswald
Best memory last season:
Pontypool reaching Schweppes
Welsh Cup final
Suggestions to improve rugby:
Nothing needed either on or off field
**Other notable landmarks in rugby
career:** Scored try for Wales U-21s
in 23–15 defeat of Scotland last
season and another in defeat of Rugby News New Zealand U-21 XV (1990)
Touchlines: Swimming, keep fit

	apps	pts
Wales U-21 (**1991**)		
Last Season	1 cap	4
v. New Zealand XV	1 app	4
Career	1 cap	4
Heineken 1990/91	4 apps	0

Mullin, B. J.   Ireland

Full Name: Brendan John Mullin
1990/91 International category:
Ireland Full
Club: Blackrock College
Position: Centre
Height: 6'1" **Weight:** 13st
Occupation: Stockbroker
Born: Israel, 31.10.63
Family: Single
Former clubs: Trinity College
Dublin, Oxford University, London
Irish
International debut: Ireland 9,
Australia 16, 1984
Five Nations' debut: Scotland 15,
Ireland 18, 1985
Best moment in rugby: Selection
for 1989 Lions
Worst moment in rugby: Ireland's
dreadful campaign at 1987 World
Cup
Most respected opponent: Former
Australian centre Brett Papworth
Serious injuries: Operation on knee
cartilage (1989/90)
Other sporting achievements:
International hurdling for Ireland
Best memory last season:
Attractive rugby played by Ireland,
especially v. Wales and Scotland
Suggestions to improve rugby:
Off-field – International Rugby
Board must give sport some direction and leadership. Rugby has outgrown
what archaic IRB was set up to administer. Disgressionary element handed
to Unions by IRB is ridiculous – has led to utter confusion
Other notable landmarks in rugby career: Jim Burns, hurdles coach at
school and still, has been major influence on career which began, in
representative terms, when played six times for Irish Schools (1981–82), three
as captain. Made B debut against Scotland in 1983 and following season broke
into full team. Played for 1986 Lions against The Rest in Cardiff to mark
centenary of IRB. Scored three tries against Tonga in 1987 World Cup. Won
two Oxford Blues (1986,87). 1988/89 Irish Player of Year. Leading try-scorer

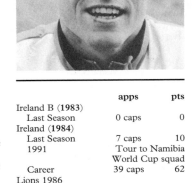

	apps	pts
Ireland B (**1983**)		
Last Season	0 caps	0
Ireland (**1984**)		
Last Season	7 caps	10
1991	Tour to Namibia	
	World Cup squad	
Career	39 caps	62
Lions 1986		
1989	1 Test	0

for 1989 Lions with seven. Played for Lions in first Test v. Australia, and v. Anzacs, and for 1989 Home Unions in 29–27 defeat of France. Scored tries v. Wales and Scotland in last season's Five Nations' Championship. Set new Irish try-scoring record with No.15 in 25–28 loss at Murrayfield
Touchlines: Tennis
Player to watch: Simon Geoghegan (London Irish)

Mullins, A. R. England

Full Name: Andrew Richard Mullins
1990/91 International category: England B
Club: Harlequins
Position: Tight-head prop
Height: 5'11" **Weight:** 16st
Occupation: Accountant
Born: Eltham, London, 12.12.64
Family: Married
Former clubs: Old Alleynians, Durham University
International debut: England 58, Fiji 23, 1989
Best moment in rugby: Running out at Twickenham against Fiji
Worst moment in rugby: Not making London team immediately after Fiji game. Knew that would determine England selection as Jeff Probyn got nod instead
Most disappointing moment: Grounding ball inches short of try-line against Fijians
Biggest problem in rugby: Wasps' England tight-head Jeff Probyn
Most respected opponent: England loose-head Paul 'Judge' Rendall – good all-rounder in bar
Serious injuries: Broken nose, broken bone in foot
Other sporting achievements: London Schools breaststroke swimming champion
Suggestions to improve rugby: Adopt a more professional (but realistic)

	apps	pts
England B (1988)		
Last Season	1 cap	0
England (1989)		
Last Season	0 caps	0
	1995 Development squad	
Career	1 cap	0

approach over training. RFU sent out training timetables which are not practical because of time involved. More helpful if they arranged memberships of local gyms and health clubs for players

Other notable landmarks in rugby career: Switched from flanker to prop aged 16 and immediately won selection to England Schools. Spent year in Army between school and Durham University. Represented England U-23s (1986) and joined Harlequins (1987/88). Share birthdate with fellow Quin Will Carling, who played in same University and England 18-Group Schools team. Played in English team at 1988 Student World Cap and same year made B debut against Australia. Represented England B in 12–9 defeat of Italy last season

Touchlines: Enjoy black and white films, especially 'The Thirty Nine Steps'

Murphy, K. J.   Ireland

Full Name: Kenneth John Murphy
1990/91 International category: Ireland Full
Club: Cork Constitution
Position: Full-back
Height: 6′ **Weight:** 12st 7lbs
Occupation: Family garage business
Born: Cork, 31.7.66
Family: Single
Family links with rugby: Father and grandfather both played for Ireland
International debut: England 23, Ireland 0, 1990
Five Nations' debut: As above
Best moment in rugby: Winning 1990/91 All-Ireland League with Cork Con
Worst moment in rugby: Missing penalty which cost Christian Brothers College Junior Schools Cup
Most respected opponents: Full-backs Gavin Hastings (Scotland) and Serge Blanco (France)
Best memory last season: All-Ireland League win
Other notable landmarks in rugby

	apps	pts
Ireland B (**1989**)		
Last Season	0 caps	0
Ireland (**1990**)		
Last Season	4 caps	0
	1 rep	
Career	8 caps	0

career: Unique family record – father and grandfather also played for country. Played Irish Schools against Junior All Blacks (1985). Represented Combined Provinces on internal tour and was a replacement for Ireland U-25s against Italy (1989). Despite losing No.15 jersey to Jim Staples last season, still made four appearances, twice replacing the unfortunate Staples

Player to watch: Philip Soden (Constitution)

Murray, N. R.   Ireland

Full Name: Niall Richard Murray
1990/91 International category:
Ireland U-21
Club: Cork Constitution
Position: Centre
Height: 6'2" **Weight:** 13st
Occupation: Bank official
Born: Cork, 5.7.69
Family: Single
Family links with rugby: Father played for Cork Constitution, Munster and Barbarians. Current International selector
International debut: Netherlands 21, Ireland U-21 7, 1990
Best moments in rugby: Winning 1989 Senior Cup and 1990/91 All-Ireland League with Cork Con. Representing Ireland U-21s
Worst moment in rugby: Shoulder injury
Best memory last season: Cork Con's All-Ireland League win
Most respected opponent: Dolphin's Michael Kiernan
Suggestions to improve rugby:
On-field – Standardise refereeing across both hemispheres

	apps	pts
Ireland U-21 (**1990**)		
Last Season	2 caps	0
Career	2 caps	0

Other notable landmarks in rugby career: Broke into Ireland U-21 team last season, making debut in Leiden v. Netherlands' senior team and winning second cap in 22–16 win over England U-21s at Moseley
Touchlines: Golf, swimming
Player to watch: Rory Moloney (University College Cork)

Nichol, S. A.   Scotland

Full Name: Scott Alan Nichol
1990/91 International category:
Scotland B
Club: Selkirk
Positions: Fly-half (U-21), left wing
(Schools)
Height: 5'10" **Weight:** 11st 7lbs
Occupation: Fireman
Born: Selkirk, 18.6.70
Family: Single
Family links with rugby: Alan Reid
(grandfather) played for Watsonians
and Edinburgh in 1930s and 1940s
International debut (U-21):
Scotland 10, Wales 24, 1990
Best moment in rugby: Being
selected to tour North America and
Canada with Scotland (1991)
Worst moments in rugby: Getting
injured at first training session in
New Zealand and missing first three
games. Missing last summer's tour
through injury
Most embarrassing moment:
Mistaking centre line at kick-off
Most respected opponent: John
Jeffrey – always gives 100 per cent
effort

	apps	pts
Scotland U-21 (**1990**)		
Last Season	1 cap	4
Career	2 caps	4
Scotland B (**1990**)		
Last Season	2 caps	0
Career	2 caps	0
Scotland VII (**1991**)	Hong Kong Sevens	
Scotland 1991	World Cup squad	

Other sporting achievements:
U-15 Border tennis champion
Best memory last season: First visit to Hong Kong Sevens
Suggestions to improve rugby: *On-field* – More running; less points for
penalty goals. *Off-field* – Scotland having parity with England and Wales in
sponsorship deals
Other notable landmarks in rugby career: Touring Canada with Selkirk
High School. Toured with Scottish Schools to New Zealand (1987/88).
Selection for South U-21s, Scotland U-19s and U-21s. Scored one of Scotland
U-21s' three tries in 15–23 loss to Wales U-21 last season before being forced
to withdraw from Scotland tour to North America with ankle ligament trouble
Touchlines: Golf (16-handicap)
Player to watch: Stuart Reid (Boroughmuir)

Nicol, A. D.   Scotland

Full Name: Andrew Douglas Nicol
1990/91 International category:
Scotland B
Club: Dundee High School FP
Position: Scrum-half
Height: 5'11.5" **Weight:** 12st 3lbs
Occupation: Estate management
student
Born: Dundee, 12.3.71
Family: Single
Family links with rugby: Alastair
(brother) plays for Scotland U-18s,
Army, and Dundee HSFP. George
Ritchie (grandfather) played for
Scotland v. England at Twickenham
(1932)
Former club: Heriot's FP
International debut (B): Scotland
10, France 31, 1991
Best moment in rugby: Selection
for Scotland's 1991 tour to North
America
Worst moment in rugby: Sprung
collarbone after two minutes of
crucial Scottish second division
match v. Watsonians last season

	apps	pts
Scotland B (**1991**)		
Last Season	1 cap	4
	1 rep	
Scotland 1991	Tour to North America	
	World Cup squad	

Other sporting achievements:
Cricket for Dundee High School CC
Most respected opponent: Jed-Forest scrum-half Gary Armstrong
Serious injuries: Sprung collarbone (five weeks out), medial ligament,
dislocated elbow, concussion
Best memory last season: Scoring try on Scotland B debut at Hughenden
Suggestions to improve rugby: *On-field* – More consistency in appreciation
of laws. *Off-field* – Allow players to benefit from rugby-related activities
Other notable landmarks in rugby career: Played three seasons for
Scotland Schools. Captained Schools and Scotland U-19s (great honour).
One game for Scotland U-21s (concussed v. Combined Services) before
earning Scotland B call-up. Bench reserve for Scotland B in 0–16 loss to
Ireland B (1990). Went on Scotland's 1991 summer tour to North America,
playing v. Alberta (won 76–7), Rugby East (won 24–12) and Ontario (won
43–3) and scoring a try in each match
Touchlines: Golf, cricket
Player to watch: Stuart Reid (Boroughmuir)

O'Hara, P. T.   Ireland

Full Name: Patrick Thomas O'Hara
1990/91 International category:
Ireland Full
Club: Sunday's Well
Position: Flanker
Height: 6'2" **Weight:** 15st
Occupation: Sales director
Born: Essex, England, 4.8.61
Family: Married with two sons
International debut: Ireland 49,
Western Samoa 22, 1988
Five Nations' debut: Ireland 21,
France 26, 1989
Best moment in rugby: First full
cap against France
Worst moment in rugby: Getting
concussed against England 1989
(lost 3–16)
Most embarrassing moment:
Playing in front of provincial
selectors in 1984/85, ended up in
centre and attempted long pass to
wing that was intercepted for try
Most respected opponent:
Scotland flanker Finlay Calder –
great reader of the game, very street
wise, and always willing to advise
Other sporting achievements:
Won a number of cross-country
races when in Essex

	apps	pts
Ireland B (**1991**)		
Last Season	1 cap	0
Career	1 cap	0
Ireland (**1988**)		
Last Season	1 caps	0
Career	10 caps	0

Best memory last season: Sunday's Well beating Dolphin to qualify for
All-Ireland League
Suggestions to improve rugby: *On-field* – Play ball on ground, within reason
Other notable landmarks in rugby career: Munster against 1984 Wallabies
and 1989 All Blacks. Cork Charity Cup (1981), Irish tours to France (1988)
and North America (1989). Irish debut 15 minutes from end v. Western
Samoa, replacing Phil Matthews. Helped Ireland B defeat England
counterparts 24–10
Touchlines: Built garden shed all by myself

Ojomoh, S. O.   England

Full Name: Stephen Oziegbe Ojomoh
1990/91 International category: England U-21
Club: Bath
Positions: No.8, blindside flanker
Height: 6'2" **Weight:** 16st
Occupation: Law/accountancy student
Born: Benin City, Nigeria, 25.5.70
Family: Single
Former club: Rosslyn Park
International debut (U-21): England 16, Ireland 22, 1990
Best moment in rugby: Helping England 18-Group beat New Zealand in 1988 Test
Worst moment in rugby: Missing pushover try playing for Bath v. Richmond (1989/90)
Most respected opponent: Bath flanker John Hall (in training)
Other sporting achievements: South West decathlon champion (1988). Runner-up in 1988 English Schools discus championship. South West long-jump and triple-jump champion. Third in All-England decathlon championship

	apps	pts
England U-21 (1990)		
Last Season	2 caps	0
Career	2 caps	0

Best memory last season: Bath winning at Leicester in English League
Suggestions to improve rugby: *On-field* – Scrap 90-degree scrummage wheel law
Other notable landmarks in rugby career: Represented South West Division, England 18-Group (1987/88), England Colts (1988/89), and England U-21s twice last season (v. Ireland U-21s and Netherlands)
Touchlines: Athletics, basketball
Player to watch: Gareth Adams (Bath)

O'Leary, S. T.   England

Full Name: Sean Thomas O'Leary
1990/91 International category:
England B
Club: Wasps
Position: Lock
Height: 6'8" **Weight:** 18st
Occupation: Doctor
Born: Plymouth, 25.9.64
Family: Single
Former clubs: Plymouth Albion,
Cambridge Univ
International debut (B): France 6,
England 18, 1988
Best moment in rugby: Cambridge
32, Oxford 6, 1984 Varsity match
Worst moment in rugby: Waking
in hospital and being told that Wasps
club mate Raph Tsagane had been
killed in the same car accident
(Easter 1990) – no rugby
disappointment can compare
Most embarrassing moment: A
certain *News of the World* headline in
1989
Most respected opponent:
Harlequins lock Paul Ackford
Other sporting achievements:
National League basketball

	apps	pts
England B (**1988**)		
Last Season	2 caps	0
England 1991	World Cup squad	
	1995 Development squad	

Best memory last season: Winning with Wasps at Neath, Bath, Orrell and
Leicester
Suggestions to improve rugby: *On-field* – More consistent refereeing of
line-outs. Fewer games, with mid-season break. Smaller English first division
(seven or eight teams) with home/away fixtures. *Off-field* – End gulf that exists
between England and other countries – Northern and Southern hemispheres
– in what players are allowed to 'earn' from off-field activities
Other notable landmarks in rugby career: Cambridge Blues (1984,85).
Selection for England tour to Argentina last summer but had to cry off through
injury. Capped three times by England Students. Represented England B v.
France B and Italy B last season. Included in original preliminary England
squad for World Cup. Meeting Janet in Vancouver – forever encouraging
Touchlines: If you are a doctor and play first-class rugby, there is hardly
sufficient time to do either properly and certainly no time for hobbies. But I

do enjoy good beer and wine, cycling, travel with good company and occasional medicine!
Player to watch: Damian Hopley (Wasps)

Oliver, G. H. Scotland

Full Name: Greig Hunter Oliver
1990/91 International category: Scotland Full (bench)
Club: Hawick
Position: Scrum-half
Height: 5′8.5″ **Weight:** 12st 8lbs
Occupation: Computer operator
Born: Hawick, 12.9.64
Family: Single
Family links with rugby: Derek (brother) plays for Hawick Linden, as did father
Former clubs: Hawick PSA, Hawick Trades
International debut: Scotland 60, Zimbabwe 21, 1987 (World Cup)
Best moment in rugby: Winning first cap
Worst moment in rugby: Any niggling injuries
Most embarrassing moment: Not being able to walk for a week because of a skin burn on my behind
Most respected opponent: Former Scotland scrum-half Roy Laidlaw – for his dedication to the game and assistance to younger players
Other sporting achievements: Won the 1986 St Ronan's Sprint. Broke 100 at Minto Golf Club
Suggestions to improve rugby: *On-field* – Make the scrum a way of starting the game, and not a means of spoiling it. When scrum comes down, if ball is in back row let play continue. *Off-field* – Give more regard to players

	apps	pts
Scotland B (**1986**)		
Last Season	0 caps	0
Scotland A (**1990**)		
Last Season	1 cap	4
Scotland (**1987**)		
Last Season	5 reps	
1991	Tour to North America World Cup squad	
Career	2 caps	4

Other notable landmarks in rugby career: Being a small part of the 1990 Grand Slam squad. Member of Scotland's 1987 World cup squad. Scored try on Scotland debut v. Zimbabwe. Toured with Scotland to Zimbabwe

(1988), Japan (1989) and New Zealand (1990), coming on as replacement for Gary Armstrong in second Test at Auckland. Scored one of six tries in Scotland A's 39–7 defeat of Spain last season. Permanent feature on full Scotland bench last season. Toured North America last summer with Scotland, partnering Craig Chalmers at half-back v. both US Eagles and Canada
Touchlines: Tennis and golf

Olver, C. J. England

Full Name: Christopher John Olver
1990/91 International category:
England Full
Club: Northampton
Position: Hooker
Height: 5'9" **Weight:** 13st 8lbs
Occupation: Teacher
Born: Manchester, 23.4.62
Family: Sue (wife) and Lisa (daughter)
Former clubs: Sandbach, Harlequins
International debut: England 51, Argentina 0, 1990
Best moments in rugby: Lifting John Player Cup after captaining Harlequins to 28–22 win over Bristol in 1988 final. Winning first England cap v. Argentina (1990/91)
Worst moment in rugby: Losing two JP Cup semi-finals with Quins
Most embarrassing moment: Every time I lose a strike against head
Most respected opponents: Former England hookers Phil Keith-Roach and Peter Wheeler
Serious injuries: Achilles tendon (operation). Dislocated shoulder (twice)
Other sporting achievements: Hit Australian cricket captain Allan Border for three consecutive sixes. 7-handicap golfer

	apps	pts
England B (1988)		
Last Season	1 cap	0
England (1990)		
Last Season	1 cap	0
	4 rep	
v. Barbarians	1 app	0
1991	Tour to Australia	
	World Cup squad	
Career	1 cap	0

Best memory last season: Representing England v. Barbarians and Argentina

Suggestions to improve rugby: *On-field* – Recruit referees who have actually played in front row. Structure season so that all League rugby is conducted on consecutive Saturdays (Sept-Nov). Then play divisionals (Dec) and then, after Christmas, Internationals. This would remove present ludicrous dilemma of players having to play major league games seven days before Internationals. *Off-field* – Compensate employers for loss of employees to rugby

Other notable landmarks in rugby career: Being invited to Mark Bailey's for dinner – this means, above all else, that I've made it in rugby. Toured with England to Argentina (1990) and Australia (1991). Represented England XV in 33–15 win over Italy XV (1989/90) and 18–16 win over Barbarians (1990/91). Captained England B in 12–9 win v. Italy last season. Made long awaited full England debut in 51-0 defeat of Argentina last season at Twickenham. Captained Northampton to 1990/91 Pilkington Cup final

Touchlines: Fly fishing and shooting

Player to watch: Paul Rendall (Wasps – has all the credentials to go far in the committee lounge)

O'MAHONY, B. G.   Ireland

Full Name: Barry Gerard O'Mahony

1990/91 International category: Ireland U-21

Club: University College Cork

Position: No.8

Height: 6′5″ **Weight:** 15st

Occupation: Student

Born: Cork, 18.9.69

Family: Single

International debut: Netherlands 21, Ireland U-21 7, 1990

Best moment in rugby: Representing UCC v. Young Munster in Munster Senior Cup final

Worst moment in rugby: Missing a penalty under posts in a school U-16 final

Most embarrassing moment: Having to make a speech

Most respected opponent: The next one

Best memory last season: Beating England U-21s at Moseley in October

Suggestions to improve rugby: *On-field* – Increase worth of try to 5 points and reduce conversion to 1 point. Shorten playing season. *Off-field* – Unions not moving as quickly as are clubs. Situation must change rapidly if Unions are not to lose power totally

Other notable landmarks in rugby career: Munster Junior and Senior School Cups with PBC. Represented Ireland U-21 v. Netherlands and England (won 22–16) last season

Touchlines: Cycling, travel, golf

Player to watch: Conor O'Shea (Lansdowne)

	apps	pts
Ireland U-21 (**1990**)		
Last Season	2 caps	0
Career	2 caps	0

O'Riordan, J.   Ireland

Full Name: James O'Riordan

1990/91 International category: Ireland B

Club: Cork Constitution

Position: Hooker

Height: 6′ **Weight:** 14st

Occupation: Army officer

Born: Cork, 10.9.66

Family: Single

Family links with rugby: Brother plays for Constitution

Former club: University College Galway

International debut (B): Ireland 16, Scotland 0, 1990

Best moment in rugby: Winning Ireland B recognition

Worst moment in rugby: Injury

Best memories last season: Two B caps and All-Ireland League success with Constitution

Other notable landmarks in rugby career: Connacht Cup medal. Represented Ireland B v. Scotland and England (won 24–10) in 1990/91

	apps	pts
Ireland B (**1990**)		
Last Season	2 caps	0
Career	2 caps	0

Touchlines: Swimming
Players to watch: Philip Soden/Paul McCarthy (both Constitution)

O'Shea, C. M. P.   Ireland

Full Name: Conor Michael Patrick O'Shea
1990/91 International category: Ireland U-21
Club: Lansdowne
Position: Full-back, fly-half
Height: 6'2" **Weight:** 14st
Occupation: Commerce student
Born: Limerick, 21.10.70
Family: Single
Family links with rugby: Brothers (Donal and Diarmid) play for Terenure
International debut: Netherlands 21, Ireland U-21 7, 1990
Best moment in rugby: Lansdowne beating Terenure to win 1990/91 Senior Cup
Worst moment in rugby: Having to settle for third place in 1990/91 All-Ireland League after making slow start
Most respected opponent: Constitution full-back Kenny Murphy
Best memory last season: Winning Senior Cup final

	apps	pts
Ireland U-21 (**1990**)		
Last Season	2 caps	0
v. Netherlands B	1 app	0
Career	2 caps	0

Suggestions to improve rugby:
On-field – Award more points for a try. *Off-field* – Nothing. Game is running very well
Other notable landmarks in rugby career: Represented Leinster U-19s (two years) and U-20s (two years). Played both cap-games for Ireland U-21s (v. Netherlands and England) last season, in addition to 11–6 win over Netherlands B
Touchlines: Golf, tennis
Player to watch: Philip Soden (Constitution)

205

O'Sullivan, E. T.   Ireland

Full Name: Eoin Thomas O'Sullivan

1990/91 International category: Ireland U-21

Club: Old Crescent

Position: Lock

Height: 6'4" **Weight:** 16st 7lbs

Occupation: Sales rep

Born: Limerick, 20.3.70

Family: Single

International debut (U-21): Italy 9, Ireland 10, 1989

Best moment in rugby: Irish Schools tour to Australia (1987)

Worst moment in rugby: Missing large part of season after chipping ankle playing for Munster

Most respected opponent: Ireland B lock Michael Galwey – tough but fair

Serious injuries: Chipped ankle

Other sporting achievements: Gaelic football for Limerick

Best memory last season: Beating England in U-21 International

Suggestions to improve rugby:
On-field – Improved refereeing and de-powering of scrum

	apps	pts
Ireland U-21 (**1989**)		
Last Season	1 cap	0
Career	3 caps	4

Other notable landmarks in rugby career: Played rugby in New Zealand in summer of 1990. Scored try for Munster U-21s in 10–13 defeat by New Zealand U-21s (1989/90). Won third Ireland U-21 cap in 22–16 win over England at Moseley

Touchlines: Parachuting, swimming

Oti, C.   England

Full Name: Christopher Oti
1990/91 International category:
England Full
Club: Wasps
Position: Wing
Height: 5'11" **Weight:** 15st
Occupation: Chartered surveyer
Born: London, 16.6.65
Family: Single
Former clubs: Nottingham,
Cambridge University
International debut: Scotland 6,
England 9, 1988
Five Nations' debut: As above
Best moment in rugby: Three tries
on England home debut in 35–3
defeat of Ireland (March 1988)
Worst moment in rugby:
Returning home early due to injury
from 1989 Lions' tour to Australia
Most embarrassing moment: Not
scoring hat-trick in every subsequent
International after Ireland 1988
Most respected opponent:
Scotland flanker Finlay Calder –
superb captain and leader
Serious injuries: Knee ligament
damage (operated on successfully in
1989), snapped left Achilles tendon
(1990/91)

	apps	pts
England B (1987)		
Last Season	0 caps	0
England (1988)		
Last Season	2 caps	0
1991	Tour to Australia	
	World Cup squad	
Career	11 caps	32
Lions 1989		

Other sporting achievements:
Hold Millfield School 100m sprint record – 10.8sec, achieved aged 17
Best memory last season: Scoring winning try for Wasps v. Orrell in English
first division
Suggestions to improve rugby: *Off-field* – Allow players to market their
own skills – advertising, speeches etc. Compensate players for time and stress
given to rugby
Other notable landmarks in rugby career: Cambridge Blues (1986,87).
Four tries on Barbarians debut (1988). Celebrated third cap with four tries
for England v. Romania in Bucharest (May 1989). Selection for 1989 Lions.
Scored try in England XV's 33–15 defeat of Italy in 1990. Injured for five

months of last season before returning in time to gain selection for England's summer tour to Australia, where regained No. 11 jersey for both Tests

---

Parfitt, S. A.   Wales

Full Name: Stuart Ashley Parfitt
1990/91 International category:
Wales Full
Club: Swansea
Position: Centre
Height: 5′11″ **Weight:** 13st 2lbs
Occupation: Financial consultant
Born: Usk, 4.3.66
Family: Single
Former club: Bridgend
International debut: Namibia 9, Wales 18, 1990
Best moment in rugby: Swansea against 1989 All Blacks – we played very well
Worst moments in rugby: Sitting on bench through 1987 Welsh Cup final which Swansea lost 15–16 to Cardiff. Losing to Pontypool in semi-finals of 1991 Schweppes Welsh Cup
Most respected opponent: Cardiff centre Mark Ring
Serious injuries: Broke collarbone at school
Best memory last season: Winning second Welsh cap v. Barbarians
Suggestions to improve rugby: *On-field* – More points for a try to make game more open. *Off-field* – Do not like idea of players being paid, but they should be entitled to anything they can get from using their names because enough of their time is given up to rugby

	apps	pts
Wales (**1990**)		
Last Season	1 cap	0
1991	World Cup squad	
Career	2 caps	0
Heineken 1990/91	13 apps	4

Other notable landmarks in rugby career: Won 8 caps for Welsh Schools before joining Bridgend, aged 18. Also represented Wales at U-20 and U-21 level before making full bow on 1990 summer tour to Namibia. Won second full cap in 24–31 loss to Barbarians at Cardiff last October
Touchlines: Golf (28-handicap), squash, cricket
Player to watch: Colin Stephens (Llanelli)

Patton, M. B.   Ireland

Full Name: Michael Brian Patton
1990/91 International category:
Ireland U-21
Club: Bangor
Position: Hooker
Height: 6′ **Weight:** 15st 2lbs
Occupation: Student
Born: Bangor, Co. Down, 15.7.69
Family: Single
Family links with rugby: Father
(Tom) was Irish Inter-Provincial
referee, brother (Philip) plays for
Hong Kong
International debut: Netherlands
21, Ireland U-21 9, 1990
Best memory last season:
Captaining Cardiff Univ to UAU
Cup final success over Swansea Univ
Worst moment in rugby: Any time
I am injured
Most respected opponent:
Ballymena's Steve Smith
Best memory last season:
Captaining Cardiff Univ to UAU
Cup final success over Swansea Univ
Suggestions to improve rugby:
On-field – Stricter refereeing. Sides

	apps	pts
Ireland U-21 (1990)		
Last Season	2 caps	0
Career	2 caps	0

get away with too much (especially offside and killing ball). *Off-field* – Too much is made of amateurism debate. The longer rugby is an amateur sport the better. However, amount of games played by top players must be limited, and they must be entitled to broken time payments
Other notable landmarks in rugby career: Captained Ireland U-21s against Netherlands (in Leiden), and England (at Moseley), in early part of 1990/91 season. Previously, captained Ulster Schools and Irish Exiles U-21s. Also represented Bangor, Welsh Universities, UAU, Irish Exiles senior XV and Irish Students
Touchlines: Squash
Player to watch: Ian Jones (Llanelli)

Pearce, G. S. England

Full Name: Gary Stephen Pearce
1990/91 International category:
England B
Club: Northampton
Position: Tight-head prop
Height: 6′ **Weight:** 15st 10lbs
Occupation: Quantity surveyor
Born: Dinton, Bucks, 2.3.56
Family: Susan (wife), Daniel and
Matthew (sons)
Former club: Aylesbury
International debut: England 7,
Scotland 7, 1979
Five Nations' debut: As above
Best moment in rugby: Clinching
second division title with
Northampton (1989/90)
Worst moment in rugby: Playing
at loose-head

Most embarrassing moment:
Watching Northampton lose 0–60 to
Orrell (1990/91)
Most respected opponent: Former
Bayonne and France prop Pierre
Dospital
Best memory last season: Playing
in Pilkington Cup final with
Northampton
Suggestions to improve rugby:

	apps	pts
England B (1988)		
Last Season	4 caps	0
Career	7 caps	4
England (1979)		
Last Season	0 caps	0
1991	Tour to Australia	
	World Cup squad	
Career	35 caps	0

On-field – Referees with better
knowledge of scrummage laws.
Off-field – Compensate players for
time lost to rugby. There is enough money in rugby generated by the players to
prevent them finishing out of pocket
Other notable landmarks in rugby career: England Schools U-16 trialist.
Played for Aylesbury Colts before moving to Northampton in Easter 1978.
Selected for England in first full season with Saints. England's most capped
prop with 35 caps to my credit between 1979–88. Captained England B on
four occasions last season (v. Emerging Australians, Spain, Ireland and
France). Only points for England came when representing B team v. France
in 1988
Player to watch: Ian Hunter (Northampton)

Pears, D.   England

Full Name: David Pears
1990/91 International category:
England B
Club: Harlequins
Position: Fly-half
Height: 5′10″ **Weight:** 12st 5lbs
Occupation: Trainee project
manager
Born: Workington, 6.12.67
Family: Single
Family links with rugby: Father
played Rugby League for Cumbria
Former clubs: Aspatria, Sale
International debut: Argentina 12,
England 25, 1990
Best moment in rugby: Winning
first full England cap
Worst moment in rugby: Missing
penalty kick which would have
earned Sale promotion to English
first division

Most embarrassing moment:
Asking Gary Pearce (England's most
capped prop with 35 to his credit),
on England B trip to Italy in 1989,
whether it was his first International
Most respected opponent: Bath's
former England fly-half Stuart
Barnes – dictates games so well
Serious injuries: Torn knee
ligaments (out for 12 weeks)
Other sporting achievements:
Cumbria Schools soccer captain
Best memory last season:
Winning Pilkington Cup final with
Harlequins

	apps	pts
England U-21 (**1989**)		
Career	1 cap	2
England B (**1988**)		
Last Season	4 caps	20
	1 rep	
Career	6 caps	45
England (**1990**)		
Last Season	0 caps	0
1991	Tour to Australia	
	World Cup squad	
	1995 Development squad	
Career	2 caps	0

Suggestions to improve rugby: Make game professional to raise standards
even higher
Other notable landmarks in rugby career: Capped six times by England
B and was a replacement when an England XV beat an Italy XV 33–15 in
Rovigo (1989/90). Scored over 700 points in three seasons of English League
rugby. Toured Argentina with England in summer 1990 and wore No.10

jersey in both Tests. Made England B debut in 9–37 loss to 1988 Wallabies. Kicked all 12 points (four penalty goals) for England B in last season's draw with Emerging Australians, contributed a conversion to 50–6 defeat of Spain, and two penalty goals in 6–10 loss to France B at Bristol
Player to watch: Ian Hunter (Northampton)

Phillips, K. H.   Wales

Full Name: Kevin Huw Phillips
1990/91 International category: Wales Full
Club: Neath
Position: Hooker
Height: 5'11" **Weight:** 14st 2lbs
Occupation: Farmer
Born: Hebron, 15.6.61
Family: Married
Former club: Cardigan
International debut: France 16, Wales 9, 1987
Five Nations' debut: As above
Best moment in rugby: Winning 1988 Welsh Cup with Neath
Worst moment in rugby: Dislocating shoulder against Swansea at The Gnoll (1987/88) and being out for three months
Most embarrassing moment: Whenever I lose strike against head
Most respected opponent: England hooker Brian Moore
Serious injuries: Dislocated shoulder
Other sporting achievements: Tug-of-war at international level
Best memory last season: Winning Heineken Welsh League with Neath

	apps	pts
Wales (**1987**)		
Last Season	6 caps	0
1991	Tour to Australia	
	World Cup squad	
Career	20 caps	0
Heineken 1990/91	13 apps	0

Suggestions to improve rugby: *Off-field* – Improve education of younger players to ensure future of game; send players into schools
Other notable landmarks in rugby career: First represented Wales in national seven at New South Wales tournament in Australia (1986). Following year was selected to senior XV. Played in 1987 World Cup and toured with

Wales to New Zealand (1988), to Namibia, as captain (1990), and to Australia last summer
Touchlines: Swimming, pool, keep-fit
Player to watch: Scott Gibbs (Neath)

Pilgrim, S. J.   England

Full Name: Stephen John Pilgrim
1990/91 International category:
England (1995 development squad)
Club: Nottingham
Position: Full-back
Height: 5′10″ **Weight:** 13st 10lbs
Occupation: Fitness advisor
Born: Sidcup, 26.10.67
Family: Single
Former club: Old Reigatians
International debut: England B 12, Fiji 20, 1989
Best moment in rugby: Running round Rory Underwood (pictured in *Daily Telegraph*) for Wasps v. Leicester, 1989
Worst moment in rugby: Wasps losing to Orrell in quarter-finals of 1991 Pilkington Cup
Most embarrassing moment: While at Wasps, intended kick-ahead for fellow Wasp Simon Smith squirted sideways – Nottingham wing caught it and scored
Most respected opponent: Former England full-back Dusty Hare – despite his age, he was always in the right place
Other sporting achievements: Basketball for Crystal Palace and Kingston

	apps	pts
England U-21 (**1989**)		
Career	1 cap	12
England B (**1989**)		
Last Season	0 caps	0
Career	1 cap	8
England	1995 Development squad	

Best memory last season: Selection for London Division at full-back despite not having played there all season
Suggestions to improve rugby: *On-field* – Better referees. *Off-field* – I would like to see a realistic appreciation of the effort put in by players. That

does not have to mean financial reward but the RFU must put themselves in players' position

Other notable landmarks in rugby career: England U-21s 53, Romania U-21 14 (Bucharest, 1989). Seeing Dick Best smile twice. Selected for England development squad for 1995 World Cup. Toured Australia with London last summer

Touchlines: Beach parties

Player to watch: Tony Underwood (Leicester)

Popplewell, N. J.   Ireland

Full Name: Nicholas James Popplewell

1990/91 International category: Ireland Full

Club: Greystones

Position: Loose-head prop

Height: 5'10" **Weight:** 16st 7lbs

Occupation: Furniture warehouse manager

Born: Dublin, 6.4.64

Family: Single

Former club: Gorey

International debut: Ireland 6, New Zealand 23, 1989

Best moment in rugby: Winning first cap v. All Blacks

Worst moment in rugby: Only lasting 20 minutes in above match before cracking a rib

Most respected opponent: Ireland prop Des Fitzgerald

Serious injuries: Broken ribs (twice)

Other sporting achievements: Played hockey for Irish Schools (3 caps)

Best memories last season: Helping Ireland B beat English in Dublin by scoring try. Winning Belvedere Sevens with Greystones

	apps	pts
Ireland B (**1991**)		
Last Season	1 cap	4
Ireland (**1989**)		
Last Season	3 caps	0
1991	Tour to Namibia	
Career	4 caps	0

Suggestions to improve rugby: *On-field* – Decrease value of penalty goal to 2 points. Scrap 90-degree scrum wheel law. *Off-field* – Compensate players for time lost away from work – not payments, just reduced hassle in claiming legitimate expenses

Other notable landmarks in rugby career: Helping to train Presentation Juniors Bray U-15s to two Leinster Junior Cups in three years. Toured with Ireland to North America, playing in 24–21 defeat of Canada (1989). Represented Ireland U-25s v. US Eagles (1990). Ireland reserve three times in 1990 Five Nations' Championship. Won second full cap in 20–18 defeat of Argentina last season in Dublin. Scored one of Ireland B's four tries in 24–10 win v. England B at Old Belvedere last March

Touchlines: Golf, tennis, squash

Porter, S. T. G.   Scotland

Full Name: Stewart Thomas Graves Porter

1990/91 International category: Scotland B

Club: Malone

Position: Wing

Height: 6′1″ **Weight:** 14st

Occupation: Company director of a shipping and removal firm

Born: Glasgow, 11.5.63

Family: Lesley (wife) and Max Thomas (son)

Family links with rugby: Richard (brother) plays for Edinburgh Academicals

Former clubs: Kilmarnock, Nottingham, Gosforth, Glasgow Academicals, Cooke

International debut (B): Scotland 22, Ireland 22, 1989

Best moment in rugby: Scotland's 1990 tour to New Zealand

Worst moment in rugby: Have not had one

Most embarrassing moment: First time my mother Jean came to watch me she came out of stand ranting and raving at referee for allowing 'those boys to trample on my son'. She was given a touchline ban

Most respected opponent: NIFC's Gordon Hamilton

	apps	pts
Scotland B (1989)		
Last Season	2 caps	0
Career	4 caps	0

Best memory last season: Second Test in Auckland: New Zealand 21, Scotland 18 (23 June, 1990)

Suggestions to improve rugby: *On-field* – Change Scottish regulation which prevents player from playing for the B team after winning a full cap. Make it after five full Internationals. Scotland introduced an A team but that should not be necessary if the regulation is revised. *Off-field* – Players should be allowed to benefit financially from off-field activities, whether or not rugby-related. Increase availablity of International tickets. Far too many are going to commercial concerns at expense of true supporters

Other notable landmarks in rugby career: Have represented Glasgow in Scottish Inter-District Championship and was selected for Notts/Lincs/Derbys in English County Championship but did not play. Became only non-Ulsterman ever to play for Ulster when represented province in 21–3 defeat by 1989 All Blacks at Ravenhill. Four appearances for Scotland B (no points scored). Toured New Zealand with Scotland (1990)

Touchlines: Golf, cricket

Player to watch: Maurice Fields (Malone)

Povoas, S. J.   England

Full Name: Simon John Povoas

1990/91 International category: England (1995 development squad)

Club: Leicester

Positions: Lock, No.8

Height: 6′2″ **Weight:** 15st 7lbs

Occupation: Sales manager

Born: Leicester, 10.6.66

Family: Single

Family links with rugby: Father played for Oadby-Wyggestonian

Former club: Oadby-Wyggestonian

Best moment in rugby: Scoring three tries for Leicester v. Ponsonby during tour of New Zealand

Worst moment in rugby: Breaking jaw playing for Leicestershire in Italy (1987)

Serious injuries: Broken hand, jaw. Damaged knee and ankle ligaments

Other notable landmarks in rugby career: Scored 25 tries for Leicester 1989/90 season – club

record for a forward. Selected to England development squad for 1995 World Cup
Touchlines: Golf

	apps	pts
England B (1989/90)	1 rep	
England	1995 Development squad	

Probyn, J. A.   England

Full Name: Jeffrey Alan Probyn
1990/91 International category: England Full
Club: Wasps
Position: Tight-head prop
Height: 5′10″ **Weight:** 15st 7lbs
Occupation: Furniture manufacturer
Born: London, 27.4.56
Family: Jennifer (wife), Jeffrey Paul (son), Steven James (son) and Rebecca (daughter)
Family links with rugby: Brother plays
Former clubs: Old Albanians, Streatham/Croydon, Richmond
International debut: France 10, England 9, 1988
Five Nations' debut: As above
Best moment in rugby: Winning 1991 Grand Slam with England
Worst moment in rugby: Leaving field concussed in Ireland (1989)
Most embarrassing moment: Getting lifted by Welsh prop Staff Jones for trying to be clever (Twickenham, 1988)
Most respected opponent: England loose-head prop Paul Rendall

	apps	pts
England B (**1986**)		
Last Season	0 caps	0
England (**1988**)		
Last Season	7 caps	4
v. Barbarians	1 cap	0
1991	Tour to Australia World Cup squad	
Career	24 caps	12

Most improved player: Harlequins prop Jason Leonard (has come on in leaps and bounds but still to reach full potential)
Serious injuries: Damaged ligaments in left knee. Ear stitches

Best memory last season: Watching Rory Underwood's England try in 16–7 defeat of Ireland – relieved massive tension

Suggestions to improve rugby: *On-field* – Better interpretation of regulations by referees (hold seminars for officials to sort out common strategy). Get touch judges more involved in running of game. *Off-field* – Improved media (especially TV). Regarding amateurism, I would like to think players could progress hand-in-hand with RFU into modern era. Allow players to benefit from off-field activities; after all, RFU market themselves on fame of players

Other notable landmarks in rugby career: Moving to Wasps. First B cap v. France. England debut in Paris. World XV v. South Africa, and Home Unions v. France (1989). Scored in England's win over Ireland (1990). Toured with England to Argentina (1990) and Australia (1991). Ever-present in England's 1991 Grand Slam side. Scored second try of England career in 28–12 win over Fiji last summer

Touchlines: Sailing, shooting, fishing, watching children grow up and play sport

Player to watch: Philip de Glanville (Bath)

Redman, N. C.   England

Full Name: Nigel Charles Redman
1990/91 International category:
England Full
Club: Bath
Position: Lock
Height: 6′4″ **Weight:** 17st 2lbs
Occupation: Electrician
Born: Cardiff, 16.8.64
Family: Married
Family links with rugby: Younger brother plays No.8 for Weston-super-Mare
Former club: Weston-super-Mare
International debut: England 3, Australia 19, 1984
Five Nations' debut: Scotland 33, England 6, 1986
Best moment in rugby: Bath beating Gloucester 48–6 in 1989 Pilkington Cup final
Worst moment in rugby: Being left out of Bath Cup final team in 1988/89 after playing in all other games

Most embarrassing moment:
South Australia v. England (1988) –
only occasion in which English team
was not on pitch while National
Anthem was being played, because I
was on the toilet
Most respected opponent: Wales
lock Robert Norster – considered
short for middle jumper but is still
one of best

	apps	pts
England B (**1986**)		
Last Season	5 caps	0
England (**1984**)		
Last Season	1 cap	0
1991	Tour to Australia	
Career	11 caps	4

Best memory last season: Winning English League Championship with
Bath
Suggestions to improve rugby: Scrap 90-degree wheel law. Bigger effort to
improve fitness of players and standard of refereeing at all levels
Other notable landmarks in rugby career: Joining Bath and playing in Cup
final (1983/84) – first of five. England debut (1984/85). Playing in first World
Cup (1987). Toured Argentina with England (1990). First-choice lock for
England B last season, playing five matches (v. Emerging Australians, Spain,
Ireland, France and Italy). Won 11th England cap in 28–12 win over Fiji last
summer
Touchlines: Volleyball, golf, DIY

Redpath, A. C.   Scotland

Full Name: Alexander Craig
Redpath
1990/91 International category:
Scotland B
Club: Melrose
Position: Full-back
Height: 6' **Weight:** 13st 10lbs
Occupation: Student
Born: Galashiels, 21.9.69
Family: Single
Family links with rugby: Andrew
(brother) played for Scotland U-18s
and U-21s. Bryan (brother) was
replacement for Scotland U-18s and
U-19s and represented the U-21s
last season. Lynne (sister) plays for
Scotland women U-21s
International debut (B): Ireland
16, Scotland 0, 1990

Best moment in rugby: Winning Scottish First Division with Melrose last season
Worst moment in rugby: Losing to Randwick in semi-finals of 1989/90 Melrose Sevens
Most respected player: Melrose's former Scotland wing Keith Robertson
Serious injuries: Broken neck (playing soccer)

	apps	pts
Scotland U-21 (**1990**)		
Last Season	1 cap	0
Career	2 caps	0
Scotland B (**1990**)		
Last Season	2 caps	0
Career	2 caps	0

Other sporting achievements: Cricket for South of Scotland U-16s
Best memory last season: Winning Border League with Melrose
Other notable landmarks in rugby career: Represented Scotland at U-19, U-21 (two seasons) and B level. Replacement also for Scotland when they beat England to clinch 1990 Grand Slam at Murrayfield. Toured with Scotland to New Zealand (1990). Made B debut in 16-0 Belfast loss to Ireland in December 1990 and kept my place for visit of France B (lost 10–31)
Suggestions to improve rugby: *On-field* – Reduce points-worth of penalties to make Scottish game more attractive. *Off-field* – None. Happy with things as they are
Touchlines: Golf, cricket
Player to watch: Stuart Reid (Boroughmuir)

Redpath, B. W.   Scotland

Full Name: Bryan William Redpath
1990/91 International category:
Scotland U-21
Club: Melrose
Position: Scrum-half
Height: 5'7" **Weight:** 10st 10lbs
Occupation: Joiner
Born: Galashiels, 2.7.71
Family: Single
Family links with rugby: Andrew
(brother) has played for Scotland
U-18s and U-21s; Craig (brother)
for Scotland U-21s and B. Lynne
(sister) plays for Scotland women
U-21s
International debut (U-21): Wales
23, Scotland 15, 1991
Best moment in rugby:
Representing Scotland U-21s last
season
Most respected opponent:
Jed-Forest scrum-half Gary
Armstrong
Other sporting achievements:
Cricket for St Boswells
Best memory last season: Playing
in Melrose seven

	apps	pts
Scotland U-21 (**1991**)		
Last Season	1 cap	0
Career	1 cap	0

Suggestions to improve rugby: *On-field* – Reduce value of penalty goal to make for more entertaining spectacle. *Off-field* – Get more youngsters involved in rugby. Instruct Melrose coach Jim Telfer not to train us so hard
Other notable landmarks in rugby career: Replacement for Scotland U-18s and U-19s. Made U-21 debut in loss to Wales at Llanelli last season
Touchlines: Golf, cricket
Player to watch: Stuart Reid (Boroughmuir)

Rees, G. W.   England

Full Name: Gary William Rees
1990/91 International category:
England Full
Club: Nottingham
Position: Flanker
Height: 6′ **Weight:** 14st 7lbs
Occupation: Financial advisor
Born: Long Eaton, 2.5.60
Family: Single
International debut: South Africa
35, England 9, 1984
Five Nations' debut: England 25,
Ireland 20, 1986
Best moment in rugby: Making
England debut as replacement in
second Test at Ellis Park
Worst moment in rugby:
Nottingham losing to Harlequins in
extra time in 1990/91 Pilkington
Cup semi-final
Most embarrassing moment:
Left-footed touch finder v. Orrell in
final game of last season – it found
their No.8!
Most respected opponent:
Australian back row Simon Poidevin
Other sporting achievements:
County Schools hockey and cricket
Best memory last season: Simon
Hodgkinson buying a round
Suggestions to improve rugby:

	apps	pts
England B (**1988**)		
Last Season	0 caps	0
England (**1984**)		
Last Season	2 caps	0
v. Barbarians	1 app	0
1991	Tour to Australia	
	World Cup squad	
Career	22 caps	8

On-field – Reduce amount of scrums. *Off-field* – Stop referees answering
players back
Other notable landmarks in rugby career: Joined Nottingham in 1978 as
full-back or scrum-half. Played for England U-23s in Italy (1982). Helped
Midlands beat 1983 All Blacks. Represented England in 1987 World Cup
and on tour in Australia (1988). Came on as 25th minute replacement for
Peter Winterbottom in England XV's 18–16 win v. Barbarians and as 69th
minute replacement for Paul Ackford (to win 21st full cap) in 51-0 defeat of
Argentina. Took tally to 22 with cap in 28-12 win over Fiji last summer
Touchlines: Golf (24-handicap), more golf

Player to watch: Stuart Potter (Nottingham) – immense natural ability; will be outstanding with experience

---

Reid, S. J. Scotland

Full Name: Stuart James Reid
1990/91 International category: Scotland B
Club: Boroughmuir
Position: No. 8
Height: 6'3.5" **Weight:** 15st 11lbs
Occupation: Bank Officer
Born: Kendal, 31.1.70
Family: Single
International debut (B): Ireland 16, Scotland 0, 1990
Best moment in rugby: Scoring two tries for Scotland XV in 41–12 win over United States (1990/91)
Most respected opponent: Stewart's Melville flanker Finlay Calder
Best memory last season: Winning Scottish League Championship with Boroughmuir
Suggestions to improve rugby: *On-field* – Less points for a penalty; too much kicking nowadays. *Off-field* – Keep encouraging youth involvement
Other notable landmarks in rugby career: Represented Scotland at U-19 (1989), U-21 (1989–91) and B levels. Last season played for U-21s in 23–15 defeat by Wales, and

	apps	pts
Scotland U-21 (**1989**)		
Last Season	1 cap	0
Career	3 caps	0
Scotland B (**1990**)		
Last Season	2 caps	0
Career	2 caps	0
Scotland 1991	Tour to North America World Cup squad	

for B team in losses to Ireland and France. Toured North America with Scotland last summer, playing in both non-cap 'tests' v. US Eagles (scoring two tries in 41–12 win) and Canada (one try in 19–24 defeat), as well as v. Alberta (one try in 76–7 win) and Rugby East
Touchlines: Squash, golf
Player to watch: Scott Nichol (Selkirk)

223

Rendall, P. A. G.   England

Full Name: Paul Anthony George Rendall

1990/91 International category: England Full (bench)

Club: Wasps

Position: Loose-head prop

Height: 5'11" **Weight:** 16st 8lbs

Occupation: Self-employed engineer

Born: London, 18.2.54

Family: Sue (wife), Kim (daughter) and Daniel (son)

Former club: Slough (1970–75)

International debut: England 15, Wales 24, 1984

Five Nations' debut: As above

Best moment in rugby: England beating France 26–7 in Paris (1990)

Worst moments in rugby: Not being selected for 1989 British Lions. Losing 1990 Grand Slam decider to Scotland

Most embarrassing moment: Being asked to pay for extra breakfast after England v. France 1989 (ate three)

Most respected opponent: Jeff Probyn – a boring so and so!

Best memory last season: Rory Underwood's decisive late try in Dublin for England

	apps	pts
England B (**1981**)		
Last Season	0 caps	0
England (**1984**)		
Last Season	0 caps	0
	4 reps	
1991	Tour to Australia World Cup squad	
Career	27 caps	0

Suggestions to improve rugby: *On-field* – Stop touch judges coming onto field. Implement two-referee system. *Off-field* – Pay for broken time. Take away fence which RFU are sitting on so it has to make a decision one way or another. International Rugby Board should start making decisions on world rugby

Other notable landmarks in rugby career: Completing Five Nations' Championship in 1988 without being dropped or injured. Gained first cap aged 30. Played for World XV against New Zealand (Tokyo 1987). Played for World XV in South Africa (1989). Toured with England to Australia, Argentina, USA, Canada, South Africa and Italy, as well as 1987 World Cup. Only International points came from a try in non-cap match v. USA (1982).

Represented centenary Barbarians in 31–24 defeat of Wales last season. Lost England place last season to Jason Leonard
Touchlines: Reading Halsbury
Player to watch: Alan Buzza (Wasps)

Renwick, W. L.   Scotland

Full Name: William Lindsay Renwick
1990/91 International category: Scotland (tour squad)
Club: London Scottish
Position: Wing
Height: 5'11" **Weight:** 13st 8lbs
Occupation: Sports Centre manager
Born: Hawick, 24.12.60
Family: Married with two children (Charlotte and Paul)
Family links with rugby: Father played for Hawick (1950)
Former clubs: Stirling County, Alsager College, Broughton Park, Sale
International debut: Scotland 32, Romania 0, 1989
Best moments in rugby: Winning first full Scotland cap. Captaining Scotland B to 18–12 away win v. France (March 1988). Gaining promotion with London Scottish to English second division (1989/90)
Worst moments in rugby: Anglo-Scots losing Scottish 1989/90 Inter-District Championship decider to Glasgow. Relegation with London Scottish (1988/89)

	apps	pts
Scotland B (**1987**)		
Last Season	0 caps	0
Scotland (**1989**)		
Last Season	0 caps	0
1991	Tour to North America World Cup squad	
Career	1 cap	0

Other notable landmarks in rugby career: Withdrew from Scotland's 1990 tour to New Zealand because wife was pregnant, but visited North America with the Scots last summer and played in wins over Alberta, Rugby East and Ontario

Revan, T. S. England

Full Name: Trevor Samuel Revan
1990/91 International category:
England B
Club: Rugby
Position: Prop
Height: 6'1" **Weight:** 17st 8lbs
Occupation: Builder
Born: Birmingham, 5.12.63
Family: Single
Former clubs: Birmingham,
Coventry
International debut (B): Ireland
24, England 10, 1991
Best moments in rugby: First time
I was selected by Coventry. Winning
English second division with Rugby
(1990/91)
Worst moment in rugby: Any time
I am on a losing side
Best memory last season:
Selection for England B v. Ireland
Suggestions to improve rugby:
On-field – Abandon 90-degree
scrum wheel law (waste of time
because penalises team going
forward. *Off-field* – Ensure that
players do not lose out financially
through playing rugby. I put a lot of time into rugby and lose a lot of money.
With all the money in the sport now that cannot be right
Other notable landmarks in rugby career: Represented Warwickshire in
County Championship and Midlands in Divisional Championship. Made
England B debut when coming on as replacement for Gary Pearce in 24–10
defeat by Ireland at Old Belvedere in March 1991
Touchlines: Music, cricket
Player to watch: Neil Back (Leicester)

	apps	pts
England B (1991)		
Last Season	1 cap	0
Career	1 cap	0

Reynolds, A. D.   Wales

Full Name: Alan David Reynolds
1990/91 International category:
Wales (World Cup squad)
Club: Swansea
Position: Flanker
Height: 6'1" **Weight:** 15st
Occupation: Plasterer
Born: 24.1.66
Family: Single
Family links with rugby:
Brother-in-law David Jacobs played
for Neath and Wales B
Former clubs: Whitland,
Laugharne
International debut: Namibia 9,
Wales 18, 1990
Best moment in rugby: Making
Welsh debut in first Test last summer
Worst moment in rugby: Being
dropped for second Test
**Other notable landmarks in
rugby career:** Represented Wales at
Youth level and Pembrokeshire
against touring US Eagles. Had
Wales U-21 trials. In Sevens, played
for Wales in Hong Kong and
Crawshays in Dubai

	apps	pts
Wales (**1990**)		
Last Season	0 caps	0
1991	World Cup squad	
Career	2 caps	0
Heineken 1990/91	10 apps	20

Richards, D.   England

Full Name: Dean Richards
1990/91 International category:
England Full
Club: Leicester
Position: No.8
Height: 6′3″ **Weight:** 17st 7lbs
Occupation: Policeman
Born: Nuneaton, 11.7.63
Family: Married
Family links with rugby: Father
played for Nuneaton
Former club: Roanne (France)
International debut: England 25,
Ireland 20, 1986
Five Nations' debut: As above
Best moment in rugby: Winning
decisive third Test with 1989 Lions
Worst moment in rugby: England
losing to Wales in Cardiff (1989)
Most respected opponent: New
Zealand No.8 Wayne Shelford
Serious injuries: Recurring
dislocated shoulder (1989/90)
Best memory last season:
England's Grand Slam
Suggestions to improve rugby:
Implement proposals on
Amateurism. Players can make
money away from field everywhere
else in world, why not in Britain?

	apps	pts
England (**1986**)		
Last Season	7 caps	0
v. Barbarians	1 app	4
1991	Tour to Australia	
	World Cup squad	
Career	27 caps	24
Lions (**1989**)	3 Tests	0

Other notable landmarks in rugby career: Joined Leicester in 1982 after
season playing in France. Played for England Schools at lock, before
graduating to England U-23s (against Romania). Also represented
Leicestershire (would like to play county rugby again after International
career) and Midlands Division. Scored two tries on International debut against
Ireland but it was one of my worst performances. Played in 1987 World Cup
and returned to Australia with 1989 Lions. Shoulder injury ruled out 1989/90
season. Lynchpin of England's 1991 Grand Slam success. Scored one of
England XV's two tries in 18–16 defeat of centenary Barbarians at
Twickenham last season. Voted Whitbread/*Rugby World* Player of the Year
for 1991
Touchlines: Squash, five-a-side soccer

Richardson, J. F   Scotland

Full Name: Jeremy Francis
Richardson
1990/91 International category:
Scotland B
Club: Edinburgh Academicals
Position: Lock
Height: 6'5" **Weight:** 16st
Occupation: Stockbroker
Born: Crawley, 7.9.63
Family: Single
Family links with rugby: Father
played for Army, Edinburgh
Academicals. Charlie (brother)
captained Edinburgh Academicals,
London Scottish, Scotland B. Guy
(brother) played for Army
International debut (B): Scotland
9, France 15, 1987
Best moment in rugby: Beating
France B 14–12 at Melrose in 1989
with brother Charlie captaining
Scotland B
Worst moment in rugby: Not
playing in 1987 World Cup
Most respected opponent:
Scotland lock Chris Gray – never
played with or against him when he
has given less than 100 per cent

	apps	pts
Scotland B (1987)		
Last Season	1 cap	0
Career	6 caps	0

Best memory last season: None: wrecked by injury. Bad concussion
followed by broken hand
Suggestions to improve rugby: *On-field* – Award more points for tries.
Penalise foul play (anywhere on pitch) with penalty kick in front of posts.
Increase quality of referees. *Off-field* – Ensure players' schedules are not
over-congested. Clarify and unify position regarding amateurism
Other notable landmarks in rugby career: Played four times for Scotland
U-21s. Included in Scotland squad for 1987 World Cup. Toured with
Scotland to Zimbabwe (1988), New Zealand (1990) and North America
(1991: three appearances). Captained Scotland B in 0–16 Belfast loss to
Ireland last season
Touchlines: Golf (15-handicap)
Player to watch: Shade Munroe (Glasgow H/K)

Rigney, B. J. — Ireland

Full Name: Brian Joseph Rigney
1990/91 International category:
Ireland Full
Club: Greystones
Position: Lock
Height: 6'4" **Weight:** 17st 8lbs
Occupation: Brewer's rep
Born: Portlaoise, 22.9.63
Family: Single
Family links with rugby: Four
brothers play for Portlaoise
Former clubs: Portlaoise,
Highfield, Bective Rangers
International debut: Ireland 13,
France 21, 1991
Five Nations' debut: As above
Best moment in rugby: Winning
first senior cap v. French
Worst moment in rugby: Being
sent-off after 14 minutes playing for
Ireland B v. Scotland B in Belfast last
season for throwing a silly punch
Most embarrassing moment: As
above
Most respected opponent: Ireland
lock Donal Lenihan – tremendous
dedication and application
Serious injuries: Broken ankle
(missed 1987 Munster Cup final as a
result). Damaged knee ligaments
(Namibia 1991)

	apps	pts
Ireland B (**1989**)		
Last Season	1 cap	0
Career	2 caps	0
Ireland (**1991**)		
Last Season	5 caps	0
1991	Tour to Namibia	
	World Cup squad	
Career	5 caps	0

Other sporting achievements: Won honours for Gaelic football and hurling
with Portlaoise. Various swimming achievements as boy
Best memory last season: Running out onto Lansdowne Road pitch for
Ireland debut
Suggestions to improve rugby: *Off-field* – Standardise Northern and
Southern hemisphere unions' attitudes towards amateurism. Reimburse
employers for time lost to rugby. Form a players' committee at top level
Other notable landmarks in rugby career: Only played rugby for four
seasons at senior level, seven in all (started aged 19). Picked for Ireland XV
v. Canada and US Eagles during 1989 North American tour. Although no
caps awarded to us, both opponents received caps. Capped after two seasons

of senior rugby by Leinster. Made Ireland B debut in 22–22 draw with Scotland (1989/90) and won second cap in ill-fated match v. same opponents last season. Called into Ireland's 1991 Five Nations' squad (aged 27) and played full campaign, earning admission into preliminary Irish World Cup squad and tour to Namibia in process. Serious knee injury, suffered in first Test v. Namibia threatens World Cup place

Player to watch: Nick Popplewell (Greystones)

Ring, M. G. Wales

Full Name: Mark Gerard Ring
1990/91 International category:
Wales Full
Club: Cardiff
Positions: Centre, full-back
Height: 6′ **Weight:** 13st 10lbs
Occupation: Company director
with Ringdale Industrial Roofing Ltd
Born: Cardiff, 15.10.62
Family: Single
Family links with rugby: Father
(Brian) played for Leicester,
Maesteg, Glamorgan Wanderers
and Tredegar
Former club: Pontypool
International debut: Wales 13,
England 13, 1983
Five Nations' debut: As above
Best moment in rugby: Welsh
Rugby Player of Year 1985
Worst moment in rugby: Injury to
left knee which meant two barren
seasons
Most embarrassing moment:
Showing off in Sevens. Ran to
try-line with ball behind back. When
placed ball over try line it slipped
from my grasp
Most respected opponents: New
Zealand centre Warwick Taylor –
showed me a new dimension to
centre play, and England's Jeremy Guscott
Serious injuries: Torn ligaments in both knees

	apps	pts
Wales B (1983)		
Last Season	0 cap	0
Career	2 caps	23
Wales (1983)		
Last Season	5 caps	0
1991	World Cup squad	
Career	28 caps	12
Heineken 1990/91	16 apps	39

Other sporting achievements: Welsh baseball international

Best memories last season: Neil Jenkins' try for Wales v. Ireland. Captaining Cardiff to win over champions Neath at The Gnoll in final round of Leagues

Suggestions to improve rugby: *On-field* – Give touch judges more authority in offside laws around fringes. In line-out, return to double-banking and lifting prevalent in shambolic 1970s (far better). Relax and enjoy every game. Take advice from coaches and fellow players. Study videos of great players. *Off-field* – Administrators are botching up the game completely. Learn from Rugby League in way they market their game. Too many people in charge are out of touch with the modern game. Invite younger men to join set-up

Other notable landmarks in rugby career: Played fly-half for Wales Youth before Cardiff (first spell) moved me to centre. Three Welsh Cup winners' medals. Cardiff's 1984 defeat of Australia. Barbarians v. Australia (1988). World XV v. South Africa (1989). Toured with Wales to New Zealand (1988) and Namibia (1990) but overlooked for 1991 trip to Australia

Touchlines: Horse racing fanatic. Fan of Rugby League (esp. Wigan). Play Sunday soccer. Interested in Brazilian soccer players who are given bad names because of off-field habits

Touchlines: All sport, especially baseball and soccer

Player to watch: Ian McKim (Cardiff)

Riordan, J. C.   Ireland

Full Name: John Cashel Riordan
1990/91 International category: Ireland B
Club: Wanderers
Position: Wing
Height: 6'2" **Weight:** 14st 7lbs
Occupation: Investment banker
Born: Cork, 30.5.66
Family: Single
Family links with rugby: Cousins include Ireland Internationals Tom Kiernan, Michael Kiernan, Noel A. Murphy and Kenny Murphy
Former club: University College Cork
Best moment in rugby: Touring Japan with Irish Universities (1987)
Worst moment in rugby: Any injuries
Most embarrassing moment:

Guesting in a Christmas 3rd XV match while being a member of Munster team and playing absolute rubbish

Most respected opponent: Ireland wing John Sexton – sheer speed

Other sporting achievements: 1982 Irish under-age 400m champion. 1984 Irish Schools athletics team. Senior county champion four times

Best memory last season: Winning Leinster League and Cup double with Wanderers

Suggestions to improve rugby: Two referees per match. Stricter disciplinary measures

Touchlines: School classmate of Ireland prop Gary Halpin. Played in same Munster Schools, Irish Schools and club side, as well as same athletics team at school, provincial and International schools level. Ireland U-25 replacement in 12–10 defeat of US Eagles at Limerick (1990). Marked Ireland B debut last season with one of four tries in 27–12 win v. touring Argentina

	apps	pts
Ireland B (**1990**)		
Last Season	1 cap	4
Career	1 cap	4

Robertson, G. B.   Scotland

Full Name: George Brian Robertson
1990/91 International category: Scotland B
Club: Stirling County
Position: Tight-head prop
Height: 6′ **Weight:** 16st 3lbs
Occupation: Potato merchant
Born: Falkirk, 9.8.59
Family: Morag (wife)
Best moments in rugby: Winning 1989/90 Scottish Inter-District Championship with Glasgow and putting on Scotland jersey for first time
Worst moment in rugby: Damaging knee ligaments so badly on Glasgow's Irish tour (1989) that thought career was over
Most respected opponent: Scotland loose-head prop David Sole
Serious injuries: Knee ligaments

Best memory last season: Making
Scotland B debut in 0–16 loss to
Ireland in Belfast
Suggestions to improve rugby:
On-field – Increase worth of tries to
5 points and reduce penalty goals to
2 points. *Off-field* – Broken time
payments

	apps	pts
Scotland B (**1990**)		
Last Season	1 cap	0
Career	1 cap	0

Other notable landmarks in rugby career: Only took up rugby at age of
22. Represented Glasgow since 1985 and toured with them to Holland and
Belgium (1985), and Ireland (1989). Joined Stirling when in Scottish third
division. Made debut for Scotland B in 0–16 loss to Ireland B last season
Player to watch: Kenny Logan (Stirling County)

Robinson, B. F.   Ireland

Full Name: Brian Francis Robinson
1990/91 International category:
Ireland Full
Club: Ballymena
Position: No.8
Height: 6'4" **Weight:** 15st
Occupation: PE teacher
Born: Belfast, 20.3.66
Family: Single
International debut: Ireland 13,
France 21, 1991
Five Nations' debut: As above
Best moment in rugby: Scoring try
for Ireland in 25–28 loss to Scotland
(1990/91)
Worst moment in rugby: Tearing
cruciate and medial ligaments in first
match after touring Zimbabwe with
Ulster (1986/87) and missing next
18 months

Most respected opponent: New Zealand back row Zinzan Brooke
Serious injuries: As above
Best memory last season: Running on for first full cap at Lansdowne Road
Suggestions to improve rugby: *On-field* – Award more points for tries.
Off-field – Relax amateur rules to allow players to earn money away from
rugby. Reimburse employers for time lost
Other notable landmarks in rugby career: Played for Irish Wolfhounds

Seven in Sicily (1989/90), and Ireland U-25s against US Eagles (1989/90). Previously represented Combined Irish Provinces (aged 20). Played for Ulster against 1989 All Blacks. Made Ireland B debut in 22–22 draw with Scotland B (1989/90) and, last season, after warming B bench v. Argentina (won 27–12), helped Ireland B beat Scots 16-0 at Ravenhill. Ever-present in Ireland's back row during 1991 Five

	apps	pts
Ireland B (**1989**)		
Last Season	1 cap	0
	1 rep	
Career	2 caps	0
Ireland (**1991**)		
Last Season	6 caps	4
1991	Tour to Namibia	
	World Cup squad	
Career	6 caps	4

Nations' Championship. Scored first International try in 25–28 loss to Scotland at Murrayfield
Touchlines: Sub-aqua diving, keep-fit
Player to watch: Simon Geoghegan (London Irish)

Robinson, R. A.   England

Full Name: Richard Andrew Robinson
1990/91 International category: England B
Club: Bath
Position: Flanker
Height: 5′9″ **Weight:** 13st 12lbs
Occupation: Schoolmaster
Born: Taunton, Somerset, 3.4.64
Family: Married
Family links with rugby: Father captained Somerset and Royal Navy and coached Somerset. Brother Sean plays for Saracens. Brother Peter plays for Taunton
Former clubs: Loughborough Students, Taunton
International debut: Australia 28, England 8, 1988
Five Nations' debut: England 12, Scotland 12, 1989

Best moment in rugby: Being told of first ever England selection on beach in Wollongong

Worst moment in rugby: England losing to Wales at Cardiff (1989) – worse feeling than being dropped

Most embarrassing moment: Welsh referee Clive Norling (wearing microphone for benefit of TV) telling me: 'British Lion or not, next time you're off'

Most respected opponents: England flankers Peter Winterbottom and Gary Rees

	apps	pts
England B (1987)		
Last Season	2 caps	0
England (1988)		
Last Season	0 caps	0
Career	7 caps	4
Lions 1989		

Serious injuries: Broken knee cap while at Loughborough

Other sporting achievements: Cricket for Somerset U-19s and West of England Schools

Best memory last season: Winning English League Championship with Bath

Suggestions to improve rugby: Retire all committee men at age of 40. Treat players better

Other notable landmarks in rugby career: Captained Loughborough to 1986 UAU title, having played in 1984 and 1985 winning teams. Played Debut for Bath at Pontypool where handed Pooler their first home defeat for twenty years. Won three Cup finals with Bath. Selected for 1989 Lions in first full International season. Toured Argentina with England in summer 1990. Captained England B to 31–16 defeat of touring Namibians at Leicester last season and also played in 12–9 win v. Italy at Waterloo

Touchlines: Golf (24-handicap)

Rodber, T. A. K.   England

Full Name: Timothy Andrew Keith Rodber
1990/91 International category: England B
Clubs: Northampton and Army
Position: No.8
Height: 6'6" **Weight:** 16st 7lbs
Occupation: Student
Born: Richmond, Yorkshire, 2.7.69
Family: Single
Family links with rugby: Father played
Former clubs: Oxford Old Boys, Petersfield
International debut (B): France 15, England 15, 1990
Best moments in rugby: Being selected for England XV v. Italy, 1990 (won 33–15). Scoring two tries for England B last season
Worst moment in rugby: Being injured by foul play v. Plymouth Albion
Most respected opponent: England No.8 Dean Richards – awesome in every department
Serious injuries: Popped ribs

	apps	pts
England B (1990)		
Last Season	3 caps	8
Career	4 caps	8
England	1995 Development squad	

Other sporting achievements: Hampshire Schools County hockey and cricket
Best memory last season: Reaching Pilkington Cup final with Saints
Suggestions to improve rugby: Anything to take away stagnant play (i.e. Gloucester scrums etc.)
Other notable landmarks in rugby career: Leaving Oxford OBs for Northampton. Played for England at U-21 and B level. Selected for England tour to Argentina (1990) and turned out v. Tucuman Selection (won 19–14), Cuyo Selection (lost 21–22) and Cordoba Selection (won 15–12). Last season scored tries for England B in 31–16 defeat of Namibia and in 10–24 loss to Ireland B. Also played v. France B (as on debut in 1990)
Touchlines: Active interest in Army

Rolland, A. C. P.   Ireland

Full Name: Alain Colm Pierre Rolland
1990/91 International category: Ireland Full
Club: Blackrock College
Position: Scrum-half
Height: 5'10" **Weight:** 11st 9lbs
Occupation: Bank official
Born: Dublin, 22.8.66
Family: Single
International debut: Ireland 20, Argentina 18, 1990
Best moments in rugby: Blackrock beating Trinity in 1988 Leinster Senior Cup final, having been given no chance. Winning first cap
Worst moment in rugby: Blackrock losing Senior Schools Cup to De La Salle, aged 18
Most embarrassing moment: Concussed playing for Leinster U-20s and talking absolute nonsense while being helped off field
Most respected opponent: Ireland scrum-half Fergus Aherne
Best memory last season: Running out for Ireland debut v. Pumas
Suggestions to improve rugby: None. Very happy with game as it is

	apps	pts
Ireland B (**1989**)		
Last Season	0 caps	0
Career	1 cap	0
Ireland (**1990**)		
Last Season	1 cap	0
	4 reps	
Career	1 cap	0

Other notable landmarks in rugby career: Played two seasons with Leinster U-20s. Three full caps for Leinster (1988/89). 1989/90 replacement for Ireland U-25s against US Eagles. One Ireland B cap came in 22–22 draw with Scotland (1989). Made full Ireland bow last season in 20–18 defeat of Argentina but relegated to bench reserve throughout 1991 Five Nations' Championship
Touchlines: Half-French – speak language fluently and have dual nationality. Enjoy cycling and running

Rooney, S. V. J.   Ireland

Full Name: Stephen Vincent John Rooney
1990/91 International category: Ireland U-21
Club: University College Dublin
Position: Flanker
Height: 6'2" **Weight:** 15st
Occupation: Commerce student
Born: Dublin, 19.11.70
Family: Single
International debut: Netherlands 21, Ireland U-21 7, 1990
Best moment in rugby: Beating England U-21s at Moseley (1990/91)
Worst moment in rugby: Playing for St Michael's College in 1988 Schools Senior Cup final defeat
Best memory last season: Winning selection to Ireland U-21s for English match
Suggestions to improve rugby: *On-field* – Abandon 90-degree scrum wheel law. Ban scrum-half dummy
Other notable landmarks in rugby career: Spent two years playing for Ireland Schools (winning seven caps), before graduating to Ireland U-21s (eligible again this season), with whom went on two-match tour of Netherlands and then played in 22–16 win over England. Also represented Leinster at U-19, U-20 and senior squad levels
Touchlines: Any sports, music
Player to watch: Gabriel Fulcher (University College Dublin)

Ireland U-21 (1990)	apps	pts
Last Season	2 caps	0
v. Netherlands B	1 app	0
Career	2 caps	0

Rowlands, J. — Wales

Full Name: Jonathan Rowlands
1990/91 International category:
Wales B (bench)
Club: Newbridge
Position: Loose-head prop
Height: 5'11" **Weight:** 15st 4lbs
Occupation: Operations manager
Born: Cardiff, 5.10.62
Family: Married
Family links with rugby: Father
played for Risca
Former clubs: Risca, Newport
International debut (B): France
28, Wales 15, 1989
Best moment in rugby: Ben
Francis Cup final when Man of
Match
Worst moment in rugby:
Newbridge losing 3–73 to Neath
Most embarrassing moment: As
above
Most respected opponent: No-one
Other sporting achievements:
Kept wicket at school
Best memory last season: First
game finished without being injured
Suggestions to improve rugby:
On-field – Give each player a ball.
Improve refereeing standards

	apps	pts
Wales B (1989)		
Last Season	1 rep	
Career	1 cap	0
Wales 1991	World Cup squad	
Heineken 1990/91	9 apps	0

Other notable landmarks in rugby career: Represented Welsh Universities, UAU and Wales B. Warmed bench for Wales B last season during 34–12 defeat of Holland in Leiden. Included in Wales' preliminary squad for 1991 World Cup
Touchlines: Member of Christians in Sport. Youth club leader
Player to watch: Richard Brown (Newbridge)

Rowntree, G. C.   England

Full Name: Graham Christopher Rowntree
1990/91 International category: England U-21
Club: Leicester
Position: Prop
Height: 6′ **Weight:** 16st 10lbs
Occupation: Insurance broker
Born: Stockton-on-Tees, 18.4.71
Family: Single
Family links with rugby: Two brothers, like myself, Dean Richards and Barry Evans, represented John Cleveland College
Former club: Nuneaton
International debut U-21: England 16, Ireland 22, 1990
Best moment in rugby: Winning first England recognition – for 16-Group back in 1987
Worst moment in rugby: England Colts' 12–6 loss to Wales at Wrexham in 1989/90 season
Most respected opponent: Wasps prop Gary Holmes
Best memory last season: Leicester's Courage League victory over Northampton

	apps	pts
England U-21 (**1990**)		
Last Season	2 caps	0
Career	2 caps	0

Suggestions to improve rugby: *On-field* – Revert to old scrummaging laws. *Off-field* – relax compensation laws
Other notable landmarks in rugby career: Broke into Leicester Tigers first team aged 19. Played in all four matches for 1989/90 England Colts. Graduated to England U-21s last season, coming on as replacement for debut in 16–22 loss to Ireland, and starting match in 7–9 loss to French Armed Forces
Touchlines: Music, synchronised swimming
Player to watch: Neil Back (Leicester)

Ryan, D.   England

Full Name: Dean Ryan
1990/91 International category:
England B
Club: Wasps
Positions: Flanker, No.8
Height: 6'6" **Weight:** 17st
Occupation: Builder
Born: Tuxford, 22.6.66
Family: Wendy (wife)
Former club: Saracens
International debut: Argentina 12,
England 25, 1990
Best moment in rugby: London
21, Australia 10, 1988
Worst moment in rugby:
Fractured arm for second time in
1989 v. Cardiff
Most embarrassing moment:
Trying to stop Australian wing
David Campese
Most respected opponent:
England No.8 Dean Richards
Serious injuries: Fractured left arm
(twice)
Best memory last season: Touring
Argentina (summer 1990) and
scoring try on full debut v. Argentina
Suggestions to improve rugby:
Off-field – Relax amateur laws
Other notable landmarks in rugby

	apps	pts
England B (**1988**)		
Last Season	4 caps	4
	1 rep	
England (**1990**)		
Last Season	0 caps	0
	1995 Development squad	
Career	2 caps	4

career: Made England B debut in 9–37 loss to 1988 touring Wallabies. Had
to withdraw from England B v. France (1989) through injury, but made four
appearances last season (v. Emerging Australians, Spain, Ireland and France),
scoring try in 50–6 win over Spain. Missed Wasps' crowning glory in 1989/90,
having left for New Zealand when club clinched English League title on final
day of season v. Saracens. Toured Argentina with England in 1990, picking
up two full caps and scoring try on debut. Toured Australia with London last
summer
Touchlines: Squash
Player to watch: Neil Back (Leicester)

Saunders, R.   Ireland

Full Name: Rob Saunders
1990/91 International category:
Ireland Full
Club: London Irish
Position: Scrum-half
Height: 5'10" **Weight:** 13st 4lbs
Occupation: Marketing executive
Born: Nottingham, 5.8.68
Family: Single
Family links with rugby: Father
(Eric) a Scottish trialist who played
for Edinburgh and Leicester, and
captained Glasgow
Former club: Queen's University,
Belfast
International debut: Ireland 13,
France 21, 1991
Five Nations' debut: As above
Best moment in rugby: Leading
Ireland out as captain on my
International debut at Lansdowne
Road
Worst moment in rugby: Being
dropped for 13–13 draw v. New
Zealand (1990)
Other sporting achievements:
Ireland U-16 squash team. Ulster
Schools shot put champion
Most respected opponent: Bath
scrum-half Richard Hill
Best memory last season: Leading
Ireland in Five Nations'
Championship

	apps	pts
Ireland U-21 (**1989**)		
Last Season	0 caps	0
Career	1 cap	0
Ireland B (**1990**)		
Last Season	1 cap	0
Career	1 cap	0
Ireland (**1991**)		
Last Season	6 caps	0
Career	6 caps	0

Suggestions to improve rugby: *On-field* – Greater awareness of fitness.
More professional approach by referees (massive gap between standards).
Reduce value of penalty goal to encourage more open play. *Off-field* – Relax
amateur status. Players should be allowed to earn money from the game (e.g.
writing for papers, appearances etc.) but should not earn from a direct salary
basis **Other notable landmarks in rugby career:** Captained Ulster Schools,
Irish Schools (v. Australia, 1987), Irish Universities and QUB. Made Ireland
U-21 debut in 10–9 away win in Italy (1989) but was dropped for 13–13
draw v. New Zealand (1990). Rose to prominence last season as one of seven

players promoted from Ireland B after 16-0 defeat of Scotland B at Ravenhill. Not only played entire 1991 Five Nations' Championship but captained side in each of four Internationals before experienced Phil Matthews took over for summer tour to Namibia

Touchlines: Squash, golf, watching any sport

Sexton, J. F.   Ireland

Full Name: John Francis Sexton
1990/91 International category: Ireland B
Club: Lansdowne
Position: Wing
Height: 5'10" **Weight:** 12st 10lbs
Occupation: Marketing representative
Born: Dublin, 27.6.63
Family: Single
Former club: Dublin Univ
International debut: Ireland 10, England 21, 1988
Five Nations' debut: Ireland 21, France 26, 1989
Best moment in rugby: Winning first cap in Millennium match
Worst moment in rugby: Underestimating Rory Underwood's pace when he ran past me for a try in Millennium match
Most embarrassing moment: As above
Most respected opponent: French wing Patrice Lagisquet
Serious injuries: Broken shoulder, dislocated shoulder, torn cruciate ligaments

	apps	pts
Ireland B (**1991**)		
Last Season	1 cap	0
Career	1 cap	0
Ireland (**1988**)		
Last Season	0 caps	0
Career	3 caps	7

Other sporting achievements: Captained Moyle Park College to Leinster Gaelic football championship. Sprinted in 100m final at National Championships
Suggestions to improve rugby: Keep game as it is but identify players' employers in match programmes
Other notable landmarks in rugby career: Played soccer and Gaelic at

school, but not rugby. Started game at 15 and went on to play for Irish Universities, Leinster and Ireland U-25s. Missed 1989/90 season through injury, after returning from 1989 summer tour to North America. Scored try for Leinster against 1990 All Blacks. Made Ireland B debut last season in 24–10 defeat of England B at Old Belvedere
Touchlines: Golf, tennis

Shaw, R. G. Wales

Full Name: Richard Gordon Shaw
1990/91 International category:
Wales U-21
Club: Llanelli
Position: Tight-head prop
Height: 6′1″ **Weight:** 16st 7lbs
Occupation: Welder
Born: Neath, 16.1.70
Family: Single
Former clubs: Glynneath, Neath Athletic
International debut (U-21): Wales 23, Scotland 15, 1991
Best moment in rugby: Selection to Wales U-21 team
Worst moment in rugby: Being dropped by Wales Youth (1987/88) after game v. Welsh Colleges
Most respected opponent: Anybody who gives me a hard time
Best memory last season: Scottish U-21 match at Llanelli
Other notable landmarks in rugby career: Represented Wales Youth (1988/89) before graduating to Wales U-21s last season. As well as game v. Scotland, also helped WRU President's (U-21) XV beat New Zealand Rugby News XV 34–13 at Pontypridd. Made three appearances for Llanelli in Heineken premier division
Touchlines: Sea fishing, shooting

	apps	pts
Wales U-21 (1990)		
Last Season	1 cap	0
v. New Zealand XV	1 app	0
Career	1 cap	0
Heineken 1990/91	3 apps	0

Shepherd, R. J. S.　　Scotland

Full Name: Rowen James Stanley Shepherd

1990/91 International category: Scotland U-21

Club: Edinburgh Academicals

Positions: Fly-half, centre

Height: 6′ **Weight:** 13st 8lbs

Occupation: PE student

Born: Edinburgh, 25.12.70

Family: Single

Family links with rugby: Father played for Caithness

Former club: Caithness

International debut (U-21): Wales 23, Scotland 15, 1991

Best moment in rugby: Scoring for Accies v. Randwick at 1990 Melrose Sevens

Worst moment in rugby: Arguing with dad while playing Sevens

Best memories last season: Winning U-21 cap and getting late call for Scotland's tour to North America

Suggestions to improve rugby: *On-field* – Alter regulation regarding rolling mauls to rule against obstructing players. *Off-field* – None. Things are okay

	apps	pts
Scotland U-21 (**1991**)		
Last Season	1 cap	3
Career	1 cap	3
Scotland 1991	Tour to North America	

Other notable landmarks in rugby career: Toured North America with Scotland last season after Scott Nichol withdrew through injury. Invited to attend Scotland's senior squad weekend at St Andrews. Previously, represented Scotland at Students and U-21 level. Kicked penalty goal for U-21s in 15–23 loss to Wales U-21s (1991)

Touchlines: Tennis, golf

Player to watch: Scott Nichol (Selkirk)

Shiel, A. G.   Scotland

Full Name: Andrew **Graham** Shiel
1990/91 International category:
Scotland U-21
Club: Melrose
Positions: Fly-half, centre, full-back
Height: 5'10" **Weight:** 13st
Occupation: Apprentice
stonemason
Born: Galashiels, 13.8.70
Family: Single
Family links with rugby: Father
played for Melrose GS
International debut (U-21):
Scotland 10, Wales 24, 1990
Best moments in rugby: First
Scotland game v. Wellington on
1990 New Zealand tour. Winning
McEwan's Scottish Championship
with Melrose (1989/90)
Worst moment in rugby: Not
making the Scottish Schools XV to
play New Zealand in 1988
Most embarrassing moment: Ball
toppled over in front of posts before I
kicked it during 1990 Hawick Sevens
Most respected opponent:
Scotland centre Sean Lineen –
always a great experience playing
against a national player in your own position

	apps	pts
Scotland U-21 (**1990**)		
Last Season	1 cap	0
Career	2 caps	6
Scotland 1990	Tour to New Zealand	
1991	Tour to North America	
	World Cup squad	

Serious injuries: Straining inner and exterior quadriceps and adductor muscle (1988/89) and missing over four months rugby. Pelvic strain (Nov 1990) – three months out
Other sporting achievements: Athletics for Borders Schools and Borders AAA
Best memories last season: Winning Border League with Melrose. Selection for Scotland tour to North America
Suggestions to improve rugby: *On-field* – Make game more attractive; too forward orientated in Scotland at present (lack of running ability). *Off-field* – Treat players better for all they put into game
Other notable landmarks in rugby career: Represented Scottish Schools three times, Scotland U-19s and U-21s (twice). Scored six points in 1989/90 defeat (10–24) to Wales U-21 and played in 15–23 loss to same opposition

last season. Made four appearances for Scotland on 1990 tour to New Zealand – Wellington (drew 16–16), Nelson Bays/Marlborough (won 23–6), Southland (won 45–12) and Manawatu (won 19–4) – scoring one try. Went to Hong Kong with European Saltires and played South Pacific Barbarians in XVs prior to Sevens tournament. Toured North America with Scotland last summer, playing in five games out of six (including Internationals v. US Eagles and Canada)

Touchlines: Social golf, cricket, swimming

Player to watch: 'Doddie' Weir (Melrose)

Sims, D. England

Full Name: David Sims

1990/91 International category: England U-21

Club: Gloucester

Positions: Lock, No.8

Height: 6'8" **Weight:** 16st 6lbs

Occupation: Student

Born: Gloucester, 22.11.69

Family: Single

Family links with rugby: Grandfather (Thomas Price) played for England (1948–49)

Former clubs: Longlevens, Sunnybank (Aus)

International debut: Netherlands 3, England U-21 24, 1990

Best moment in rugby: Putting on Gloucester senior shirt for first time

Worst moment in rugby: Watching 1990 Pilkington Cup final defeat to Bath from Gloucester replacements' bench

Most respected opponent: Gloucester lock John Gadd (in training)

	apps	pts
England U-21 (**1990**)		
Last Season	3 caps	0
Career	4 caps	0

Serious injuries: Damaged neck muscles

Other sporting achievements: Basketball for Gloucester Jets

Other notable landmarks in rugby career: Attended England Schools (16-Group) and Colts final trials. Played for South West U-21s before graduating to senior team. Won England Students cap against Combined

Services and was replacement for England U-21s against French Armed forces. Played for Brisbane club Sunnybank in summer of 1990 before returning to play for England U-21s in 16–22 loss to Ireland U-21s at Moseley and, last May, v. Netherlands and French Armed Forces again

Touchlines: Swimming, training, music

Skinner, M. G. England

Full Name: Michael Gordon Skinner
1990/91 International category: England Full (bench)
Club: Harlequins
Positions: Flanker (6 or 7), No.8
Height: 6'4" **Weight:** 16st 6lbs
Occupation: Freelance computer consultant
Born: Newcastle upon Tyne, 26.11.58
Family: Single
Former clubs: Blaydon, Blackheath
International debut: France 10, England 9, 1988
Five Nations' debut: As above
Best moment in rugby: Mike Teague's admission to being on a mission from God
Worst moment in rugby: Referee Fred Howard awarding Nottingham a kickable penalty in our 1990/91 Pilkington Cup semi-final, with the scores at 15–15 in extra-time. Guess who it was given against?
Most embarrassing moment: Playing blind-side for Barbarians v. NZ Barbarians (1987/88). Still bound to scrum when Michael Jones was scoring on blind side from 10-yard scrum. The worst feeling I have ever felt

	apps	pts
England B (**1987**)		
Last Season	1 cap	0
England (**1988**)		
Last Season	1cap	0
	4 reps	
1991	Tour to Australia	
	World Cup squad	
Career	13 caps	4

Most respected opponent: Billy Mordue, captain and No.8 of Ryton RFC – great commitment and loyalty to club
Serious injuries: Knee operation – file and drill knee cap

Best memory last season: Celebrations in the winning changing room after both Grand Slam (England) and Pilkington Cup final (Quins)

Suggestions to improve rugby: *On-field* – Standards of refereeing. Players, administrators and coaches put so much work in to improve and then we get Fred Howard in the Cup semi-final against Nottingham! The RFU is promoting the game brilliantly at junior level. Maybe they could improve it for us older ones by improving the TV coverage (edited highlights and commentators are not good)

Other notable landmarks in rugby career: Scored winning try on debut for Blaydon at Stockton (1975/76) and received hero's welcome afterwards on return from having eye stitched at hospital. Started career as centre at school, and played No.8 and flanker for Northumberland Colts. Joined Blackheath in 1979 and represented Kent in 1986 County Championship final. Became fixture in London divisional team after moving to Harlequins. Made England B debut in 1987 match v. France. Represented second string again last season in 31–16 defeat of touring Namibians. Ever-present on England bench during Grand Slam prior to touring Australia last summer where came on as 40th minute replacement for Mike Teague in 28–12 win over Fiji to gain 13th cap

Touchlines: Cuddling girlfriend Anna Palmer (Hong Kong Sevens), fishing, squash, DIY, drinking

Player to watch: Marcus 'spartacus' Acott (Charlton Park) – because his father is Kevin Acott

Smith, G. B.   Scotland

Full Name: Graham Bernard Smith
1990/91 International category:
Scotland A
Club: Moseley
Position: Tight-head prop
Height: 6′1″ **Weight:** 17st 5lbs
Occupation: Building operative
Born: Wolverhampton, 5.3.61
Family: Karen (wife) and child
International debut: Spain 7,
Scotland A 39, 1990
Best moment in rugby: Scoring
first try for Scotland (v. British
Columbia) on last summer's tour to
North America
Worst moment in rugby: Moseley
losing 6–3 to Aspatria in third round
of 1988/89 Pilkington Cup
Most respected opponent: Former
Wales loose-head prop Ian Stephens
Best memory last season: Gaining
selection to Scotland A – totally out
of the blue
Suggestions to improve rugby: *On-field* – Standards of refereeing are
getting left behind. There are only
one or two top class referees; only one
or two who can interpret the scrummage professionally. It is not the
referees' fault. They are not given

	apps	pts
England U-23 (**1984**)		
Career	1 cap	0
Scotland B (**1990/91**)	1 rep	
Scotland A (**1990**)		
Last Season	1 cap	0
Career	1 cap	0
Scotland 1991	Tour to North America	

enough help from the authorities. *Off-field* – Expected to do so much as a
player. Never asked/wanted to be paid to play but seems unreasonable that
we cannot earn a little bit from the sport off the field
Other notable landmarks in rugby career: Qualified to play for Scotland
through grandparents (from Castle Douglas), having represented England
U-23s v. Spain in 1984. Played for Anglo-Scots in Scottish Inter-District
Championship. Bench reserve for Scotland B v. France at Hughenden last
season, having played for Scotland A before Christmas. Toured North
America with Scotland last summer, making appearances v. British Columbia
(scored try in 29–9 win), Rugby East (won 24–12) and Ontario (won 43–3)
Touchlines: 'Showing' bull mastiff dogs
Player to watch: Stuart Reid (Boroughmuir)

Smith, I. R.   Scotland

Full Name: Ian Richard Smith
1990/91 International category:
England B (bench)/Scotland B
Club: Gloucester
Position: Flanker
Height: 6′ **Weight:** 13st 10lbs
Occupation: Civil engineer
Born: Gloucester, 16.3.65
Family: Single
Family links with rugby: Father
Dick was an England trialist who
played for (and captained)
Gloucester and Barbarians
Former club: Longlevens
International debut (England):
Spanish Select 15, England B 32,
1989
International debut (Scotland):
Ireland B 16, Scotland B 0, 1990
Best moment in rugby: Reaching
Twickenham with Gloucester in
1989/90 Pilkington Cup final
Worst moment in rugby: Losing
1989/90 Pilkington Cup final 6–48
to Bath
Most embarrassing moment:
Above match – we were humiliated
Most respected opponent: Neath
flanker Lyn Jones

	apps	pts
England B (1989/90)		Tour to Spain
(1990/91)	1 rep	
Scotland B (**1990**)		
Last Season	2 caps	0
Career	2 caps	0

Suggestions to improve rugby: Relax amateur laws
Other notable landmarks in rugby career: England 18-Group trialist.
Played 200th game for Gloucester in 1989/90 Pilkington Cup final. Spent
1988 Australian season playing in Wollongong. Selected to England's 1991
World Cup squad, having spent summer of 1990 on standby for Argentine
tour, but then decided to switch allegiances to Scotland and played twice for
Scotland B last season (v. Ireland and France). 1991/92 Gloucester captain
Touchlines: Shooting, squash

Smith, S. J.   Ireland

Full Name: Stephen James Smith
1990/91 International category:
Ireland Full
Club: Ballymena
Position: Hooker
Height: 6′ **Weight:** 16st
Occupation: Sportswear rep
Born: Belfast, 18.7.59
Family: Single
Family links with rugby: Brother
Oliver plays for Ballymena
International debut: Ireland 10,
England 21, 1988
Five Nations' debut: Ireland 21,
France 26, 1989
Best moment in rugby: Selection
for 1989 Lions
Worst moment in rugby: Having
to leave field at Twickenham after
damaging rib cartilage against
England in 1990 clash
Most respected opponent: All
Blacks hooker Sean Fitzpatrick
Serious injuries: Damaged rib
cartilage (1990)
Best memory last season: Scoring
try for Ireland in 13–21 loss to
France in comeback match from rib
cartilage sustained previous season v.
England

	apps	pts
Ireland B (1990/91)	1 rep	
Ireland (**1988**)		
Last Season	6 caps	4
1991	Tour to Namibia	
	World Cup squad	
Career	15 caps	8
Lions 1989		

Suggestions to improve rugby:
On-field: – Welcome any laws to speed up game. *Off-field* – More professional
approach away from field to match greater commitment being made by players
Other notable landmarks in rugby career: Called out to 1987 World Cup
as Ireland's second replacement hooker but did not feature. Following season
broke into Ireland team and became first Irishman to mark debut with a try
since Hugo MacNeill in 1981. Represented Barbarians against 1988 Wallabies,
1989 Home Unions against France, and 1989 Lions in Australia, playing 5
games and scoring 2 tries. Toured South Africa with 1989 World XV and
found experince awe-inspiring – a real eye-opener. Helped Ballymena win
1989/90 Ulster League and Cup double for second consecutive season (first
team to achieve feat since 1907). Although only bench reserve for Ireland B

v. Argentina early last season, was a regular for Ireland in ensuing Five Nations' Championship, scoring try in loss to France
Touchlines: Golf (15-handicap)
Player to watch: Nicky Barry (Garryowen)

Soden, P. J.   Ireland

Full Name: Philip Joseph Soden
1990/91 International category: Ireland B
Club: Cork Constitution
Position: Loose-head prop
Height: 6' **Weight:** 16st 10lbs
Occupation: Owner of dry-cleaning business
Born: London, 6.9.69
Family: Single
Former club: Christian Brothers College (Cork)
International debut (B): Ireland 16, Scotland 0, 1990
Best moment in rugby: Playing in above match
Best memory last season: Cork Con's All-Ireland League victory
Other notable landmarks in rugby career: Played for Irish Schools (1986–88) and Munster at Schools and U-20 level, before graduating to U-21 team in 1989 for 13–13 draw with touring New Zealand XV. Won second U-21 cap in 22–16 defeat of England last season before graduating to B team for 16-0 win v. Scotland B at Ravenhill
Touchlines: Golf, swimming
Player to watch: Paul McCarthy (Constitution)

	apps	pts
Ireland U-21 (**1989**)		
Last Season	1 cap	0
Career	2 caps	0
Ireland B (**1990**)		
Last Season	1 cap	0
Career	1 cap	0

254

Sole, D. M. B.   Scotland

Full Name: David Michael Barclay Sole
1990/91 International category: Scotland Full
Club: Edinburgh Academicals
Position: Prop
Height: 5'11″ **Weight:** 16st 4lbs
Occupation: Grain buyer
Born: Aylesbury, 8.5.62
Former clubs: Exeter University, Toronto Scottish, Bath
International debut: Scotland 18, France 17, 1986
Five Nations' debut: As above
Best moment in rugby: Captaining Scotland to 1990 Five Nations' Grand Slam
Worst moments in rugby: Suffering broken nose and cheekbone playing in Bath's 12–3 win against Moseley in the 1987 John Player Cup quarter-final. Coming so close to winning second Test v. New Zealand (Auckland, 1990) but failing 18–21
Most respected opponents: Scotland's Iain Milne and France's Jean-Pierre Garuet – two of the world's strongest scrummagers. They don't bend the rules, but use their strength to succeed

	apps	pts
Scotland B (**1983**)		
Last Season	0 caps	0
Career	5 caps	
Scotland (**1986**)		
Last Season	5 caps	0
1991	World Cup squad	
Career	32 caps	8
Scotland VII (**1991**)	Hong Kong Sevens	
Lions 1989	3 Tests	0

Serious injuries: Broken nose, cheekbone
Best memory last season: Imposing a £2 fine on anyone who kicked to touch during Barbarians' Easter Tour match at Cardiff
Suggestions to improve rugby: *On-field* – Award more points for a try to take emphasis off kicking. *Off-field* – More constructive dialogue between players and committee men
Other notable landmarks in rugby career: 1987 John Player Cup winners' medal. Appointed Scotland captain (Scotland 38, Fiji 17, Murrayfield, 28 October, 1989). Captained Lions against New South Wales B and the Anzacs during 1989 tour of Australia. Captained Barbarians against 1989 All Blacks.

Captained Home Unions against Europe in April 1990 in aid of Romanian Appeal. Captained Scotland on 1990 tour of New Zealand
Player to watch: Ronnie Kirkpatrick (Jed-Forest)

Southern, D. V.   England

Full Name: David Vincent (**Sammy**) Southern
1990/91 International category: England B
Club: Orrell
Position: Prop
Height: 5'10" **Weight:** 15st 8lbs
Occupation: Motor mechanic
Born: Wigan, 29.12.52
Family: Janice (wife), Martin (son) and Alison (daughter)
International debut: England B 31, Namibia 16, 1990
Best moments in rugby: First time captaining Orrell. Lancashire's 1990 tour to Zimbabwe
Worst moment in rugby: Orrell's 1990/91 Pilkington Cup semi-final loss to Northampton
Most respected opponent: Former Pontypool prop Charlie Faulkner
Best memory last season: Winning at Gloucester with Orrell
Suggestions to improve rugby: *On-field* – Less pressure on referees from assessors. *Off-field* – No complaints

	apps	pts
England B (**1990**)		
Last Season	1 cap	0
Career	1 cap	0

Other notable landmarks in rugby career: Orrell captain. Represented Lancashire, North and Barbarians last season, in addition to making England B debut in 31–16 win of Namibia
Touchlines: Keeping fit to play rugby
Player to watch: Martin Hynes (Orrell)

Stanger, A. G. Scotland

Full Name: Anthony George Stanger
1990/91 International category: Scotland Full
Club: Hawick
Position: Wing
Height: 6'2" **Weight:** 13st 7lbs
Occupation: Bank officer
Born: Hawick, 14.5.68
Family: Single
Family links with rugby: Peter (brother) plays for Hawick, Scotland U-18s
International debut: Scotland 38, Fiji 17, 1989
Five Nations' debut: Ireland 10, Scotland 13, 1990
Best moment in rugby: Scoring try in Grand Slam decider against England
Worst moment in rugby: Getting dropped by Hawick in 1986/87 as an 18-year-old
Most respected opponents: Rory Underwood and Arthur Emyr
Other sporting achievements: Hawick High School athletics champion (three times)

Scotland (**1989**)	apps	pts
Last Season 1991	5 caps	8
	World Cup squad	
Career	13 caps	36

Suggestions to improve rugby: *On-field* – Increase value of a try, reduce value of a penalty goal. *Off-field* – Do not try to bring about too much change too quickly. The SRU are doing very well, but they must ensure that everyone is treated equally when it comes to peripheral benefits

Other notable landmarks in rugby career: Scored 6 tries in first 6 Internationals (2 on debut against Fiji, 3 against Romania and 1 against England in Grand Slam decider). Toured with Scotland in Japan (summer 1989), scoring 3 tries in 3 games, and to New Zealand last summer. Made debut for Hawick while 17-year-old student – 5 caps for Scottish Schools at centre in 1985/86, followed by 2 for Scotland U-21s. Began last season with two tries in 49–3 defeat of Argentina (9 tries in 9 Internationals)

Player to watch: Peter Stanger (Hawick)

Stanhope, B. G.   England

Full Name: Benjamin Guy Stanhope
1990/91 International category:
England U-21
Club: Harlequins
Position: Hooker
Height: 5′9.5″ **Weight:** 15st
Occupation: Medical student
Born: British Columbia, Canada,
24.9.69
Family: Single
Former club: Guy's Hospital
International debut (U-21):
England 16, Ireland 22, 1990
Best moment in rugby: Captaining
England Schools to their first ever
win over Italy (20–14) at 16-Group
level in April 1986
Worst moments in rugby: Losing
to France (18-Group) in 1987, and
Ireland (U-21) in October 1990
Best memory last season: Being
capped by England at U-21 level
Suggestions to improve rugby:
On-field – I think the current rules of
the game, when properly enforced,
provide as good a game as possible.
I just wish more referees knew even
vaguely what 90-degrees is! *Off-field*

	apps	pts
England U-21 (1990)		
Last Season	1 cap	0
Career	1 cap	0

– Amateurism is rugby union's greatest strength. To preserve this I think
players should be able to benefit from any non-playing capacity (including
after-dinner speeches) so as to avoid payments to players under tenuous and
false pretences, which, really, we all know is widespread in the game
Other notable landmarks in rugby career: Capped by England at
16-Group (1986), 18-Group (1987) and U-21s (1990)
Touchlines: Singing, acting, basketball, all sports
Player to watch: Gavin Thompson (Harlequins) – a complete centre; fast
and elusive runner, solid tackler

Staples, J.   Ireland

Full Name: James (Jim) Staples
1990/91 International category:
Ireland Full
Club: London Irish
Positions: Full-back, wing
Height: 6'2" Weight: 13st 7lbs
Occupation: Commercial property
agent
Born: London, 20.10.65
Family: Single
Family links with rugby: Younger
brother plays for Westcombe Park
Former clubs: St Mary's, Bromley,
Sidcup
International debut: Wales 21,
Ireland 21, 1991
Five Nations' debut: As above
Best moment in rugby: Making
Ireland debut in Cardiff last season
Worst moments in rugby: Missing
out on promotion to English first
division with London Irish in
1988/89 after losing 22–21 to
last-minute dropped goal by
Blackheath, having led 21-0 at
half-time. Rory Underwood's try for
England in Dublin last season
Most embarrassing moment:
Missing flight home from Spain on
first county senior trip
Most respected opponent:
Scotland full-back Gavin Hastings –
strong, fast and always a threat

	apps	pts
Ireland U-25 (**1990**)		
Last Season	1 cap	0
Career	1 cap	0
Ireland B (**1989**)		
Last Season	0 caps	0
Career	1 cap	0
Ireland (**1991**)		
Last Season	5 caps	12
	1 rep	
1991	Tour to Namibia	
Career	5 caps	12

Other sporting achievements:
Played soccer in same forward line as Crystal Palace FC's Ian Wright for
Greenwich Borough
Best memory last season: Scoring debut try for Ireland in draw with Wales
Suggestions to improve rugby: *On-field* – No kicks to be allowed into touch
on full, even those taken inside own 22. *Off-field* – None. Just happy to be
playing at top level
Other notable landmarks in rugby career: Took over from former Ireland
full-back Hugo MacNeill at No.15 in London Irish team. Represented

Connacht v. 1989 All Blacks and Irish Wolfhounds in 1988/89 Hong Kong Sevens. Played twice for Ireland U-25s before reaching B grade in 1989/90 with appearance in 22–22 draw with Scotland. Selected for senior bench v. France in Five Nations' opener last season before playing in next three games, scoring try in 21–21 draw with Wales

Touchlines: Soccer, most other sports
Player to watch: Simon Geoghegan (London Irish)

Steele, J. D. England

Full Name: John David Steele
1990/91 International category:
England B
Club: Northampton
Position: Fly-half
Height: 5'10" **Weight:** 12st 5lbs
Occupation: Surveyor
Born: Cambridge, 9.8.64
Family: Sophie (wife)
Former club: Shelford
International debut: England B 31, Namibia 16, 1990
Best moment in rugby: Kicking six penalty goals to help Northampton beat Orrell in 1990/91 Pilkington Cup semi-finals
Worst moment in rugby: Northampton's 0–60 loss to Orrell (1990/91)
Most respected opponent: Former Leicester fly-half Les Cusworth
Best memory last season: Beating Orrell to reach 1990/91 Pilkington Cup final
Suggestions to improve rugby:
On-field – More flexible interpretation of certain rules by referees. Sort out chaos at scrums.
Off-field – Compensation for loss of earnings

		apps	pts
England B (**1990**)			
Last Season		1 cap	0
Career		1 cap	0
England	1995 Development squad		

Other notable landmarks in rugby career: Combined Services captain v. Australia. Toured New Zealand in 1988 with Combined Services & Police. Winning 1989/90 English second division title and 1990 National Sevens with Northampton. Played in 1990/91 Pilkington Cup final with Saints. Made

England B debut, two years after first being B replacement. Bench reserve v. 1988 touring Wallabies. Debut v. Namibia last season. Included in England's 1995 development squad
Touchlines: Sandhurst (1983/84). Five years as army officer. Joined first first-class club aged 24. Hockey, squash
Player to watch: Gavin Baldwin (Northampton)

Strett, M. G. England

Full Name: Martin Gerard Strett
1990/91 International category: England B
Club: Orrell
Position: Fly-half
Height: 6′ **Weight:** 12st 8lbs
Occupation: Student
Born: St Helens, Lancs, 4.4.68
Family: Single
Family links with rugby: Brian (father) played for West Park
Former club: West Park
International debut (B): England 12, Italy 9, 1991
Best moment in rugby: Lancashire's 1990 tour to Zimbabwe
Worst moment in rugby: Orrell's 1990 Pilkington Cup semi-final loss to Northampton
Best memory last season: Selection for England B

Most respected opponent: None. I don't worry about them
Suggestions to improve rugby: *On-field* – Greater consistency in refereeing. *Off-field* – None. Happy with way game is going
Other notable landmarks in rugby career: Replacement for England B v. Irish and French second strings. Given debut in 12–9 defeat of Italy and scored all English points (try, conversion and two penalty goals)

	apps	pts
England B (1991)		
Last Season	1 cap	12
	2 reps	
Career	1 cap	12

Swindells, S. R.   England

Full Name: Stephen Richard Swindells
1990/91 International category: England U-21
Club: Manchester
Position: Full-back
Height: 6′2″ **Weight:** 13st 4lbs
Occupation: Work in family's delicatessen
Born: Altrincham, 25.10.69
Family: Single
Family links with rugby: Chris (father) played for Manchester
Former club: Sale
International debut (U-21): England 16, Ireland 22, 1990
Best moment in rugby: Representing England U-21s
Worst moment in rugby: Missing ball playing for Cheshire v. Lancashire at U-16 level. Lancs scored from mistake (fortunately, I kicked last-minute penalty goal to tie game)
Other sporting achievements: Cricket for Cheshire Schools – had North and England U-16 trials

	apps	pts
England U-21 (**1990**)		
Last Season	2 caps	24
Career	2 caps	24

Best memory last season: Kicking 12 points on England U-21 debut at Moseley
Suggestions to improve rugby: *On-field* – None. Rules constantly changing and I would like to see game stay as it is. *Off-field* – A return to playing for enjoyment not the lure of money. Sad that everyone is going to rugby league
Other notable landmarks in rugby career: Represented North at U-16, U-18, U-21 (two seasons) and Full levels. Landed four penalty goals in England U-21's 16–22 loss to Ireland last season and repeated feat in 20–18 win over Netherlands
Player to watch: Damian Hopley (Wasps)

Taylor, B.   Wales

Full Name: Bleddyn Taylor
1990/91 International category:
Wales (World Cup squad)
Club: Swansea
Position: Wing
Height: 5'9" **Weight:** 13st 7lbs
Occupation: Area sales manager
Born: Bangor, 17.1.59
Family: Pamela (wife), Bleddyn
Rhys (son) and Nia (daughter)
Family links with rugby: Father
(Graham) played for Pontypool.
Uncle (Ivor) played for Pontypool
and Newport
Former clubs: Neath, Pontypool,
Llanelli
Best moments in rugby: Winning
1983 Welsh Cup with Pontypool.
Inclusion in Wales' preliminary 1991
World Cup squad
Worst moment in rugby: Being left
out of Swansea side to play 1989 All
Blacks
Most respected opponent: Llanelli
wing Ieuan Evans
Best memory last season: Topping
try-scoring charts in inaugural
Heineken Welsh premier division with 11

	apps	pts
Wales 1991	World Cup squad	
Heineken 1990/91	15 apps	44

Suggestions to improve rugby: *On-field* – Leave laws alone – too much chopping and changing goes on. *Off-field* – Look at possibility of reimbursing players for time lost to work
Other notable landmarks in rugby career: Represented Wales in 1986 Sports Aid Sevens at Cardiff Arms Park
Touchlines: Golf (12-handicap)
Player to watch: Ian Jones (Llanelli)

Teague, M.   England

Full Name: Michael Clive Teague
1990/91 International category:
England Full
Club: Gloucester
Positions: No. 8, flanker
Height: 6'3" **Weight:** 16st
Occupation: Bricklayer
Family: Lorraine (wife)
Family links with rugby:
Grandfather played for
Gloucestershire
Former clubs: Cardiff, Gloucester
Old Blues
International debut: France 32,
England 18, 1984
Five Nations' debut: As above
Best moment in rugby: 1989 Lions
winning decisive third Test against
Australia
Worst moment in rugby: England
losing 1990 Grand Slam decider to
Scotland
Most embarrassing moment:
Giving Wales three seconds of hell in
1989 and then being carried off
Most respected opponent: All
Black Murray Mexted
Serious injuries: Torn shoulder,
knee ligaments
Best memory last season: Winning
Grand Slam with England
Suggestions to improve rugby:

	apps	pts
England B (**1981**)		
Last Season	1 cap	0
England (**1985**)		
Last Season	6 caps	8
v. Barbarians	1 app	0
1991	Tour to Australia	
	World Cup squad	
Career	17 caps	12
Lions 1989	2 Tests	0

On-field – Cannot improve the game that much, it's improving itself. More points for a try, less for a penalty goal
Other notable landmarks in rugby career: Represented England at U-23 and B levels. Also played for 1989 Lions in Australia, where voted man of the series. Lost England place to John Hall for Argentina game last season but regained it throughout Five Nations' Grand Slam campaign, and contributed vital tries v. Wales and Ireland. Also represented England B in 12–12 draw with Emerging Australians
Touchlines: Moto cross
Players to watch: David Sims/Neil Matthews (Gloucester)

Thomas, A.   Wales

Full Name: Andrew Thomas
1990/91 International category:
Wales B
Club: Neath
Position: Hooker
Height: 5'10.5" **Weight:** 14st
Born: Neath, 28.5.64
Family: Single
Family links with rugby: Uncle
(Robert Flay) played for Aberavon
Former clubs: Maesteg, Seven
Sisters, Llanelli, Glynneath
International debut: Netherlands
12, Wales B 34, 1990
Best moment in rugby: Joining
Neath from Glynneath
Most respected opponent: All
hookers
Best memory last season: Making
Wales B debut

	apps	pts
Wales B (**1990**)		
Last Season	1 cap	0
Career	1 cap	0
Heineken 1990/91	6 apps	4

Other notable landmarks in rugby career: Kevin Phillips' understudy at The Gnoll, played only six League games for the Welsh champions last season. However, given Wales B debut in solitary match at that level, a 34–12 defeat of Netherlands at Leiden
Touchlines: All sports
Player to watch: Matthew McCarthy (Aberavon)

Thomas, D. J. Wales

Full Name: David Jonathon Thomas
1990/91 International category:
Wales U-21
Club: Neath
Position: Centre
Height: 5'11" **Weight:** 13st
Occupation: Mechanical
engineering student
Born: Carmarthen, 6.9.70
Family: Single
Family links with rugby: Father
(Myron) played for Pontyberem
International debut (U-21): Wales
23, Scotland 15, 1991
Best moment in rugby: Wales
debut v. Scots at Llanelli
Serious injuries: Torn knee
cartilage (required operation)
Best memory last season: Beating
Scotland U-21s
**Other notable landmarks in rugby
career:** Represented Wales at
Schools and Youth level before
getting U-21 call-up last season.
Made just one League appearance
for Neath in 1990/91
Touchlines: Javelin, golf, tennis
Player to watch: Scott Gibbs
(Neath)

	apps	pts
Wales U-21 (**1991**)		
Last Season	1 cap	0
Career	1 cap	0
Heineken 1990/91	1 app	0

Thomas, P. J.   Wales

Full Name: Philip John Thomas
1990/91 International category:
Wales U-21
Club: Glamorgan Wanderers
Position: Flanker
Height: 5'11" **Weight:** 13st
Occupation: Apprentice fitter
Born: Barry, 27.7.69
Family: Single
Former club: Llantwit Major
International debut (U-21):
Scotland 10, Wales 24, 1990
Best moment in rugby: Playing for
Wales U-21s
Worst moment in rugby: Losing
front teeth playing for Llantwit
Major, aged 17
Most respected opponent:
Llanelli's Lyn Jones
Other sporting achievements:
Welsh lifeguard team for last four
years
Best memory last season: Beating
Scotland U-21s at Llanelli
Suggestions to improve rugby:
On-field – Remove sin-bin. It gives
referees and players an 'easy' option.
Encourage better standards of touch
judging. *Off-field* – Like to see game
going semi-professional

	apps	pts
Wales U-21 (**1990**)		
Last Season	1 cap	0
v. New Zealand XV	1 app	0
Career	2 caps	0
Heineken 1990/91	14 apps	0

Other notable landmarks in rugby career: Represented Wales Youth in
three non-cap matches (1987/88) and Wales U-20s against North Wales
U-23s. During 1989/90 helped Wales U-21s beat Combined Services U-21s
83–3 and Scotland U-21s at Ayr. Last season played in WRU President's XV
which beat New Zealand Rugby News Youth XV 34–13 at Pontypridd, and
in Wales U-21 side that beat Scotland 23–15 at Llanelli
Touchlines: Lifeguard coaching
Player to watch: Scott Gibbs (Neath)

Thompson, G. J.   England

Full Name: Gavin John Thompson
1990/91 International category:
England B
Club: Harlequins
Position: Centre
Height: 6′ **Weight:** 13st 6lbs
Occupation: Insurance underwriter
Born: Croydon, Surrey, 30.8.69
Family: Single
Former club: Rosslyn Park
International debut: England B 12,
Emerging Australians 12, 1990
Best moment in rugby: Final
whistle of Harlequins' 1990/91
Pilkington Cup semi-final v.
Nottingham which we won after 20
minutes' extra-time
Worst moment in rugby:
Attempting to play scrum-half v.
Coventry – we lost by 50 points
Most embarrassing moment: As
above
Most respected opponent:
England fly half Rob Andrew – he
can read and run a game as he likes
Other sporting achievements:
Represented Surrey at hockey and
cricket at U-15 and U-16 levels
Best memory last season: Beating
Leicester in English first division with
a Harlequins 'second' team

	apps	pts
England U-21 (**1989**)		
Last Season	0 caps	0
Career	3 caps	12
England B (**1990**)		
Last Season	5 caps	0
Career	5 caps	0
England	1995 Development squad	

Suggestions to improve rugby: *On-field* – Reduce size of English first division and play League games on home and away basis. Alter points system to encourage sides to play more expansive rugby and make it less of an incentive to kick for goal. *Off-field* – Finally clear up the 'grey' areas in the Pro-Am situation. Allow players to be rewarded for non-playing matters
Other notable landmarks in rugby career: England 18-Group, 4 caps (1987). England Colts, 3 caps (1988). Toured Kenya with Penguins (1989). Appointed England U-21 captain for two Internationals in 1989/90 and selected for England tour of Argentina (1990). Scored tries in each of three U-21 Internationals played (v. Romania, Netherlands and French Armed Forces). Toured in summer of 1990 to Argentina with England (playing v.

Tucuman XV, Buenos Aires XV and Cordoba XV) and warming bench in both Tests v. Pumas. Graduated to England B last season where made five appearances (v. Emerging Australians, Spain, Ireland, France and Italy)
Touchlines: Reading, especially autobiographies
Player to watch: Mark Russell (Harlequins) – strong and mobile, with correct attitude to succeed

---

Thorburn, P. H.   Wales

Full Name: Paul Huw Thorburn
1990/91 International category: Wales Full
Club: Neath
Position: Full-back
Height: 6′ **Weight:** 13st 5in
Occupation: Sales manager for telecom company
Born: Rheindalen, West Germany, 24.11.62
Family: Married with daughter
Family links with rugby: Father played for Cardiff 2nd XV. Brother had England Schools Trial
Former clubs: Swansea University, Ebbw Vale
International debut: France 14, Wales 3, 1985
Five Nations' debut: As above
Best moments in rugby: Kicking last-minute penalty which beat Australia 22–21 and gave Wales third place in 1987 World Cup. Scoring first ever try for Wales against Namibia last summer
Worst moment in rugby: Being dropped by Wales for 1988 game against England
Most embarrassing moment: Taking easy penalty kick for Neath against Sale. Scoreboard was directly behind posts and as I was about to strike ball it registered 3 extra points. I promptly missed
Most respected opponent: French full-back Serge Blanco

	apps	pts
Wales B (1984)		
Last Season	0 caps	0
Career	2 caps	32
Wales (1984)		
Last Season	6 caps	34
1991	Tour to Australia	
	World Cup squad	
Career	37 caps	300
Heineken 1990/91	16 apps	166

Serious injuries: Broken leg, collarbone. Dislocated shoulder
Best memory last season: Neath winning inaugural Welsh League title
Other sporting achievements: Cricket for Hereford and Worcester
Suggestions to improve rugby: Make it easier for players to compete in events all over world by compensating employers for time away from work
Other notable landmarks in rugby career: Born in Europe, grew up in England, but played for Welsh Universities, UAU and Ebbw Vale before joining Neath. Record points scorer in Welsh rugby. Failed to score only twice in 37 appearances for Wales (v. Scotland 1989 and Ireland 1990). Set Welsh record when scoring 52 points in 1986 Five Nations' Championship. Among other fondest memories are 70-yard penalty which helped Wales beat Scotland in 1986, and injury-time penalty that beat Ireland in 1988 to secure Welsh Triple Crown. Captained Wales nine times, including throughout five-match schedule last season. Broke Welsh single-match points-scoring record with 21 points (try, conversion and five penalty goals) in 24–31 loss to centenary Barbarians (caps awarded). Previous best (19) held by Jack Bancroft, Keith Jarrett and Phil Bennett
Touchlines: Waterskiing, squash, golf
Player to watch: Scott Gibbs (Neath)

Tobin, D.   Ireland

Full Name: Derek Tobin
1990/91 International category:
Ireland U-21
Club: Young Munster
Position: Scrum-half
Height: 5'6" **Weight:** 11st 7lbs
Occupation: International shipping clerk
Born: Limerick, 15.9.69
Family: Single
Family links with rugby: Most of my relations are involved with various clubs throughout Limerick
Former clubs: St Edna's (Limerick), Invercargill Marist (NZ)
International debut: Netherlands 21, Ireland U-21 7, 1990
Best moment in rugby: Beating England U-21s at Moseley last season
Worst moment in rugby: Losing 1991 Senior Cup final to Shannon

Most embarrassing moment:
Missing conversion in front of posts
Most respected opponent: Lex
Chisolm
Best memory last season:
Qualifying for first division of
All-Ireland League
Suggestions to improve rugby:
On-field – Introduce sin-bin (as used in NZ and Aus). *Off-field* – Laws on amateurism should be relaxed regarding advertising etc. Players do not want to be paid for playing but should be able to take advantage of cash deals
Other notable landmarks in rugby career: Playing for Munster Schools team. Winning U-20 Inter-Provincial series. Representing Ireland U-21s twice last season (v. Netherlands and England U-21s) in cap-matches and also in win over Irish Exiles
Touchlines: Canoeing, outdoor activities
Player to watch: Simon Geoghegan (London Irish) – probably the most dynamic wing to hit Irish rugby in years

	apps	pts
Ireland U-21 (1990)		
Last Season	2 caps	0
Career	2 caps	0

Tonge, S. P.   Ireland

Full Name: Simon Peter Tonge
1990/91 International category:
Ireland U-21
Club: Wanderers
Position: Prop
Height: 5'11" **Weight:** 17st
Occupation: Electrical engineer
Born: Dublin, 19.11.69
Family: Single
International debut (U-21):
England 16, Ireland 22, 1990
Best moment in rugby: Beating English in above match at Moseley
Most respected opponent:
Lansdowne prop Des Fitzgerald
Best memory last season: Playing v. Cork Constitution in All-Ireland league
Suggestions to improve rugby:
On-field – Slacken offside rules regarding rucking and mauling (too strict at present)

Other notable landmarks in rugby career: Represented Leinster at U-19 and U-20 level before attracting national selection last season at U-21 level
Touchlines: Travelling
Player to watch: Mark Evans (Wanderers)

	apps	pts
Ireland U-21 (**1990**)		
Last Season	1 cap	0
Career	1 cap	0

Tukalo, I. Scotland

Full Name: Iwan Tukalo
1990/91 International category: Scotland Full
Club: Selkirk
Position: Left wing
Height: 5'9″ **Weight:** 13st
Occupation: Senior engineer with British Gas, Scotland
Born: Edinburgh, 5.3.61
Family: Wife (Susan)
Former club: Royal High
International debut: Scotland 15, Ireland 18, 1985
Five Nations' debut: As above
Best moment in rugby: Beating England to win 1990 Grand Slam
Worst moment in rugby: Playing for South of Scotland v. New Zealand (1983)
Most embarrassing moment: Running to listen to captain's instructions in Scotland's match v. Fiji (1989) and arriving too late
Best memory last season: Returning to national side for Five Nations' match against Ireland for first time since previous summer's tour to New Zealand
Worst memory: Only lasting 35 mins in above match before sustaining badly bruised back
Most respected opponent:

	apps	pts
Scotland B (**1982**)		
Last Season	0 caps	0
Career	5 caps	
Scotland A (**1990**)		
Last Season	1 cap	12
Career	1 cap	12
Scotland (**1985**)		
Last Season	1 cap	0
1991	World Cup squad	
Career	24 caps	40

Australia wing David Campese – electrifying pace over five yards and excellent side-step

Serious injuries: Torn ligaments, ankle and knee. Torn hamstring

Suggestions to improve rugby: *On-field* – To make it more competitive, reduce size of Scottish first division to eight clubs and play matches on home and away basis. *Off-field* – Let events take their natural course. Sad for game when people just look to it for making a bit of extra money

Other notable landmarks in rugby career: Played three times at scrum-half for Scottish Schools in 1978–79, captaining side against France; toured with Scotland to Romania (1984), North America (1985), Spain and France (1986), Japan (1989) and New Zealand (1990); lost place on Scotland left wing to Alex Moore during 1990 New Zealand tour (character-building experience), but returned in 28–25 defeat of Ireland because of injury to Moore (only to be forced off field myself before half-time); scored three tries for Scotland A XV in 39–7 defeat of Spain in Seville on 22 December 1990

Touchlines: Squash, golf

Player to watch: Scott Nichol (Selkirk)

Turnbull, D. J.   Scotland

Full Name: Derek James Turnbull
1990/91 International category:
Scotland Full
Club: Hawick
Position: Flanker
Height: 6'3" **Weight:** 16st
Occupation: Sales rep
Born: Hawick, 2.10.61
Family: Angie (wife)
Family links with rugby: Father past president of Hawick Trades RFC
Former clubs: Hawick PSA, Hawick Trades
International debut: New Zealand 30, Scotland 3, 1987 World Cup
Five Nations' debut: Scotland 23, France 12, 1988
Best moment in rugby: Coming on as a replacement in the 1990 Grand Slam decider against England at Murrayfield

Worst moment in rugby: Losing to New Zealand in World Cup quarter-finals

Most embarrassing moment: Leading a Hawick Sevens side out at Gala Sports on 1 April, 1989. The rest of the side stayed in the dressing room until I was out on the pitch – all by myself!

Most respected opponent: Willie Duggan – he knew how to cheat well

Other sporting achievements: Completed London Marathon in 1982

	apps	pts
Scotland B (**1982**)		
Last Season	0 caps	0
Career	6 caps	
Scotland A (**1990**)		
Last Season	1 cap	0
Career	1 cap	0
Scotland (**1987**)		
Last Season	4 caps	0
1991	Tour to North America World Cup squad	
Career	8 caps	0

Best memory last season: Scotland's home wins v. Wales and Ireland

Suggestions to improve rugby: *On-field* – Don't allow anyone to kick the ball in opponents' half of the field. More liberal interpretations by referees, like in southern hemisphere. *Off-field* – None. We have a good relationship with our governing body in Scotland

Other notable landmarks in rugby career: Scotland tours to North America (1985), France and Spain (1986), World Cup (1987), Zimbabwe (1988), Japan (1989), New Zealand (1990) and North America (1991)

Touchlines: Enjoy golf – especially the 19th hole

Player to watch: Stuart Reid (Boroughmuir)

Ubogu, V. E.   England

Full Name: Victor Eriakpo Ubogu
1990/91 International category:
England B
Club: Bath
Position: Loose-head prop
Height: 5′9″ **Weight:** 16st
Occupation: Surveyor
Born: Lagos, Nigeria, 8.9.64
Family: Single
Former clubs: Moseley, Richmond
International debut: England B 12,
Emerging Australians 12, 1990
Best moment in rugby: Bath
beating Toulouse in 1989/90
Worst moment in rugby: Not
reaching last four with England in
inaugural Student World Cup
(1988) after losing to USSR and NZ
Best memory last season: Scoring
two tries for England B v. Spain
Suggestions to improve rugby:
There should be more regard for
players. We tend to be ignored – not
listened to enough
**Other notable landmarks in rugby
career:** Played for Oxford in 10–15
loss to Cambridge in 1987 Varsity
match. Won Pilkington Cup winners'

	apps	pts
England B (1990)		
Last Season	2 caps	8
Career	2 caps	8
England	1995 Development squad	

medal with Bath in 1990 after helping demolish Gloucester 48–6 at
Twickenham. Scored two tries for England B in 50–6 defeat of Spain last
season on second B appearance

Underwood, R.   England

Full Name: Rory Underwood
1990/91 International category:
England Full
Club: Leicester
Position: Wing
Height: 5′9″ **Weight:** 13st 7lbs
Occupation: RAF pilot
Born: Middlesbrough, 19.6.63
Family: Wendy (wife) and Rebecca
(daughter)
Family links with rugby: Brother
Tony plays for Leicester, Cambridge
Univ and England B
Former club: Middlesbrough
International debut: England 12,
Ireland 9, 1984
Five Nations' debut: As above
Best moments in rugby: Scoring
try seven minutes from time in 16–7
win over Ireland which secured 1991
Triple Crown for England
Worst moment in rugby:
England's 9–12 loss to Wales at
Cardiff (1989)
Most embarrassing moment:
Making error which led to Wales
scoring crucial try against England in
above match
Most respected opponent: French
wing Patrice Lagisquet

	apps	pts
England B (**1982**)		
Last Season	0 caps	0
England (**1984**)		
Last Season	7 caps	20
v. Barbarians	1 app	0
1991	Tour to Australia	
	World Cup squad	
Career	45 caps	108
Lions 1986		
1989	3 Tests	0

Other sporting achievements:
Swam and played cricket for Barnard
Castle School, which England
team-mate Rob Andrew also
attended
Best memory last season: England's Grand Slam
Suggestions to improve rugby: *On-field* – Leave alone. *Off-field* –
Continued improvement by Unions in looking after players and wives.
International Board must make unambiguous rulings concerning amateurism
Other notable landmarks in rugby career: Scored two tries for Leicester
against Barbarians in 1983 – three months later was in England team. Missed
tour to Argentina in summer of 1990, due to RAF commitments, having

become England's most-capped back and highest try-scorer during 1989/90 season. Equalled Douglas Lambert's 82-year-old England record of 5 tries in an International (v. Fiji). Previously played for England Colts, U-23 and B teams. Toured Australia with 1989 Lions, playing in all three Tests. Try scored in 16–7 defeat of Ireland during last season's Grand Slam was most important of career (26th England try). Also scored in 21–19 win over France (1991 Grand Slam decider) and in 28–12 summer defeat of Fiji

Touchlines: Crosswords, reading
Player to watch: Neil Back (Leicester)

Underwood, T.   England

Full Name: Tony Underwood
1990/91 International category:
England B
Clubs: Leicester/Cambridge Univ
Position: Wing
Height: 5'9" **Weight:** 12st 10lbs
Occupation: Student
Born: Ipoh, Malaysia, 17.2.69
Family: Single
Family links with rugby: Brother
Rory is England's record try-scorer
International debut: England B 12,
Fiji 20, 1989
Best moments in rugby: Playing
for Barbarians v. 1989 All Blacks,
and for Irish Wolfhounds in Hong
Kong Sevens. Any time I score tries
Worst moments in rugby:
Cambridge's 1990 Varsity match
loss (12–21) to Oxford. England's
1990 Tour to Argentina
Most respected opponents: Wings
Ian Hunter (Northampton) and
David Campese (Australia)
Serious injuries: Broken jaw, torn
hamstring and damaged knee
cartilage – all in second half of
1989/90 season

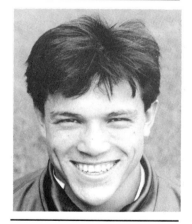

	apps	pts
England B (1989)		
Last Season	2 caps	0
England 1991	World Cup squad	
v. Barbarians	1 app	0
	1995 Development squad	

Best memory last season: Scoring
four tries in Barbarians' Easter Tour match at Cardiff
Suggestions to improve rugby: *On-field* – Expansion of League programme

to home and away. *Off-field* – Take necessary steps to prevent player drain to rugby league. Greater representation of players' views in Union

Other notable landmarks in rugby career: Played for England Schools (18-Group) before graduating to England team for inaugural Student World Cup (1988). Played for Barbarians in 10–21 defeat by 1989 All Blacks at Twickenham and for England in 18–16 win over Barbarians (1990/91). Represented Irish Wolfhounds in 1989 Hong Kong Sevens. Gone on to represent Combined Students, England B, North of England and, latterly, England in 1990 summer tour of Argentina. Represented England B last season v. Emerging Australians (12–12) and Ireland (lost 10–24)

Touchlines: Cricket, squash, girlfriend Heidi

Player to watch: Philip de Glanville (Bath) – silky smooth skills

---

Wainwright, R. I   Scotland

Full Name: Robert Iain Wainwright
1990/91 International category: Scotland B
Club: Edinburgh Academicals
Position: Flanker
Height: 6′5″ **Weight:** 15st 7lbs
Occupation: Medical student
Born: Perth, 22.3.65
Family: Single
Family links with rugby: Father (J. F. Wainwright) a 1956 Cambridge Blue
Former club: Cambridge Univ
International debut (B): Italy 3, Scotland 26, 1988
Best moment in rugby: Watching Scotland win 1990 Grand Slam at Murrayfield
Worst moment in rugby: Cambridge Univ v. Durham Univ (Jan 1988)
Most respected opponent: Scotland flanker John Jeffrey
Serious injuries: Broken cheekbone (Jan 1990), ankle (Sept 1990)
Other notable landmarks in rugby career: Cambridge Blue (1986), Barbarians Easter tour (1988), Hong Kong Sevens (1988,89), Scotland B

	apps	pts
Scotland B (1988)		
Last Season	1 cap	0
Career	2 caps	0

(1988 and last season in 0–16 loss to Ireland), touring Japan with Scotland –
two games, two tries (1989)
Touchlines: Wildlife, fishing, photography, whisky

Wallace, R. M.   Ireland

Full Name: Richard Michael
Wallace
1990/91 International category:
Ireland B
Club: Garryowen
Position: Wing
Height: 5'11" **Weight:** 13st
Occupation: Sales executive
Born: Cork, 16.1.68
Family: Single
Former club: Cork Constitution
International debut (B): Ireland
16, Scotland 0, 1990
Best moment in rugby: Selection
for Ireland's 1991 Namibia tour and
World Cup squad
Most respected opponent:
Leicester's Tony Underwood
Other sporting achievements:
Sailed (Laser class) for Ireland at
1990 European Championships
(France)
**Other notable landmarks in rugby
career:** Munster U-18s and U-21s
(1988). Irish Colleges (1987/88).
Scored try in 24–10 defeat of
England B at Old Belvedere on
second appearance for Ireland B last
season. Made full debut as
replacement for Simon Geoghegan in first Test loss to Namibia (6–15)
Touchlines: Flying (hold private licence), sailing, reading, music
Player to watch: Simon Geoghegan (London Irish)

	apps	pts
Ireland B (**1990**)		
Last Season	2 caps	4
Career	2 caps	4
Ireland (**1991**)		
Last season	1 cap	0
Career	1 cap	0

Waters, K.   Wales

Full Name: Ken Waters
1990/91 International category:
Wales Full (bench)
Club: Newbridge
Position: Hooker
Height: 5′10″ **Weight:** 15st 10lbs
Occupation: Day Care Centre
officer
Born: Cwmbran, 9.10.61
Family: Yvette (wife) and Gregory
(son)
Former club: Cwmbran
Best moment in rugby: Playing for
Newbridge in 1990/91 Schweppes
Welsh Cup semi-final v. Llanelli
Worst moment in rugby: Losing
above match
Most respected opponent:
Llanelli's David Fox
Best memory last season:
Watching Andrew Sutton catch a ball
in a line-out

	apps	pts
Wales B (1990/91)	1 rep	
Wales (1990/91)	4 reps	
1991	Tour to Australia	
	World Cup squad	
Heineken 1990/91	18 apps	20

**Other notable landmarks in rugby
career:** Within touching distance of
international action last season, as
No.2 to Kevin Phillips on Wales
replacements' bench throughout Five
Nations' Championship, and deputy
to Andrew Thomas for Wales B during 34–12 win over Netherlands. However,
got a game for centenary Barbarians v. Swansea, albeit as a replacement.
Reward for loyalty to national cause was invitation to tour Australia last
summer and to join Wales' preliminary World Cup squad. Ever-present for
Newbridge in Heineken premier division
Touchlines: Spending time with wife and child
Player to watch: Andrew Sutton (Newbridge) – because he caught a line-out
ball!

Watkins, I. J. — Wales

Full Name: Ian John Watkins
1990/91 International category:
Wales (World Cup squad)
Club: Cardiff
Position: Hooker
Height: 5'10" **Weight:** 14st 8lbs
Occupation: Sales executive
Born: Blaina, 10.3.63
Family: Married with a son
Family links with rugby: Father
John played scrum-half for
Pontypool, Abertillery and Ebbw
Vale and captained Monmouth
Police and British Police
Former clubs: RTB Youth, Ebbw
Vale
International debut: England 3,
Wales 11, 1988
Five Nations' debut: As above
Best moment in rugby: Coming on
as last-minute replacement in 1988
at Twickenham
Worst moment in rugby: 1988
Welsh tour to New Zealand
Most embarrassing moment:
Being sent off v. Pontypridd on
Boxing Day, 1990
Most respected opponent: New
Zealand hooker Sean Fitzpatrick –
excellent thrower-in of ball

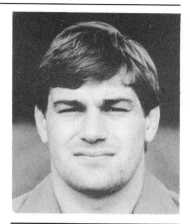

	apps	pts
Wales B (**1986**)		
Last Season	0 caps	0
Career	4 caps	4
Wales (**1988**)		
Last Season	0 caps	0
	1 rep	
1991	World Cup squad	
Career	10 caps	4
Heineken 1990/91	3 apps	4

Serious injuries: Knee ligaments, badly strained back
Other sporting achievements: Soccer trials for Coventry City
Suggestions to improve rugby: End midweek matches to allow players to train harder during week
Other notable landmarks in rugby career: Started career as scrum-half and centre before moving into pack at senior school. Scored try v. Scotland (1988) in first game I started. Captained 1988 Barbarians at Leicester and on 1989 Easter tour. Younger half of only father and son combination to play for Ebbw Vale. First hooker from Ebbw Vale to play for Wales. Bench reserve for Wales v. Barbarians last season
Touchlines: Weight training, golf

Watt, A. G. J.   Scotland

Full Name: Alan Gordon James Watt
1990/91 International category: Scotland A
Club: Glasgow High/Kelvinside
Positions: Prop, lock
Height: 6′5″ **Weight:** 18st 10lbs
Occupation: Plant Hire employee
Born: Glasgow, 10.7.67
Family: Single
Family links with rugby: Father played for Jordanhill FP, grandfather played for Hutchesons'
International debut (A): Spain 7, Scotland 39, 1990
Best moment in rugby: Winning B cap
Most respected opponent: Kelso's John Jeffrey
Best memories last season: Selection for Scotland's North American tour. GHK retaining Scottish first division status
Suggestions to improve rugby: *On-field* – Scrummage to restart game

	apps	pts
Scotland B (**1991**)		
Last Season	1 cap	0
Career	1 cap	0
Scotland A (**1990**)		
Last Season	1 cap	0
Career	1 cap	0
Scotland 1991	Tour to North America World Cup squad	

Other notable landmarks in rugby career: Represented Scotland Schools, scoring try v. Wales in 1987. Called into Scotland A team as prop for 39–7 defeat of Spain in Seville (1990) despite club position being lock. Also given Scotland B debut, in 10–31 defeat by France at Hughenden, before touring North America with Scotland last summer and playing v. US Eagles (won 41–12) and Canada (lost 19–24). Scored two tries in 76–7 win over Alberta and one in 24–12 defeat of Rugby East
Touchlines: Waterskiing
Player to watch: Andy Ness (Glasgow High/Kelvinside)

Webb, J. M.   England

Full Name: Jonathan Mark Webb
1990/91 International category:
England Full
Club: Bath
Position: Full-back
Height: 6'2" **Weight:** 13st 8lbs
Occupation: Surgeon
Born: London, 24.8.63
Family: Amanda (wife) and Harriet
(daughter)
Former clubs: Bristol Univ,
Northern, Bristol
International debut: England 6,
Australia 19, 1987
Five Nations' debut: France 10,
England 9, 1988
Best moment in rugby: Helping
England beat Australia in 1988
Worst moment in rugby: Sitting
on England bench during 1990
Murrayfield defeat
Most respected opponent: France
full-back Serge Blanco
Best memory last season: Winning
English League Championship with
Bath in first full season at club
Suggestions to improve rugby:
On-field – Greater consistency
between northern and southern
hemisphere referees. *Off-field* –
Clarify financial side of game (relating to amateurism)

	apps	pts
England B (**1987**)		
Last Season	0 caps	0
England (**1987**)		
Last Season	2 caps	21
	4 reps	
Career	18 caps	123
	1995 Development squad	

Other notable landmarks in rugby career: Educated in Newcastle and
played for Northern before medical studies forced move to West Country.
Represented England B before making England debut as replacement for
concussed Marcus Rose in 1987 World Cup. Returned to Australia on 1988
and 1991 England tours. Lost England full-back slot to Simon Hodgkinson
in May 1989. Moved to Bath at tail-end of 1989/90 season to revitalise career
and was recalled to full England squad last season. Recently graduated from
doctor (Dr) to surgeon (Mr) status and became Fellow of Royal College of
Surgeons (FRCS). Played in both Tests (v. Fiji and Australia) last summer
Touchlines: Playing oboe, golf
Player to watch: Adedayo Adebayo (Bath)

Webster, R. E.   Wales

Full Name: Richard Edward Webster
1990/91 International category: Wales Full
Club: Swansea
Position: Flanker
Height: 6'2" **Weight:** 15st 8lbs
Occupation: Sales rep
Born: Morriston, 9.7.67
Family: Kelly (daughter)
Former club: Bonymaen
International debut: Wales 22, Australia 21, 1987
Best moment in rugby: Winning first Wales cap in World Cup third place play-off
Worst moment in rugby: Getting injured
Most respected opponent: Swansea flanker Alan Reynolds
Serious injuries: Five operations on knee
Best memory last season: Winning second Wales full cap in 24–31 loss to Barbarians
Suggestions to improve rugby: *Off-field* – All committee members to retire at 35

	apps	pts
Wales (1987)		
Last Season	1 cap	0
1991	Tour to Australia	
	World Cup squad	
Career	2 caps	0
Heineken 1990/91	10 apps	16

Other notable landmarks in rugby career: Won six caps for Welsh Youth (1984–86). Selected for Wales' 1991 World Cup squad. Represented Wales v. centenary Barbarians in cap-match last season
Touchlines: Horse riding, weightlifting, DIY
Player to watch: Stuart Davies (Swansea)

Weir, G. W.   Scotland

Full Name: George Wilson (Doddie) Weir
1990/91 International category: Scotland Full
Club: Melrose
Positions: No.8, lock
Height: 6'7" **Weight:** 15st
Occupation: Agricultural student
Born: Edinburgh, 4.7.70
Family: Single
Family links with rugby: Father played for Gala. Brother plays for Stewart's-Melville School
International debut: Scotland 49, Argentina 3, 1990
Best moment in rugby: Getting capped v. Argentina
Most respected opponents: Scotland's John Jeffrey and David Sole

Other sporting achievements: Stow sprint champion. Completing Thirlestone cross-country on horse
Best memory last season: Winning first cap at Murrayfield
Suggestions to improve rugby:
On-field – Abolish conversions and instead increase worth of tries.
Off-field – Allow players to benefit from rugby-related activities

	apps	pts
Scotland U-21 (**1990**)		
Last Season	1 cap	0
Career	2 caps	0
Scotland A (**1990**)		
Last Season	1 cap	0
Career	1 cap	0
Scotland (**1990**)		
Last Season	1 cap	0
	1 rep	
1991	Tour to North America	
	World Cup squad	
Career	1 cap	0

Other notable landmarks in rugby career: Toured New Zealand with Scottish Schools (1988) and Scotland (1990). Represented South of Scotland in Inter-District Championship, Scotland B (22–22 draw with Ireland, 1990) and Scotland U-21s (v. Wales, 1990 and 1991). Made full debut in pre-Christmas 1990 defeat of Argentina. Toured North America with Scotland last summer, playing in all six matches (including two non-cap internationals v. US Eagles and Canada)
Touchlines: Horse riding (one-day eventing), clay pigeon shooting, training six days per week
Player to watch: Carl Hogg (Melrose)

Westwood, J. Wales

Full Name: Jonathan Westwood
1990/91 International category:
Wales U-21
Club: Newbridge
Positions: Full-back/wing
Height: 5'11" **Weight:** 12st
Occupation: Welsh Brewers sales
representative
Born: Pontypool, 14.7.71
Family: Single
Family links with rugby: Father
(Keith) played for Ebbw Vale and
Newbridge. Uncle (Ray Knott)
played for Ebbw Vale and
Newbridge
Former club: Abercarn
International debut (U-21): Wales
23, Scotland 15, 1991
Best moment in rugby: Gaining
Youth and U-21 caps for Wales
Worst moment in rugby: Losing to
Pontypool in 1991 Schweppes
Welsh Cup
Most embarrassing moment:
Running into a tree during squad
session in Cardiff
Most respected opponent:
Newbridge's David Rees – simply
because he always seems to be
running my way, even though he's on the same side

	apps	pts
Wales U-21 (**1991**)		
Last Season	1 cap	0
v. New Zealand XV	1 app	0
Career	1 cap	0
Heineken 1990/91	16 apps	8

Best memories last season: Winning Snelling Sevens and helping Welsh
President's (U-21) XV beat New Zealand U-21 XV
Suggestions to improve rugby: *On-field* – Less whistle-happy referees.
More points for a try. *Off-field* – Payment for loss of wages through rugby
commitments
Other notable landmarks in rugby career: Represented Wales Youth,
Welsh Colleges, Wales U-20 and U-21, Crawshays, Gwent County and
Estiddfoed XV
Touchlines: Indian food, horse racing, golf, cricket
Player to watch: Richard Brown (Newbridge)

White, D. B.   Scotland

Full Name: Derek Bolton White
1990/91 International category:
Scotland Full
Club: London Scottish
Positions: No.8, lock, flanker
Height: 6′4″ **Weight:** 16st
Occupation: Financial advisor
Born: Haddington, 30.1.58
Family: Audrey (wife)
Family links with rugby: Brother
(Kenyan) plays for Harlequins
Former clubs: Dunbar,
Haddington, Gala
International debut: Scotland 16,
France 7, 1982
Five Nations' debut: As above
Best moment in rugby: Winning
1990 Grand Slam
Worst moment in rugby: 1989
Lions' first Test defeat (12–30) v.
Australia
Most embarrassing moment:
Missing an opponent and hitting
John Jeffrey instead
Most respected opponent: John
Beattie. He combined strength, skill,
and a determination to win with a
really mean streak
Serious injuries: Severed medial
ligament in left knee (New Zealand
1981)
Best memory last season: Making
it back into Scotland team after
broken cheekbone

	apps	pts
Scotland B (**1982**)		
Last Season	0 caps	0
Career	1 cap	
Scotland A (**1990**)		
Last Season	1 cap	0
Career	1 cap	0
Scotland (**1982**)		
Last Season	4 caps	8
1991	World Cup squad	
Career	30 caps	32
Scotland VII (**1991**)	Hong Kong Sevens	
Lions 1989	1 Test	0

Suggestions to improve rugby:
On-field – Shorten second half of matches. *Off-field* – Get the Unions into
the 20th century. Appoint team managers. Allow payments for books, articles,
appearances etc. More promotion of rugby at grass-roots level
Other notable landmarks in rugby career: Toured with Scotland to New
Zealand (1981), Australia (1982), France (1986) and World Cup (1987),
and went to Australia (1989) with Lions. Have played in each of back five
positions for country. Played in seven games for 1989 Lions, scoring 1 try.

Scotland replacement 13 times. Have played Inter-District rugby for Edinburgh, the South and Anglo-Scots. Scored brace of tries in 32–12 defeat of Wales last season
Player to watch: Mark Moncrieff (Gala) – possesses pace, skill and dedication

Wilkinson, C. R. Ireland

Full Name: Colin Robert Wilkinson
1990/91 International category: Ireland B
Club: Malone
Positions: Full-back, fly-half, centre
Height: 5'11" **Weight:** 13st 7lbs
Occupation: Solicitor
Born: Belfast 4.4.61
Family: Claire (wife) and Ben (son)
Family links with rugby: Brother-in-law (John Martin) is the Ireland physio
International debut: Ireland B 27, Argentina 12, 1990
Best moment in rugby: Selection to Ireland's 1991 World Cup squad as an over–30 – big thrill
Worst moment in rugby: Captaining Malone to defeat by Ballymena in 1989/90 Ulster Senior Cup final
Most respected opponent: Instonians wing Keith Crossan
Best memory last season: Winning Melrose Sevens with Malone

	apps	pts
Ireland B (**1990**)		
Last Season	3 caps	5
Career	3 caps	5

Suggestions to improve rugby:
On-field – More consistency in refereeing. *Off-field* – Reimbursement for time lost to rugby
Other notable landmarks in rugby career: Played for Ulster at Schools, U-19, U-20, U-21, U-23 and senior levels. Played 18 times for Ulster since 1985. Landed conversion and penalty goal for Ireland B in 24–10 defeat of England B at Old Belvedere last season. Also played in wins over Argentina (27–12) and Scotland B (16-0). Included in Ireland's squad for 1991 World Cup
Touchlines: Golf (18-handicap)
Player to watch: Richard Wallace (Garryowen)

288

Williams, B. V.   Wales

Full Name: Brian Victor Williams
1990/91 International category:
Wales Full
Club: Neath
Position: Prop
Height: 6'1" **Weight:** 13st 10lbs
Occupation: Farmer
Born: Pennffordd, 9.7.62
Family: Married
Family links with rugby: Younger
brother played for Wales U-15s
Former club: Narberth
International debut: Wales 9,
Scotland 13, 1990
Five Nations' debut: As above
Best moment in rugby: Winning
first full cap, at Cardiff
Worst moment in rugby:
Dislocating shoulder three times and
needing two operations and two
years' away from game to solve
problem
Most respected opponent: Ireland
prop Des Fitzgerald
Serious injuries: Shoulder
dislocations
Best memory last season: Neath
winning Welsh premier division title
**Other notable landmarks in rugby
career:** Did not take up game until
aged 17 when joined Narberth.
Spotted by Neath in Pembrokeshire
team that beat Japan. Won first and
only B cap six years ago. After playing v. Barbarians, England and Scotland
last season, lost place to Mike Griffths for matches v. Ireland and France

	apps	pts
Wales B (**1985**)		
Last Season	0 caps	0
Career	1 cap	0
Wales (**1990**)		
Last Season	3 caps	0
	2 reps	
1991	World Cup squad	
Career	5 caps	0
Heineken 1990/91	13 apps	4

Williams, O. L. — Wales

Full Name: Owain Llewellyn Williams
1990/91 International category: Wales Full (bench)
Club: Bridgend
Position: No.8
Height: 6'6" **Weight:** 15st 7lbs
Occupation: Freelance film and TV designer
Born: Bridgend, 10.10.64
Family: Single
Family links with rugby: Brother Gareth played for Bridgend and Wales. Father played for Pontypridd
Former clubs: Glamorgan Wanderers, Queensland (Aus)
International debut: Namibia 30, Wales 34, 1990
Best moment in rugby: Winning first cap in second Test at Windhoek
Worst moment in rugby: Bridgend losing 1990 Welsh Cup final
Most respected opponent: Any back row player
Other sporting achievements: Basketball and cross-country for Mid-Glamorgan Schools
Best memory last season: Bench reserve for Barbarians v. Argentina

	apps	pts
Wales B (**1990**)		
Last Season	1 cap	0
Career	1 cap	0
Wales (**1990**)		
Last Season	1 rep	
1991	World Cup squad	
Career	1 cap	4
Heineken 1990/91	18 apps	12

Suggestions to improve rugby: *On-field* – Throw out half the rules: make game more simple and less technical. *Off-field* – Clarify amateurism question. Don't really know what is going on
Other notable landmarks in rugby career: Represented Welsh Schools (U-18), Students and Academicals. Also played for Crawshays, Public School Wanderers and Barbarians (v. Penarth). Played against England and New Zealand while with Queensland in 1988. Toured Namibia with Wales summer 1990. Included on senior Wales bench for 'International' defeat by centenary Barbarians last season and helped Wales B beat Netherlands 34–12 in Leiden
Touchlines: Cinema, helping out on dad's farm
Player to watch: Garin Jenkins (Pontypool)

Williams, S. M.   Wales

Full Name: Steven Michael
Williams
1990/91 International category:
Wales B
Club: Neath
Positions: No.8, flanker, lock
Height: 6'5" **Weight:** 17st
Occupation: Trainee quantity
surveyor
Born: Neath, 3.10.70
Family: Single
Former clubs: Bryncoch, Swansea
International debut: Netherlands
12, Wales B 34, 1990
Best moment in rugby: Scoring try
for Wales against Singapore in Hong
Kong Sevens
Worst moment in rugby:
Namibian tour – did not go as
planned

Most respected opponent: Bath's
England lock Nigel Redman – he
gave me a good hiding in my first
game for Swansea
Serious injuries: Torn ankle
ligaments (1989/90), dislocated
thumb (1990/91)

	apps	pts
Wales U-21 (**1990**)		
Last Season	2 caps	0
Career	3 caps	0
Wales B (**1990**)		
Last Season	1 cap	0
Career	1 cap	0
Heineken 1990/91		
(with Swansea)	10 apps	4

Best memory last season: Helping
Wales U-21s defeat New Zealand
XV 34–13 at Pontypridd
Suggestions to improve rugby:
On-field – Change training times from evenings to mornings. Simplify rules:
don't know if coming or going at present. *Off-field* – Preserve midweek games:
don't allow Leagues to demean them
Other notable landmarks in rugby career: Played for Welsh Schools and
Welsh Tertiary Colleges. Captained Wales U-21s (1989/90) and represented
them again last season in 23–15 defeat of Scotland. Toured Namibia with
Wales (1990) and represented Wales at 1990 Hong Kong Sevens. Missed
two and half months of last season after having operation to repair dislocated
thumb. Made Wales B debut in 34–12 defeat of Netherlands in Leiden
(1990/91). Moved to Neath at tail-end of last season
Touchlines: Cycling
Player to watch: Ian Jones (Llanelli)

Williams-Jones, H.   Wales

Full Name: Hugh Williams-Jones
1990/91 International category:
Wales Full
Club: South Wales Police
Position: Prop
Height: 6′ **Weight:** 16st 4lbs
Occupation: Police officer
Family: Karyn (wife), Lloyd (son)
and Nia (daughter)
Family links with rugby: Brother
(Richard) is Grade III WRU referee
Former clubs: Bridgend,
Pontypridd
International debut: Scotland 23,
Wales 7, 1989
Five Nations' debut: As above
Best moment in rugby: Winning
first full cap

Worst moment in rugby: After
coming on as replacement against
Scotland, not being selected for next
match against Ireland
Most embarrassing moment:
South Wales Police's Welsh Cup
quarter-final defeat against
Llanharan in 1988/89
Most respected opponent:
Scotland prop David Sole
Other sporting achievements:
Glamorgan County Cricket U-15
cap

	apps	pts
Wales B (**1989**)		
Last Season	0 caps	0
Wales (**1989**)		
Last Season	1 caps	0
1991	Tour to Australia	
Career	4 caps	0
Heineken 1990/91	13 apps	0

Best memory last season: Gaining selection to Wales' summer tour to
Australia
Suggestions to improve rugby: *On-field* – Scrap 90-degree scrum wheel
law altogether as too negative. *Off-field* – IRB must clarify regulations relating
to amateurism and then insist on worldwide adherence
Other notable landmarks in rugby career: Winning three Welsh Youth
caps and one at B level. Tour to Australia last summer was third with Wales
Touchlines: All sport
Player to watch: Scott Quinnell (Llanelli)

Wilson, G. D.   Scotland

Full Name: Grant Douglas Wilson
1990/91 International category:
Scotland (Tour squad)
Club: Boroughmuir
Position: Prop
Height: 5'11" **Weight:** 16st 7lbs
Occupation: Police officer
Born: Edinburgh, 10.11.66
Family: Single
Family links with rugby: Named
after great Hawick rugby brothers of
Jake, Oliver and Derrick Grant
Former club: Preston Lodge
International debut (B): Scotland
22, Ireland 22, 1989
Best moment in rugby: Being
selected by Scotland at tight-head for
non-cap Test v. Japan in Tokyo
(1989) in front of specialist
tight-heads
Worst moment in rugby: Losing
9–31 to France B (1990)
Most embarrassing moment:
Catching ball inside own 22,
somebody else calling 'mark', and
having to take resulting kick myself
Most respected opponents:
Scotland props Iain Mine and David
Sole

	apps	pts
Scotland B (**1989**)		
Last Season	0 caps	0
Career	2 caps	0
Scotland 1991	Tour to North America	

Other sporting achievements: 1989 Scottish Youth sprint and marathon
canoeing champion
Best memory last season: Touring North America with Scotland
Suggestions to improve rugby: Establish a Scottish knock-out cup
competition and reduce size of First Division from fourteen to ten clubs
Other notable landmarks in rugby career: Played for South of Scotland
U-16s, Edinburgh and Scotland U-18s (1983–85), U-21s (1985–89), British
Police, and Edinburgh District side. During busy 1989/90 season represented
Scotland XV v. Japan, Scotland B v. Ireland and France, and was on
replacements' bench for Scotland v. Fiji. Toured North America with Scotland
last summer, appearing in defeats of British Columbia (29–9) and Ontario
(43–3), and scoring a try against the latter side

Winterbottom, P. J.　　　England

Full Name: Peter James
Winterbottom
1990/91 International category:
England Full
Club: Harlequins
Position: Flanker
Height: 6′ **Weight:** 14st 10lbs
Occupation: Inter-dealer
Euro-bond broker
Born: Horsforth, Leeds, 31.5.60
Family: Single
Family links with rugby: Father
played for Headingley and is past
President
Former clubs: Fleetwood,
Headingley, Exeter, Napier HS OBs
(NZ), Hawkes Bay (NZ), Durban
HS OBs (SA), Merolomas
(Vancouver, Can)
International debut: England 15,
Australia 11, 1982
Five Nations' debut: Scotland 9,
England 9, 1982
Best moment in rugby: Making
England debut against touring
Wallabies
Most embarrassing moment:
Being caught from behind by Gareth
Chilcott, playing touch rugby
Most respected opponent: Former
French flanker Jean-Pierre Rives – a
legend

	apps	pts
England B (**1981**)		
Last Season	0 caps	0
England (**1982**)		
Last Season	5 caps	0
v. Barbarians	1 app	0
1991	Tour to Australia	
	World Cup squad	
Career	42 caps	8
Lions 1983	4 Tests	0

Serious injuries: My brain
Other sporting achievements: School U-16 tennis champion
Best memory last season: Grand Slam
Other notable landmarks in rugby career: Much travelled and vastly
experienced player who shot up the representative ranks following impressive
displays for Yorkshire, and England against France in 1981 B International.
Represented England Colts at No.8, before switching to flanker, where played
for Yorkshire. Tours include New Zealand with 1983 Lions, and South Africa
(1984), World Cup (1987), Argentina (1990) and Australia (1991) with

294

England. Played club rugby all over world. Ever-present during Grand Slam campaign last season

Wyllie, D. S.   Scotland

Full Name: Douglas Stewart Wyllie
1990/91 International category: Scotland Full (bench)
Club: Stewart's-Melville
Positions: Fly-half, centre
Height: 6′1″ **Weight:** 13st 10lbs
Occupation: Sports sales rep
Born: Edinburgh, 20.5.63
Family: Jennifer (wife)
International debut: Scotland 12, Australia 37, 1984
Five Nations' debut: Scotland 21, Wales 25, 1985
Best moment in rugby: Winning 1982 Middlesex Sevens at Twickenham with Stewart's-Melville as an 18-year old
Worst moment in rugby: Playing in Scotland XV which lost 1989 'Test' 24–28 to Japan in Tokyo – we took them for granted
Most embarrassing moment: As above
Most respected opponents: Former Scotland players Jim Renwick and John Beattie (most aggressive player I have ever come up against)
Serious injury: Broken bone in foot (1987/88)
Other sporting achievements: Soccer for England U-13 Schoolboys

	apps	pts
Scotland B (**1984**)		
Last Season	0 caps	0
Career	3 caps	
Scotland A (**1990**)		
Last Season	1 cap	0
Career	1 cap	0
Scotland (**1984**)		
Last Season	5 reps	
1991	Tour to North America	
Career	10 caps	

Best memory last season: Stewart's-Melville beating Currie in Scottish National League match with a last-minute penalty goal to avoid relegation. Delighted for the young players at the Stew-Mel club
Suggestions to improve rugby: *On-field* – If the scrum goes down when the ball is at the No.8's feet, let play continue. Finish Scottish League

programme before Christmas – New Year diary is too cluttered at present.
Off-field – Allow game at top level to go semi-pro. Standards would improve immeasurably if players had longer to spend on their skills. Clarify amateur laws and allow players to benefit from off-field activities (e.g. speech-making) related to the game

Other notable landmarks in rugby career: Called into Scotland senior squad aged 19, having twice represented Scotland B in 1982. Selected to Scotland bench in 1983. Spent early years in England, where I was educated at Dulwich College in south London. Did not take up rugby until aged 14. Ever-present for Scotland in 1987 World Cup, moving from centre to fly-half after John Rutherford broke down in opening match. Captained Scotland during last summer's tour of North America, playing in all six games (including Internationals v. USA and Canada)

Touchlines: Golf (15-handicap at Baberton GC), Hearts soccer fan
Player to watch: Kenny Milligan (Stewart's-Melville)

Appendix

AITKEN, Scott. **1990/91 International category:** Scotland U-21. **Position:** Lock. **Debut:** Wales U-21 23, Scotland 15, 1991. **Caps:** 1. **Points:** 0. **Club:** Melrose. **Born:** 13.7.70. **Height:** 6′5″ **Weight:** 14st. **Occupation:** Student.

ANDREOU, Dinos. **1990/91 International category:** England U-21. **Position:** Lock. **Debut:** French Armed Forces 9, England U-21 7, 1991. **Caps:** 1. **Points:** 0. **Club:** Coventry. **Born:** 29.9.69. **Height:** 6′4″ **Weight:** 16st 8lb. **Occupation:** Buyer for Dunlop Automotives.

BALDWIN, David Neil. **1990/91 International category:** England (1995 Development squad). **Position:** Lock. **Debut:** England B 18, USSR 10, l989. **Caps:** 0. **Points:** 0. **Club:** Sale. **Born:** 3.9.64. **Height:** 6′6″ **Weight:** 17st 8lb. **Occupation:** Screen printer.

BALDWIN, Gavin Paul Samuel. **1990/91 International category:** England (1995 Development squad). **Position:** Prop. **Debut:** Netherlands 3, England U-21 24, 1990. **Caps:** 2. **Points:** 0. **Club:** Northampton. **Born:** 6.12.68. **Height:** 6′1″ **Weight:** 17st **Occupation:** Health & fitness advisor.

BENNETT, Stewart. **1990/91 International category:** Scotland U-21. **Position:** Flanker. **Debut:** Wales U-21 23, Scotland U-21 15, 1991. **Caps:** 1. **Points:** 0. **Club:** Kelso. **Born:** 15.10.69. **Height:** 6′1″ **Weight:** 14st **Occupation:** Farmer.

BLACKMORE, Andrew George. **1990/91 International category:** England (1995 Development squad). **Position:** Lock. **Debut:** None. **Club:** Bristol. **Born:** 1.11.65. **Height:** 6′7″ **Weight:** 17st 8lb. **Occupation:** Life assurance clerk.

BULLOCK, Warwick **1990/91 International category:** England U-21. **Position:** Lock. **Debut:** Netherlands 18, England U-21 20, 1991. **Caps:** 1. **Points:** 0. **Club:** Coventry. **Born:** 9.2.70. **Height:** 6′ **Weight:** 16st 6lb. **Occupation:** Family garage salesman.

CALLARD, Jonathan Edward Brooks. **1990/91 International category:** England (1995 Development squad). **Position:** Full-back. **Debut:** Spain 9, England B 31, 1989. **Caps:** 1. **Points:** 4. **Club:** Bath. **Born:** 1.1.66. **Height:** 5′10″ **Weight:** 12st 7lb. **Occupation:** PE Teacher.

CHALLINOR, Andrew Paul. **1990/91 International category:** England U-21 (bench). **Position:** Fly-half. **Debut:** None (replacement: England U-21 16, Ireland U-21 22, 1990). **Club:** Harlequins. **Born:** 5.12.69. **Height:** 5′11.5″ **Weight:** 13st.

CHANGLENG, David Michael. **1990/91 International category:** Scotland U-21 (bench). **Position:** Fly-half. **Debut:** None (replacement: Wales U-21, 23, Scotland U-21 15, 1991). **Club:** Gala. **Born:** 25.4.70. **Height:** 6′ **Weight:** 12st. **Occupation:** PE Student.

COCKERILL, Richard. **1990/91 International category:** England U-21. **Position:** Hooker. **Debut:** Netherlands 18, England U-21 20, 1991. **Caps:** 1. **Points:** 0. **Club:** Coventry. **Born:** 16.12.70. **Height:** 5'9" **Weight:** 13st 7lb. **Occupation:** Antique furniture restorer.

DAVIS, Everton. **1990/91 International category:** England (1995 Development squad). **Position:** Wing. **Debut:** England B 12, Fiji 20, 1989. **Caps:** 2. **Points:** 0. **Club:** Harlequins. **Born:** 30.5.60. **Height:** 5'9" **Weight:** 11st 10lb. **Occupation:** Senior computer analyst.

DAVIS, Julian. **1990/91 International category:** England (1995 Development squad). **Position:** Scrum-half. **Debut:** Netherlands 3, England U-21 24, 1990. **Caps:** 1. **Points:** 0. **Club:** Bristol. **Born:** 1.10.68. **Height:** 5'7" **Weight:** 11st 7lb. **Occupation:** Draughtsman.

DINEEN, Leonard Michael. **1990/91 International category:** Ireland U-25 (bench). **Position:** Prop. **Debut:** Bench, Ireland U-25 12, US Eagles 10, March 1990 (bench also: Ireland U-25 36, Spain 17, Sept 1990. Capt 1985 Irish Schools v. New Zealand). **Club:** Cork Constitution. **Born:** 14.12.66. **Height:** 6'2" **Weight:** 16st 7lb. **Occupation:** Building Society employee.

DIXON, Simon. **1990/91 International category:** England U-21. **Position:** Wing. **Debut:** French Armed Forces 9, England U-21 7, 1991. **Caps:** 1. **Points:** 0. **Club:** Rosslyn Park. **Born:** 3.4.70. **Height:** 6'1" **Weight:** 13st **Occupation:** Student.

DOW, Aidan William Hunter. **1990/91 International category:** Scotland U-21 (bench). **Positions:** Centre, wing. **Debut:** England Schools 3, Scotland Schools 3, 1987. **Caps:** 0. **Points:** 0. **Clubs:** Glasgow High/Kelvinside. **Born:** 15.9.69. **Height:** 5'10" **Weight:** 12st **Occupation:** Business studies student.

DUNSTON, Ian Charles. **1990/91 International category:** England (1995 Development squad). **Position:** Tight-head prop. **Debut:** England Colts 22, Italy Youth 10, 1987. **Caps:** 0. **Points:** 0. **Club:** Wasps. **Born:** 11.6.68. **Height:** 5'10" **Weight:** 16st 4lb. **Occupation:** Trainee accountant.

FALLON, James (**Jim**) Anthony. **1990/91 International category:** England (1995 Development squad). **Position:** Wing. **Debut:** France B 15, England B 15, 1990. **Caps:** 1. **Points:** 0. **Club:** Bath. **Born:** 27.3.65. **Height:** 6'1" **Weight:** 15st **Occuaption:** Builder.

FIELDS, Andrew Richard Ian. **1990/91 International category:** England U-21. **Position:** Hooker. **Debut:** French Armed Forces 9, England U-21 7, 1991. **Caps:** 1. **Points:** 0. **Club:** Nottingham. **Born:** 20.5.70. **Height:** 5'11" **Weight:** 14st 7lb. **Occupation:** Student.

FLOOD, Jonathan Paul. **1990/91 International category:** England U-21. **Position:** Centre. **Debut:** Netherlands 18, England U-21 20, 1991. **Caps:** 2 (also: French Armed Forces 9, England U-21 7, 1991). **Points:** 0. **Club:** Bridgend. **Born:** 25.11.70. **Height:** 6' **Weight:** 13st 7lb. **Occupation:** Student.

FULCHER, Gabriel Mark. **1990/91 International category:** Ireland U-21. **Position:** Lock. **Debut:** Netherlands 21, Ireland U-21 7, 1990. **Caps:** 2

(also: England U-21 16, Ireland U-21 22, 1990). **Points:** 0. **Club:** University College Dublin. **Born:** 27.11.69. **Height:** 6'5" **Weight:** 16st 7lb. **Occupation:** Science/business student.

GLENNON, Brian Thomas. **1990/91 International category:** Ireland U-25 (bench)/World Cup squad. **Position:** Centre/fly-half. **Debut:** Bench, Ireland U-25 36, Spain 17, 1990 (5 caps for Irish Schools). **Club:** Lansdowne. **Born:** 17.4.67. **Height:** 6' **Weight:** 12st 7lb. **Occupation:** Trainee accountant.

GRECIAN, Nicholas James Grecian. **1990/91 International category:** Scotland B. **Position:** Wing. **Debut:** Ireland B 16, Scotland B 0, 1990. **Caps:** 1. **Points:** 0. **Club:** London Scottish. **Born:** 1.9.64. **Height:** 5'8" **Weight:** 13st 7lb. **Occupation:** Account Sales Manager.

HACKNEY, Stephen Thomas. **1990/91 International category:** England 1995 Development squad). **Position:** Wing. **Debut:** England B 9, Australia 37, 1988. **Caps:** 2. **Points:** 4. **Club:** Nottingham. **Born:** 13.6.68. **Height:** 5'11" **Weight:** 13st 4lb. **Occupation:** Sales manager.

HALY, Charles Michael. **1990/91 International category:** Ireland U-25 (bench). **Position:** Full-back. **Debut** (U-21, capt): Ireland 22, Italy 13, 1988 (also: Irish Schools, Irish Univs, Irish Students). **Clubs:** University College Cork/Oxford Univ/London Irish. **Born:** 13.10.67. **Height:** 5'11" **Weight:** 13st. **Occupation:** Pol/Econ student.

HAMLIN, Michael Paul. **1990/91 International category:** England (1995 Development squad). **Position:** Fly-half. **Debut:** Spain 9, England B 31, l989. **Caps:** 1. **Points:** 7. **Club:** Gloucester. **Born:** 10.3.60. **Height:** 5'11" **Weight:** 12st. **Occupation:** Building consultant.

HARRIS, Michael Anthony. **1990/91 International category:** England (1995) Development squad). **Position:** Blind-side flanker. **Debut:** Romania U-21 13, England U-21 54, 1989. **Caps:** 1. **Points:** 0. **Club:** Wasps. **Born:** 7.9.67. **Height:** 6'4" **Weight:** 16st 7lb. **Occupation:** Ironmongery warehouse assistant.

HENNEBRY, Paul Joseph. **1990/91 International category:** Ireland World Cup squad. **Position:** Fly-half. **Debut:** Ireland U-25 12, US Eagles 10, 1990. **Caps:** 1. **Points:** 8. **Club:** Terenure College. **Born:** 12.4.65. **Height:** 6'1" **Weight:** 13st. **Occupation:** Area sales manager (catering).

HENNESSY, Raymond Gerald. **1990/91 International category:** Ireland U-21. **Position:** Wing. **Debut:** Netherlands 21, Ireland U-21 7, l990. **Caps:** 2 (also: England U-21 16, Ireland U-21 22, 1990). **Points:** 4 (try v. England). **Club:** Lansdowne. **Born:** 18.2.70. **Height:** 6'0.5" **Weight:** 13st. **Occupation:** Bank official.

JACKSON, Andrew James. **1990/91 International category:** England U-21. **Position:** Loose-head prop. **Debut:** Netherlands 18, England U-21 20, 1991. **Caps:** 1. **Points:** 0. **Club:** West Hartlepool. **Born:** 30.1.70. **Height:** 5'8" **Weight:** 15st 7lb. **Occupation:** Box-making apprentice.

LANGLEY, Colin. **1990/91 International category:** Wales U-21. **Position:** Lock. **Debut:** Wales U-21 23, Scotland U-21 15, 1991. **Caps:** 1 (also:

WRU President's XV 34, New Zealand XV 13, 1990). **Points:** 0. **Club:** Cardiff. **Born:** 17.10.71. **Height:** 6'6" **Weight:** 17st 2lb. **Occupation:** Student.

LILEY, Robert James. **1990/91 International category:** England U-21. **Position:** Full-back. **Debut:** French Armed Forces 9, England U-21 7, 1991. **Caps:** 1. **Points:** 0. **Club:** Cahors (France). **Born:** 3.4.70. **Height:** 6' **Weight:** 12st 6lb. **Occupation:** Bank employee (Credit Agricole) and French interpreter.

McBRYDE, Robin Currie. **1990/91 International category:** Wales U-21 (bench). **Position:** Hooker. **Debut:** None. **Club:** Swansea. **Born:** 3.7.70. **Height:** 6' **Weight:** 15st 7lb. **Occupation:** Overhead linesman.

McGAULEY, Conor Francis. **1990/91 International category:** England (1995 Development squad). **Position:** Tight-head prop. **Debut:** None. **Club:** Rosslyn Park. **Born:** 6.5.66. **Height:** 6'3" **Weight:** 17st 10lb. **Occupation:** Options broker.

MACNAUGHTON, Robert Carlo. **1990/91 International category:** England (1995 Development squad). **Position:** Centre. **Debut:** French Students 18, English Students 37, 1989. **Caps:** 6. **Points:** 4. **Club:** Liverpool St Helens. **Born:** 21.9.65. **Height:** 6' **Weight:** 13st. **Occupation:** Architectural student.

MALONE, Niall Gareth. **1990/91 International category:** Ireland U-21. **Position:** Fly-half. **Debut:** Netherlands 21, Ireland U-21 7, 1990. **Caps:** 2 (also: England U-21 16, Ireland U-21 22, 1990). **Points:** 21 (1pg v. Netherlands, 5pg and 1dg v. England). **Clubs:** Loughborough Students/Collegians. **Born:** 30.4.71. **Height:** 5'11" **Weight:** 12st. **Occupation:** Student.

MURCHISON, Ewen Alexander. **1990/91 International category:** Scotland U-21 (bench). **Debut:** None (replacement: Wales U-21 23, Scotland U-21 15, 1991). **Club:** Loughborough University. **Born:** 26.7.71. **Height:** 6' **Weight:** 13st. **Occupation:** Student.

O'CONNELL, Ken. **1990/91 International category:** Ireland U-25. **Position:** Blindside flanker. **Debut:** Ireland U-25 36, Spain 17, 1990. **Caps:** 1. **Points:** 0 (Played for Irish Schools, and twice for Ireland U-21s in 1989/90, capt v. New Zealand XV). **Club:** Sunday's Well. **Height:** 6'2" **Weight:** 15st 7lb. **Occupation:** Sales manager.

ORRELL, Tony. **1990/91 International category:** Wales U-21 (bench). **Position:** Loose-head prop. **Debut:** Scotland U-21 10, Wales U-21 24, 1990. **Caps:** 1. **Points:** 0. **Club:** Cardiff. **Born:** 7.12.70. **Height:** 6'1" **Weight:** 18st 8lb. **Occupation:** Quantity surveyor.

PARTON, Andrew Richard. **1990/91 International category:** England (1995 Development squad). **Positions:** Full-back, wing. **Debut:** None. **Clubs:** Coventry/Cambridge Univ. **Born:** 31.1.68. **Height:** 6'3" **Weight:** 14st. **Occupation:** Management studies student.

PEARSON, Joel Timothy Vernon. **1990/91 International category:** England U-21. **Position:** Flanker. **Debut:** Netherlands 18, England U-21 20, 1991.

Caps: 2 (also: French Armed Forces 9, England U-21 7, 1991). **Points:** 0. **Club:** Bristol. **Born:** 8.3.70. **Height:** 6′ **Weight:** 14st 6lb. **Occupation:** Trainee insurance underwriter.

POOLE, Matthew David. **1990/91 International category:** England (1995 Development squad). **Position:** Lock. **Debut:** Romania U-21 13, England U-21 54, 1989. **Caps:** 3. **Points:** 0. **Club:** Leicester. **Born:** 6.2.69. **Height:** 6′7″ **Weight:** 17st 9lb. **Occupation:** Business systems salesman.

POTTER, Stuart. **1990/91 International category:** England (1995 Development squad). **Position:** Inside centre. **Debut:** None. **Club:** Nottingham. **Born:** 11.11.67. **Height:** 5′11″ **Weight:** 13st 8lb. **Occupation:** Insurance broker.

RENNELL, Mark Ian. **1990/91 International category:** England U-21. **Position:** No.8. **Debut:** French Armed Forces 9, England U-21 7, 1991. **Caps:** 1. **Points:** 0. **Club:** Bedford. **Born:** 17.1.71. **Height:** 6′2″ **Weight:** 16st 7lb. **Occupation:** Student.

RICHARDSON, Brian James. **1990/91 International category:** Scotland B (bench). **Position:** Prop. **Debut:** None (replacement: Scotland B 10, France B 31, 1991). **Club:** Boroughmuir. **Born:** 8.6.59. **Height:** 6′6′ **Weight:** 17st. **Occupation:** Royal Air Force sergeant.

ROBERTS, Harry. **1990/91 International category:** Scotland B. **Position:** Hooker. **Debut:** Ireland B 16, Scotland B 0, 1990. **Caps:** 1. **Points:** 0. **Club:** London Scottish. **Born:** 3.12.60. **Height:** 5′11″ **Weight:** 15st 8lb.

ROY, Stuart. **1990/91 International category:** Wales preliminary World Cup squad. **Debut:** Scotland U-21 10, Wales U-21 24, 1990. **Caps:** 1. **Points:** 0. **Position:** Lock. **Club:** Cardiff. **Born:** 25.12.68. **Height:** 6′6″ **Weight:** 17st 4lb. **Occupation:** Medical student. Heineken League 1990/91 – Apps: 15. **Points:** 4 (try).

RUSSELL, Jonathan James. **1990/91 International category:** Ireland U-21. **Position:** Centre. **Debut:** Netherlands 21, Ireland U-21 7, 1990. **Caps:** 2 (also: England U-21 16, Ireland U-21 22, 1990). **Points:** 0. **Clubs:** Instonians/Heriot's FP. **Born:** 8.2.70. **Height:** 5′11″ **Weight:** 13st. **Occupation:** Student.

SHARP, Alan Victor. **1990/91 International category:** England (1995 Development squad). **Debut:** Spain 9, England B 31, 1989. **Caps:** 1. **Points:** 0. **Position:** Loose-head prop. **Club:** Bristol. **Born:** 17.10.69. **Height:** 5′10″ **Weight:** 16st 7lb. **Occupation:** Builder.

SHORTLAND, Stephen Michael. **1990/91 International category:** England (1995 Development squad). **Position:** Lock. **Caps:** 1. **Points:** 0. **Club:** Headingley. **Born:** 12.1.68. **Height:** 6′7″ **Weight:** 17st. **Occupation:** PE Student.

SIMKINS, Gavin Joshua. **1990/91 International category:** England U-21. **Position:** Scrum-half. **Debut:** Netherlands 18, England U-21 20, 1991. **Caps:** 1. **Points:** 0. **Club:** Bedford. **Born:** 18.11.69. **Height:** 5′11″ **Weight:** 12st 10lb. **Occupation:** Agricultural student.

TANNER, Michael John. **1990/91 International category:** England U-21.

Position: Lock. **Debut:** England U-21 16, Ireland U-21 22, 1990. **Caps:** 1. **Points:** 0. **Club:** Royal Navy. **Born:** 4.12.69. **Height:** 6'5" **Weight:** 17st 7lb. **Occupation:** Royal Marines (second Lieutenant).

TANNER, Paul John. **1990/91 International category:** England U-21 (bench). **Position:** Lock. **Debut:** None (replacement for England U-21 16, Ireland U-21 22, 1990). **Clubs:** Northampton/RAF. **Born:** 30.12.69. **Height:** 6'7" **Weight:** 17st 10lb. **Occupation:** Royal Air Force Police.

TAYLOR, Roger John. **1990/91 International category:** England (1995 Development squad). **Position:** Hooker. **Debut:** None. **Club:** Nottingham. **Born:** 23.6.67. **Height:** 6' **Weight:** 15st 7lb. **Occupation:** Mechanical engineer.

TIMMS, Douglas Leonard. **1990/91 International category:** Scotland U-21 (bench). **Position:** Hooker. **Debut:** None. **Club:** Dunfermline. **Born:** 15.12.71. **Height:** 6' **Weight:** 13st 10lb. **Occupation:** PE Student.

WARD, Raymond. **1990/91 International category:** Ireland U-25. **Position:** Loose-head prop. **Debut:** Ireland U-25 36, Spain 17, 1990. **Caps:** 1. **Points:** 0. **Club:** Dublin Univ. **Height:** 6'2" **Weight:** 17st. **Occupation:** Student.

WAREHAM, Richard Antony (**Biff**). **1990/91 International category:** England (1995 Development squad). **Position:** Tight/loose-head prop. **Debut:** Romania U-21 13, England U-21 54, 1989. **Caps:** 1. **Points:** 0. **Club:** Leicester. **Born:** 24.1.68. **Height:** 5'11" **Weight:** 15st 10lb. **Occupation:** PE Teacher.

WEST, Richard John. **1990/91 International category:** England U-21. **Position:** Lock. **Debut:** Netherlands 20, England U-21 20, 1991. **Caps:** 1. **Points:** 0. **Club:** Ledbury. **Born:** 20.3.71. **Height:** 6'8" **Weight:** 16st 7lb. **Occupation:** Agricultural student.

WILLS, Stephen Richard. **1990/91 International category:** England U-21. **Position:** Wing. **Debut:** Netherlands 18, England U-21 20, 1991. **Caps:** 1. **Points:** 4 (try). **Club:** Leicester. **Born:** 26.12.70. **Height:** 5'10" **Weight:** 12st 10lb. **Occupation:** Policeman.

Retirees

BATEMAN, Allan Glen. **International history:** Wales 1990 (4 caps, 0 pts). **Reason for retiring:** Switched codes to join Warrington RLFC. **Former Union clubs:** Maesteg Celtic, Maesteg, Neath. **Born:** Maesteg, 6.3.65.

JONES, Mark Alun. **International history:** Wales 1987-90 (14 caps, 8 pts). **Reason for retiring:** Switched codes to join Hull. **Former Union clubs:** Tredegar, Neath. **Born:** Tredegar, 22.6.65.

NORSTER, Robert Leonard. **International history:** Wales 1982-89 (34 caps, 8 pts), British Lions 1983 (2 Tests), 1989 (1 Test) – Former Wales captain who shared record with Allan Martin as country's most-capped lock. **Reason for retiring:** Shoulder injury. **Former Union clubs:** Abertillery, Cardiff. **Born:** Ebbw Vale, 23.6.57.

PHILLIPS, Rowland David. **International history:** Wales 1987-90 (10 caps, 0 pts). **Reason for retiring:** Switched codes to join Warrington. **Former Union club:** Neath. **Born:** St David's, Pembrokeshire, 28.7.65.

SMITH, Brian Anthony. **International history:** Australia 1987 (6 caps, 8 pts), Ireland 1989-91 (9 caps, 27 pts). **Reason for retiring:** Switched codes to join Balmain (Aus). **Former Union clubs:** Wests (Aus), Manly (Aus), Oxford Univ, Leicester. **Born:** St George (Aus), 9.9.66.

Rugby World Cup 1991

ORDER OF PLAY

Date	Game		Venue	PM	Pool
29 Sept	Opening ceremony		Twickenham	2.00	–
3 Oct	England	v. New Zealand	Twickenham	3.00	1
4 Oct	Australia	v. Argentina	Llanelli	3.00	3
	France	v. Romania	Beziers	8.00	4
5 Oct	Italy	v. USA	Otley	1.00	1
	Scotland	v. Japan	Edinburg	3.00	2
	Fiji	v. Canada	Bayonne	8.00	4
6 Oct	Wales	v. Western Samoa	Cardiff	1.00	3
	Ireland	v. Zimbabwe	Dublin	3.00	2
8 Oct	New Zealand	v. USA	Gloucester	1.00	1
	England	v. Italy	Twickenham	3.00	1
	France	v. Fiji	Grenoble	8.00	4
9 Oct	Australia	v. Western Samoa	Pontypool	1.00	3
	Ireland	v. Japan	Dublin	3.00	2
	Scotland	v. Zimbabwe	Edinburgh	3.00	2
	Wales	v. Argentina	Cardiff	8.00	3
	Canada	v. Romania	Toulouse	8.00	4
11 Oct	England	v. USA	Twickenham	3.00	1
12 Oct	Scotland	v. Ireland	Edinburgh	1.30	2
	Wales	v. Australia	Cardiff	3.15	3
	Fiji	v. Romania	Brive	7.00	4
13 Oct	Argentina	v. Western Samoa	Pontypridd	3.00	3
	New Zealand	v. Italy	Leicester	3.00	1
	France	v. Canada	Agen	8.00	4
14 Oct	Zimbabwe	v. Japan	Belfast	3.00	2
19 Oct	Winner Pool 2	v. RU Pool 3	Edinburgh	2.30	C
	Winner Pool 4	v. RU Pool 1	Paris	3.00	B
20 Oct	Winner Pool 3	v. RU Pool 2	Dublin	1.00	D
	Winner Pool 1	v. RU Pool 4	Lille	3.00	A
26 Oct	B v. C. – Semi-final		Edinburgh	2.30	
27 Oct	A v. D. – Semi-final		Dublin	2.30	
30 Oct	Third/Fourth place play-off		Cardiff	2.30	
2 Nov	RUGBY WORLD CUP FINAL 1991		Twickenham	2.30	

HOW THEY QUALIFIED
(Win=3pts, Draw=2, Loss=1)

EUROPE

FRANCE PRE-QUALIFYING TOURNAMENT: Switzerland 22, Israel 15 (30.4.89); Denmark 0, Sweden 39 (30.4.89); Switzerland 12, Denmark 26 (2.5.89); Sweden 26, Israel 10 (2.5.89); Israel 6, Denmark 16 (4.5.89); Switzerland 15, Sweden 33 (4.5.89). **Sweden** progress to qualifying round.

	P	W	D	L	F	A	Pts
Sweden	3	3	0	0	98	25	9
Denmark	3	2	0	1	42	57	7
Switzerland	3	1	0	2	49	74	5
Israel	3	0	0	3	31	64	3

QUALIFYING ROUNDS: First – Czechoslovakia 23, Yugoslavia 6 (9.9.89). **Second** – Czechoslovakia 12, Portugal 15 (1.10.89); West Germany 6, Netherlands 12 (17.9.89). **Third** – Portugal 3, Netherlands 32 (8.10.90). **Fourth** – Netherlands 24, Sweden 3 (15.10.89). **Netherlands** qualify to European preliminary pool.

MADRID QUALIFYING TOURNAMENT: Poland 25, Belgium 23 (29.10.89); Spain 29, Netherlands 15 (29.10.89); Belgium 12, Netherlands 32 (1.11.89); Spain 23, Poland 9 (1.11.89); Spain 58, Belgium 6 (5.11.89); Netherlands 33, Poland 27 (5.11.89). **Spain** and **Netherlands** progress.

	P	W	D	L	F	A	Pts
Spain	3	3	0	0	110	27	9
Netherlands	3	2	0	1	80	68	7
Poland	3	1	0	2	61	79	5
Belgium	3	0	0	3	38	115	3

FINAL QUALIFYING TOURNAMENT (Italy: Rovigo, Treviso and Padua): Italy 30, Spain 6 (30.9.90); Romania 45, Netherlands 7 (30.9.90); Romania 19, Spain 6 (3.10.90); Netherlands 11, Italy 24 (3.10.90); Italy 29, Romania 21 (7.10.90); Netherlands 12, Spain 22 (7.10.90). **Italy** (into Pool 1) and **Romania** (into Pool 4) qualify for World Cup finals.

	P	W	D	L	F	A	Pts
Italy	3	3	0	0	83	38	9
Romania	3	2	0	1	85	42	7
Spain	3	1	0	2	34	60	5
Netherlands	3	0	0	3	30	91	3

ASIA/PACIFIC

HONG KONG PRELIMINARY TOURNAMENT (12–19.11.88): **Pool A**
– Korea 102, Malaysia 0; Hong Kong 45, Sri Lanka 3; Korea 39, Hong Kong
19; Malaysia 6, Sri Lanka 12; Korea 68, Sri Lanka 6; Hong Kong 50, Malaysia
0.

	P	W	D	L	F	A	Pts
Korea	3	3	0	0	209	25	9
Hong Kong	3	2	0	1	114	42	7
Sri Lanka	3	1	0	2	21	119	5
Malaysia	3	0	0	3	6	164	3

Pool B – Japan 82, Singapore 0; Thailand 9, Taiwan 32; Japan 108, Thailand
7; Singapore 3, Taiwan 86; Japan 20, Taiwan 19; Thailand 17, Singapore 3.

	P	W	D	L	F	A	Pts
Japan	3	3	0	0	210	26	9
Taiwan	3	2	0	1	137	32	7
Thailand	3	1	0	2	33	143	5
Singapore	3	0	0	3	6	185	3

Play-off: Hong Kong 19, Taiwan 4. **Final:** Japan 13, Korea 17. **Korea** and
Japan progress to Tokyo qualifying tournament.

TOKYO QUALIFYING TOURNAMENT: Korea 7, Western Samoa 74
(8.4.90); Tonga 16, Japan 28 (8.4.90); Tonga 3, Western Samoa 12 (11.4.90);
Korea 10, Japan 26 (11.4.90); Korea 22, Tonga 45 (15.4.90); Western Samoa
37, Japan 11 (15.4.90). **Western Samoa** (into Pool 3) and **Japan** (into Pool
2) qualify for finals.

	P	W	D	L	F	A	Pts
W.Samoa	3	3	0	0	123	21	9
Japan	3	2	0	1	65	63	7
Tonga	3	1	0	2	64	62	5
Korea	3	0	0	3	39	145	3

AFRICA

ZIMBABWE QUALIFYING TOURNAMENT (Harare): Zimbabwe 22,
Ivory Coast 9 (5.5.90); Morocco 12, Tunisia 16 (5.5.90); Tunisia 12, Ivory
Coast 7 (9.5.90); Zimbabwe 16, Morocco 0 (9.5.90); Morocco 11, Ivory

Coast 4 (12.5.90 – abandoned 70 mins); Zimbabwe 24, Tunisia 13 (12.5.90).
Zimbabwe (into Pool 2) qualify for finals.

	P	W	D	L	F	A	Pts
Zimbabwe	3	3	0	0	62	22	9
Tunisia	3	2	0	1	41	43	7
Morocco	3	1	0	2	23	36	5
IvoryCoast	3	0	0	3	20	45	3

AMERICA

AMERICAN ZONE CLASSIFICATION TOURNAMENT: Canada 21,
United States 3 (23.9.89); Argentina 23, United States 6 (11.11.89); Canada
15, Argentina 6 (30.3.90); Argentina 13, United States 6 (7.4.90); Canada
12, United States 14 (9.6.90); Argentina 15, Canada 19 (16.6.90). **Canada**
(into Pool 4), **Argentina** (into Pool 3) and **United States** (into Pool 1) qualify
for finals.

	P	W	D	L	F	A	Pts
Canada	4	3	0	1	67	38	10
Argentina	4	2	0	2	57	46	8
United States	4	1	0	3	29	69	6

The Teams

POOL 1
ENGLAND

Qualification: Automatic
Colours: White jerseys with red rose, white shorts
World Cup record: 1987 – Quarter-finalists. Lost controversial opening
match to Australia (6–19) but rebounded well to account for Japan (60–7)
and the United States (34–6) and book a quarter-final tie against **Wales**. The
match proved disastrous for England as they lost 3–16, although Wales' later
feat of beating Australia in the third place play-off showed England's defeat
in a slightly more favourable light. **1991** – Automatic qualification.
Results since 1987 World Cup: 1988 – France 10, England 9; England 3,
Wales 11; Scotland 6, England 9; England 35, Ireland 3; Australia 22, England
16; Australia 28, England 8; Fiji 12, England 25; England 28, Australia 19.
1989 – Romania 3, England 58; England 12, Scotland 12; Ireland 3, England

16; England 11, France 0; Wales 12, England 9; England 58, Fiji 23. **1990 –** England 23, Ireland 0; France 7, England 26; England 34, Wales 6; Scotland 13, England 7; Italy XV 15, England XV 33; Argentina 12, England 25; Argentina 15, England 12; England 51, Argentina 12. **1991 –** Wales 6, England 25; England 21, Scotland 12; Ireland 7, England 16; England 21, France 19; Fiji 12, England 28; Australia 40, England 15.

Survivors from 1987 (squad members in 1990/91): Jon Webb, Rory Underwood, Rob Andrew, Richard Hill, Dean Richards, Peter Winterbottom, John Hall, Mickey Skinner, Gary Rees, Wade Dooley, Paul Rendall, Jeff Probyn, Brian Moore.

Unlike France, who have maintained their back division while overhauling the pack, England will field a very similar set of forwards to 1987, while Rory Underwood is the only likely back survivor from the 1987 quarter-final loss to Wales. Up front, Jeff Probyn and Jason Leonard might have unseated Paul Rendall and Gary Pearce as Brian Moore's front row cohorts but the latter two remain in contention, as do Nigel Redman (lock) and Gary Rees (flanker) in the shadows of Paul Ackford and Mike Teague/John Hall respectively.

Pool pointers: As in 1987 (when they lost to Australia), the key to England's Pool fortunes is contained in their opening game, when they face the World champion All Blacks at Twickenham. As Grand Slam holders, England will be confident, although less so after their summer beating by Australia, but mindful of the form New Zealand showed when touring Britain (though not England) in 1989. The critical factor is likely to be goal kicking. England learnt the value of discipline during the 1991 Five Nations' Championship, committing precious few infringements, and if they can maintain that form and reduce the influence of Grant Fox, the holders could be troubled. With Simon Hodgkinson's prolific boot threatening, providing he can make the team, New Zealand will be equally diligent. Italy, despite their continued improvement, and the United States, whom England disposed of (34–6) in 1987, should be relevant only in terms of points-difference.

NEW ZEALAND

Qualification: Automatic (holders)
Colours: Black jerseys with silver fern, black shorts
World Cup record: 1987 – Webb Ellis Trophy winners. Qualified from Pool 3 with maximum points and a points-difference of plus 156, courtesy of wins over Italy (70–6), Fiji (74–13) and Argentina (46–15). Never troubled by either **Scotland** in Christchurch quarter-final (30–3), or **Wales** in Brisbane semi-final (49–6). Even the French were powerless as New Zealand, steered by the unerring boot of Grant Fox (17 pts in final, 126 overall) won the Auckland final 29–9. **1991 –** Automatic qualification.
Results since 1987 World Cup: 1988 – Australia 16, NZ 30; NZ 52, Wales 3; NZ 54, Wales 9; Australia 7, NZ 32; Australia 19, NZ 19; Australia 9, NZ

30. **1989** – NZ 25, France 17; NZ 34, France 20; NZ 60, Argentina 9; NZ 49, Argentina 12; NZ 24, Australia 12; Wales 9, NZ 34; Ireland 6, NZ 23. **1990** – NZ 31, Scotland 16; NZ 21, Scotland 18; NZ 21, Australia 6; NZ 27, Australia 17; NZ 9, Australia 21; France 3, NZ 24; France 12, NZ 30. **1991** – Argentina 14, NZ 28; Argentina 6, NZ 36.

Survivors from 1987 (squad members in 1990/91): Kieran Crowley, John Kirwan, Terry Wright, Joe Stanley, Grant Fox, Wayne Shelford, Zinzan Brooke, Alan Whetton, Gary Whetton, Richard Loe, Steve McDowell, Sean Fitzpatrick.

It was thought that the exodus of All Blacks to rugby league in the summer of 1990 (John Gallacher, Frano Botica, John Schuster, Matthew Ridge etc) might cause New Zealand to fall from their perch as the world's best team; that the three-Test Bledisloe Cup series against Australia followed by a two-Test series in France would expose the New Zealanders' new-found vulnerability. Not a bit of it. While Australia won the third 'dead rubber' Test (21–9) to hand the All Blacks their first defeat in 1373 days, 50 games and 23 Tests (since they were beaten by France in Nantes on 15 Nov, 1986), New Zealand retained the Cup and then, with Grant Fox in splendid form, accounted for the French in Europe by a 2–0 Test margin. If any Englishman might question the All Blacks' mastery of the game, they need only recall how Wayne Shelford transformed Northampton during the 1990/91 season, or how coach Doug Wyllie got Coventry buzzing during his short stint at Coundon Road at the beginning of 1990.

Pool Pointers: Will likely start the tournament as favourites to repeat their 1987 triumph, but with the prospect of England at a packed Twickenham in their opening Pool match, NZ will immediately discover the magnitude of their 'double' quest. That match will decide, barring a catastrophe against the USA or Italy, who journeys to the Parc des Princes for an equally unappealing tie against France, in all probability, in the quarter-final stage. The Twickenham winners avoid Paris and head for Lille for a less daunting match against either Romania, Fiji or Canada.

ITALY

Qualification: European zone winners
Colours: Blue shirts, white shorts
World Cup record: **1987** – After being crushed by New Zealand (6–70) in Pool opener, Italy improved markedly against Argentina (lost 16–25) before scoring one of the tournament's biggest upsets by beating Fiji (18–15). **1991** – Qualified by winning European pool (played in Italy) with 100 per cent record against Spain (30–6), Netherlands (24–11) and Romania (29–21).
Players to watch: Ivan Francescato, Massimo Benomi, Massimo Brunello, Luigi Troiani, Massimo Cuttitta, Franco Properzie, Gianbattista Croci.
Pool pointers: Italy showed the world what they were capable of achieving

when beating Fiji (18–15) in the 1987 World Cup. An Italian XV entertained an **England XV** in Rovigo (1990) and kept the deficit to a respectable 15–33. Nevertheless, Italy will do well to repeat the feat against England, whilst success against New Zealand would seem even more unlikely (even though they did restrict the All Blacks to narrow victories of 17–9 in 1976 and 18–12 in 1979). That leaves the United States (at Otley) as Italy's one real chance of World Cup success. Lost both Tests to Namibia last summer (7–17 and 19–33).

UNITED STATES

Qualification: Third place in American zone
Colours: Red jerseys, white shorts
World Cup record: 1987 – Marked debut with shock 21–18 win over Japan in Brisbane, where Los Angeles full-back Ray Nelson bagged 13 points. From there the only way was down, losing to England (7–60) and Australia (12–47). **1991** – Continued to develop in qualifying, despite propping up the American zone. Two defeats by Argentina (6–23 and 6–13) following an opening loss to zone-winners Canada (3–21) painted a bleak picture, but the horizon brightened considerably for the US of A when they went to Seattle and beat the Canucks 14–12, with tries by Barry Daily and Rory Lewis and penalty goals from Mike DeJong and Mark Williams.
Recent results: Beaten 46–0 by Wales in Nov 1987, 32–7 by Ireland XV in Sept 1989, 12–10 by Ireland U–25s in March 1990, and 41–12 by Scotland last May. Had to cancel proposed tour of USSR in autumn 1990 due to shortage of funds. (Proceeds from 1987 World Cup were divided up between competing nations so USA covered most of expenses. This is not happening in 1991.) World Cup preparations, therefore, consigned to six-match tour of Australia where lost 9–67 in Test. Last summer, defeated Japan twice (20–9 and 27–15) but lost both Tests v. France (9–41 and 3–10★). ★Abandoned at half-time.
Players to watch: Brian Vizard (capt), Mike DeJong, Chris O'Brien, Mark Williams, Gary Hein, Don James.
Pool pointers: Lost to **England** (6–34) in 1987 World Cup, having previously succumbed 11–37 (1977) and 0–59 (1982), so unlikely to provide more than a distraction to the English challenge, especially before a full house at Twickenham. Although, as Eagles wing Gary Hein proved when helping Oxford upset the odds against Cambridge in the 1991 Varsity match, nothing should be taken for granted. Japan, who fell to the Eagles in 1987 competition, will testify to that. A 6–53 loss to New Zealand in 1980 gives little cause for optimism either when the sides meet at Gloucester. So it looks like Italy or bust. The form which accounted for Canada in qualifying would trouble Italy, but that which led to a 9–67 loss at the hands of Australia would probably not.

POOL 2
IRELAND

Qualification: Automatic
Colours: Green jerseys, white shorts
World Cup record: 1987 – Quarter-finalists. Having lost 6–13 to Wales in their opening game, Ireland collected wins over Canada (46–19) and Tonga (32–9) to qualify as runner-up. That earned them the doubtful privilege of facing Australia in Sydney for a place in the semi-finals. Ireland lost 33–15. **1991** – Automatic qualification.
Results since 1987 World Cup: 1988 – Ireland 22, Scotland 18; France 25, Ireland 6; Ireland 9, Wales 12; England 35, Ireland 3; Ireland 49, Western Samoa 22. **1989** – Ireland 21, France 26; Wales 13, Ireland 19; Ireland 3, England 16; Scotland 37, Ireland 21; Canada 21, Ireland XV 24; United States 7, Ireland XV 32; Ireland 6, New Zealand 23. **1990** – England 23, Ireland 0; Ireland 10, Scotland 13; France 31, Ireland 12; Ireland 14, Wales 8; Ireland 20, Argentina 18. **1991** – Ireland 13, France 21; Wales 21, Ireland 21; Ireland 7, England 16; Scotland 28, Ireland 25; Namibia 15, Ireland 6; Namibia 26, Ireland 15.
Survivors from 1987 (squad members in 1990/91): Keith Crossan, Michael Kiernan, Brendan Mullin, Michael Bradley, Philip Matthews, Neil Francis, Donal Lenihan, Des Fitzgerald, Jim McCoy, John McDonald, Steve Smith, Terry Kingston.

Despite their disappointing summer tour to Namibia, Ireland have many reasons for optimism going into the tournament, having produced a team of flair and ability virtually overnight last season. One minute they were struggling desperately to beat a weak Argentina side in Dublin, the next they had brought in half the B team and transformed into an outfit bubbling with optimism. True, they still shared the Five Nations' Wooden Spoon with Wales, but with the youthful zeal of, amongst others, London Irish quartet Rob Saunders, Simon Geoghegan, David Curtis and Jim Staples, combining with the experience of Donal Lenihan, Phil Matthews, Brendan Mullin, Steve Smith and Keith Crossan, a change in fortunes cannot be far away.
Pool pointers: As in 1987, Ireland have been pitted against Home Union opposition (Scotland) and, as last time round, that match will, in all likelihood, decide the Pool winner. Ireland must travel to Murrayfield for the tie but they will not mind that, bearing in mind their performance there in the 1991 Five Nations' Championship in defeat by 25–28. Of their other opponents, Japan will be the most unknown, as Western Samoa came to Lansdowne Road in 1989 and were beaten 49–22.

SCOTLAND

Qualification: Automatic
Colours: Navy blue jerseys, white shorts
World Cup record: **1987** – Quarter-finalists. To lose the inspirational John Rutherford in the opening Pool match against France and to be paired with New Zealand in the quarter-finals were two factors which conspired against the Scots. However, they had the satisfaction of sharing a 20–20 draw with the French, who had just won a splendid Grand Slam and were en route for the World Cup final. Comprehensive wins over Zimbabwe (60–21) and Romania (55–28) ensured that the Scots qualified unbeaten, but they lost that tag to the All Blacks next time out (30–3). **1991** – Automatic qualification.
Results since 1987 World Cup: **1987** – Scotland XV 15, France XV 12. **1988** – Ireland 22, Scotland 18; Scotland 23, France 12; Wales 25, Scotland 20; Scotland 6, England 9; Zimbabwe 10, Scotland XV 31; Zimbabwe 7, Scotland XV 34; Scotland 13, Australia 32. **1989** – Scotland 23, Wales 7; England 12, Scotland 12; Scotland 37, Ireland 21; France 19, Scotland 3; Japan 28, Scotland XV 24; Scotland 38, Fiji 17; Scotland 32, Romania 0. **1990** – Ireland 10, Scotland 13; Scotland 21, France 0; Wales 9, Scotland 13; Scotland 13, England 7; New Zealand 31, Scotland 16; New Zealand 21, Scotland 18; Scotland 49, Argentina 3. **1991** – France 15, Scotland 9; Scotland 32, Wales 12; England 21, Scotland 12; Scotland 28, Ireland 25; USA 12, Scotland XV 41; Canada 24, Scotland XV 19.
Pool pointers: Scotland beat Ireland 28–25 at Murrayfield in the 1991 Five Nations' Championship and, by their own admission, were fortunate to win. The pair meet again in Edinburgh in the key final Pool match. The Scots have been rewarded for their adventurous tours to developing rugby nations over the past three years by being drawn with Japan and Zimbabwe who they visited in 1988 and 1989 respectively. Those who played in a Scotland XV beaten 24–28 by Japan in Tokyo will be keen to turn the tables this time round. Scotland's home is very much their castle – unbeaten at Murrayfield since the Wallabies visited in 1988 – and, provided they keep winning, they will play every match at home until the final.
Survivors from 1987 (squad members in 1990/91): Gavin Hastings, Peter Dods, Iwan Tukalo, Scott Hastings, Doug Wyllie, Greig Oliver, John Jeffrey, Finlay Calder, Derek Turnbull, David Sole, Jeremy Richardson, Iain Milne.

The memory of a somewhat lacklustre campaign in the 1991 Five Nations' Championship, a hangover from their 1990 Grand Slam followed by a fine tour to New Zealand, should spur the Scots on. Gavin Hastings scored 62 points in the 1987 competition and is one of many returning squad members. Add the 'newcomers' – Craig Chalmers, Gary Armstrong, Tony Stanger and Paul Burnell, to name but four – and Scotland have a useful blend.

JAPAN

Qualification: Asian/Pacific zone runners-up
Colours: Red and white hooped jerseys, white shorts
World Cup record: 1987 – Made worst possible start when beaten by rank outsiders United States (18–21) in Brisbane, despite outscoring Eagles by three tries to two, and were then swept aside by England (7–60) and Australia (23–42). **1991** – Reached Tokyo qualifying tournament by beating Singapore (82–0), Thailand (108–7) and Taiwan (20–19), although lost 13–17 to Korea in final. Gained revenge on Koreans in Tokyo (winning 26–10) and also got the better of Tonga (28–16), but loss to Western Samoa (11–37) consigned them to the role of Asian/Pacific zone bridesmaids.
Players to watch: Seiji Hirao, Toshi Hayashi, Takahiro Hosokawa, Tsuyoshi Fujita, Atsushi Oyagi, Yoshito Yoshida, Sinali Latu (ex-Tongan No.8), Nofomuli Taumoefolau (ex-Tongan centre).
Pool pointers: Despite 28–24 defeat of Scotland XV in May 1989, Japan lost twice to British Columbia (3–41 and 10–41) in September 1989 on tour to Canada which was effectively a training camp. Thrashed by New Zealand in two Tests straight after 1987 World Cup (0–74 and 6–104) before losing to Korea in final of Asian Championship for second straight year, prompting dismissal of entire coaching staff. Akihiro Shukuzawa appointed new coach. Benefited mightily from home advantage in Asian/Pacific zone qualifying tournament where 75,000 helped them on their way. Lost 15–27 to USA in Chicago in May 1991. The kicking of Hosokawa is vital (21 v. Tonga, 18 v. Korea in qualifying), as is the leadership of prop Toshi Hayashi, who helped Oxford win the 1991 Varsity match.

ZIMBABWE

Qualification: African zone winners
Colours: White with olive green hoops, white shorts
World Cup record: 1987 – Turned in an excellent performance when losing narrowly to Romania (20–21) in Pool 4 opening match. But could offer little resistance against Scotland (lost 21–60) and France (lost 12–70). **1991** – Qualified by winning African pool with 100 per cent record against Tunisia (24–13), Morocco (16–0) and Ivory Coast (22–9).
Survivors from 1987 World Cup (squad members in 1990/91): Andre Buitendang, Greig Brown, Grant Davidson, George Elcombe, Andy Ferreira, Kevin Graham, Mike Martin, Malcolm Sawyer, Richard Tsimba.
Players to watch: Andy Ferreira (capt), Richard Tsimba, Honeywell Nguruve, Zivanai Dzinomurumbi, Peter Albasini, Anthony Horton, Brendan Dowson, Bedford Chimbima.
Pool pointers: Recent defeats by Spain, Romania, Italy and Namibia do not augur well for the challenge of Ireland and Scotland who, in addition to their

comprehensive 61–20 victory in the 1987 World Cup, won both unofficial Tests when the nations met at Bulawayo (31–10) and Harare (34–7) in 1988. Japan would appear to offer their only chance of success.

POOL 3
WALES

Qualification: Automatic
Colours: Red jersey, white shorts
World Cup record: 1987 – Third place. As is the case this time, Wales went to the 1987 World Cup as joint holders (with England) of the Wooden Spoon but produced a memorable month of performances to claim third place. They were made to work for their place in the second stage, winning Pool 2 only after close matches against **Ireland** (won 13–6) and Tonga (won 29–16) and a less taxing 46–19 win over Canada, thanks largely to four tries from Ieuan Evans. However, that achieved, Wales were good value for their 16–3 quarter-final triumph over **England**, although it has to be said that the opposition were far from impressive. The 49–6 beating handed out by New Zealand in the semi-final looked to have shattered Wales (their biggest ever defeat) but, to their enormous credit, they regrouped and defeated Australia 22–21 in a thrilling third place play-off after Paul Thorburn goaled from the touchline in the final minute. 1991 – Automatic qualification.
Results since 1987 World Cup: 1987 – Wales 46, United States 0. **1988 –** England 3, Wales 11; Wales 25, Scotland 20; Ireland 9, Wales 12; Wales 9, France 10; New Zealand 52, Wales 3; New Zealand 54, Wales 9; Wales 24, Western Samoa 6; Wales 9, Romania 15. **1989** – Scotland 23, Wales 7; Wales 13, Ireland 19; France 31, Wales 12; Wales 12, England 9; Wales 9, New Zealand 34. **1990** – Wales 19, France 29; England 34, Wales 6; Wales 9, Scotland 13; Ireland 14, Wales 8;Namibia 9, Wales 18, Namibia 30, Wales 34. 1991 – Wales 31, Barbarians 24; Wales 6, England 25; Scotland 32, Wales 12; Wales 21, Ireland 21; France 36, Wales 3.
Survivors from 1987 World Cup (squad members in 1990/91): Paul Thorburn, Ieuan Evans, Mark Ring, Robert Jones, Phil Davies, Richie Collins, Richard Webster, Kevin Phillips.

Considering the turmoil Welsh rugby has been in since winning the 1988 Triple Crown, it is little wonder that so few of the 1987 squad remain this time round. The loss of Jonathan Davies, John Devereux, Paul Moriarty and David Young to rugby league has sapped the Principality's strength and morale and it is largely the New Guard – Neil Jenkins and Scott Gibbs to name but two – in whose hands Wales' fortunes will be placed. Yet, in Thorburn, Ieuan Evans, Robert Jones and Phil Davies, Wales possess four players of genuine international class. The team's balance is not right but if they can hold off Western Samoa and Argentina, Wales could secure the runners-up spot behind Australia. More than that is most unlikely.

Pool pointers: After their summer misery Down Under, Wales has little reason for confidence, especially as there are no obvious weaker links in the Pool, with Western Samoa having demonstrated their ability when holding Wales to a 24–6 scoreline in Cardiff in 1988, and the enigmatic Pumas world renowned for the heights they are capable of reaching. The order of matches should suit Wales, with the toughest opponent, Australia, saved until last. It is unthinkable to look beyond an Australian Pool win but who progresses as runners-up will be one of the fascinations of the preliminary stage.

AUSTRALIA

Qualification: Automatic
Colours: Gold jersey, green shorts
World Cup record: 1987 – Semi-finalists. Australia's problem was one of endurance. 79 minutes was okay, but the full 80 minutes became a problem later in the tournament. Wins over **England** (19–6), the United States (47–12) and Japan (42–23) augured well for the knock-out stage but, after dismantling Ireland 33–15 in Sydney to reach the semi-finals, they bowed out at the same venue to France. Remembered as one of the greatest games ever, the Wallabies succumbed to a last-gasp try from Serge Blanco (lost 24–30). They then met **Wales** in the third place play-off and lost out to a final minute penalty by Paul Thorburn (21–22). **1991** – Automatic qualification.
Results since 1987 World Cup: 1987 – Australia 16, New Zealand 30; Argentina 19, Australia 19; Argentina 27, Australia 19. **1988** – Australia 22, England 16; Australia 28, England 8; Australia 7, NZ 32; Australia 19, NZ 19; Australia 9, NZ 30; England 28, Australia 19; Scotland 13, Australia 32. **1989** – Australia 30, British Lions 12; Australia 12, Lions 19; Australia 18, Lions 19; France 15, Australia 32; France 25, Australia 19; NZ 24, Australia 12. **1990** – Australia 21, France 9; Australia 48, France 31; Australia 19, France 28; Australia 67, USA 9; NZ 21, Australia 6; NZ 27, Australia 17; NZ 21, Australia 21. **1991** – Australia 63, Wales 6; Australia 40, England 15.
Survivors from 1987: David Campese, Michael Lynagh, Nick Farr-Jones, Troy Coker, Simon Poidevin, Steve Tuynman, Bill Campbell, Steve Cutler, Tom Lawton, Mark Hartill, Mark McBain, Cameron Lillicrap.

Australia's challenge will once again be based around their two match winners behind the scrum, Michael Lynagh and David Campese. Everybody knows of what the pair are capable – Lynagh with his prolific boot and Campese his magical running – but none have developed a method of blotting them out as a threat. In Nick Farr-Jones, captain and scrum-half, Australia also have a great general, a fine tactician, running their show. It will be interesting to see how the many young Wallabies introduced over the past year cope with the unique pressures of the World Cup.
Pool pointers: By ending New Zealand's 50-match unbeaten record last season, Australia proved that they can rule the world, if only for one brief day.

It might have been a 'dead' rubber in the Bledisloe Cup series but **Wales**, Argentina and Western Samoa will have taken note. Australia have lost two of their last four meetings with Wales (1981 and 1987), although on last summer's evidence they would appear to currently hold a firm advantage, while Argentina sneaked the two-Test series with the Wallabies following the 1987 World Cup.

WESTERN SAMOA

Qualification: Asian/Pacific zone winners
Colours: Blue jersey, white shorts
World Cup record: 1987 – Reserves. **1991** – Qualified by winning Asian/Pacific pool with 100 per cent record against Japan (37–11), Tonga (12–3) and Korea (74–7).
Players to watch: Peter Fatialofa (capt), Afato Leu'u, Silo Vaifale, Harry Schuster, Timo Tagaloa, Tupo Faamasino, Philip Saena, Too Manoo, Taufusi Salesa, Aneterea Aoilupo.
Pool pointers: The Western Samoans have suffered from the player-drain to New Zealand. Joe Stanley, John Schuster and Viaga Tuigamala, for example, all opted for the All Blacks, leaving the Samoans to struggle on. That said, the South Pacific island, who had only been reserves in 1987, had few problems in qualifying this time, scoring an encouragingly big win over fellow finalists Japan in the process. Samoa showed, when running Wales close in 1988, that the ability is there and with the outside pace of wing Timo Tagaloa they could well prove one of the surprises of the Pool stage.

ARGENTINA

Qualification: American zone runners-up
Colours: Light blue and white hooped jersey, white shorts
World Cup record: 1987 – Sandwiched defeat of Italy (25–16) between losses to Fiji (9–28) and New Zealand (15–46). **1991** – Disappointing in qualifying from pressure-free American zone where all three competing nations were guaranteed passage to finals. Despite twice defeating the United States (23–6 and 13–6) they failed to get the better of pool winners Canada on either of their meetings. After going down 6–15 away from home, the Pumas failed to gain revenge at home, losing 15–19.
Players to watch: Jorge Allen, Diego Cuesta-Silva, Lisandro Arbizu, Diego Cash.
Pool pointers: If the World Cup was being played in South America, Argentina would fancy their chances, but Europe is an entirely different prospect, especially without the inspirational Hugo Porta. The Pumas might have beaten England in Buenos Aires (August 1990) but, two months later at Twickenham, they were routed 51–0, followed by 49–3 at Murrayfield.

However, the form they displayed when coming so close to beating Ireland (18–20) on the same tour, underscores the need for **Wales** and Western Samoa to be vigilant against the Pumas.

POOL 4
FRANCE

Qualification: Automatic
Colours: Blue jerseys, white shorts
World Cup record: 1987 – Runners-up. Unbeaten in Pool 4 although held to a draw by **Scotland** (20–20) in opening game. Progressed after beating Romania (55–12) and Zimbabwe (70–12). Better points difference assured them of avoiding New Zealand until final, whereas Scotland were obliged to play them in last eight. Beat Fiji (31–16) in quarter-finals before squeezing past Australia 30–24 in Sydney semi-final which many believed to be the greatest ever International. Serge Blanco's last-minute try pipped the hosts to the final berth. Against New Zealand, who had been given a far easier semi-final ride by **Wales**, France were unable to rescale the heights attained against Australia, and Grant Fox (17 points) condemned France to the runners-up spot. **1991** – Automatic qualification.
Results since 1987 World Cup: 1987 – Scotland XV 15, France 12. **1988** – France 10, England 9; Scotland 23, France 12; France 25, Ireland 6; Wales 9, France 10; Argentina 15, France 18; Argentina 18, France 6; France 29, Argentina 9; France 28, Argentina 18. **1989** – Ireland 21, France 26; France 31, Wales 12; England 11, France 0; France 19, Scotland 3; New Zealand 25, France 17; France 20, New Zealand 34; France 27, Home Unions 29; France 15, Australia 32; France 25, Australia 19. **1990** – Wales 19, France 29; France 7, England 26; Scotland 21, France 0; France 31, Ireland 12; France 6, Romania 12. **1991** – France 15, Scotland 9; Ireland 13, France 21; France 36, Wales 3; England 21, France 19; USA 9, France 41; Romania 21, France 33.
Survivors from 1987: Serge Blanco, Didier Camberabero, Patrice Lagisquet, Jean-Baptiste Lafond, Eric Bonneval, Philippe Sella, Denis Charvet, Franck Mesnel, Pierre Berbizier, Pascal Ondarts, Eric Champ, Laurent Rodriguez, Louis Armary, Jean Condom.

France's back division is still pretty much intact from 1987; indeed all seven who played in the final (Blanco, Camberabero, Sella, Charvet, Laqisquet, Mesnel and Berbizier) participated in the 1991 Five Nations' Championship. However, the French pack has undergone reconstruction. Of the forwards who played against England in the 1991 Grand Slam decider, only Pascal Ondarts featured in the last World Cup.
Pool pointers: France were a joy to watch last season. Under the coaching of Daniel Dubroca the expression and passion returned. Again we thrilled to Blanco, Sella, Saint-Andre and the like in open play while Olivier Roumat

and Xavier Blond were among the notables up front. Their meeting with Fiji promises to be a thrilling exhibition of rugby but whether it proves to be the Pool decider will largely depend on Romania, who dispatched France 12–6 in Auch in 1990, but lost 21–33 to the same opponents last summer.

FIJI

Qualification: Automatic
Colours: White jerseys with black palm tree, black shorts
World Cup record: 1987 – After a bright start against Argentina (won 28–9), Fiji were crushed mercilessly by the All Blacks in Christchurch (74–13) and, perhaps still dazed, then lost to Italy (15–18). **1991** – Automatic qualification.
Players to watch: Waisale Serevi, Noa Nadruku, Tomasi Cama, Mesake Rasari, Pauliasi Tabulutu.
Pool pointers: Fiji are like a film which works on video but not the big screen. As a sevens team they rule the world roost yet they are unable to translate that prowess to the XV-a-side format. They demonstrated their fallability by losing to Italy in the 1987 tournament yet defeated Argentina with little trouble. Guaranteed to entertain the French crowds, win or lose, but what results they will achieve against Canada and Romania, only they know.

ROMANIA

Qualification: European zone runners-up
Colours: Yellow jerseys, blue shorts
World Cup record: 1987 – Struggled to beat Zimbabwe (21–20) in opening match and not allowed to find rhythm thereafter, losing heavily to both France (12–55) and Scotland (28–55). **1991** – Qualified as runners-up in European zone, beating Spain (19–6) and Netherlands (45–7) but going down to Italy (21–29).
Players to watch: Gheorghe Ion, Costica Cojecariu, Stefan Chirila, Niculae Racean, Nicolai Nichitgean.
Pool pointers: Romania, like Fiji, are the enigmas of the world game. Brilliant one minute – beating Wales 15–9 at Cardiff in 1988 (their first away win against a Big Eight nation) – appalling the next – losing 15–22 to Tunisia and 0–60 to Ireland in 1985. Their build-up has been characteristic. Having earned their first win on French soil in the rain at Auch in 1990, beating France 12–6, they then threw away all the good work by losing 18–21 to Italy early in 1991. Out went coach Theodor Radulescu and his assistant Florin Popovici after that, to be replaced by Petre Ianusievici. After Ceauscescu and the Revolution, an episode which cost the lives of so many Romanians including the great Florica Murariu, no-one deserves success more than Romania.

CANADA

Qualification: American zone winners
Colours: Red jerseys, white shorts
World Cup record: 1987 – Opened account in impressive form when trouncing Tonga 37–4 in Napier, scoring seven tries in process. Unable to reproduce winning form against Ireland (19–46) or Wales (9–40) but, nevertheless, had good reason to be proud of their campaign. **1991 –** Qualified as winners of American zone. However, 100 per cent record, which seemed assured after two wins over Argentina and an away triumph in the United States, alluded them when the Eagles scored a surprise win in Seattle.
Players to watch: Mark Wyatt, Gareth Rees, Shayne Brown, Ian Stuart, Paul Szabo, John Robertsen.
Pool pointers: Canada's success is very much dependent on the form of captain Mark Wyatt, whose boot has served as a barometer to their form throughout so much of the past decade. Only last summer he kicked a world record eight penalty goals in Canada's 24–19 defeat of Scotland. A very hard Pool to call, the Canucks seem unlikely to trouble Romania or Fiji (France are out of the question) and, yet, they could beat them both.

World Cup Referees

England: F A Howard, E F Morrison. **Scotland**: J Fleming, B Anderson. **Wales**: W D Bevan, L J Peard. **Ireland**: O E Doyle, S R Hilditch. **France:** R Hourquet, P Robin. **Australia:** K V J Fitzgerald, A R MacNeill. **New Zealand**: D J Bishop, K H Lawrence. **Argentina**: E Sklar. **Canada**: K J Morrison. **Fiji:** L Colati. **Italy:** N Cadamuro. **Japan:** H Yagi. **Romania:** I Vasilica. **United States:** D Reordan. **Zimbabwe:** K J Went. Western **Samoa:** F Vito. **Belgium:** D Roelands.

1987 World Cup Records

Most points in competition 126 – G Fox (New Zealand)
Best British/Irish performances 62 – G Hastings (Scotland) 43 – J Webb (England) 37 – P Thorburn (Wales) 36 – M Kiernan (Ireland)
Most tries in competition 6 – C Green/J Kirwan (New Zealand)
Best British/Irish performances – M Harrison (England) 4 – M Duncan/A

Tait/J Jeffrey (Scotland) 4 – I Evans (Wales) 3 – B Mullin/H MacNeill (Ireland)

Most conversions in competition 30 – G Fox (New Zealand)
Best British/Irish performances 16 – G Hastings (Scotland) 11 – J Webb (England) 11 – P Thorburn (Wales)
7 – M Kiernan (Ireland)

Most penalty goals in competition 21 – G Fox (New Zealand)
Best British/Irish performances
7 – J Webb (England)
6 – G Hastings (Scotland)
5 – M Kiernan (Ireland)
5 – P Thorburn (Wales)

Most dropped goals in competition
3 – J Davies (Wales)
Best other British/Irish performances
1 – M Kiernan (Ireland)
   T Ward (Ireland)
0 – England
0 – Scotland

Most points in a match (individual) 30 – D Camberabero (France, v. Zimbabwe) **Best British/Irish performances** 27 – G Hastings (Scotland, v. Romania) 20 – J Webb (England, v. Japan) 19 – M Kiernan (Ireland, v. Canada) 16 – I Evans (Wales, v. Canada)

Most tries in a match (individual) 4 – I Evans (Wales, v. Canada)
4 – C Green (New Zealand, v. Fiji)
J Gallagher (New Zealand, v. Fiji) **Best other British/Irish performances**

3 – B Mullin (Ireland, v. Tonga)
3 – M Harrison (England, v. Japan)
3 – J Jeffrey (Scotland, v. Romania)
Most tries in a match (team) 13 – France (v. Zimbabwe) **Best British/Irish performances** 11 – Scotland (v. Zimbabwe) 10 – England (v. Japan)
8 – Wales (v. Canada)
6 – Ireland (v. Canada)

Most conversions in a match (individual/team) 10 – G Fox (New Zealand, v. Fiji) **Best British/Irish performances**
8 – G Hastings (Scotland, v. Zimbabwe and Romania)
7 – J Webb (England, v. Japan)
5 – M Kiernan (Ireland, v. Canada)
4 – P Thorburn (Wales, v. Canada)

Most penalty goals in a match (individual/team)
6 – G Fox (New Zealand, v. Scotland and Argentina) **Best British/Irish performances**
4 – J Webb (England, v. USA)
4 – G Hastings (Scotland, v. France)

2 – P Thorburn (Wales, v. Tonga and England)
2 – M Kiernan (Ireland, v. Canada and Wales)
T Ward (Ireland, v. Tonga)
Most dropped goals in a match (team)
2 – Wales (v. Ireland)
2 – Ireland (v. Canada) **Most dropped goals in a match (individual)** 2 –
J Davies (Wales, v. Ireland)

International Results

Details are given of every International match played during season 1990/91
(at or above U-21 level) involving the four Home Unions and a selection of
others played around the globe. Players' clubs are given in brackets. In the
case of tours: results, appearances (signified by the relevant match number
after the player's name), and scorers have been logged. 'R' indicates an
appearance as a replacement. Brackets after scorer indicates time of score;
number after scorer's name indicates quantities of score.

FRANCE TO AUSTRALIA
June 1990: 8 games

The disappointment of France's 2–1 Test series defeat is magnified by the
death of 26-year-old Dax prop Dominique Bouet, who was found dead in his
hotel bed in New Caledonia where the team stopped for two days rest on their
way home. He had won five caps.
Results: (1) New South Wales 12, France 19 (Sydney); (2) ACT 21, France
22 (Canberra); (3) first Test: **Australia 21, France 9** (Sydney); (4) Australian
Universities 19, France 26 (Brisbane); (5) Queensland 15, France 3
(Brisbane); (6) Sydney 36, France 26 (Sydney); (7) second Test: **Australia
48, France 31** (Brisbane); (8) third Test: **Australia 19, France 28** (Sydney).
Record: P8 W4 D0 L4 F164 A191.

USA TO AUSTRALIA
June–July 1990: 6 games

PARTY: E Whitaker (Old Blues), **R Nelson** (Los Angeles), **C Williams**
(Cal-Berkeley), **G Hein** (Oxford Univ), **K Higgins** (OMBAC), **B Corcoran**
(Old Blues), **M Williams** (BATS), **J Burke** (Albany Knicks), **C O'Brien**
(Old Blues), **M DeJong** (Denver Barbarians), **G Goodman** (Dallas
Harlequins), **B Daily** (San Jose), **B Clark** (Boston), **D James** (Oxford Univ),
C Lippert (OMBAC), **S Goodkind** (Life College), **F Paoli** (Denver
Barbarians), **P Johnson** (Louisville), **J Schrami** (Wisconsin), **B Leversee**
(OMBAC), **K Swords** (Beacon Hill), **T Ridnell** (OPSB), **B Farley**

(Philadelphia), **D Gonzalez** (OMBAC), **J Wilkerson** (Belmont Shore), **B Vizard** (OMBAC, capt).

Results: (1) Queensland B 13, USA 13 (Rockhampton, 26 June); (2) NSW Country 6, USA 19 (Grenfell, 1 July); (3) South Australia 12, USA 16 (Adelaide, 4 July); (4) **Australia 67, USA 9** (Brisbane, 8 July); (5) Victoria 13, USA 37 (Melbourne, 11 July); (6) Western Australia 33, USA 23 (Perth, 15 July).

Record: P6 W3 D1 L2 F117 A142.

AUSTRALIA TO NEW ZEALAND
July–August 1990: 12 games

Results: (1) Waikato 21, Australia 10 (Hamilton, 11 July); (2) Auckland 16, Australia 10 (Auckland, 14 July); (3) West Coast-Buller 0, Australia 62 (Westport, 17 July); (4) first Test: **New Zealand 21, Australia 6** (Christchurch, 21 July); (5) Timaru Hanan Shield 0, Australia 34 (Timaru, 25 July); (6) Otago 20, Australia 24 (Dunedin, 28 July); (7) North Auckland 14, Australia 28 (Whangarei, 31 July); (8) second Test: **New Zealand 27, Australia 17** (Auckland, 4 Aug); (9) North Harbour 12, Australia 23 (Takapuna, 8 Aug); (10) Taranaki 3, Australia 27 (New Plymouth, 11 Aug); (11) Bay of Plenty 12, Australia 4 (Rotorua, 14 Aug); (12) third Test: **New Zealand 9, Australia 21** (Wellington, 18 Aug).

Record: P12 W7 D0 L5 F266 A155.

BARBARIANS CENTENARY
September 1990-April 1991: 9 games

Results: (1) England XV 18, Barbarians 16 (Twickenham, 29 Sept); (2) Bradford & Bingley 7, Barbarians 52 (2 Oct); (3) Wales 24, Barbarians 31 (Cardiff, 6 Oct); (4) Newport 43, Barbarians 6 (30 Oct); (5) Barbarians 34, Argentina 22; (Cardiff, 17 Nov); (6) Leicester 21, Barbarians 26 (27 Dec); (7) East Midlands 34, Barbarians 46 (Northampton, 6 March); (8) Cardiff 25, Barbarians 42 (30 March); (9) Swansea 33, Barbarians 31 (1 April).

Scorers: 16 – Chalmers (2t, 4c), Dods (1t, 6c), T Underwood (4t). 15 – Barnes (3c, 3p). 14 – D Evans (3t, 1c), Hodgkinson (4c,2p), Wyatt (3t,1c). 13 – Lafond (1t,3c,1dg). 12 – Harriman (3t). 8 – Carter (2t), Clarke (2t), Crossan (2t), Gomez (2t), Guscott (2t), Lynagh (1c, 2p), Moon (2t), Murphy (4c), Titley (2t). 6 – G Hastings (1t, 1c), B Smith (1t, 1c). 4 – Campese (1t), Champion (1t), Donovan (1t), P Davies (1t), Dear (1t), I Evans (1t), Farr-Jones (1t), Harrison (1t), Hunter (1t), R Jones (1t), Marshall (1t), O'Riordan (1t), Pool-Jones (1t), Rush (1t), Stanley (1t), Wells (1t), penalty try (4). 2 – Andrew (1c).

Record: P9 W6 D0 L3 F284 A227.

ROMANIA TO ENGLAND AND WALES
September 1990: 3 games

Results: (1) Bath 38, Romania 9 (2 Sept); (2) Leicester 15, Romania 12 (4 Sept); (3) Newbridge 35, Romania 21 (8 Sept).
Record: P3 W0 D0 L3 F42 A88.

NAMIBIA TO ENGLAND AND FRANCE
October–November 1990: 6 games

Results: (1) Lancashire 15, Namibia 23 (Liverpool St Helens, 30 Oct); (2) England B 31, Namibia 16 (Leicester, 2 Nov); (3) Combined Services 13, Namibia 16 (Portsmouth, 6 Nov); (4) France A 30, Namibia 20 (Dijon, 20 Nov); (5) French Selection 33, Namibia 0 (Arras, 13 Nov); (6) French Forces XV 3, Namibia 12 (Bourges, 16 Nov).
Record: P6 W3 D0 L3 F87 A125.

England B (16) 31, Namibia (10) 16
Leicester, 2 November 1990

Welford Road brings the best out of John Liley on his B debut. The Leicester full-back converts two of England's three tries and lands five penalty goals for a 19-point haul. Consolation for the tourists is that they match England's tally of three tries.

England B: J Liley (Leicester); B Evans (Leicester), B Barley (Wakefield), P de Glanville (Oxford University), P Hull (Bristol); J Steele (Northampton), C Luxton (Harlequins); G Holmes (Wasps), N Hitchen (Orrell), S Southern (Orrell), R Kimmins (Orrell), S Dear (Rosslyn Park), M Skinner (Harlequins), A Robinson (Bath, capt), T Rodber (Northampton). **Repl: Not used** – G Ainscough (Orrell), G Childs (Wasps), M Hancock (Richmond), M Linnett (Moseley), S Davies (Rosslyn Park), I Smith (Gloucester).
Scorers – Tries: Rodber, Hull, penalty try. **Conversions:** Liley 2. **Penalty goals:** Liley 5.
Namibia: A Stoop (Wanderers); G Mans (Wanderers, capt), J Swart (Wanderers), J Deysel (Windhoek), B Swartz (Windhoek); M Olivier (United), B Buitendag (Wanderers); C Derks (Windhoek), E Beukes (Walvis Bay), H Grobler (United), S Losper (United), A van der Merwe (Grootfontein), W Maritz (Police), A Skinner (Wanderers), T Oosthuizen (Windhoek).
Scorers – Tries: Mans, Oosthuizen, Stoop. **Conversions:** Olivier 2.
Referee: J Fleming (Scotland).

SPAIN TO IRELAND
September 1990: 3 games

Results: (1) Connacht 31, Spain 19 (Galway, 1 Sept); (2) Ulster 28, Spain 13 (Belfast, 4 Sept); (3) **Ireland U-25 36, Spain 17** (Limerick, 8 Sept).
Record: P3 W0 D0 L3 F49 A95.

Ireland U-25 36, Spain 17
Limerick, 8 September 1990
Ireland U-25: J Staples (London Irish); J Riordan (Wanderers), V Cunningham (St Mary's College), J Clarke (Dolphin), S Geoghegan (London Irish); N Barry (Garryowen), A Rolland (Blackrock College); R Ward (Dublin University), T Kingston (Dolphin), G Halpin (Wanderers), P Johns (Dublin University), M Galwey (Shannon), K Leahy (Wanderers, capt), K O'Connell (Sunday's Well), P Lawlor (Bective Rangers). **Repl: Not used** – C Haly (UCC), B Glennon (UCD), R Saunders (London Irish), L Dineen (Constitution), S McKinty (Bangor).
Scorers – Tries: Barry 2, Rolland, Clarke, Geoghegan, Leahy, Riordan. **Conversions:** Barry 3, Cunningham.
Spain: F Puertes; J Azkargorta, J Moreno, S Torres, D Saenz; C Camarero, J Diaz; J Alvarez, S Santos, J Diez, G Amunarriz, J Chocarro, J Gutierrez, A Malo, H Massono. **Repl:** A Altuna for Diez, 54 mins; J Torres for Camarero, 70 mins.
Scorers – Tries: Puertas, Santos, Saenz. **Conversion:** Diaz. **Penalty goal:** Diaz.
Referee: J Fleming (Scotland).

England (9) 18, Barbarians (7) 16
Twickenham, 29 September 1990

Simon Hodgkinson hints at his potent season to come with 14 points in England's entertaining win over the centenary Barbarians before a packed Twickenham gallery. But the most eyecatching display comes from Barbarians replacement Neil Back, the Leicester open-side flanker.

England: S Hodgkinson (Nottingham); R Underwood (Leicester), W Carling (Harlequins, capt), J Guscott (Bath), T Underwood (Leicester); R Andrew (Wasps), R Hill (Bath); J Leonard (Harlequins), J Olver (Northampton), J Probyn (Wasps), W Dooley (Preston Grasshoppers), P Ackford (Harlequins), M Teague (Gloucester), P Winterbottom (Harlequins), D Richards (Leicester). **Repl: Used** – G Rees (Nottingham) for Winterbottom, 26 mins. **Not used** – D Morris (Orrell), J Buckton (Saracens), D Pears (Harlequins), B Moore (Harlequins), V Ubogu (Bath).
Scorers – Tries: Richards, Hodgkinson. **Conversions:** Hodgkinson 2. **Penalty goals:** Hodgkinson 2.
Barbarians: K Murphy; J-B Lafond, J Stanley, D Charvet, D Campese; M Lynagh, N Farr-Jones (capt); R Loe, I Watkins, P Burnell, I Jones (North Auckland), S Cutler, K Janik, E Rush, P Davies. **Repl:** N Back for Janik, 49 mins.
Scorers – Tries: Campese, Davies. **Conversion:** Lynagh. **Penalty goals:** Lynagh 2.
Referee: D Bevan (Wales).

Wales (21) 24, Barbarians (21) 31
Cardiff, 6 October 1990

Wales create a stir amongst traditionalists by awarding caps against a scratch side and captain Paul Thorburn celebrates by establishing a Welsh single-match points-scoring record. His tally of 21 points comprises one try, one conversion and five penalty goals. Unfortunately, for the Principality, the Barbarians have the final say.

Wales: P Thorburn (Neath, capt); S Ford (Cardiff), M Ring (Cardiff), S Parfitt (Swansea), A Edmunds (Neath); D Evans (Cardiff), C Bridges (Neath); B Williams (Neath), K Phillips (Neath), M Griffiths (Cardiff), G D Llewellyn (Neath), P Arnold (Swansea), M Morris (Neath), R Webster (Swansea), M Jones (Neath). **Repl: Used** – P Knight (Pontypridd) for Williams, 14 mins; A Davies (Cambridge Univ) for Ring, 47 mins. **Not used** – R Jones (Swansea), A Clement (Swansea), I Watkins (Cardiff), O Williams (Bridgend).

Scorers – Try: Thorburn. **Conversion:** Thorburn. **Penalty goals:** Thorburn 5. **Dropped goal:** Evans.

Barbarians: D Campese; J B Lafond, J Stanley, J Guscott, D Charvet; S Barnes, N Farr-Jones (capt); P Rendall, S Smith, R Loe, I Jones (North Auckland), S Cutler, M Teague, E Rush, D Erbani. **Repl: Not used** – H Davies, F Gomez, H Taylor, R Lee, G Dawe, T Underwood (Leicester).

Scorers – Tries: Stanley (20), Farr-Jones (32), Rush (67), Guscott (79). **Conversions:** Barnes 3 (20,32,67). **Penalty goals:** Barnes 3 (1,6,39).

Referee: F Howard (England).

IRELAND U-21s TO NETHERLANDS
September 1990: 2 games

PARTY: C O'Shea (Lansdowne – 1,2), D Hernan (UCD – 1,2), J Russell (Instonians – 1,2), G Lavin (St Mary's Coll – 1), N Murray (Constitution – 2), R Hennessy (Lansdowne – 1,2), N Malone (Loughborough Univ – 2), D Tobin (Young Munster – 2), D O'Mahony (UCC – 1), N Hogan (Terenure Coll – 2), P Soden (Constitution – 2), L Murphy (UCC – 1), M Patton (Bangor, capt – 1,2), A Stewart (Portadown – 2), S Cully (Malone – 1), E O'Sullivan (Old Crescent – 1,2), G Fulcher (UCD – 1,2), S Rooney (UCD – 1,2), B O'Mahony (UCC – 2), K McKee (CIYMS – 2), S Duncan (Malone – 1), S Kirkpatrick (Malone – 1).

Results: (1) Netherlands B 6, Ireland U-21 11 (Leiden, 18 Sept); (2) Netherlands 21, Ireland U-21 7 (Leiden, 21 Sept).

Scorers: Hennessy 8 (2t), O'Sullivan 4 (1t), D O'Mahony 3 (1dg), Malone 3 (1p).

Record: P2 W1 D0 L1 F18 A27.

Netherlands 21, Ireland U-21 7
Leiden, 21 September 1990
Ireland U-21: C O'Shea; D Hernan, J Russell, N Murray, R Hennessy; N

Malone, D Tobin (Young Munster); P Soden, M Patton (capt), A Stewart, E O'Sullivan, G Fulcher, S Rooney, B O'Mahony, K McKee.
Scorers – Try: O'Sullivan. **Penalty goal:** Malone.

ARGENTINA TO IRELAND, ENGLAND AND SCOTLAND
October-November 1990: 8 games

PARTY: A Scolni (Asociacion Alumni – 1,3,5,7R); **G Angaut** (La Plata – 2*,4*,6*,7,8*), **S Ezcurra** (Club Universatario de Buenos Aires – 1,3,5), **G M Jorge** (Pucara – 2,3,5,6,8), **G L Romero Acuna** (Gimnasia y Egscrima de Rosario – 1,3,4), **M Allen** (Club Athletico de San Isidro – 2,4,5,6,7,8), **D Cuesta Silva** (San Isidro Club – 1,3,5,6,7,8), **H M Garcia Simon** (Pueyrredon – 2,3), **S Meson** (Tucuman Rugby – 1,4,6,7,8), **H Porta** (Banco de la Nacion, capt – 1,3,5,7), **L Arbizu** (Belgrano AC – 2,3R,4,6,7,8), **H Vidou** (Buenos Aires Cricket & Rugby – 2,4), **G Camardon** (Asociacion Alumni – 1,4,5,8), **R H Crexell** (Jockey Club, Rosario – 2,3,6,7), **H H Ballatore** (Asociacion Alumni – 1,2,4), **D M Cash** (San Isidro Club – 3,5,6,7,8), **L E Lonardi** (San Isidro Club – 1), **O Fascioli** (Mendoza – 2,4,6), **M Aguirre** (Asociacion Alumni – 4,6,7,8); **A Cubelli** (Belgrano AC – 1,4,6,7), **R A Le Fort** (Tucuman Rugby – 2,3,5,8), **R Etchegoyen** (Banco de la Nacion – 4,6,8), **G Llanes** (La Plata – 1,3,5,6,7,8), **F Mendez** (Tucuman Rugby – 1R,2,3,5), **J Simes** (Tala – 1,2,4,6R), **P Sporledor** (Curupayti – 2R,3,5,7,8), **M J S Bertranou** (Los Tordos – 2,3,5,6R,7), **E Ezcurra** (Newman – 1,4,6,7), **P A Garreton** (Circule Universatario de Tucuman – 1,3,5,7,8), **R Villalonga** (Asociacion Alumni – 2,4,6,8), **A M Macome** (Tucuman Rugby – 1,2,3,5,8R).
Manager: F M Alvarez. **Assistant manager:** E Gonzalez del Solar. **Coach:** L Gradin. **Assistant coach:** G Lamarca. **Medical officer:** Dr L Garcia Yanez.
Results: (1) Ireland B 27, Argentina 12 (Limerick, 20 Oct); (2) Irish Students 6, Argentina 23 (Cork, 23 Oct); (3) **Ireland 20, Argentina 18** (Dublin, 27 Oct); (4) Eastern Counties 15, Argentina 28 (Cambridge, 30 Oct); (5) **England 51, Argentina 0** (Twickenham, 3 Nov); (6) South of Scotland 10, Argentina 13 (Kelso, 6 Nov); (7) **Scotland 49, Argentina 3** (Edinburgh, 10 Nov); (8) Barbarians 34, Argentina 22 (Cardiff, 17 Nov).
Scorers: Vidou 33 (2t, 2c, 7p), Meson 23 (1t, 2c, 5p), Porta 22 (2c, 6p), Arbizu 9 (3dg), Allen 8 (2t), Cuesta Silva 8 (2t), Macome 4 (1t), Jorge 4 (1t), Scolni 4 (1t), penalty try (4).
Record: P8 W3 D0 L5 F119 A212.

Ireland B (12) 27, Argentina (3) 12
Limerick, 20 October 1990
Ireland B are helped on their way to victory by indiscipline in the tourists' ranks, highlighted midway through the first half when referee Clayton Thomas dismisses Pumas' prop Luis Lonardi for stamping in a maul. Hugo Porta, Argentina's inspirational captain, is fortunate not to follow suit following a

heavy challenge on Irish centre Vincent Cunningham. The Irish lead 12–3 at the midway point and extend the spread soon after the break through lock forward Mick Galwey's fourth try in three matches. Ireland's fourth try comes from Simon Geoghegan, who sprints 40 yards along the touchline to confirm his burgeoning talent.

Ireland B: C Wilkinson (Malone); J Riordan (Wanderers), V Cunningham (St Mary's College), J Clarke (Dolphin), S Geoghegan (London Irish); N Barry (Garryowen), M Bradley (Constitution, capt); J Fitzgerald (Munster), T Kingston (Dolphin), G Halpin (Wanderers), K Potts (St Mary's College), M Galwey (Shannon), K Leahy (Wanderers), D McBride (Malone), P Lawlor (Bective Rangers). **Repl: Not used –** F Aherne (Lansdowne), R Keyes (Constitution), P Danaher (Garryowen), S Smith (Ballymena), J McCoy (Bangor), B Robinson (Ballymena).
Scorers – Tries: Riordan, Galwey, Bradley, Geoghegan. **Conversion:** Barry. **Penalty goals:** Barry 2, Cunningham.
Argentina: A Scolni; G Romero Acuna, D Cuesta Silva, S Meson, S Ezcurra; H Porta (capt), G Camardon; L Lonardi, A Cubelli, H Ballatore, G Llanes, J Simes, P Garreton, E Ezcurra, A Macome. **Repl:** F Mendez for Simes, 32 mins.
Scorers – Try: Scolni. **Conversion:** Porta. **Penalty goals:** Porta 2.
Referee: C Thomas (Wales)

Ireland (7) 20, Argentina (9) 18
Dublin, 27 October 1990

Argentina field nine new caps against Ireland and lead the match five times before cruelly being deprived of victory by Michael Kiernan's 40-metre penalty goal six minutes into injury time. Kiernan claims 16 points in all, adding four penalty goals to a try, to move to within 1 International point of the 300-mark. Ken Hooks' try is his first in International rugby. Ireland give debuts to scrum-half Alain Rolland, lock forward Paddy Johns and No.8 Peter Lawlor.

Ireland: K Murphy (Constitution); K Hooks (Bangor), B Mullin (Blackrock College), M Kiernan (Dolphin), K Crossan (Instonians); B Smith (Leicester), A Rolland (Blackrock College); N Popplewell (Greystones), J McDonald (Malone), D Fitzgerald (Lansdowne), N Mannion (Lansdowne), D Lenihan (Constitution, capt), P Johns (Dublin University), D McBride (Malone), P Lawlor (Bective Rangers) **Repl: Used –** V Cunningham (St Mary's College) for Mullin, 40 mins. **Not used –** M Bradley (Constitution), R Keyes (Constitution), J Fitzgerald (Young Munster), T Kingston (Dolphin), M Galwey (Shannon).
Scorers – Tries: Hooks (32), Kiernan (42). **Penalty goals:** Kiernan 4 (14,62,72,86).
Argentina: A Scolni; S Ezcurra, D Cuesta Silva, H Garcia Simon, G Jorge; H Porta (capt), R Crexell; F Mendez, R Le Fort, D Cash, G Llanes, P Sporledor, P Garreton, M Bertranou, A Macome. **Repl: Used –** L Arbizu

for Garcia Simon, 70 mins. **Not used** – G Camardon, H Ballatore, A Cubelli, O Faccioli, R Villalonga.
Scorers – Try: Macome (84). **Conversion:** Porta. **Penalty goals:** Porta 4 (13,23,40,53).
Referee: C Hawke (New Zealand).

England (18) 51, Argentina 0
Twickenham, 3 November 1990

Simon Hodgkinson breaks England record for points scored in a single match with 23-point haul in what is England's highest ever total without reply. The Nottingham full-back converts each of England's seven tries in addition to landing three penalty goals. Northampton hooker John Olver makes his long-awaited debut in an England front row, who have their task eased considerably with the 69th minute dismissal of Federico Mendez, the 18-year-old loose-head prop, who becomes the first Argentine to be sent off in a senior International match after flooring Paul Ackford with a blatant haymaker. Mendez is later suspended for four weeks. Rory Underwood's try-treble makes him the first Englishman to pass 100 points scoring only tries. Pumas' captain Hugo Porta fails to score for only the second time in 17 years of International rugby.

England: S Hodgkinson (Nottingham); R Underwood (Leicester), W Carling (Harlequins, capt), J Guscott (Bath), N Heslop (Orrell); R Andrew (Wasps), R Hill (Bath); J Leonard (Harlequins), J Olver (Northampton), J Probyn (Wasps), W Dooley (Preston Grasshoppers), P Ackford (Harlequins), J Hall (Bath), P Winterbottom (Harlequins), D Richards (Leicester). **Repl: Used** – G Rees (Nottingham) for Ackford, 69 mins. **Not used** – J Webb (Bath), J Buckton (Saracens), D Morris (Orrell), P Rendall (Wasps), B Moore (Harlequins).
Scorers – Tries: Hill (11), Underwood 3 (15,47,80), Guscott 2 (50,77), Hall (73). **Conversions:** Hodgkinson 7. **Penalty goals:** Hodgkinson 3 (4,40,44).
Argentina: A Scolni; S Ezcurra, D Cuesta Silva, M Allen, G Jorge; H Porta (capt), G Camardon; F Mendez, R Le Fort, D Cash, G Llanes, P Sporledor, P Garreton, M Bertranou, A Macome. **Repl: Not used** – M Aguirre, A Cubelli, O Faccioli, R Villalonga, R Crexell, L Arbizu.
Referee: C Hawke (New Zealand)

Scotland (17) 49, Argentina (0) 3
Edinburgh, 10 November 1990

Gavin Hastings becomes Scotland's all-time leading points-scorer when his 17-point tally (one try, five conversions and one penalty goal) gives him 286 points in 27 Internationals and overhauls the previous incumbent, Andy Irvine, who had amassed 273 points in 51 matches. Two tries for Tony Stanger maintains his remarkable scoring record – nine tries in nine Internationals. Kenny Milne becomes the first Scotland hooker to score a brace of tries.

Scotland: G Hastings (Watsonians); A Stanger (Hawick), S Hastings

(Watsonians), S Lineen (Boroughmuir), A Moore (Edinburgh Academicals); C Chalmers (Melrose), G Armstrong (Jed-Forest), D Sole (Edinburgh Academicals, capt), K Milne (Heriot's FP), P Burnell (London Scottish), C Gray (Nottingham), G Weir (Melrose), J Jeffrey (Kelso), A Buchanan-Smith (Heriot's FP), G Marshall (Selkirk). **Repl: Not used –** P Dods (Gala), D Wyllie (Stewart's-Melville FP), G Oliver (Hawick), I Milne (Heriot's FP), J Allan (Edinburgh Academicals), J Laing (Gala).
Scorers – Tries: Stanger 2, Milne 2, Moore, Armstrong, Gray, Chalmers, G Hastings. **Conversions:** G Hastings 5. **Penalty goal:** G Hastings.
Argentina: G Angaut; D Cuesta Silva, L Arbizu, S Meson, M Allen; H Porta (capt), R Crexell; M Aguirre, A Cubelli, D Cash, G Llanes, P Sporledor, P Garreton, E Ezcurra, M Bertanou. **Repl: Used –** A Scolni for Porta, 16 mins. **Not used –** H Ballatore, R-A Le Fort, G Jorge, R Etchegoyen, G Camardon.
Scorer – Penalty goal: Meson.
Referee: F Burger (South Africa).

England U-21 (10) 16, Ireland U-21 (6) 22
Moseley, 29 October 1990

England suffer their first defeat at U-21 level to an accomplished Irish team, powered by a cohesive pack and rewarded by outside-half Malone, who kicks 18 points in addition to laying the foundations for Hennessy's try. England, whose previous matches against Romania (1989), the Netherlands and French Armed Forces (both 1990) ended victorious, lead until the final quarter when Malone's dropped goal nudges Ireland ahead and Hennessy's injury-time score cements their advantage.

England U-21: S Swindells (Manchester); S Bromley (Liverpool St Helens), L Boyle (Moseley, capt), M Hutton (Richmond), L McKenzie (Coventry); N Matthews (Gloucester), R Booth (Sale); D Hilton (Bristol), B Stanhope (Harlequins), N Lyman (Moseley), M Tanner (Royal Navy), D Sims (Gloucester), R Jenkins (Cambridge Univ), G Adams (Bath), S Ojomoh (Bath). **Repl: Used –** G Rowntree (Leicester) for Lyman. **Not used –** P Challinor (Harlequins), J Wray (Morley), S Douglas (Newcastle-Gosforth), P Tanner (Northampton).
Scorers – Try: Jenkins. **Penalty goals:** Swindells 4.
Ireland U-21: C O'Shea (Lansdowne); D Hernan (UCD), J Russell (Instonians), N Murray (Constitution), R Hennessy (Lansdowne); N Malone (Loughborough University), D Tobin (Young Munster); P Soden (Constitution), M Patton (Bangor, capt), S Tonge (Wanderers), E O'Sullivan (Old Crescent), G Fulcher (UCD), S Rooney (UCD), B O'Mahoney (UCC), K McKee (CIYMS).
Scorers – Try: Hennessy. **Penalty goals:** Malone 5. **Dropped goal:** Malone.
Referee: A Thompson (Manchester).

NEW ZEALAND TO FRANCE
October-November 1990: 8 games

PARTY: K Crowley (Taranaki), **S Philpott** (Canterbury), **J Kirwan** (Auckland), **T Wright** (Auckland), **V Tuigamala** (Auckland), **J Timu (Otago), C Innes** (Auckland), **J Stanley** (Auckland), **B McCahill** (Auckland), **W Little** (North Harbour), **G Fox** (Auckland), **W Mannix** (Wellington), **G Bachop** (Canterbury), **P McGahan** (North Harbour), **R Loe** (Waikato), **G Purvis** (Waikato), **S McDowell** (Auckland), **L Hullena** (Wellington), **S Fitzpatrick** (Auckland), **W Gatland** (Waikato), **I Jones** (North Auckland), **G Whetton** (Auckland, capt), **M Pierce** (Wellington), **S Gordon** (Waikato), **M Jones** (Auckland), **A Whetton** (Auckland), **Z Brooke** (Auckland), **M Brewer** (Otago), **R Gordon** (Waikato), **P Henderson** (Waikato).

Results: (1) Cote d'Azur 19, New Zealand 15 (Toulon, 17 Oct); (2) Languedoc 6, New Zealand 22 (Narbonne, 20 Oct); (3) Centre-Limousin 24, New Zealand 27 (Brive, 24 Oct); (4) French Barbarians 13, New Zealand 23 (Agen, 27 Oct); (5) Cote Basque 18, New Zealand 12 (Bayonne, 30 Oct); (6) **France 3, New Zealand 24** (first Test: Nantes, 3 Nov); (7) French Selection 15, New Zealand 22 (La Rochelle, 6 Nov); (8) **France 12, New Zealand 30** (second Test: Paris, 10 Nov).

Record: P8 W6 D0 L2 F175 A110.

First Test: **France (3) 3, New Zealand (18) 24**
Nantes, 3 November 1990

Those doubting New Zealand's ability to maintain their position as the world's best, in the light of their heavy summer losses to Rugby League, are straightened out as the All Blacks crush France in the first of two Tests, on the back of another overpowering kicking display from Grant Fox, 16 points, including the conversions of tries by Craig Innes and Alan Whetton, both scored in the opening ten minutes.

France: S Blanco (Biarritz, capt); S Weller (Grenoble), J C Langlade (Nimes), F Mesnel (Racing Club de Paris), P Saint-Andre (Montferrand); D Camberabero (Beziers), A Hueber (Lourdes); P Ondarts (Biarritz), L Armary (Lourdes), L Seigne (Agen), A Benazzi (Agen), O Roumat (Dax), E Champ (Toulon), E Melville (Toulon), L Rodriguez (Dax). Repl: Used – P Marocco (Montferrand) for Seigne, 70 mins. Not used – P Berot (Agen), D Berty (Toulouse), H Sanz (Narbonne), P Benetton (Agen), J Condom (Biarritz).

Scorer – Penalty goal: Camberabero (34).

New Zealand: K Crowley; J Kirwan, C Innes, W Little, T Wright; G Fox, G Bachop; S McDowell, S Fitzpatrick, R Loe, I Jones, G Whetton (capt), A Whetton, M Jones, M Brewer. **Repl: Used** – Z Brooke for Brewer, 40 mins. **Not used** – V Tuigamala, J Stanley, P McGahan, M Pierce, L Hullena.

Scorers – Tries: Innes (5), A Whetton (12). **Conversions:** Fox 2. **Penalty goals:** Fox 3 (26,30,44). **Dropped goal:** Fox (79).

Referee: S MacNeill (Australia).

Second Test: **France (6) 12, New Zealand (15) 30**
Paris, 10 November 1990

Grant Fox resumes from where he left off in the previous week's first Test
with 22 points as New Zealand clinch the series by a 2–0 margin against a
French side which, in making nine changes from the first Test, give debuts
to Berty, Gourragne, Dal Maso and replacement Cabannes. What is so
remarkable about Fox's display is not so much that he lands six penalty goals
and two conversions, but rather that his eight kicks represent a 100 per cent
success rate. France, despite 12 points from Didier Camberabero, finish a
distant second.

France: S Blanco (capt); J B Lafond, F Mesnel, P Saint-Andre, D Berty;
D Camberabero, H Sanz; M Pujolle (Nice), M Dal Maso (Mont de Marsan),
P Ondarts, J F Gourragne (Beziers), O Roumat, P Benetton, A Benazzi,
C Deslandes (Racing Club). **Repl: Used** – L Cabannes (Racing Club) for
Benazzi, 65 mins. **Not used** – P Berot, J-C Langlade, A Hueber, J Condom,
P Marocco.
Scorer – Penalty goals: Camberabero 3. **Dropped goal:** Camberabero.
New Zealand: K Crowley; J Kirwan, C Innes, W Little, T Wright; G Fox,
G Bachop; S McDowell, S Fitzpatrick, R Loe, I Jones, G Whetton (capt),
A Whetton, M Jones, M Brewer.
Scorers – Tries: Crowley, M Jones. **Conversions:** Fox 2. **Penalty goals:**
Fox 6.
Referee: S MacNeill (Australia).

England B (12) 12, Emerging Australians (3) 12
Wasps, 4 November 1990

England B let slip a 12-point lead, created by the boot of Harlequin David
Pears who lands four out of five attempts on goal, as David Knox kicks four
penalty goals, three in the second half, to earn the tourists a share of the spoils.
England B: I Hunter (Northampton); A Harriman (Harlequins), J Buckton
(Saracens), D Hopley (Wasps), T Underwood (Cambridge Univ); D Pears
(Harlequins), R Moon (Llanelli); V Ubogu (Bath), G Dawe (Bath), G Pearce
(Northampton, capt), N Redman (Bath), M Bayfield (Bedford), M Teague
(Gloucester), N Back (Leicester), D Ryan (Wasps). **Repl:** G Thompson
(Harlequins) for Underwood.
Scorer – Penalty goals: Pears 4.
Australians: M Pini (Royals); M Anderson (Queensland Univ), J Little
(Souths, Brisbane), P Cornish (Royals), C Newman (Canberra Whites);
D Knox (Randwick), P Slattery (Queensland Univ); M Ryan (Brothers),
D Nucifora (Queensland Univ), D Crowley (Souths), T Kava (Randwick,
capt), D Rix (Sydney Univ), W Ofahengaue (Manly), J Ross (Royals), J Eales
(Brothers).
Scorer – Penalty goals: Knox 4.
Referee: B Stirling (Ireland).

Wales U-21 (WRU President's XV) 34, New Zealand U-21 (Rugby News XV) 13

Pontypridd, 8 November 1990

Wales U-21s, playing under the title of WRU President's XV because their opponents are not the official New Zealand U-21 side, score 13 points in as many minutes to spark an impressive victory at Sardis Road. Fly-half Neil Jenkins, a product of the host club, weighs in with 14 points by landing two penalty goals and converting four of his side's five tries.

Wales U-21: L Evans (Llanelli); A Donovan (Cardiff), I Jones (Llanelli), M Kehoe (Newbridge), J Westwood (Newbridge); N Jenkins (Pontypridd), P John (Cardiff, capt); M Davis (Newport), A Lamerton (Llanelli), R Shaw (Llanelli), L Mruk (Pontypool), C Langley (Cardiff), O Lloyd (Bridgend), P Thomas (Glamorgan Wanderers), S Williams (Swansea). **Repl: Used** – R McBride (Swansea) for Lamerton. **Not used** – K Allen (New Dock Stars), B Shenton (Aberavon), D Llewellyn (Newport), M Lewis (Glamorgan Wanderers), I Bebb (CIHE).
Scorers – Tries: Donovan, Evans 2, Mruk, John. **Conversions:** Jenkins 4. **Penalty goals:** Jenkins 2.

New Zealand U-21 XV: W Burton; T Barrel, F Hecka, G Beam, T Fawdray; S Hall, R Le Bas; G Halford, D Heaps, T Barchard, S Nicholson, G Taylor, A Slater, M Webber (capt), R Hilton-Jones.
Scorers – Try: Hilton-Jones. **Penalty goals:** Barrel 3.
Referee: S Griffiths (England).

Barbarians 34, Argentina 22

Cardiff, 17 November 1990

Argentina put aside the disappointment of their heavy defeats at the hands of England and Scotland, to produce a lively display. But unfortunately for them Simon Hodgkinson, who kicked a record 23 points against them a fortnight earlier, lands another 14, including four conversions from a possible five.

Barbarians: S Hodgkinson; I Evans, M Ring, C Innes, K Crossan; C Chalmers, R Jones; L Hullena, T Kingston, P Knight, C Gray, I Jones, G Rees, R Webster, P Davies. **Repl: Not used** – A Clement (Swansea & Wales), D Evans, D Llewellyn, O Williams (Bridgend & Wales), I Buckett, A Lamerton (Llanelli).
Scorers – Tries: Crossan 2, Evans, Chalmers, Jones. **Conversions:** Hodgkinson 4. **Penalty goals:** Hodgkinson 2.

Argentina: G Angaut (capt); D Cuesta Silva, S Meson, M Allen, G Jorge; L Arbizu, G Camardon; M Aguirre, R Le Fort, D Cash, G Llanes, P Sporledor, R Villalonga, P Garreton, R Etchegoyen. **Repl:** A Macome for Garreton, 34 mins.
Scorers – Tries: Meson, penalty try, Cuesta Silva. **Conversions:** Meson 2. **Penalty goals:** Meson 2.
Referee: J Fleming (Scotland).

Netherlands (6) 12, Wales B (15) 34
Leiden, 2 December 1990

Pontypridd outside-half Neil Jenkins makes an impressive start to his International campaign with 18 points in Wales' only B fixture of the season, while Anthony Clement runs the show and scores one of Wales' five tries. However, Wales (Paul Arnold and Andrew Kembury) lose out at the line-out to a team which were late replacements when annual opponents France pulled out.

Netherlands: M Marcker (Castricumse); B Verhofstad (Castricumse), S Hadinegoro (Haagse), D Pace (Delftse), B Wisse (Diok); M Mickelsen (Diok), M Eman (Haagse); W van Altena (Hilversum), Y Kummer (Diok, capt), R Broers (Diok), J Dam (Castricumse), E J Berendsen (Diok), G de Vries (Amsterdam), M Visser (Hilversum), W van der Kleij (Haagse).

Scorers – Tries: Kummer 2. **Conversions:** Mickelsen 2.

Wales B: A Clement (Swansea); S Ford (Cardiff), S Lewis (Pontypridd), S Gibbs (Neath), S Bowling (Llanelli); N Jenkins (Pontypridd), P John (Cardiff); I Buckett (Swansea), A Thomas (Neath), J Davies (Neath), P Arnold (Swansea), A Kembury (Neath), S Williams (Swansea), G George (Newport, capt), O Williams (Bridgend). **Repl: Used** – E Lewis (Llanelli) for S Williams, 76 mins. **Not used** – K Waters (Newbridge), J Rowlands (Newbridge), R Howley (Bridgend), S Hill (Cardiff), L Evans (Llanelli).

Scorers – Tries: Ford 2, Jenkins, Gibbs, Clement. **Conversions:** Jenkins 4. **Penalty goals:** Jenkins 2.

Referee: R Williams (England)

Spain (0) 7, Scotland A (19) 39
Seville, 22 December 1990

Scotland achieve their biggest winning margin over Spain, and their third win in the fixture's history in a match which allows No.8 Derek White to confirm his recovery after three months out with a broken cheek bone. The 'A' concept permits several of Scotland's leading players, who would otherwise miss out, to get valuable International experience. Iwan Tukalo, the Selkirk wing, scores three of Scotland A's six tries, and captain Peter Dods weighs in with 11 points.

Spain: F Puertas; D Saenz, J Morote, J Moreno, J Azkargorta; E Candau, J Diaz; J Alvarez, J Aguiar, J Diez, M Justiniano, G Amunarriz, J Gutierrez, J Etxebarria, F Mendez. **Repl: Not used** – S Santos, D Torres, J Perez, J Mazariegos.

Scorers – Try: Moreno. **Penalty goal:** Puertas.

Scotland: P Dods (Gala, capt); M Moncrieff (Gala), D Caskie (Gloucester), R Maclean (Moseley), I Tukalo (Selkirk); D Wyllie (Stewart's-Melville FP), G Oliver (Hawick); G Isaac (Gala), J Allan (Edinburgh Academicals), G Smith (Moseley), D Cronin (Bath), G Weir (Melrose), D Turnbull (Hawick), G Marshall (Selkirk), D White (London Scottish). **Repl: Not used** – G Breckenridge (Glasgow High/Kelvinside), D Bryson (Gala), A Watt

(Glasgow High/Kelvinside), J Hay (Hawick), B Edwards (Allòa), N McIlroy (Jed-Forest).
Scorers – Tries: Tukalo 3, Oliver, Weir, Cronin. **Conversions:** Dods 4.
Penalty goal: Dods.
Referee: Y Bressy (France).

Ireland B (3) 16, Scotland B 0
Ravenhill, 22 December 1990

Ireland lock Brian Rigney receives his marching orders 14 minutes after the start for throwing a wild punch but, rather than handicap the home side, his dismissal galvanises them. Jack Clarke and David Hernan cross for tries while Ballymana fly-half Derek McAleese kicks 8 points. Scotland's misery is sealed by their failure to register a single point in 66 minutes against 14 men.

Ireland B: C Wilkinson (Malone); D Hernan (UCD), D Curtis (London Irish), J Clarke (Dolphin), R Wallace (Garryowen); D McAleese (Ballymena), R Saunders (London Irish); P Soden (Constitution), J O'Riordan (Constitution), P McCarthy (Constitution), M Galwey (Shannon), B Rigney (Greystones), K Leahy (Wanderers, capt), G Hamilton (NIFC), B Robinson (Ballymena).
Scorers – Tries: Clarke, Hernan. **Conversion:** McAleese. **Penalty goals:** McAleese 2.
Scotland B: D Barrett (West of Scotland); N Grecian (London Scottish), C Redpath (Melrose), S Nichol (Selkirk), S Porter (Malone); S McGauchie (Pontypool), S Jardine (Glamorgan Wanderers); P Jones (Gloucester), H Roberts (London Scottish), B Robertson (Stirling County), J Richardson (Edinburgh Academicals, capt), A Macdonald (Heriot's FP), R Wainwright (Edinburgh Academicals), I Smith (Gloucester), S Reid (Boroughmuir).
Repl: Not used – I Jardine (Stirling County), C Glasgow (Heriot's FP), A Nicol (Dundee HSFP), C Hogg (Melrose), I Corcoran (Gala), D Milne (Heriot's FP).
Referee: S Griffiths (England).

1991 FIVE NATIONS' CHAMPIONSHIP

France (9) 15, Scotland (3) 9
Paris, 19 January 1991

Scotland, the Grand Slam holders, stumble at the first hurdle in Paris, where they have not won since 1969, to a rejuvenated France who, despite their failure to register a try, signal their expansive intentions for the season. Scotland, uncharacteristically sloppy, are finally undone by three dropped goals, after pulling back to 9–9 early in the second half.

France: S Blanco (Biarritz, capt); J B Lafond (Racing Club de Paris),

F Mesnel (Racing), D Charvet (Racing), P Lagisquet (Bayonne); D Camberabero (Beziers), P Berbizier (Agen); G Lascube (Agen), P Marocco (Montferrand), P Ondarts (Biarritz), O Roumat (Dax), M Tachdjian (Racing), X Blond (Racing), L Cabannes (Racing), M Cecillon (Bourgoin). **Repl: Not used** – P Saint-Andre (Montferrand), T Lacroix (Dax), H Sanz (Narbonne), C Deslandes (Racing), L Seigne (Agen), V Moscato (Begles).
Scorers – Penalty goals: Camberabero 2 (3,20). **Dropped goals:** Blanco (11), Camberabero 2 (57,72).
Scotland: G Hastings (Watsonians); A Stanger (Hawick), S Hastings (Watsonians), S Lineen (Boroughmuir), A Moore (Edinburgh Academicals); C Chalmers (Melrose), G Armstrong (Jed-Forest); D Sole (Edinburgh Academicals, capt), K Milne (Heriot's FP), P Burnell (London Scottish), C Gray (Nottingham), D Cronin (Bath), D Turnbull (Hawick), J Jeffrey (Kelso), D White (London Scottish). **Repl: Not used** – P Dods (Gala), D Wyllie (Stewart's-Melville), G Oliver (Hawick), J Allan (Edinburgh Academicals), D Milne (Heriot's FP), G Marshall (Selkirk).
Scorer – Penalty goals: Chalmers 2 (43,54). **Dropped goal:** Chalmers (8).
Referee: E Morrison (England).

Wales (3) 6, England (12) 25
Cardiff, 19 January 1991

After 28 years of coming and going without success, England finally succeed at Cardiff and it is full-back Simon Hodgkinson whom they have to thank. The Nottingham player slots a world record seven penalty goals and Mike Teague bulldozes over for a close-range try to confirm England's authority and restore their self-belief inside the Arms Park. 'That score made up for all the wet Wednesday nights I have spent travelling down to play in Wales and all the lessons I have been given down there over the years,' recalls Teague.
Wales: P Thorburn (Neath, capt); I Evans (Llanelli), M Ring (Cardiff), S Gibbs (Neath), S Ford (Cardiff); N Jenkins (Pontypridd), R Jones (Swansea); B Williams (Neath), K Phillips (Neath), P Knight (Pontypridd), G D Llewellyn (Neath), G O Llewellyn (Neath), G George (Newport), A Carter (Newport), P Arnold (Swansea). **Repl: Used** – C Bridges (Neath) for Jones, 59 mins. **Not used** – A Clement (Swansea), D Evans (Cardiff), M Griffiths (Cardiff), K Waters (Newbridge), E Lewis (Llanelli).
Scorers – Penalty goals: Thorburn (3), Jenkins (46).
England: S Hodgkinson (Nottingham); N Heslop (Orrell), W Carling (Harlequins, capt), J Guscott (Bath), R Underwood (Leicester); R Andrew (Wasps), R Hill (Bath); J Leonard (Harlequins), B Moore (Harlequins), J Probyn (Wasps), P Ackford (Harlequins), W Dooley (Preston Grasshoppers), M Teague (Gloucester), P Winterbottom (Harlequins), D Richards (Leicester). **Repl: Not used** – J Webb (Bath), D Hopley (Wasps), D Morris (Orrell), P Rendall (Wasps), J Olver (Northampton), M Skinner (Harlequins).

Scorers – Try: Teague (64). **Penalty goals:** Hodgkinson 7 (5,14,21,25,51,54,69).
Referee: R Megson (Scotland).

Scotland (13) 32, Wales (6) 12
Edinburgh, 2 February 1991
Scotland bounce back from the disappointment of Paris with a stunning display against a Welsh side showing none of the forward spirit that characterised their display against the English. Derek White and Gary Armstrong control the game at the base of the Scottish pack and claim three of the four home tries. Craig Chalmers scores the fourth and completes his collection with a conversion, dropped goal and two penalty goals in Scotland's second biggest win over Wales.
Scotland: G Hastings; A Stanger, S Hastings, S Lineen, A Moore; C Chalmers, G Armstrong; D Sole (capt), J Allan, P Burnell, C Gray, D Cronin, D Turnbull, J Jeffrey, D White. **Repl: Used** – K Milne for Allan, 47 mins. **Not used** – P Dods, D Wyllie, G Oliver, G Marshall, D Milne.
Scorers – Tries: White 2 (20,80), Armstrong (25), Chalmers (53). **Conversions:** Chalmers (25), G. Hastings (80). **Penalty goals:** Chalmers (2), G Hastings 2 (71,76). **Dropped goal:** Chalmers (51).
Wales: P Thorburn (capt); I Evans, M Ring, S Gibbs, S Ford; N Jenkins, R Jones; B Williams, K Phillips, P Knight, G D Llewellyn, G O Llewellyn, G George, A Carter, P Arnold. **Repl: Used** – A Clement for Thorburn, 69 mins. **Not used** – C Bridges, D Evans, M Griffiths, K Waters, E Lewis.
Scorers – Try: Ford (60). **Conversion:** Thorburn. **Penalty goal:** Thorburn 2 (4,32).
Referee: D J Bishop (New Zealand).

Ireland (10) 13, France (6) 21
Dublin, 2 February 1991
Ireland's belated entry into the Five Nations' Championship shows a massive improvement from their last outing in October, when so fortunate to beat Argentina. With London Irish newcomers Simon Geoghegan and Rob Saunders, given the responsibility of captaining the side on his debut, providing a breath of fresh air to the Irish cause, France require a 77th minute try by Cabannes to finally subdue the home challenge.
Ireland: K Murphy (Constitution); S Geoghegan (London Irish), B Mullin (Blackrock College), M Kiernan (Dolphin), K Hooks (Bangor); B Smith (Leicester), R Saunders (London Irish, capt); J Fitzgerald (Young Munster), S Smith (Ballymena), D Fitzgerald (Lansdowne), M Galwey (Shannon), B Rigney (Greystones), P Matthews (Wanderers), G Hamilton (NIFC), B Robinson (Ballymena). **Repl: Not used** – J Staples (London Irish), V Cunningham (St Mary's College), A Rolland (Blackrock College), T Kingston (Dolphin), G Halpin (Wanderers), N Mannion (Lansdowne).
Scorers – Try: S Smith (7). **Penalty goals:** Kiernan 3 (15,32,55).

France: S Blanco (capt); J B Lafond, F Mesnel, D Charvet, P Lagisquet; D Camberabero, P Berbizier; G Lascube, P Marocco, P Ondarts, O Roumat, M Tachdjian, X Blond, L Cabannes, M Cecillon. **Repl: Used** – P Saint-Andre for Lagisquet, 51 mins. **Not used** – T Lacroix, H Sanz, C Deslandes, P Gimbert (Begles), V Moscato.
Scorers – Tries: Lagisquet (51), Cabannes (77). **Conversions:** Camberabero 2. **Penalty goals:** Camberabero 3 (4,11,62).
Referee: D Bevan (Wales).

England (9) 21, Scotland (6) 12
Twickenham, 16 February 1991

The stigma of March 17, 1990 is laid to rest as England gain adequate revenge for the disappointment suffered at Murrayfield in the Grand Slam decider to the previous Five Nations' Championship. If England were tactically naiive in Edinburgh they are the opposite before a passionate Twickenham crowd who delight in seeing Simon Hodgkinson methodically add another 17 points to his ever-increasing collection. Orrell wing Nigel Heslop scores the game's only try shortly into the second period.

England: S Hodgkinson; N Heslop, W Carling (capt), J Guscott, R Underwood; R Andrew, R Hill; J Leonard, B Moore, J Probyn, P Ackford, W Dooley, M Teague, P Winterbottom, D Richards. **Repl: Not used** – J Webb, S Halliday, D Morris, P Rendall, J Olver, M Skinner.
Scorers – Try: Heslop (44). **Conversion:** Hodgkinson. **Penalty goals:** Hodgkinson 5 (14,17,35,68,76).
Scotland: G Hastings; A Stanger, S Hastings, S Lineen, A Moore; C Chalmers, G Armstrong; D Sole (capt), K Milne, P Burnell, C Gray, D Cronin, D Turnbull, J Jeffrey, D White. **Repl: Not used** – P Dods, D Wyllie, G Oliver, G Marshall, D Milne, J Hay (Hawick).
Scorer – Penalty goals: Chalmers 4 (21,27,51,61).
Referee: S Hilditch (Ireland).

Wales (9) 21, Ireland (9) 21
Cardiff, 16 February 1991

The match billed as 'the Wooden Spoon decider', despite coming so early in the Championship programme, produces a thrilling spectacle if an inconclusive result. Both teams gain comfort from staving off defeat, although Wales are probably the most satisfied with the draw as they are outscored by four tries to two. Each Ireland touchdown earns a special cheer: Brendan Mullin's score, his 14th, equals the Irish record, there are debut tries for wing Jack Clarke and full-back Jim Staples, while the exciting Simon Geoghegan marks his second appearance with the draw-clinching score 13 minutes from time.

Wales: P Thorburn (capt); I Evans, M Ring, S Gibbs, S Ford; N Jenkins, C Bridges; M Griffiths, K Phillips, J Davies (Neath), G D Llewellyn, P Arnold,

E Lewis, M Morris (Neath), P Davies (Llanelli). **Repl: Not used** – R Jones, A Clement, D Evans, K Waters, A Carter, B Williams.
Scorers – Tries: Arnold (21), Jenkins (50). **Conversions:** Thorburn 2. **Penalty goals:** Thorburn 2 (16,56). **Dropped goal:** Jenkins (62).
Ireland: J Staples; S Geoghegan, D Curtis (London Irish), B Mullin, J Clarke (Dolphin); B Smith, R Saunders (capt); J Fitzgerald, S Smith, D Fitzgerald, M Galwey, B Rigney, P Matthews, G Hamilton, B Robinson. **Repl: Used** – K Murphy for Staples, 40 mins. **Not used** – V Cunningham, A Rolland, T Kingston, G Halpin, N Mannion.
Scorers – Tries: Staples (17), Mullin (52), Clarke (59), Geoghegan (67). **Conversion:** B Smith (17). **Dropped goal:** B Smith (5).
Referee: D Bishop (New Zealand).

Ireland (3) 7, England (3) 16
Dublin, 2 March 1991
England are told by all and sundry that Ireland will help warm them up for their Grand Slam decider against France a fortnight hence, nothing more. Fortunately, the team have the good sense to take little notice of such misguided advice, because Ireland turn in a fine performance on their home patch. Simon Geoghegan notches his second try in three games but it is Rory Underwood's score, seven minutes from time, which decides the game as England lead for the first time.
Ireland: J Staples; S Geoghegan, D Curtis (London Irish), B Mullin, K Crossan (Instonians); B Smith, R Saunders (capt); J Fitzgerald, S Smith, D Fitzgerald, B Rigney, N Francis (Blackrock College), P Matthews, G Hamilton, B Robinson. **Repl: Not used** – K Murphy, V Cunningham, A Rolland, T Kingston, G Halpin, N Mannion.
Scorers – Try: Geoghegan (44). **Penalty goal:** B Smith (24).
England: S Hodgkinson; N Heslop, W Carling (capt), J Guscott, R Underwood; R Andrew, R Hill; J Leonard, B Moore, J Probyn, P Ackford, W Dooley, M Teague, P Winterbottom, D Richards. **Repl: Not used** – J Webb, S Halliday, D Morris, P Rendall, J Olver, M Skinner.
Scorers – Tries: Underwood (72), Teague (83). **Conversion:** Hodgkinson (83). **Penalty goals:** Hodgkinson 2 (40,63).
Referee: A Ceccon (France).

France (14) 36, Wales (3) 3
Paris, 2 March 1991
The Welsh visit to Parc des Princes is always going to be an exercise in damage limitation and so it proves. Serge Blanco, making his farewell Five Nations' appearance for France in Paris, scores a breathtaking try after only two minutes to set the tempo and, in an emotional finale, steps up to convert France's sixth and final try from the touchline before accepting the accolade of the crowd. Paul Thorburn's massive first half penalty goal is Wales' only solace.
France: S Blanco (capt); J B Lafond, P Sella (Agen), F Mesnel, P

Saint-Andre; D Camberabero, P Berbizier; G Lascube, P Marocco, P Ondarts, O Roumat, J F Gourragne (Beziers), X Blond, L Cabannes, C Deslandes. **Repl: Used** – T Lacroix for Sella, 72 mins. **Not used** – E Bonneval (Toulouse), H Sanz, P Gimbert (Begles), M Tachdjian, M Cecillon. **Scorers – Tries:** Blanco (2), Saint-Andre (11), Mesnel (51), Roumat (57), Sella (72), Lafond (79). **Conversions:** Camberabero 2 (57,72), Blanco (79). **Penalty goals:** Camberabero 2 (32,36). **Wales:** P Thorburn (capt); I Evans, M Ring, S Gibbs, A Emyr (Swansea); N Jenkins, C Bridges; M Griffiths, K Phillips, J Davies (Neath), G D Llewellyn, P Arnold, E Lewis, M Morris (Neath), P Davies (Llanelli). **Repl: Not used** – R Jones, A Clement, D Evans, K Waters, A Carter, B Williams. **Scorer – Penalty goal:** Thorburn (27). **Referee:** K Fitzgerald (Australia).

Scotland (15) 28, Ireland (15) 25
Edinburgh, 16 March 1991

Scotland maintain their unbeaten record at Murrayfield, which dates back to the visit of the 1988 Wallabies, although victory in the outstanding match of the International Championship is somewhat fortuitous. Inhibitions are nowhere to be seen as the two sides give a splendid rendition of the way the game should be played. As against Wales, Ireland outscore their opponents in the try-count and yet fail to win. Brendan Mullin establishes a new Irish try-scoring record with his 15th score in the green jersey while Brian Smith signs off, before joining Balmain Rugby League Club in Australia, by failing with a last ditch drop goal attempt which would have levelled the scores.
Scotland: G Hastings; A Stanger, S Hastings, S Lineen, I Tukalo; C Chalmers, G Armstrong; D Sole (capt), J Allan, P Burnell, C Gray, D Cronin, D Turnbull, J Jeffrey, D White. **Repl: Used** – P Dods for Tukalo, 35 mins. **Not used** – D Wyllie, G Oliver, G Marshall, D Milne, K Milne. **Scorers – Tries:** G Hastings (40), Stanger (48), S Hastings (58). **Conversions:** Chalmers 2 (40,48). **Penalty goals:** Chalmers 3 (2,15,55), G Hastings (31). **Ireland:** J Staples; S Geoghegan, D Curtis (London Irish), B Mullin, K Crossan (Instonians); B Smith, R Saunders (capt); J Fitzgerald, S Smith, D Fitzgerald, B Rigney, N Francis (Blackrock College), P Matthews, G Hamilton, B Robinson. **Repl: Used** – K Murphy for Staples, 70 mins. **Not used** – V Cunningham, A Rolland, T Kingston, G Halpin, N Mannion. **Scorers – Tries:** Crossan (19), Robinson (38), Geoghegan (43), Mullin (73). **Conversions:** B Smith 3 (19,38,73). **Dropped goal:** B Smith (29). **Referee:** K Fitzgerald (Australia).

England (18) 21, France (9) 19
Twickenham, 16 March 1991

The day England have dreamed of for eleven years, since Bill Beaumont skippered the last All White Grand Slam in 1980, finally arrives. Amid emotional scenes at Twickenham, England cling on to their advantage – attained through Rory Underwood's 30th minute try and another 14 points from Simon Hodgkinson – despite Franck Mesnel crossing for a last-minute try which his captain Serge Blanco converts. France have the consolation of scoring the game's outstanding try, through Saint-Andre. Hodgkinson finishes season with Five Nations' record haul of 60 points.

England: S Hodgkinson; N Heslop, W Carling (capt), J Guscott, R Underwood; R Andrew, R Hill; J Leonard, B Moore, J Probyn, P Ackford, W Dooley, M Teague, P Winterbottom, D Richards. **Repl: Not used** – J Webb, S Halliday, D Morris, P Rendall, J Olver, M Skinner.

Scorers – Try: Underwood (30). **Conversion:** Hodgkinson. **Penalty goals:** Hodgkinson 4 (2,23,33,63). **Dropped goal:** Andrew (17).

France: S Blanco (capt); J B Lafond, P Sella (Agen), F Mesnel, P Saint-Andre; D Camberabero, P Berbizier; G Lascube, P Marocco, P Ondarts, M Tachdjian, O Roumat, X Blond, L Cabannes, A Benazzi. **Repl: Used** – M Cecillon for Tachdjian, 54 mins. **Not used** – T Lacroix, E Bonneval (Toulouse), H Sanz, P Gimbert (Begles), C Deslandes.

Scorers – Tries: Saint-Andre (13), Camberabero (56), Mesnel (79). **Conversions:** Camberabero 2 (13,79). **Penalty goal:** Camberabero (27).

Referee: L Peard (Wales).

Ireland B (7) 24, England B (10) 10
Old Belvedere, 1 March 1991

England give away a 10–7 half-time lead as they suffer their first defeat of the season at B level. Ireland show themselves to be the hungrier team on the day and, set alongside their win in the U-21 fixture, have every reason to look forward to the future in confident mood.

Ireland B: C Wilkinson (Malone); R Wallace (Garryowen), J Clarke (Dolphin), M Kiernan (Dolphin), J Sexton (Lansdowne); N Barry (Garryowen), M Bradley (Constitution, capt); N Popplewell (Greystones), J O'Riordan (Constitution), P McCarthy (Constitution), M Galwey (Shannon), P Johns (Dublin Univ), P O'Hara (Sunday's Well), M Fitzgibbon (Shannon), P Lawlor (Bective Rangers).

Scorers – Tries: Johns, Clarke, Wallace, Popplewell. **Conversion:** Wilkinson. **Penalty goals:** Kiernan, Wilkinson.

England B: J Liley (Leicester); I Hunter (Northampton), J Buckton (Saracens), G Thompson (Harlequins), T Underwood (Leicester); D Pears (Harlequins), R Moon (Llanelli); G Holmes (Wasps), G Dawe (Bath), G Pearce (Northampton, capt), N Redman (Bath), S Dear (Rosslyn Park), D Ryan (Wasps), N Back (Leicester), T Rodber (Northampton). **Repl: Used** – T Revan (Rugby) for Pearce. **Not used** – M Strett (Orrell), A Kardooni (Leicester), K Dunn (Gloucester), B Clarke (Saracens), P de Glanville (Bath).

Scorers – Tries: Rodber, Hunter. **Conversion:** Liley.

Referee: K McCartney (Scotland).

Scotland B (3) 10, France B (21) 31
Glasgow, 2 March, 1991
Scotland suffer their second disappointing result of the season at B level when
they are outclassed by France at Hughenden. Encouraging performances from
scrum-half Andy Nicol and No.8 Stuart Reid are very much isolated plusses
as Scotland fall to their 11th defeat in a series dating back over 19 matches
and 20 years.
Scotland B: C Redpath (Melrose); S Porter (Malone), S Nichol (Selkirk),
R Maclean (Moseley, capt), M Moncrieff (Gala); C Glasgow (Heriot's FP),
A Nicol (Dundee HSFP); D Milne (Heriot's FP), J Hay (Hawick), A Watt
(Glasgow High/Kelvinside), C Hogg (Melrose), A Macdonald (Heriot's FP),
D McIvor (Edinburgh Academicals), I Smith (Gloucester), S Reid
(Boroughmuir). **Repl: Not used** – M Dods (Gala), R Adam (Edinburgh
Academicals), M Allingham (Heriot's FP), B Richardson (Boroughmuir),
G Smith (Moseley), I Corcoran (Gala).
Scorers – Try: Nicol (80). **Penalty goals:** Glasgow 2 (38,52).
France B: J L Sadourney (Colomiers); S Viars (Brive), E Nicol
(Montferrand), M Marfaing (Toulouse), J-P Bullich (Narbonne); P Montlaur
(Agen), G Camberabero (Beziers, capt); P Tapie (Grenoble), C Garcia
(Beziers), S Graou (Auch), C Mougeot (Begles), H Chaffardon (Grenoble),
J-F Tordo (Nice), M Courtiols (Begles), S Dispagne (Perpignan). **Repl:
Used** – J-M Cadieu (Toulouse) for Mougeot, 64 mins; P Soula (Toulouse)
for Garcia, 78 mins. **Not used** – P Toussent (Castre), S Milhas (Auch),
E Vergniol (Dax), L Bontemps (La Rochelle).
Scorers – Tries: Bullich (7), Sadourney (28), Camberabero (60).
Conversions: Montlaur 2 (7,28). **Penalty goals:** Montlaur 4 (15,34,54,67).
Dropped goal: Montlaur (40).
Referee: J Groves (Wales).

England B 6, France B 10
Bristol, 15 March 1991
England's campaign at B level, which began so promisingly with two victories
and a draw in their three opening matches, continues to deteriorate as France,
despite playing three-quarters of the match without dismissed hooker Pierre
Tapie, still have enough in hand.
England B: I Hunter; A Harriman (Harlequins), J Buckton, G Thompson
(Harlequins), A Adebayo (Bath); D Pears, R Moon; G Holmes, G Dawe, G
Pearce (capt), N Redman, S O'Leary (Wasps), D Ryan, N Back, T Rodber.
Repl: Not used – P de Glanville, M Strett, A Kardooni, M Hynes (Orrell),
K Dunn, B Clarke.
Scorer – Penalty goals: Pears 2.
France B: J-L Sadourney; L Bontemps, S Viars, E Nicol, M Marfaing;
J-P Bullich, P Montlaur; S Milhas (capt), P Tapie, J-F Tordo, G Pages
(Rodez), S Graou, J-M Cadieu, M Courtiols, S Dispagne. **Repl: Used** – C
Barriere (Nimes) for Dispagne.

341

Scorers – **Try:** Viars. **Dropped goals:** Montlaur 2.
Referee: R Yemen (Wales).

FINAL FIVE NATIONS' TABLE 1990/91

1990 positions in brackets

	P	W	D	L	F	(t, c, p, dg)	A	(t, c, p, dg)	Pts
England (2)	4	4	0	0	83	(5, 3, 18, 1)	44	(4, 2, 8, 0)	8
France (3)	4	3	0	1	91	(11,7, 8, 3)	46	(2, 1, 10, 2)	6
Scotland (1)	4	2	0	2	81	(7, 4, 13, 2)	73	(6, 5, 9, 4)	4
Ireland (4)	4	0	1	3	66	(10,4, 4, 2)	86	(9, 7, 11, 1)	1
Wales (5)	4	0	1	3	42	(3, 3, 7, 1)	114	(15,6, 12, 2)	1

SCORERS – 60 – S Hodgkinson (England) 3c,18p. 46 – D Camberabero
(France) 1t,6c,8p,2dg; C Chalmers (Scotland) 1t,10p,2dg,3c. 24 –
P Thorburn (Wales) 6p,3c. 17 – B Smith (Ireland) 4c,1p,2dg. 15 –
G Hastings (Scotland) 1t,1c,3p. 12 – S Geoghegan (Ireland) 3t. 10 –
N Jenkins (Wales) 1t,1p,1dg. 9 – M Kiernan (Ireland) 3p; S Blanco (France)
1t,1c,1dg. 8 – F Mesnel (France) 2t; B Mullin (Ireland) 2t; P Saint-Andre
(France) 2t; M Teague (England) 2t; R Underwood (England) 2t; D White
(Scotland) 2t. 4 – G Armstrong (Scotland) 1t; P Arnold (Wales) 1t;
L Cabannes (France) 1t; J Clarke (Ireland) 1t; K Crossan (Ireland) 1t; S Ford
(Wales) 1t; S Hastings (Scotland) 1t; N Heslop (England) 1t; J-B Lafond
(France) 1t; P Lagisquet (France) 1t; B Robinson (Ireland) 1t; O Roumat
(France) 1t; P Sella (France) 1t; S Smith (Ireland) 1t; T Stanger (Scotland)
1t; J Staples (Ireland) 1t. 3 – R Andrew (England) 1dg. TOTAL: 363
(36t,21c,50p,9dg).

England B (18) 50, Spain (0) 6
Gloucester, 20 January 1991

After the percentage game of Cardiff, England B turn on the style at
Kingsholm to account for a Spanish side with nine tries. The try spree is
inspired by the ubiquitous Leicester flanker Neil Back, with Bath wing Ade
Adebayo, clubmate and hooker Victor Ubogu, and Llanelli scrum-half Rupert
Moon claiming two touchdowns apiece.
England B: J Liley (Leicester); I Hunter (Northampton), P de Glanville
(Bath), G Thompson (Harlequins), A Adebayo (Bath); D Pears (Harlequins),
R Moon (Llanelli); V Ubogu (Bath), G Dawe (Bath), G Pearce
(Northampton, capt), N Redman (Bath), S Dear (Rosslyn Park), D Ryan
(Wasps), N Back (Leicester), B Clarke (Saracens). **Repl: Not used** – M Strett
(Orrell), A Kardooni (Leicester), G Holmes (Wasps), K Dunn (Gloucester),
T Rodber (Northampton).

Scorers – Tries: Adebayo 2, Moon 2, Ubogu 2, Ryan, Hunter, penalty try.
Conversions: Liley 3, Pears. **Penalty goals:** Liley 2.
Spain: F Puertas; D Saenz, S Torres, J Moreno, C Garcia; M Sanchez, J
Diaz; J Elvarez (capt), F Castro, A Altuna, F Mendez, J Rodriguez, A Malo,
J Gutierrez, E Illaregui. **Repl: Used** – J A Gonzalez for Castro; J Candau for
Rodriguez.
Scorer – Try: Sanchez. **Conversion:** Sanchez.
Referee: G Simmonds (Wales).

Cathay Pacific/Hong Kong Bank Invitation Sevens
Hong Kong, 24–25 March 1991

Scotland's first official representation at the Hong Kong Sevens ends in
disappointment when the VII are eliminated by Canada in the quarter-finals.
The Barbarians reach the last four before bowing out to eventual winners Fiji,
who then repeat their 1990 final win over New Zealand.
Scotland squad: G Armstrong (Jed-Forest), C Chalmers (Melrose),
S Hastings (Watsonians), J Jeffrey (Kelso, capt), R Kirkpatrick (Jed-Forest),
G Marshall (Selkirk), S Nichol (Selkirk), D Sole (Edinburgh Academicals),
D White (London Scottish). **Manager:** G Young. **Coach:** I McGeechan.
Pool matches: A – Fiji 48, Singapore 0; Spain 32, Singapore 0; Fiji 30, Spain
0. **B** – Western Samoa 20, Malaysia 9; Tonga 38, Malaysia 0; Western Samoa
16, Tonga 6. **C** – Barbarians 18, Germany 6; Germany 13, Korea 10;
Barbarians 34, Korea 0. **D** – Australia 30, Papua New Guinea 10; US Eagles
22, Papua New Guinea 10; Australia 22, US Eagles 0. **E** – Scotland 28, Sri
Lanka 6; Soviet Bears 18, Sri Lanka 8; Scotland 20, Soviet Bears 6. **F** –
Argentina 32, Thailand 0; Canada 28, Thailand 0; Canada 26, Argentina 0.
G – France 38, Arabian Gulf 0; Hong Kong 20, Arabian Gulf 6; France 4,
Hong Kong 0. **H** – New Zealand 40, Taipei 0; Taipei 12, Japan 6; New
Zealand 40, Japan 0.
Quarter-finals: Fiji 21, Western Samoa 6; Barbarians 16, Australia 6; Canada
24, Scotland 4; New Zealand 30, France 8. **Semi-finals:** Fiji 22, Barbarians
14; New Zealand 26, Canada 0. **Final:** Fiji 18, New Zealand 14.
Plate final: Argentina 36, US Eagles 6. **Bowl final:** Korea 36, Thailand 0.
Final: Fiji 18, New Zealand 14.

England B (6) 12, Italy B (3) 9
Waterloo, 27 March 1991

Martin Strett, the Orrell fly-half, celebrates his debut for England B with all
the points in their less than convincing defeat of their Italian counterparts at
Waterloo. England end their B programme with three wins, one draw and
two defeats.
England B: A Buzza (Wasps); A Harriman (Harlequins), J Buckton
(Saracens), G Thompson (Harlequins), A Adebayo (Wasps); M Strett
(Orrell), S Bates (Wasps); G Holmes (Wasps), J Olver (Northampton, capt),
A Mullins (Harlequins), N Redman (Bath), M Bayfield (Bedford), J Hall

(Bath), A Robinson (Wasps), D Egerton (Bath). **Repl: Used:** – I Hunter (Northampton) for Thompson. **Not used** – D Pears (Harlequins), R Moon (Llanelli), G Dawe (Bath), M Hynes (Orrell), D Ryan (Wasps).
Scorer – Try: Strett. **Conversion:** Strett. **Penalty goals:** Strett 2.
Italy B: D Tebaldi (Noceto); P Vaccari (Calvisano), F Gaetaniello (Livorno), S Bordon (Rovigo), M Brunello (Rovigo); D Dominguez (Milano), F Pietrosanti (L'Aquila); R de Bernardo (Petrarca Padova), A Marengoni (Milano), G Rosai (Parma, capt), A Colella (L'Aquila), C Checchinato (Rovigo), R Saetti (Padova), M Giovanelli (Milano), P Pedroni (Milano).
Scorer – Try: Dominguez. **Conversion:** Dominguez. **Penalty goal:** Dominguez.
Referee: C Rouve (France).

Wales U-21 (20) 23, Scotland U-21 (0) 15
Llanelli, 20 April 1991

Wales impress by opening up a 20–0 lead in 40 minutes, with senior cap Neil Jenkins weighing in with 15 points, but then go off the boil. Inspired by New Zealand-born No.8 Dale McIntosh, who plays his club rugby alongside Jenkins at Pontypridd, Scotland stage a spirited rally with three second half tries. But Wales, who have never been beaten in the fixture, hang on.

Wales U-21: L Evans (Llanelli); J Westwood (Newbridge), S Gibbs (Neath), J Thomas (Neath), A Donovan (Cardiff); N Jenkins (Pontypridd), P John (Cardiff, capt); M Davis (Newport), A Lamerton (Llanelli), R Shaw (Llanelli), L Mruk (Pontypool), C Langley (Cardiff), O Lloyd (Bridgend), P Thomas (Glamorgan Wanderers), S Williams (Swansea). **Repl: Used** – I Bebb (CIHE) for Donovan, 73 mins. **Not used** – M McCarthy (Aberavon), D Llewellyn (Newport), T Orrell (Cardiff), R McBride (Swansea), A Williams (Maesteg).
Scorers – Tries: Mruk (11), Donovan (18), Jenkins (21). **Conversion:** Jenkins 18. **Penalty goals:** Jenkins 3 (3,40,62).
Scotland U-21: C Redpath (Melrose); R Adam (Edinburgh Academicals), S Nichol (Selkirk), G Shiel (Melrose), D Macrae (Cambridge Univ); R Shepherd (Edinburgh Academicals), B Redpath (Melrose); J Couper (Glasgow High/Kelvinside), D McAndrew (Stirling County), G McKee (Glasgow High/Kelvinside, capt), S Aitken (Melrose), G Weir (Melrose), S Reid (Boroughmuir), S Bennett (Kelso), D McIntosh (Pontypridd). **Repl: Not used** – A Dow (Glasgow High/Kelvinside), D Changleng (Gala), K Robertson (Hillhead/Jordanhill), I Murchison (Loughborough Univ), A Kittle (Stewart's-Melville), D Timms (Dunfermline).
Scorers – Tries: Nichol (45), Macrae (66), Adam (78). **Penalty goal:** Shepherd (59).
Referee: D Matthews (England).

SCOTLAND TO NORTH AMERICA
May 1991: 6 games

PARTY: P Dods (Gala – 1,4,5,6), **M Dods** (Gala – 2,3,5), **M Moncrieff** (Gala – 1,2,4,6), **L Renwick** (London Scottish – 2,3,5), **A Stanger** (Hawick – 1,3,4,6), **I Jardine** (Stirling County – 2,5), **G Shiel** (Melrose – 1,3,4,5,6), **R Shepherd** (Edinburgh Academicals – 2,3), **D Wyllie** (Stewart's-Melville, capt – 1,2,3,4,5,6), **C Chalmers** (Melrose – 1,4,6), **A Nicol** (Dundee HSFP – 2,3,5), **G Oliver** (Hawick – 1,4,6), **G Wilson** (Boroughmuir – 1,5), **D Milne** (Heriot's FP – 2,4,6), **G Smith** (Moseley – 1,3,5), **A Watt** (Glasgow High/Kelvinside – 2,3,4,6), **J Allan** (Edinburgh Academicals – 1,4,6), **K Milne** (Heriot's FP – 2,3,5), **A Macdonald** (Heriot's FP – 1,2,4,6), **B Richardson** (Boroughmuir – 2,3,5), **G Weir** (Melrose – 1,R2,3,4,5,6), **J Amos** (Gala – 1,3,5), **R Kirkpatrick** (Jed-Forest – 2,3,5,6), **G Marshall** (Selkirk – 1,4,5), **D Turnbull** (Hawick – 1,2,4,6), **S Reid** (Boroughmuir – 2,3,4,6).

Results: (1) British Columbia 9, Scotland 29 (Vancouver, 8 May); (2) Alberta 7, Scotland 76 (Edmonton, 11 May); (3) Rugby East 12, Scotland 24 (New York City, 15 May); (4) **US Eagles 12, Scotland 41** (Hartford, 18 May); (5) Ontario 3, Scotland 43 (Toronto, 22 May); (6) **Canada 24, Scotland 19** (New Brunswick, 25 May).

Scorers: P Dods 56 (10c,12p), M Dods 44 (3t,13c,2p), Stanger 20 (5t), Moncrieff 16 (4t), Reid 16 (4t), Kirkpatrick 12 (3t), Nichol 12 (3t), Watt 12 (3t), Renwick 8 (2t), Shiel 8 (2t), Wyllie 8 (2t), Amos 4 (1t), Macdonald 4 (1t), Turnbull 4 (1t), Smith 4 (1t), Wilson 4 (1t).

Record: P6 W5 D0 L1 F232 A67.

US Eagles 12, Scotland 41
Hartford, 18 May 1991

Two wins over Japan have not prepared the US Eagles for the class of opposition which Scotland provide at the Dillon Stadium in Connecticut and after an early exchange of penalty goals by Peter Dods and Eagles' Mike DeJong, the tourists settle down to dismantling their hosts, with tries by Andy Macdonald, Stuart Reid (2) and Tony Stanger (2).

USA: R Nelson (Belmont Shore); R Lewis (Washington), K Higgins (Old Blues), J Burke (Albany Knicks), C Williams (Old Blues); M DeJong (Denver Barbarians), B Daily (San Jose Seahawks); C Lippert (OMBAC), T Flay (Old Puget Sound), N Mottram (Boulder), T Ridnell (Old Puget Sound), K Swords (Beacon Hill), B Leversee (OMBAC), K Farley (Whitemarsh), B Vizard (OMBAC, capt).

Scorer – Penalty goals: DeJong 4.

Scotland: P Dods; A Stanger, D Wyllie (capt), G Shiel, M Moncrieff; C Chalmers, G Oliver; D Milne, J Allan, A Watt, G Weir, A Macdonald, D Turnbull, G Marshall, S Reid.

Scorers – Tries: Macdonald, Reid 2, Stanger 2. **Conversions:** Dods 3. **Penalty goals:** Dods 5.

Referee: G Gadovich (Canada).

Canada 24, Scotland 19
New Brunswick, 25 May 1991

Scotland, fielding only four players with Five Nations' experience, are beaten by Canada, or more precisely their captain and full-back Mark Wyatt who lands a world-record eight penalty goals (beating Simon Hodgkinson's seven against Wales earlier in the season). Despite going down, Scotland have the consolation of scoring the game's two tries, through Stuart Reid and Tony Stanger.

Canada: M Wyatt (capt); S Gray, C Stewart, J Lecky, J Woods; G Rees, J Graf; E Evans, M Cardinal, D Jackart (all British Columbia), A Charron (Ontario), N Hadley, G McKinnon, B Breen, G Ennis (all British Columbia).

Scorer – Penalty goals: Wyatt 8.

Scotland: P Dods; A Stanger, D Wyllie (capt), G Shiel, M Moncrieff; C Chalmers, G Oliver; D Milne, J Allan, A Watt, G Weir, A Macdonald, D Turnbull, R Kirkpatrick, S Reid.

Scorers – Tries: Reid, Stanger. **Conversion:** Dods. **Penalty goals:** Dods 3.

Referee: S Griffiths (England).

Netherlands 18, England U-21 20
's-Hertogenbosch, 18 May 1991

England open up a 20–6 lead at Vliert Park but are left clinging desperately to a 2-point advantage after a sterling display of Dutch courage. Full back Stephen Swindells takes his penalty goal count to eight in two matches this season, while wings Leroy McKenzie and Steve Wills cross for tries against a Dutch senior side which has lost seven of its previous eight Internationals during the course of the season.

Netherlands: B Wisse (Leiden); J van Esseveld (Eemland), S Hadinegoro (The Hague), P Hengeveld (Amstelveen), K Sanchez (The Hague); M Michelsen (Leiden), M Eman (The Hague); M Tielrooij (Hilversum), M Visser (Hilversum, capt), G de Vries (Amsterdam), M van Loon (Leiden), E-J Berendsen (Leiden), R Broers (Leiden), Y Kummer (Leiden), W van Altena (Hilversum)

Scorers – Tries: Kummer, Broers. **Conversions:** Michelsen 2. **Penalty goal:** Michelsen. **Dropped goal:** Hengeveld.

England U-21: S Swindells (Manchester); L McKenzie (Coventry), P Flood (Bridgend), L Boyle (Moseley), S Wills (Leicester); N Matthews (Gloucester), G Simkins (Bedford); A Jackson (West Hartlepool), R Cockerill (Coventry), W Bullock (Coventry), R West (Ledbury), D Sims (Gloucester), J Pearson (Bristol), G Adams (Bath, capt), S Ojomoh (Bath).

Scorers – Tries: Wills, McKenzie. **Penalty goals:** Swindells 4.

Referee: D Leslie (Scotland).

French Armed Forces U-21 9, England U-21 7
Dunkirk, 22 May 1991

Despite scoring the only try of the game, a neat effort by Gloucester fly-half Neil Matthews, poor goal kicking costs England U-21s victory. Although Richard Booth lands one, the French take revenge for their 16–23 loss in last season's fixture with two penalty goals by full-back Rolland and a drop goal from second half replacement Fiard.

F. A. F. : R Rolland (Nice); P Passicousset (Bayonne), Y Croes (Istres), L Chambiard (Nimes), O Duboscq (Pau); J-M Soubira (Brive), P Ladouce (Bourgoin, capt); L Benezech (Racing Club), F Lavergne (Aurillac), P Carrere (PUC), P Baixeras (Chateaurenard), E Lecomte (Montferrand), F Simiand (Grenoble), A Agueb (Tarbes), S Dispagne (Perpignan). **Repl:** R Crespy (Brive) for Carrere, 55 mins; P Fiard (Romans) for Croes, 58 mins.
Scorers – Penalty goals: Rolland 2. **Dropped goal:** Fiard.

England U-21: R Liley (Cahors); L McKenzie (Coventry), L Boyle (Moseley), P Flood (Bridgend), S Dixon (Rosslyn Park); N Matthews (Gloucester), R Booth (Sale); G Rowntree (Leicester), A Fields (Nottingham), N Lyman (Moseley), D Andreou (Coventry), D Sims (Gloucester), J Pearson (Bristol), G Adams (Bath, capt), M Rennell (Bedford).
Scorers – Try: Matthews. **Penalty goal:** Booth.
Referee: D Roelands (Belgium).

WALES TO AUSTRALIA
June–July 1991: 6 games

PARTY: L Evans (Llanelli – 5), **P Thorburn** (Neath – 1,2,4,6), **A Clement** (Swansea – 3,5,R6), **I Evans** (Llanelli – 1,2,3,4,6), **I Jones** (Llanelli – 1,3), **S Ford** (Cardiff – 2,4,6), **D Evans** (Cardiff – 1,5,R6), **S Gibbs** (Neath – 1,2,3,4,6), **M Hall** (Cardiff – 2,4,5,6), **S Lewis** (Pontypridd – 3,5), **A Davies** (Neath – 1,2,5,6), **N Jenkins** (Pontypridd – 3,4), **C Bridges** (Neath – 2,5,6), **R Jones** (Swansea – 1,R2,3,4), **M Davis** (Newport – 3,4,6), **M Griffiths** (Cardiff – 1,2,5), **P Knight** (Pontypridd – 2,3), **H William-Jones** (South Wales Police – 1,4,5,6), **K Phillips** (Neath – 2,5,6), **K Waters** (Newbridge – 1,3,4), **P Arnold** (Swansea – 2,3,4,6), **R Goodey** (Pontypool – 1,5), **G D Llewellyn** (Neath – 3,4,6), **G O Llewellyn** (Neath – 1,2,5,R6), **R Collins** (Cardiff – 1,3,4,5,6), **E Lewis** (Llanelli – 1,3,6), **M Morris** (Neath – 2,5), **R Webster** (Swansea – 2,4), **P Davies** (Llanelli – 1,2,4,6), **Hembrow** (Cardiff), **S Legge** (Glamorgan Wanderers – 1,3,5).
Results: (1) Western Australia 6, Wales 22 (Perth, 30 June); (2) Queensland 35, Wales 24 (Brisbane, 7 July); (3) Australia Capital Territory 3, Wales 7 (Canberra, 10 July); (4) New South Wales 71, Wales 8 (Sydney, 14 July); (5) Queensland Country 7, Wales 35 (Rockhampton, 17 July); (6) **Australia 63, Wales 6** (Brisbane, 21 July).
Scorers: A Davies (1t,5dg), D Evans 15 (1t,1p,4c), Hall 12 (3t), L Evans 8 (2t), R Jones (2t), Webster 8 (2t), Thorburn 5 (1c,1dg), Clement 4 (1t), Ford

4 (1t), Legge 4 (1t), E Lewis 4 (1t), G O Llewellyn 4 (1t), penalty try (4), Jenkins 3 (1p).
Record: P6 W3 L3 F102 A185.

ENGLAND TO AUSTRALIA AND FIJI
July 1991: 6 games

PARTY: **S Hodgkinson** (Nottingham – 2,3,R4,6), **J Webb** (Bath – 1,4,5), **N Heslop** (Orrell – 1,4,6), **I Hunter** (Northampton – 2,4,6), **C Oti** (Wasps – 2,3,5), **R Underwood** (Leicester – 1,3,5), **W Carling** (Harlequins, capt – 1,3,5), **J Guscott** (Bath – 1,3,R4,5), **S Halliday** (Harlequins – 2,4,6), **D Hopley** (Wasps – 2,4,6), **R Andrew** (Wasps – 1,3,5), **D Pears** (Harlequins – 2,4,6), **R Hill** (Bath – 1,3,5), **D Morris** (Orrell – 2,4,6), **J Leonard** (Harlequins – 1,3,5), **G Pearce** (Northampton – 3,4,6), **J Probyn** (Wasps – 1,2,5), **P Rendall** (Wasps – 2,4,6), **B Moore** (Harlequins – 1,3,5), **J Olver** (Northampton – 2*,4*,6*), **P Ackford** (Harlequins – 1,3,6), **W Dooley** (Preston Grasshoppers – 1,3), **N Redman** (Bath – 2,4,5,6), **M Bayfield** (Northampton – 2,4,5), **J Hall** (Bath – 1,4), **G Rees** (Nottingham – 2,4,5), **M Skinner** (Harlequins – R1,2,4,R5,6), **M Teague** (Gloucester – 1,3,5,6), **P Winterbottom** (Harlequins – 1,3,6), **D Richards** (Leicester – 2,3,5).

Results: (1) New South Wales 21, England 19 (Sydney, 7 July); (2) Victoria President's XV 9, England 26 (Melbourne, 10 July); (3) Queensland 20, England 14 (Brisbane, 14 July); (4) Fiji B 27, England 13 (Lautoka, 16 July); (5) Fiji 12, England 28 (Suva, 20 July); (6) Emerging Australians 3, England 36 (Gosford, 23 July); (7) **Australia 40, England 15** (Sydney, 27 July).

Scorers: Webb 41 (1t,9p,5c), Hodgkinson 17 (1p,7c), Andrew 10 (1t,2dg), Guscott 8 (2t), Heslop 8 (2t), Hopley 8 (2t), Hunter 8 (2t), Morris 8 (2t), Underwood 8 (2t), Pears 7 (1t1dg), Hill 4 (1t), Oti 4 (1t), Probyn 4 (1t), Rees 4 (1t), Richards 4 (1t), Skinner 4 (1t), Teague 4 (1t).
Record: P7 W3 D0 L4 F151 A132 .

IRELAND TO NAMIBIA
July 1991: 4 games

PARTY: **J Staples** (London Irish – 2,4), **K Murphy** (Constitution – 1,3), **S Geoghegan** (London Irish – 2), **B Mullin** (Blackrock Coll – 1,2,4), **D Curtis** (London Irish – 2,3,4), **K Crossan** (Instonians – 1,3,4), **R Wallace** (Garryowen – 1,R2,3), **J Clarke** (Dolphin – 1,2,3,4), **V Cunningham** (St Mary's Coll – 1,2,4), **N Barry** (Garryowen – R4,3), **R Saunders** (London Irish – 2,4), **F Aherne** (Lansdowne – 1,3), **J Fitzgerald** (Young Munster – 3), **S Smith** (Ballymena – 1,2,4), **D Fitzgerald** (Lansdowne – 1,2,4), **N Popplewell** (Greystones – 1,2,4), **T Kingston** (Dolphin – 3), **G Halpin** (Wanderers – 3), **B Rigney** (Greystones – 2), **D Lenihan** (Constitution – 3,4), **M Galwey** (Shannon – 1,3,R4), **N Francis** (Blackrock Coll – 1,2,4), **P Matthews** (Wanderers, capt – 1,2), **G Hamilton** (NIFC – 3,4), **B Robinson**

(Ballymena – 1,2,4), **P O'Hara** (Sunday's Well – 1,2,3), **N Mannion** (Lansdowne – R2,3,4).

Results: (1) Namibia B 16, Ireland 45 (Windhoek, 17 July); (2) **Namibia 15, Ireland 6** (first Test: Windhoek, 20 July); (3) Namibia South Sub-Union 4, Ireland 35 (Keetmanshop, 23 July); (4) **Namibia 26, Ireland 15** (second Test Windhoek, 27 July).

Scorers: Wallace 20 (5t), Mullin 17 (2p,1dg,4c), Aherne 14 (1t,2p,2c), Barry 8 (2p,1c), Staples 8 (1t,2c), Crossan 4 (1t), Cunningham 4 (1t), D Fitzgerald 4 (1t), Galwey 4 (1t), Popplewell 4 (1t), Smith 4 (1t), penalty try (4), Curtis 3 (1dg), Murphy 3 (1p). Tries: Stoop, Mans, Maritz, Barnard, Coetzee. Conversions: Coetzee 3.

Record: P4 W2 D0 L2 F101 A61.

Full list of entries

ENGLAND

Ackford, P.J.
Adams, G.E.
Adebayo, A.A.
Ainscough, G.C.
Andreou, D.
   (Appendix)
Andrew, C.R.
Back, N.A.
Baldwin, D.N.
   (Appendix)
Baldwin, G.P.S.
   (Appendix)
Barley, B.
Bates, S.M.
Bayfield, M.C.
Blackett, P.M.
   (Appendix)
Blackmore, A.G.
   (Appendix)
Booth, R.D.
Boyle, L.S.
Buckton, J.R.
Bullock, W.
   (Appendix)
Buzza, A.J.
Callard, J.E.B.
   (Appendix)
Carling, W.D.C.
Challinor, A.P.
   (Appendix)
Childs, G.C.
Clarke, B.B.
Clough,
Cockerill, R.
   (Appendix)
Davies, S.L.
Davis, E. (Appendix)

Davis, J. (Appendix)
Dawe, R.G.R.
Dear, S.J.
De Glanville, P.R.
Dixon, S. (Appendix)
Dooley, W.A.
Douglas, S.M.
Dunn, K.A.
Dunston, I.C.
   (Appendix)
Egerton, D.W.
Fallon, J.A. (Appendix)
Fields, A.R.I.
   (Appendix)
Flood, J.P. (Appendix)
Guscott, J.C.
Hackney, S.T.
   (Appendix)
Hall, J.P.
Halliday, S.J.
Hamlin, M.P.
   (Appendix)
Hancock, M.E.
Harriman, A.T.
Harris, M.A.
   (Appendix)
Heslop, N.J.
Hill, R.J.
Hilton, D.I.W.
Hitchen, N.
Hodgkinson, S.D.
Holmes, G.
Hopley, D.P.
Hull, P.A.
Hunter, I.
Hutton, M.J.
Hynes, M.P.
Jackson, A.J.
   (Appendix)

Jenkins, R.J.H
Kardooni, A.
Kimmins, R.
Leonard, J.
Liley, J.G.
Liley, R.J. (Appendix)
Linnett, M.S.
Luxton, C.T.
Lyman, N.M.
McGauley, C.F.
   (Appendix)
McKenzie, L.
MacNaughton, R.C.
   (Appendix)
Matthews, N.J.
Moon, R.H.StJ.B.
Moore, B.C.
Morris, C.D.
Mullins, A.R.
Ojomoh, S.O.
O'Leary, S.T.
Olver, C.J.
Oti, C.
Parton, A.R.
   (Appendix)
Pearce, G.S.
Pears, D.
Pearson, J.T.V.
   (Appendix)
Pilgrim, S.J.
Poole, M.D.
   (Appendix)
Potter, S. (Appendix)
Povoas, S.J.
Probyn, J.A.
Redman, N.C.
Rees, G.W.
Rendall, P.A.G.

Rennell, M.I.
  (Appendix)
Revan, T.S.
Richards, D.
Robinson, R.A.
Rodber, T.A.K.
Rowntree, G.C.
Ryan, D.
Sharp, A.V.
  (Appendix)
Shortland, S.M.
  (Appendix)
Simkins, G.J.
  (Appendix)
Sims, D.
Skinner, M.G.
Southern, D.V.
Stanhope, B.G.
Steele, J.D.
Strett, M.G.
Swindells, S.R.
Tanner, M.J.
  (Appendix)
Tanner, P.J.
  (Appendix)
Taylor, R.J.
  (Appendix)
Teague, M.C.
Thacker, T.A.
  (Appendix)
Thompson, G.J.
Ubogu, V.E.
Underwood, R.
Underwood, T.
Wareham, R.A.
  (Appendix)
Webb, J.M.
West, R.J. (Appendix)
Wills, S.R. (Appendix)
Winterbottom, P.J.

IRELAND

Aherne, L.F.P.
Barry, N.

Bradley, M.T.
Clarke, J.D.
Crossan, K.D.
Cunningham, V.J.G.
Curtis, D.M.
Danaher, P.P.A.
Dineen, L.M.
  (Appendix)
Field, M.J.
Fitzgerald, D.C.
Fitzgerald, J.J.
Fitzgibbon, M.J.
Francis, N.P.
Fulcher, G.M.
  (Appendix)
Galwey, M.J.
Geoghegan, S.P.
Glennon, B.T.
  (Appendix)
Halpin, G.F.
Haly, C.M.
  (Appendix)
Hamilton, G.F.
Hennebry, P.J.
  (Appendix)
Hennessy, R.G.
  (Appendix)
Hernan, D.C.
Hooks, K.J.
Johns, P.S.
Keyes, R.P.
Kiernan, M.J.
Kingston, T.J.
Lawlor, P.J.
Leahy, K.T.
Lenihan, D.G.
McAleese, D.R.
McBride, W.D.
McCarthy, P.D.
McCoy, J.J.
McDonald, J.P.
McKee, K.J.
McKinty, S.J.
Malone, N.G.
  (Appendix)

Mannion, N.P.S.
Matthews, P.M.
Mullin, B.J.
Murphy, K.J.
Murray, N.R.
O'Connell, K.
  (Appendix)
O'Hara, P.T.
O'Mahony, B.G.
O'Riordan, J.
O'Shea, C.M.P.
O'Sullivan, E.T.
Patton, M.B.
Popplewell, N.J.
Rigney, B.J.
Riordan, J.C.
Robinson, B.F.
Rolland, A.C.P.
Rooney, S.V.J.
Russell, J.J. (Appendix)
Saunders, R.
Sexton, J.F.
Smith, B.A. (Retiree)
Smith, S.J
Soden, P.J.
Staples, J.
Tobin, D.
Tonge, S.P.
Wallace, R.M.
Ward, R. (Appendix)
Wilkinson, C.R.

SCOTLAND

Adam, D.R.W.
Aitken, S. (Appendix)
Allan, J.
Allingham, M.J.de G.
Amos, J.P.
Armstrong, G.
Barrett, D.
Bennett, S. (Appendix)
Breckenridge, G.M.
Bryson, D.

Buchanan-Smith,
 G.A.E.
Burnell, A.P.
Calder, F.
Caskie, D. (Appendix)
Chalmers, C.M.
Changleng, D.M.
 (Appendix)
Corcoran, I.
Couper, J.A.
Cronin, D.F.
Dods, M.
Dods, P.W.
Dow, A.W.H.
 (Appendix)
Edwards, B.
Glasgow, I.C.
Gray, C.A.
Grecian, N.J.
 (Appendix)
Hastings, A.G.
Hastings, S.
Hay, J.A.
Hogg, C.D.
Isaac, G.R.
Jardine, I.C.
Jardine, S.
Jeffrey, J.
Jones, P.M.
Kirkpatrick, R.M.
Laing, J.
Lineen, S.R.P.
McAndrew, D.C.
McGauchie, S.
McKee, G.T.
McIlroy, N.A.
McIntosh, D.L.M.
McIvor, D.J.L.
Macdonald, A.E.D.
Maclean, R.R.W.L.
Macrae, D.
Marshall, G.R.
Milne, D.F.
Milne, I.G.
Milne, K.S.

Moncrieff, M.
Moore, A.
Murchison, E.A.
 (Appendix)
Nichol, S.A.
Nicol, A.D.
Oliver, G.H.
Porter, S.T.G.
Redpath, A.C.
Redpath, B.W.
Reid, S.J.
Renwick, W.L.
Richardson, B.J.
 (Appendix)
Richardson, J.F.
Roberts, H.
 (Appendix)
Robertson, G.B.
Shepherd, R.J.S.
Shiel, A.G.
Smith, G.B.
Smith, I.R.
Sole, D.M.B.
Stanger, A.G.
Timms, D.L.
 (Appendix)
Tukalo, I.
Turnbull, D.J.
Wainwright, R.I.
Watt, A.G.J.
Weir, G.W.
White, D.B.
Wilson, G.D.
Wyllie, D.S.

WALES

Arnold, P.
Bateman, A.G.
 (Retiree)
Booth, A.H.
Bowling, S.A.
Bridges, C.J.
Buckett, I.
Budd, M.

Carter, A.J.
Clement, A.
Collins, R.G.
Davies, A.
Davies, J.D.
Davies, P.T.
Davis, M.E.
Donovan, A.W.
Edmunds, D.A.
Emyr, A.
Evans, D.W.
Evans, I.C.
Evans, I.L.
Ford, S.P.
Fox, D.C.
George, G.M.
Gibbs, I.S.
Goodey, R.
Griffiths, M.
Hall, M.R.
Hembrow, I.L.
Hill, S.D.
Howley, R.
Jenkins, N.R.
John, P.
Jones, I.W.
Jones, M.A. (Retiree)
Jones, R.N.
Kembury, A.J.
Knight, P.
Laity, C.
Lamerton, A.E.
Langley, C.
 (Appendix)
Lewis, E.W.
Lewis, S.L.
Llewellyn, D.S.
Llewellyn, G.D.
Llewellyn, G.O.
Lloyd, O.S.
McBryde, R.C.
 (Appendix)
Morris, M.S.
Moseley, K.
Mruk, L.M.

Norster, R.L. (Retiree)
Orrell, T. (Appendix)
Parfitt, S.A.
Phillips, K.H.
Phillips, R.D. (Retiree)
Reynolds, A.D.
Ring, M.G.
Rowlands, J.

Roy, S. (Appendix)
Shaw, R.G.
Taylor, B.
Thomas, A.
Thomas, D.J.
Thomas, P.J.
Thorburn, P.H.
Waters, K.

Watkins, I.J.
Webster, R.E.
Westwood, J.
Williams, B.V.
Williams, O.L.
Williams, S.M.
Williams-Jones, H.